Latinx Environmentalisms

Edited by
SARAH D. WALD, DAVID J. VÁZQUEZ,
PRISCILLA SOLIS YBARRA, AND SARAH JAQUETTE RAY

Latinx Environmentalisms
PLACE, JUSTICE, AND THE DECOLONIAL

With a Foreword by LAURA PULIDO and
an Afterword by STACY ALAIMO

TEMPLE UNIVERSITY PRESS
Philadelphia • Rome • Tokyo

TEMPLE UNIVERSITY PRESS
Philadelphia, Pennsylvania 19122
tupress.temple.edu

Copyright © 2019 by Temple University—Of The Commonwealth System
   of Higher Education
All rights reserved
Published 2019

Library of Congress Cataloging-in-Publication Data

Names: Wald, Sarah D., editor. | Vázquez, David J., editor. | Ybarra,
   Priscilla Solis, editor. | Ray, Sarah Jaquette, editor. | Pulido, Laura,
   writer of foreword. | Alaimo, Stacy, 1962- writer of afterword.
Title: Latinx environmentalisms : place, justice, and the decolonial /
   edited by Sarah D. Wald, David J. Vázquez, Priscilla Solis Ybarra, and
   Sarah Jaquette Ray ; with a foreword by Laura Pulido and an afterword by
   Stacy Alaimo.
Description: Philadelphia : Temple University Press, 2019. | Includes
   bibliographical references and index. | Summary: "Latinx
   Environmentalisms brings the environmental humanities into dialogue with
   Latinx literary and cultural studies. By considering how Latinx cultures
   are environmental but often refuse to identify as environmentalist, the
   volume explores the possibilities and challenges of Latinx environmental
   representations, especially how they broaden environmental justice to
   address decolonial frameworks"— Provided by publisher.
Identifiers: LCCN 2019009195 (print) | LCCN 2019980311 (ebook) | ISBN
   9781439916667 (cloth) | ISBN 9781439916674 (paperback) | ISBN
   9781439916681 (ebook)
Subjects: LCSH: American literature—Hispanic American authors—History and
   criticism. | Ecocriticism. | Environmentalism in literature. | Hispanic
   Americans—Social conditions. | Environmentalism—United States. |
   Environmental justice—United States.
Classification: LCC PS153.H56 L45 2019 (print) | LCC PS153.H56 (ebook) |
   DDC 810.9/98073—dc23
LC record available at https://lccn.loc.gov/2019009195
LC ebook record available at https://lccn.loc.gov/2019980311

9 8 7 6 5 4 3 2 1

This book is dedicated to all the unsung Latinx environmental activists and thinkers.

Contents

Foreword | *Laura Pulido* — ix

Acknowledgments — xvii

1 Introduction: Why Latinx Environmentalisms?
   | *Sarah D. Wald, David J. Vázquez, Priscilla Solis Ybarra,
   and Sarah Jaquette Ray* — 1

PART I Place: Racial Capital and the Production of Place

2 Greenwashing the White Savior: Cancer Clusters, Supercrips,
   and *McFarland, USA* | *Julie Avril Minich* — 35

3 The National Park Foundation's "American Latino Expedition":
   Consumer Citizenship as Pathway to Multicultural National
   Belonging | *Sarah D. Wald* — 52

4 "A Story Is a Physical Space": An Interview with Héctor Tobar
   | *Shane Hall* — 76

5 Speculative Futurity and the Eco-cultural Politics of
   Lunar Braceros: 2125–2148 | *Christopher Perreira* — 87

6 Sun Ma(i)d: Art, Activism, and Environment in Ester
   Hernández's Central Valley | *Jennifer Garcia Peacock* — 104

7 "An Organic Being in the Middle of Chicago": An Interview
   with Ana Castillo | *Priscilla Solis Ybarra and Sarah D. Wald* — 131

PART II Justice: Expanding Environmentalism

8 Environmental Justice and the Ecological Other in
   Ana Castillo's *So Far from God* | Sarah Jaquette Ray   147

9 "We Carry Our Environments within Ourselves": An Interview
   with Helena María Viramontes | David J. Vázquez, Sarah D. Wald,
   and Paula M. L. Moya   164

10 "Between Water and Song": Maria Melendez and the Contours
   of Contemporary Latinx Ecopoetry | Randy Ontiveros   177

11 "Justice Is a Living Organism": An Interview with
   Lucha Corpi | Gabriela Nuñez   189

PART III The Decolonial: Alternative Kinships and Epistemologies of Futurity

12 Memory, Space, and Gentrification: The Legacies of the Young
   Lords and Urban Decolonial Environmentalism in Ernesto
   Quiñonez's *Bodega Dreams* | David J. Vázquez   203

13 Postcards from the Edges of Haiti: The Latinx Ecocriticism
   of Mayra Montero's *In the Palm of Darkness* | Ylce Irizarry 227

14 "Against the Sorrowful and Infinite Solitude": Environmental
   Consciousness and Streetwalker Theorizing in Helena María
   Viramontes's *Their Dogs Came with Them* | Paula M. L. Moya   250

15 Oedipal Wrecks: Queer Animal Ecologies in Justin Torres's
   We the Animals | Richard T. Rodríguez   267

16 "The Body Knows and the Land Has Memory": An Interview
   with Cherríe Moraga | Priscilla Solis Ybarra   281

   Afterword: What Is Absent; Fields, Futures, and
   Latinx Environmentalisms | Stacy Alaimo   295

   Contributors   303

   Index   307

Foreword

LAURA PULIDO

Allow me to begin with a confession: I have not always been a big fan of ecocriticism, especially as it relates to environmental justice. I recall clearly the first time I was introduced to Latinx ecocriticism. It was in the early 1990s, and I was attending a small conference that examined the intersections between environmentalism, environmental justice, Latin America, and U.S. Latinx populations. There were several sessions focused on literary criticism, and I admit to being baffled as to why such presentations were included in the event: Wasn't this supposed to be about the *actual* environment? I could not grasp how cultural analysis could be useful to the larger project of building an antiracist movement to smash capitalism (my preoccupation at the time). I recall, in particular, a discussion of Raymond Barrio's *The Plum Plum Pickers*. How could a piece of fiction, let alone an analysis of it, be of consequence when people were dying? Yes, the novel focused on farmworkers, and I certainly enjoyed reading fiction, but because the scholarship was not based on empirical methods, such as the archive or ethnography, I could not appreciate its value. Though I cringe as I share this memory, I can now say that I "get it." It is all too apparent to me today the importance of questions of representation, futurity, imagination, and memory and the need to examine complexities that exceed social science tools. Although I still very much identify and work as a social scientist, I am convinced that whatever impact my work has had is due to my propensity to borrow concepts and tools from any intellectual tradition, including the humanities. Thus, while I am honored to be invited to write the foreword to *Latinx Environmentalisms*, I cannot help but note the irony. I share this anecdote not only in the interest of full disclosure but also because my long engagement in the field gives me a certain vantage point—one that I hope is useful in terms of historically contextualizing *Latinx Environmentalisms.*

The publication of *Latinx Environmentalisms* marks a milestone. To date, there is one other comparable volume that I am aware of that focuses exclusively on the environmental histories, experiences, and imaginations of the Latinx population or a subset of it, and that is *Subversive Kin: Chicana/o Studies and Ecology,* edited by Devon Peña. *Latinx Environmentalisms* is distinct in several ways. First, despite being heavily weighted toward the Chicanx experience, *Latinx Environmentalisms* includes other groups as well, such as Nuyoricans and Haitians. Indeed, the concept of "Latina/o studies" was just emerging in the late nineties, whereas today it is increasingly the norm. Second, while *Subversive Kin* was very much an interdisciplinary text, it was predominantly social science in orientation. In contrast, *Latinx Environmentalisms* focuses on literary and cultural analysis. Seen in this light, as the editors note, it is indeed overdue and most welcome. Third, *Subversive Kin* was published relatively early on in the development of environmental justice, whereas the present book is twenty years later. Consequently, the two texts are intervening in two different intellectual landscapes. Whereas *Subversive Kin* was part of a nascent challenge to mainstream environmentalism, *Latinx Environmentalisms* is contributing to a more established body of work. Consequently, *Latinx Environmentalisms* goes beyond environmental justice and explores what Latinx studies can contribute to our understanding of the environment, while at the same time critiquing environmentalism itself. This brings me to the last distinction of the text, the emphasis on a (de)colonial framework. Arguably, most studies of Latinx environmentalisms are rooted in race, reflecting a U.S. framework, which typically privileges racism over other processes of domination. But foregrounding the decolonial also reflects a particular moment in the evolution of critical ethnic studies, which have been heavily influenced by both indigenous and Latin American studies.

> All discussions about the environment ought to engage colonialism, or they risk extending colonialism by ignoring this ongoing legacy. Inversely, decolonial efforts must address the environment, and failing to do so simply because of the environmental movement's prevailing investment in whiteness risks perpetuating the notion that land, geography, and spatial sovereignty are separate from ecosystemic conditions and their dynamic . . . relationship to cultural identities. (Chapter 1, this volume)

This, to me, is one of the most exciting aspects of this project, one, I might add, that is largely absent from most social science scholarship. Moreover, I appreciate the extent to which such a framework is drawn from the Latin

American context and therefore reflects a transnational or hemispheric perspective. I firmly believe that *all* environmental analyses must be grounded in larger materialist processes, and all social processes must be connected to the transformation of nature. While most environmental justice scholarship is rooted in an antiracist framework, with the exception of indigenous experiences, rarely is (de)colonization given equal treatment.

Reading *Latinx Environmentalisms* raises several additional provocative questions for me—questions that I have been thinking about more generally in regard to environmental justice, Latinx studies, and critical race theory. Engaging this volume signaled for me their urgency as we consider how to move the field forward. My comments seek to amplify the generative nature of *Latinx Environmentalisms*. Three specific political-intellectual questions arise: What are the boundaries of environmentalism and environmental justice? How might we envision the full range of Latinx populations' environmental positions and roles? And finally, how do we conceptualize Latinx peoples, especially ethnic Mexicans, in terms of settler colonization?

The Boundaries of Environmentalism and Environmental Justice

The editors begin the introduction to *Latinx Environmentalisms* by foregrounding crucial questions that many of those invested in environmentalism grapple with: What constitutes the environment? Who is an environmentalist? What are the implications of labeling issues and people as "environmental" when they may not see themselves that way? What is gained? What is lost? Wald, Vázquez, Ybarra, and Ray (Chapter 1, this volume) explain the relative lateness of this volume as resulting from the fact that numerous Latinx writers have been slow to identify themselves or their work as environmentally related. They provide a compelling set of reasons as to why they have chosen to identify various artists and texts as environmental. Besides pushing against the whiteness of environmentalism, they argue that Latinx cultures can broaden and enhance what counts as environmentalism by linking it to larger issues, including racism, colonization, and economic exploitation. Yet there are also some drawbacks to such a strategy. My desire to "pause" has less to do with this text and is more a commentary on the larger ideological and political trajectory of the environmental justice movement, which the current volume also scrutinizes. Since the emergence of environmental justice in the 1980s, there has been a continual call to broaden the conception of the environment, with scant attention to the costs.

Some of the works analyzed in this volume are easily identifiable as environmentally related; others can be read as environmental, although that was not necessarily their primary purpose; and others push the bounds of what constitutes the environment. These multiple positions are, of course, deliberate and intended to reframe the relationship between Latinx cultural production and the environment. When this practice of broadening the conception of the environment began in the 1980s, environmental justice activists *needed* to challenge the terrain and authority of mainstream environmentalism in order to assert themselves and their concerns. That could happen only through redefining the environment, what became known as "where we live, work, and play." Though there has been significant progress on this front, as seen by funders and numerous mainstream organizations, there is still significant work to be done, as the editors note. Indeed, the absence of such a discussion reflects the limited degree to which diversity has been embraced and analyzed by both mainstream and environmental justice activists.

While a broadened conception of the environment is still foundational to environmental justice, this assumption has not been interrogated: What are the consequences, if any, of consistently advocating for a broadened conception of the environment? There are at least three possible points to consider. First is the loss of ambiguity. Often, political and moral clarity requires cutting through ambiguity in order to identify a clear path forward. But other times ambiguity can provide important insights regarding ourselves and our relationships to the larger world. I would suggest that it is worth lingering, however briefly, in the ambiguity of what constitutes the environment. It could be that after such reflection one may emerge convinced of the merits of such a position. This, in itself, would be worthwhile, because presumably one would have carefully analyzed the merits and drawbacks of such a strategy instead of taking it for granted. Conversely, one might emerge more cautious about such a strategy, advocate for a refinement, or perhaps seek to create something altogether distinct from "environmentalism." I am not wedded to any particular outcome, but I do know that the places we tend to avoid, what might be called spaces of "surplus ambiguity," are often potentially rich sites for close inspection.

The second question that arises stems from including people, places, and struggles under the environmental umbrella when they do not identify as such. I feel a general unease when employing this practice. I say this as someone who has done this myself. Conversely, I have also been categorized in a multitude of ways that did not reflect my own sense of self. Undoubtedly this happens to everyone at some point, but the practice is especially weighted and complex for people who have routinely had names and categories imposed on them through larger processes of domination, dispossession, and violence. In short, however well intended, there is a politics to this practice that we must be cognizant of.

And finally, there are multiple issues related to political strategy and organizing. At the heart of advocating for a broadened conception of the environment is a belief in the moral value of environmentalism and the desire not only to make it available to all people but also to reconceptualize it so that it can better capture the lived experiences and realities of those who are not white and from the Global North. Sarah Jaquette Ray, in her chapter on Ana Castillo's *So Far From God* (Chapter 6), highlights a whole set of power dynamics that compel colonized people, people of color, immigrants, and others relegated to the margins to adopt an environmental framing. Though a complex calculus, the bottom line is that this framing offers such people the possibility of enhanced support and political leverage. These are powerful assets that do not come easily to subordinated communities.

As the bounds of the environment expand, what does this mean for strategy and for building a broad-based movement? Might such diffuseness lead to political fragmentation? On one hand, one could argue that such diffuseness gives environmentalism its strength; on the other, one could also argue that it may lead to splintering and balkanization. Conventional thinking maintains there is great power in creating as broad a movement as possible, but recent history from U.S. conservatives suggests that adhering to a coherent political line can also lead to real change. As the world faces new and unprecedented ecological crises, in terms of both global warming and the massive political opposition to addressing this crisis, it is unclear what conception of the environment will be most helpful. Should the environment be divided by topic or power geometries (Massey), as some of us believe that global warming is fundamentally a crisis of capitalism (Klein)? Do we need a short-term and a long-term strategy? Once again, I do not know the answers, but these are important questions we need to be asking.

The Environmental Positionality of Latinx Peoples

How do we conceptualize the subjectivity of Latinx people in terms of the environment? The editors situate this volume as part of the "third wave" of environmental literature, which focuses on historically silenced voices. As such, the book contributes to a much larger literature that challenges the erasure of Latinx people (and others) as responsible environmental actors, or depicts them as agents of environmental destruction devoid of a larger structural analysis. In response to this, many writers have articulated two alternative positions for Chicanx people: either as victims of environmental degradation, capitalist exploitation, and colonization, or as overlooked sources of environmental values and knowledge. Such efforts to ecologically salvage Latinx peoples permeate the environmental justice literature. They have most recently been articulated by Ybarra in her important book *Writing the Goodlife*. She writes, "We never needed to become environmentalists in the first place, and we therefore have an array of strategies at our disposal for how to live well with Earth" (28). While it may be true that Mexican American writers do convey such an environmental ethic in their writing (and we do possess a range of strategies), we must also exercise caution around such claims. I say this as someone who actively participated in this repositioning in my dissertation (Pulido, *Environmentalism and Economic Justice*).

We first need to historicize such claims. Drawing on the editors' framing of *Latinx Environmentalisms* as a "recovery model," such claims can be seen as part of a "first wave" of Latinx or people of color environmentalism, in which such arguments were necessary to challenge mainstream environmentalism and to reconceive the subject position of those deemed peripheral or hostile to the environment. The initial task was to excavate, document, and assert the legitimacy of diverse Latinx environmental heritages and experiences. This included close attention to the uneven power dynamics associated with the materiality of the global economy, as well as reframing denigrated cultural practices, such as curanderas, as valuable assets in our collective struggle to create more ecologically and culturally sustainable lifeways. This is essential work, and *Latinx Environmentalisms* takes us far along that road—but it is not complete.

What is missing is a more complex reading of Latinx environmental subjectivity. This collection brings us closer to that goal by providing a launchpad to reconsider this question. By focusing on either victim or ecological innovator, other possibilities are obscured—namely, Latinx peoples as perpetrators of environmental harms. While this may be an unpopular idea, we cannot ignore environmentally problematic practices and values—especially in a place like the United States. Given that the United States consumes almost 25 percent of the world's energy, it is difficult *not* to see U.S. Latinx peoples as consumers at the very least—albeit at lower levels than other groups. Indeed, Wald's chapter on the American Latino Expedition (Chapter 3, this volume) clearly shows consumption as one of the key pathways to an expanded environmental consciousness and practice on the part of Latinx people (mostly women). This is a crucial insight that must not be glossed over. A similar theme can be seen in the concept of Latino Urbanism (Irazabal), which has argued that Latinx peoples live more environmentally friendly lifestyles, including using mass transit, high-density living, and recycling. These are all true—but what about lowriders?

A further complication stems from the term *Latinx*, which erases the multiplicity of environmental experiences that are located under a single heading. Specifically, the intraclass politics and racial differentiation in this category are silenced. Because of a lack of attention to intra-Latinx distinctions, only a certain set of practices tend to be offered as new additions or improvements to our conception of "the environment." For example, what are the environmental traditions of agricultural labor subcontractors—the vast majority of whom are Latinx? How are these experiences distinct from those of the farmworkers they manage and often exploit? While I fully support the effort to more accurately understand and depict the diverse environmental consciousness of Latinx peoples, we must not overlook the contradictions.

Latinx People and Settler Colonization

The final question I wish to raise is regarding Latinx people, especially ethnic Mexicans, as settler colonizers. The editors write, "Latinxs share an uneasy relationship with settler colonialism as both perpetrators of colonial violence and objects of settler colonial dispossession" (Chapter 1, this volume). This statement builds on important work by scholars such as Guidotti-Hernández and Saldaña-Portillo, who have begun excavating this complex terrain. Despite the fact that the editors offer a detailed analysis of the subjectivity of Latinx people in the introduction, there are no chapters that explore the role of Latinx people as colonizers, although several of the interviews hint at it. This should not be surprising, as it reflects a much larger lacuna within Chicanx and Latinx studies, as well as within the larger environmental justice literature. In both fields of study, Latinx people and especially ethnic Mexicans are regularly depicted as the colonized, not the colonizer (Pulido, "Geographies of Race and Ethnicity"). Of course, the vast majority of Latinx peoples live and labor under conditions not of their own making, and I do not wish to assert an agency or power that may not exist. Yet we cannot overlook the fact that in many places in the southwestern United States, especially in California, New Mexico, and Arizona, ethnic Mexicans actively participated in the conquest and dispossession of Native peoples. This is thorny, as not only are Mexicans partly indigenous themselves, but such questions go to the heart of some of the most basic assumptions of Chicanx studies (Pulido, "Geographies of Race and Ethnicity"). The very term *Latinx* is challenging in this regard. Though it offers us something valuable, foregrounding the colonization of las Américas, it also costs us something. We risk losing the intrapower dynamics within the "Latinx" umbrella, especially the multiple subjectivities of Mexicans as colonizers and the colonized.

In this particular historical moment when indigeneity is exploding in critical ethnic studies, it is especially incumbent on those of us who identify as Mexican American and Chicanx to take the lead in broaching this difficult conversation. As the field of Latinx environmentalisms develops, we will hopefully reach the point where we will be able to offer nuanced analyses of Latinx people as indigenous, brown, black, and white; as colonized and colonizer; as trabajador y jefe; as land based, urban, and immigrant. This is the full complexity of Latinx life en las Américas. We have a long way to go, but we will get there only through the kind of painstaking and collective work that *Latinx Environmentalisms* represents.

WORKS CITED

Barrio, Raymond. *The Plum Plum Pickers*. Bilingual Review Press, 1984.
Guidotti-Hernández, Nicole. *Unspeakable Violence: Remapping U.S. and Mexican National Imaginaries*. Duke UP, 2011.

Irazabal, Clara. "Beyond 'Latino New Urbanism': Advocating Ethnourbanisms." *Journal of Urbanism: International Research on Placemaking and Urban Sustainability*, vol. 5, no. 2, 2012, pp. 241–268.
Klein, Naomi. *This Changes Everything: Capitalism vs. the Climate*. Simon and Schuster, 2014.
Massey, Doreen. "A Global Sense of Place." *Space, Place and Gender*, U of Minnesota P, 1994, pp. 146–156.
Peña, Devon, editor. *Subversive Kin: Chicana/o Studies and Ecology*. U of Arizona P, 1999.
Pulido, Laura. *Environmentalism and Economic Justice: Two Chicano Struggles in the Southwest*. U of Arizona P, 1996.
——. "Geographies of Race and Ethnicity III: Settler Colonialism and Nonnative People of Color." *Progress in Human Geography*, vol. 42, no. 2, 2018, pp. 309–318.
Saldaña-Portillo, María Josefina. *Indian Given: Racial Geographies across Mexico and the United States*. Duke UP, 2016.
Ybarra, Priscilla Solis. *Writing the Goodlife: Mexican American Literature and the Environment*. U of Arizona P, 2016.

Acknowledgments

We learned so much from collaborating, and we believe in making that process visible. The model of academic individualism ignores the fact that we are all doing work and generating thoughts within many material and emotional relations. If one of the injustices we seek to counter by putting this volume together is the atomistic view that Western individuals can ignore their dependence on the well-being of other communities and species, then recognizing the ways we are sustained by them here reinforces our intention.

Many communities, family members, friends, colleagues, and funders have supported this project over the years. We first thank the professional conferences that brought the four of us together: the Association for the Study of Literature and Environment (ASLE), the American Studies Association (ASA), the biennial U.S. Latina/o Literary Theory and Criticism conference at John Jay College of Criminal Justice, and the Latina/o Studies Association (LSA). It was at the 2013 First Biennial Latina/o Literary Theory and Criticism Conference at John Jay College of Criminal Justice in New York City and the 2013 ASLE conference at the University of Kansas where we first came together around the themes in this volume. At the 2014 ASA conference in Los Angeles, this book took form in our imaginations as we reunited over lunch after attending and participating in the panel "The Land and the Fury: Land, Space, and Legacies of Cultural Nationalism in Latina/o Environmentalism." In 2015, Priscilla, Sarah, and Sarah co-led an ASLE pedagogy workshop on "The Depths of Latina/o Environmentalism," which further pulled key members into our conversation. At multiple gatherings at John Jay and LSA during the intervening years, contributors to this volume gathered as we collaborated further and got to know each other; these organizations provided the conditions needed for collaborations to take shape. We extend a special thanks to Belinda Rincón and Richard Pérez, John Jay organizers, for their enthusiasm about this project. Their detailed facilitation made that conference particularly productive for us on two different occasions.

Panelists and audiences at these conferences were seminal in generating the main arguments of *Latinx Environmentalisms*. We are grateful to these communities of scholars, activists, and students who kept us thinking about this book's purpose, audience, and value, and who keep working on the intersections of Latinx cultural production and environmental values.

The four of us were able to come together to work collectively on this project at a symposium at the University of Oregon because of a grant from the Oregon Humanities Center and the University of Oregon English Department Diversity Committee. Further, the Oregon Humanities Center provided additional funds to support the project's production and publication. The University of North Texas (UNT) Department of English and UNT's College of Liberal Arts and Social Sciences provided funds to support production and publication as well. We also thank Pedro for his fabulous Airbnb in D.C. Spending a full day writing a second draft of our introduction there together was excellent, and within walking distance of great Ethiopian cuisine and a beautiful park!

We had the distinct pleasure of working with Sara Jo Cohen at Temple University Press. Sara has managed to work with four coeditors with grace, and her enthusiasm for the project and capacity for big-picture thinking were indispensable in helping us conceive both the broad contours of the book and the fine details. We thank Ashley Petrucci, Gary Kramer, and Nikki Miller of Temple University Press for their work in bringing our book to print. We are also grateful to Noël Sturgeon and Hsuan L. Hsu, who provided superb suggestions that improved the project. We thank Ainsley Davis for her invaluable editorial assistance. Thank you to Gina Filo for providing indexing support at a critical moment.

Our interviewees deserve special thanks, as does Stuart Bernstein, who acted as an eager interlocutor for Cherríe Moraga and Helena María Viramontes. For those of us who had the privilege to spend some time in conversation with writers Ana Castillo, Lucha Corpi, Cherríe Moraga, Héctor Tobar, and Helena María Viramontes, we want you to know that this volume takes shape not just from the words you shared with us on those occasions but also because of your inspiring work over the years. We love teaching your work, writing about your work, and now including your ideas in this collection. It is a true honor to be in conversation with all of you.

And to our courageous contributors: because your work pushes into the fraught intersection of environmental studies and Latinx studies, it can sometimes feel it rubs against the grain of both. It has been a privilege for us to develop these conversations at that complex intersection.

Sarah D. Wald especially thanks Priscilla Solis Ybarra, David J. Vázquez, and Sarah Jaquette Ray for fostering a collaboration built on friendship and intellectual exchange. I am a better person and a better scholar for the work we have done together. Our work is more than the sum of its parts, and what we have achieved extends far beyond this volume. I am forever grateful to have you as friends. Caleb Connolly, Akya Sackos-Connolly, and Thumper were patient, gracious, and supportive with the time and energy this project required. You have my love, always. I also thank and celebrate Alan, Angela, Mike, Debbie, Corinne, Jisun, and Kyla for their love and support. This book would not have taken its current form without conversations with Kirby Brown, Tara Fickle, Carolyn Finney, Janet Fiskio, Jennifer James, Amy Harwood, Stephanie LeMenager, Mireya Loza, Julie Minich, Salma Monani, Paula Moya, Kari Norgaard, Laura Pulido, Courtney Rae, Erica Rand, Jeannie Shinozuka, and Nicole Seymour. This book was improved through feedback from the attendees of the Environmental Justice, Race, and Public Lands symposium at the University of Oregon. I would also like to give special recognition to the graduate students in English 660: Ecocritical Approaches to Race and Ethnicity and the undergraduate students in English 343: Latinx Literary Environmentalisms whose insights and conversations contributed in many ways to my thinking in this volume. Shout-outs to Latifa, Justin, Amias, Jasmine, Audrey, Winnie, Carley, Luke, Millie, Andrew, Carol, Kyung, Eric, Angela, Ralph, Karl, Arlene, Matt, Hannah, Sharon, Cindy, Ovide, Aimee, Julie, Sherry, Leslie, Chris, Barney, Cayenne, Kaleo, Taryn, and Noa. Additional colleagues, mentors, family members, and friends too numerous to name deserve further acknowledgment for conversations, insights, cheerleading, and advice. The communities out of which books, articles, or other types of publications arise are always broader and extend much further than the listed authors.

Priscilla Solis Ybarra would like to thank Sarah Jaquette Ray, Sarah D. Wald, and David J. Vázquez. I learned so much from you in this process, and you are all a model for me of broad knowledge, quick wit, generous spirit, agile writing, organizational wisdom, and collaborative spirit. I'm so happy and all the better off that this project brought us closer together. I'll miss our regular conversations; the glimpses of your homes, offices, kids, and pets over Skype; our thinking and writing together; and most of all, our laughter and kindness to one another. But I also know the collaborations will continue. I would also like to thank my colleagues at the UNT Department of English; my always-game undergrads and graduate students at UNT; la familia en Lubbock, especially Ibai for her fighting spirit; Laila Amine and Michael Thompson, who were stolen away by Wisconsin, but you know you'll always be Texans, too; and my Denton family: Annette Lawrence, Shay Youngblood, Irene Klaver, Brian O'Connor, Alicia Re Cruz, Mariela Nuñez-Janes, Tanya Darby, Andrea Silva, Diego Esparza, Brad Leali, Jennifer Wallach, Michael Wise, and Yolanda Flores Niemann.

I also send out special thanks to friends and colleagues who have taken care of me alma y cuerpo in the time I was working on this project (and beyond), feeding me, housing me, inviting me to give talks, hanging with me at conferences, and having so many beautiful conversations. Love to all, in no particular order: Paula Gaetano Adi, Alejandro Borsani, Theresa Delgadillo, Walton Muyumba, Juan Muñoz, Estella B. Leopold, Tony Anella, Cara McCulloch, Barry Lopez, Joni Adamson, Aby Pérez Aguilera, Leonardo Figueroa Helland, Melina Vizcaíno Aleman, Jesse Aleman, Heather Houser, John Moran González, Domino Renee Pérez, Stacy Alaimo, Jorge Marcone, Juan Carlos Galeano, Carolyn Finney, Chip Blake, Lauret Savoy, Claudia J. Ford, Scott Russell Sanders, Kyle Powys Whyte, Baird Callicott, Curt Meine, Camille Dungy, Cecilia Balli, Juanita Mantz, Tony Díaz, Bryan Parras, Liana Lopez, Karen Clark, John Escobedo, Lourdes Alberto, Jennifer Snead, Chad Covey, Linus! and Scout, Chaone Mallory, Krista Comer, Stephanie Elizondo Griest, Tammy Gomez, Mayra Guardiola, Virginia Smith, and Sandra Postel. My family went through some tough times in the course of this book coming together. I thank the universe for bringing us closer and stronger together. I'm also so happy to welcome new familia: Yessenia Marte Lanfranco, Yesslin Marte Rocque, and Debbie Monroe. José Aranda y los Talleristas: I couldn't do any of it without you. Esti keeps me grounded every day. And my soulmates: Rosario Daza and Willem Versluis, you've taught me so much. Trips to Seattle and Oz are way overdue. Willem, my love, I'll never forget the piraña, the rainbow, or the kayaks with the tiny penguins.

David J. Vázquez sends the warmest thanks and the highest props to my brilliant coeditors and friends Sarah D. Wald, Priscilla Solis Ybarra, and Sarah Jaquette Ray. I am proud to know you and to have deepened our friendship through this project. To say thank you is to underestimate the contributions that Rhonda Zimlich, Gabriella Zimlich-Vázquez, Veronica Zimlich-Vázquez, and Wally and Ramona Vázquez make to my daily life. Honorable mentions to Shasta, Osiris, Athena, and the late, great Luna. I am forever indebted to all of you for your patience with and enduring confidence in me. I would also like to thank the Institute for Humanities Research at Arizona State University and the Oregon Humanities Center for providing funding that contributed to the formation of this project. Shout-outs to Allison Carruth, Lee Bebout, Elena Machado Sáez, Randy Ontiveros, Ylce Irizarry, Eliza Rodríguez y Gibson, John Riofrio, Julie Minich, Tanya González, Kirby Brown, John Moran González, Shane Hall, Daniel Platt, Alex Cavanaugh, Jennifer Harford-Vargas, Ramón Saldívar, Paula Moya, Kari Norgaard, Stephanie LeMenager, and Karen Ford, all of whom contributed crucial support, challenges, and conversation that made this work possible. My weekly conversations with Stephanie Schlagel and NiCole Buchanan have become sustaining in so many ways. Special thanks to the graduate students in ENG 660: Monsters in the Anthropocene and ENG 660:

Latina/o Speculative Realism & Environmental Justice and to the numerous undergraduates who contributed vital conversations that helped shape my thinking on all things environmental.

Sarah Jaquette Ray would like to thank Sarah D. Wald, Priscilla Solis Ybarra, and David J. Vázquez for their friendship and intellectual support. Working with so many coeditors may seem cumbersome, but in this case, it was truly a pleasure to collaborate. Writing together in the same space, writing together over Skype, delegating work, supporting each other when our lives got in the way of progress, and working on these themes over the past four years as American culture undergoes so many tectonic shifts has been both a career highlight and an existential buoy. David, Sarah, and Priscilla have become beloved mentors and friends to me because of this project.

A handful of students have also been crucial to my thinking about these topics by collaborating on research, coteaching, attending conferences, and taking leadership roles on campus and beyond: Noemi Pacheco, Carlrey Delcastillo, Ashley Torres, Shiloh Green, Ivan de Soto, Angelica Muñoz, Paradise Martinez Graff, Kristian Salgado, Jessica Suarez, Ryan Sandejas, Karina Coronado, and Irán Ortiz. These students are my teachers, and not a day goes by that I am not in awe of their passion and skills.

Other colleagues I want to thank are Renée Byrd, Janelle Adsit, and Rosemary Sherriff, for being my core of Humboldt State University colleagues who support each other's scholarly lives. Fernando Paz, Loren Collins, and Rob Keever graciously integrate faculty like me in their brilliant projects. Alma Zechman and the Environmental Studies Program community at Humboldt State make it all happen.

Together, the editors want to acknowledge the many unsung and unheard voices of Latinx activists, thinkers, and creators whose environmental contributions have gone unnoticed or rejected, for being transgressive to the status quo but also for not registering as "environmental." We dedicate this book to you.

And last, but certainly not least, thanks to all the vibrant matter that went into keeping us sustained in body and mind and that went into the production of this book you hold in your hands.

Latinx Environmentalisms

1

Introduction

Why Latinx Environmentalisms?

SARAH D. WALD,
DAVID J. VÁZQUEZ,
PRISCILLA SOLIS YBARRA,
AND SARAH JAQUETTE RAY

When Priscilla Solis Ybarra asked the poet, playwright, and feminist theorist Cherríe Moraga, "Do you personally identify as an environmentalist?" Moraga responded definitively, "I wouldn't say that." Similarly, Lucha Corpi told Gabriela Nuñez, "I don't identify myself as an environmentalist." It is a repeated refrain throughout the interviews in this volume: creative writers discussed the environmental themes in their work while disidentifying with the term *environmentalist*. Likewise, many of the scholars we approached about this project initially expressed surprise, and sometimes even distaste, at being hailed as writing about environmental issues. Given this hesitation, why bother to make such a label explicit? And, what, specifically, makes this work "environmental"? Moreover, how should we interpret the hesitancy of some contributors to see their work as environmental, while others openly embrace it?

Environmentalism in the United States is most often associated with a middle- to upper-class white demographic, working on behalf of nonhuman nature for the preservation of wilderness or the conservation of species. As Chicanx studies scholar Randy Ontiveros observes, "Conventional wisdom often sees environmentalism as a 'white thing' comprised of boutique shopping, organic cooking, wilderness escapes, and other racially coded activities. It even gets represented occasionally as a twenty-first century update to the colonial nineteenth-century 'white man's burden.'" Although Ontiveros is quick to point out that "the reality of environmentalism . . . is considerably more complex" (87), his critique of the cultural and demographic whiteness of mainstream environmental movements is still largely correct. As environmental justice scholar Dorceta E. Taylor documented in 2014 for Green 2.0, "despite increasing racial diversity in the United States, the racial composition of environmental organizations and agencies has not broken the 12 percent to 16 percent 'green ceiling' that has been in place for decades." This remains the case despite widespread polling data attesting to stronger levels of support for environmental initiatives among Asian Americans and Pacific Islanders, Latinxs, and African Americans than among white populations.[1] Not only are mainstream environmentalism's practices and disciplines "racially coded" but, as the disavowal of Moraga and Corpi attest, its investment in whiteness, class distinction, and even national belonging serve to occlude environmental values that exist outside of the mainstream.[2]

Before the emergence of the environmental justice movement in the 1980s, which worked to protect low-income communities and communities of color from enduring a disproportionate burden of environmental destruction,[3] the whiteness of mainstream environmentalism often obscured environmental racism and the connections between social and environmental health. This initial environmental justice activism and scholarship, which emerged from a civil rights framework, called for equal access to environmental benefits and equal distribution of environmental ills. It also challenged the wilderness focus of mainstream environmental organizations to redefine the environment as "where we live, work, and play" (Bullard, *Dumping in Dixie*; Gottlieb; Di Chiro).

Indigenous activists and indigenous studies scholars expanded this initial civil rights framework to identify colonialism's role in causing and perpetuating environmental injustice and to argue for sovereignty's place within environmental justice movements. This sovereignty framework is visible in documents like the Principles of Environmental Justice authored by participants in the First National People of Color Environmental Leadership Summit (1991) and continues in more recent scholarship such as Traci Brynne Voyles's *Wastelanding* (2015) and the special issue in *Environment and Society* on "Indigenous Resurgence, Decolonization, and Movements for Environmental Justice" (2018), edited by Jaskiran Dhillon, as well as in political activism like that of water protectors at Standing Rock. Latinx activists and scholars, most notably Devon Peña and Laura Pulido, also expanded the environmental justice frame to include the farmworkers movement, especially its campaign against pesticides, and land-based movements of the Southwest.

Building on insights of the environmental justice movement and environmental justice scholarship, academics in fields such as history, geography, literature, and cultural studies including Joni Adamson, Bruce Braun, Denis Cosgrove, William Cronon, Richard Grove, Donna Haraway, Jake Kosek, Carolyn Merchant, Mary E. Mendoza, and Mark Spence (as only a few examples) have firmly articulated mainstream environmentalism as a racial project. Postcolonial ecocritic Rob Nixon, for example, observes that the mainstream environmental movement in the United States has placed undue emphasis on "wilderness preservation, on wielding the Endangered Species Act against developers, and on saving old-growth forests" (252), leading some antiracist and anticolonial thinkers to dismiss "environmentalism as either irrelevant or complicit in imperialism" (253). At the very least, the whiteness of mainstream environmentalism fails to account for the diverse environmental ethics at work in communities of color, including Latinx cultures.

Thus, this volume seeks to account, in part, for the variety of ways in which Latinx cultures are often (although certainly not always) environmental but hardly ever identify as environmentalist. Indeed, we argue that Latinx cultures redefine and broaden what counts as environmentalism, even as they sometimes reject the term entirely. Part of this redefinition concerns how Latinx cultures make evident the racism inherent in some of the assumptions of environmentalism through a variety of forms of rejection, acceptance, or revision of the term itself. Perhaps most importantly, Latinx cultures hold the potential to make visible key aspects of the exploitation of the earth (introduced and exacerbated by colonization and capital) that figure into the historical marginalization of Latinx communities. This insight emerges both from the variety of cultural values that circulate in different Latinx communities, including indigenous and Afro-Latinx communities, and from the lived experience of being exploited alongside the land through the processes of colonization and present-day coloniality and ongoing neoliberal abstraction. Latinx literatures and cultural productions often offer deep and significant insights about environmental issues, environmental ethics, and the intertwining of environmental ills with the social ills of racism, capitalism, and colonialism. Our decision to use the term *environmentalisms* here, even with authors who may not identify in this way, represents a political choice to redress the vacuum of attention given to Latinx environmental thought, particularly in literature and cultural productions. We argue that this vacuum emerges from the colonialist and white supremacist ideologies embedded in the formulation of mainstream environmentalism.

We foreground the work of literary and cultural studies scholars and creative writers, as opposed to work in the social sciences or politics, as central to the project of *Latinx Environmentalisms*. Although literary critics have been writing about the environmental aspects of Latinx literature for at least twenty years, this is the first such collection of essays on Latinx environmentalisms in literary and cultural productions.[4] As we contend throughout this volume, literary and cultural production are crucial to the processes through which social and environmental inequality are constructed. Social inequalities and the expendability of particular populations of people, plants, animals, and ecosystems are produced in part through narratives that either erase their existence or justify their disposal. As Julie Avril Minich argues in this volume, as opposed to other methodologies, "cultural critique offers an account of the unjust social relations that shape policy and of the narrative processes that naturalize and reify systemic injustice." Similarly, as many ecocritics ask, to what extent is narrative itself caught up in environmental degradation? Textual and visual analyses are key strategies for contesting the epistemological processes of colonialism and racial capitalism and the policies they underwrite. Moreover, the literary, cinematic, and visual arts provide essential sites for envisioning radical alterities, as we take up in the third section of this volume, "The Decolonial: Alternative Kinships and Epistemologies of Futurity." Latinx literary and cultural environmentalisms in particular offer new ways for scholars, students, and activists to apprehend the world as it is and envision (and thus work toward) the world as it might be.

Critical Approaches to the Environment within Latinx Studies

Social, political, and scholarly interventions generally understood to be "environmental" prioritize healing a rupture between humans and nature. We trace the genealogy of this rupture to the rise of Western modernity and the colonial encounter, instead of the dominant environmental historiography, which roots the rupture in Enlightenment dualistic thinking and the capitalist forms of production that followed. That is, environmental studies often invokes the Cartesian split between mind and body as a key moment that enabled the objectification of nature and eventual abuse of the environment.[5] However, environmental studies rarely accompanies this critique of the Cartesian split with a similar assessment of the colonial encounter. This is where considering Latinx cultures alongside environmentalism becomes uniquely generative, particularly in relation to developing a decolonial environmental approach to Latinx cultural productions.

Part of our goal in this volume is to reevaluate environmental ideas through the lens of Latinx studies, particularly the focus on critical race theory that guides much of the scholarship in this field. Scholars such as Juan Flores, Marta Caminero-Santangelo, and Rosaura Sánchez and Beatrice Pita have noted that a focus on processes of race and racialization is a key theoretical concern in Latinx studies. Similarly, scholars such as Walter Mignolo and Aníbal Quijano have argued that the projects of Western humanism cannot be understood as separable from the advent of racism and colonialism in the seventeenth and eighteenth centuries. When considered from these perspectives, it is important to note that the insufficient attention environmental studies pays to processes of race and racialization, the colonial encounter, and sexualization and heteronormativity is both a manifestation of Western Enlightenment rationality and a result of Eurocentric forms of knowledge. In short, we contend that a fundamental contribution of this volume is as a corrective to forms of knowledge that do not take sufficient account of how racism, colonialism, capitalist exploitation, patriarchy, heteronormativity, anthropocentrism, and environmental degradation emerge from similar logics of domination and the Western will to know. Following the lead of Franz Fanon and Edward Said, whose ideas are considered more decolonial than environmental, we agree that given, as Said writes, "empire is an act of geographical violence," (225) discussions about the environment ought to engage colonialism, or they risk extending colonialism by ignoring this ongoing legacy. Inversely, decolonial efforts must address the environment, and failing to do so simply because of the environmental movement's prevailing investment in whiteness risks perpetuating the notion that land, geography, and spatial sovereignty are separate from ecosystemic conditions and their dynamic (as opposed to deterministic or anachronistic) relationship to cultural identities.

Thus, this volume is not strictly an environmental justice project, as it takes seriously these broader historical, geographical, epistemological, and biopolitical schisms between environment-as-geography (echoing Said) and "justice." That is, environmental justice as a framework does not capture the myriad forms of Latinx environmental expression and activism and has thus far failed to fully engage the ways that colonization as a form of geographical violence perhaps constitutes, as some scholars such as Voyles, Kyle Whyte, and Dhillon argue, the first environmental injustice: the colonial project itself.[6] It is therefore helpful to look to the decolonial and to critical geography to expand beyond the analyses delimited by any framework described as centering the "environment." In other words, land sovereignty can be an environmental justice issue, but it is also fruitful to understand it as geographical (i.e., relating to space) or as colonial. And if we take Said seriously, these two concepts cannot be separated.

Therefore, while environmental justice has been crucial for bringing questions of race and environmental inequality into the scholarly conversation, we hope to extend the frameworks from which these issues can be approached. Critical race studies scholarship by thinkers such as Michelle Alexander, Eduardo Bonilla-Silva, Mel Y. Chen, Kimberlé Crenshaw, Angela Davis, Emmanuel Chukwudi Eze, Cheryl Harris, Lisa Lowe, George Lipsitz, Charles Mills, Aileen Moreton-Robinson, Michael Omi and Howard Winant, Natalia Molina, Laura Pulido, David Roediger, and others have underscored the structural relationship between racism, capitalism, and social inequality. This body of scholarship also credits the innovative ways people of color resist their marginalization, including by mobilizing forms of power that leverage environmental ideas to consolidate existing social relations, as the opening story about our interviewees suggests. Although many of the essays included in this volume invoke environmental justice, we note the ways much of this work also extends conversations between Latinx studies and environmental studies by crediting authors and artists for the innovations they bring to environmental thinking, precisely through their intertwining of resistance to social, political, and environmental concerns. For these authors and artists, it is simply impossible to separate these struggles. They shift the terrain on which environmentalism takes place, emphasizing instead how racism, colonialism, and environmental racism are manifestations of a larger capitalist logic of power—what Quijano calls the "coloniality of power."

Latinx cultures often resist participating in the ruptures caused by the Cartesian split between human and nature, and Latinx cultural productions offer frequent and rich environmental representations.[7] It is, in fact, arguable that Latinx cultural productions evidence engagements with environmental ideas that precede the modern environmental movement (popularly dating to Rachel Carson's publication of *Silent Spring* in 1962). Authors such as Doña María Amparo Ruiz de Burton, Jovita González, Fabiola Cabeza de Baca, Josefina Niggli, and José Antonio Villarreal evidence keen environmental awareness of issues like land use, farmworker justice, culture and geography, and conservation that anticipates many of the concerns of the contemporary environmental movement. In such texts, we suggest, we can identify a tradition of decolonial environmental thought in Latinx cultural productions—thought that serves as precursors to the rich varieties of Latinx decolonial environmentalisms evident in the more contemporary (post-1950s) cultural productions explored in this collection.

Our use of such a term, *Latinx decolonial environmentalisms*, raises certain questions as to how we are using the concept of "the decolonial." For this volume, we define "the decolonial" as both an epistemological and a material project that emerges in large part from Latin American thought. Scholars such as Mignolo and Quijano have described the projects of modernity, coloniality, and racism as inextricable from one another as the "colonial matrix of power." In particular, Mignolo has debunked Western epistemology as a normative logic from which all knowledge might emerge. He instead demonstrates how this epistemological project has served as an ideological cover for the very material projects of capitalism, racism, and colonialism. The essays in this volume expand on these lines of reasoning by making visible the contributions of previously marginalized Latinx epistemologies to environmental thought. As author Helena María Viramontes explains in an interview for this volume, "when I refer to decolonizing the imagination, I begin with us—the colonized. We who have to question our assumptions and realities to break our chains of colonization and to decolonize ourselves into another form of thinking about who and what we are." In centering the decolonial, this collection supports a claim Paula Moya makes in Chapter 14: "Not merely challenging current relations of power and the logics that structure them, decolonial thinkers seek to subvert a colonial way of being by setting aside inherited assumptions to envision new social, political, and environmental possibilities."

We recognize that our use of the decolonial in a Latinx settler-colonial context may raise some red flags among indigenous studies scholars. This is because a certain incommensurability exists between the ways that indigenous studies scholars approach the decolonial, such as Eve Tuck and K. Wayne Yang's compelling argument against the use of the decolonial as metaphor, and the decolonial projects of Latin American studies, the framework from which the editors and the contributors of this volume most often draw. However, we find the intersections of these two approaches to the decolonial to be generative, especially from the unique perspective of Latinx creativities. Indeed, we might note that both indigenous studies scholars and decolonial Latin American studies thinkers caution against totalizing narratives, the erasure of incommensurabilities (Tuck and Yang 17, 28), and the creation of "new abstract universals" in decolonial thought (Mignolo and Walsh 1). Moreover, both conversations recognize the interconnections between the epistemological, ontological, and material workings of colonialism, especially the centrality of the process through which indigenous relationships to lands suffer a process of ongoing erasure by colonialist claims to land as property.

We note, as well, the complexities of Latinx engagement with Tuck and Yang's definitions of the decolonial given Latinx subject positions. Latinxs share an uneasy relationship with settler colonialism as both perpetrators of colonial violence and objects of settler-colonial dispossession. It is without question that Spanish conquistadors and mestizos were part of the force that appropriated indigenous lands during the conquest of the Americas, as well as participants in other colonial and neocolonial projects from the Civil War to the ongoing imperial violence of the Iraq and Afghanistan Wars. Yet it is also true that, as the Chicano Movement and ongoing social movement groups dedicated to decolonizing the island of Puerto Rico attest, Latinxs have experienced the theft of lands by settlers. As a group that also claims historical ties to indigenous communities from what is now the United States and other parts of the Americas, Latinxs share complicated relationships with the decolonial that can neither be encapsulated by indigeneity nor be easily dismissed. Additionally, Latinx identities include formerly enslaved African populations, adding another dimension to settler-colonial dynamics.

Consequently, the essays in this volume explore the complex relationship between Latinx identities and lived experiences and the sometimes conflicting ways Latinxs seek to engage, disrupt, and amend decolonial forms of environmentalism. For example, the resistance to the neoliberal production of space by Latinx authors and artists sits in uneasy relation to settler-colonial thought as Latinx land reclamation projects always simultaneously serve and disturb settler-colonial logics. A "Latinx environmental" focus reveals new possibilities from the tensions within decolonial approaches. Latinxs inherit genealogies of both colonizer and colonized, so the Latinx experience positions this community to develop what Chela Sandoval calls a "differential consciousness," a capacity to enter into a "'third meaning,' which is that which always haunts any other two meanings in binary opposition" (Sandoval 141). In this volume, we argue that the discourse surrounding environmental issues and the material realities that shape the human relation to the earth offer an especially unique and powerful opportunity to show the Latinx differential consciousness in action. We remain committed to the possibilities for interethnic, antiracist coalitions as a form of decolonial environmentalist practice. Part of what we find compelling about the essays and interviews included in this volume are the ways decolonial thought reveals that antiracism and critical environmentalism are not necessarily at odds. As the essays we include indicate, we take seriously the contribution of cultural analysis and production to the decolonial, even as we take seriously the idea that such work is always partial and incomplete if not accompanied by material changes and may even reinforce "settler moves to innocence" (Tuck and Yang 3).

Race and Ethnicity in the Environmental Humanities

Like mainstream environmentalism broadly, subfields within the environmental humanities (e.g., ecocriticism, environmental history, environmental anthropology) have grappled with legacies of exclusion and racialization. We can look to the development of ecocriticism as a particular example, but similar dynamics have occurred in the other relevant subfields. Early literature-and-environment studies, or what Lawrence Buell calls "first wave" ecocriticism, privileged descriptions of the pastoral wilderness retreat in nature writing, which reflected the political aims of the early environmental movement: to preserve pristine nature for aesthetic appreciation and transcendence. Like environmentalism, ecocriticism has largely ignored myriad environmental identities that did not fit into this narrow politics. "Waves" of ecocriticism since its inception have taken race much more seriously, drawing on ethnic studies, postcolonial studies, environmental justice, and critical race theory to interrogate environmentalism's "possessive investment in whiteness," to use Lipsitz's concept. At a minimum, these more recent waves bring more voices to the environmental table by showing how many communities appreciate nature and articulate traditional environmentalist values.

However, simply including nondominant writers who express traditional environmental values ignores how those traditional environmental values rest on what Denis Cosgrove calls "hidden attachments" (36) to white supremacy and colonialism. That is, if environmental values are inherently based on an ideology of exclusion that preserves beautiful landscapes for certain communities deemed to be desirable citizens, then what does it mean when the abject, subaltern, or colonized performs those traditional environmental forms? Put another way, does including more voices, simply because they reference existing environmental ideology, undermine the radical work these authors do outside of environmentalism, such as negotiating sovereignty, articulating an "active subjectivity," or decolonizing cultural production? In *Writing the Goodlife*, Priscilla Solis Ybarra goes as far as to say that the word *environment* itself reinforces the separation between humans and nature, even as, ironically, "environmentalism struggles to reunite humans with our natural environment," and that many writers ignored by the ecocritical canon are disregarded precisely because they do not see their work as primarily about the politics of preserving nature because "they never needed to become environmentalists in the first place" (28). As Ybarra asks, does the word *environment* remain relevant when different communities "may understand nature in a different way as to merit a different term" (25)? Even calling non-Western, nondominant works "environmental" holds the potential to ignore the intersections of social justice, identity, national belonging, and cultural tradition that shape different communities' environmentalisms.

While an analysis of the critical turns or "waves" ecocriticism has undergone is one useful way to understand how the field has incorporated questions of race, a more expansive genealogy might argue that there are three ways that ecocriticism has dealt with race, all of which radically challenge what counts as ecocriticism. One approach distinguishes mainstream environmental works and ecocriticism from environmental justice activism and scholarship. Where the former privileges wilderness, for example, the latter privileges places where people "live, work, play, and pray." Some of the key scholars and texts in early environmental justice ecocriticism are Julie Sze, Joni Adamson, Giovanna Di Chiro, Mei Mei Evans, Rachel Stein, Noël Sturgeon, T. V. Reed, and the edited collections *The Environmental Justice Reader* and *New Perspectives on Environmental Justice: Gender, Sexuality, and Activism*. This scholarship identified environmental justice themes in literature and sought to understand how literary criticism could further the aims of the environmental justice social movement. As Sze argues, literature freed representations of environmental injustice from the modes of documentary and statistics. Through experimental forms and figurative language, Sze shows that literature may theorize and communicate the experiences of environmental injustices in ways that social science methodologies typically do not. Building on these earlier scholars, Rob Nixon argues that literature and cultural production may be able to address the representational challenges of what he terms "slow violence," or violence that is hard to apprehend because it often results from the exponential magnification of multiple harms, or because its scale in time and space is either too large or too small for human forms of knowing. The binary between mainstream environmental works and environmental justice is useful not only in that it includes many previously underrepresented voices in an environmental framework but also for these new frameworks and themes it brings to environmental inquiry.

A second approach centers the epistemological moorings of critical race theory in environmental literary analysis and is exemplified in the works of

Giovanna Di Chiro, Ian Finseth, Janet Fiskio, John Gamber, Robert Hayashi, Hsuan L. Hsu, Jennifer James, Jeffrey Myers, Paul Outka, Shazia Rahman, Sarah Jaquette Ray, Karen Salt, Noël Sturgeon, Julie Sze, David J. Vázquez, and Sarah D. Wald, to mention only a few. These scholars critique ecocriticism from the perspective of critical race studies, untangling the field's investments in racial hierarchy and focusing on cultural productions that sometimes elude obvious environmental categories. Further, ecocriticism and the environmental humanities have productively engaged disability studies (Chen; Kafer; Ray and Sibara), queer theory (Mortimer-Sandilands and Erickson; Seymour), animal studies (Huggan and Tiffin; Gaard; Haraway; Wolfe), and new materialism (Alaimo; Iovino and Oppermann). Although this list of critical works is far from exhaustive, we do want to note that ecocriticism and the environmental humanities have connected with these latter areas in ways that contribute meaningfully to Latinx literary analysis, as this volume highlights.

The social justice turn in ecocriticism and the environmental humanities and the environmental justice turn in critical race theory set the stage for this project. The work herein suggests that environmental justice is not the only useful tool resulting from the synergy between critical race theory and environmental thought, even as environmental justice has proved to be essential to bridging social justice and the environment and to challenging the race and class privilege within the environmental movement, as Phaedra Pezzullo and Ronald Sandler (*Environmental Justice and Environmentalism*) and David Schlosberg (*Environmental Justice and the New Pluralism*) have argued. But the engagement of critical race theory and the social justice direction of environmental studies opens possibilities for a range of new forms of theorizing and cultural production. This volume seeks to chart some of that terrain by advancing a third approach, which might be understood as a recovery model, that neither adds more voices to the existing environmental table without questioning the very terms of that category nor assigns all nonwhite environmental concerns to environmental justice. This recovery mode demonstrates the myriad ways that communities excluded from the dominant environmental and national imaginary have long held environmental values and continue to create new ways of thinking about environmental issues. The question shifts from "How do we get more diversity in environmental humanities?" to "How can environmental humanists recognize the ways that diverse groups have always been 'environmental'?" Exemplary recovery scholars are Camille T. Dungy, John Claborn, Carolyn Finney, Salma Monani, Kimberly N. Ruffin, Whyte, and Ybarra.

In forwarding a recovery model, this project seeks to correct assumptions that Latinxs do not care about the environment and to serve as a check to environmentalist moralizing, which often positions Latinxs as "ecologically other," to use Ray's term. In contrast, our approach considers the writers analyzed herein as bearers of environmental knowledge and as practitioners of sustainable cultural praxis with traditions that stretch longer than contemporary U.S. environmental thought. We further argue that these authors, artists, and other cultural workers are minoritarian precisely because of the very processes of colonialism, empire, and the Cartesian will to know that made environmentalism as we now know it necessary in the first place. As is clear in the organization of our book, we do not advance a recovery model as exclusionary of environmental justice concerns or the necessary scholarship of critical race theory. In fact, these other approaches are foundational to the work of a recovery project.

Recovery efforts have proved to be somewhat uneven in relation to the cultures and populations they engage. For example, there are built-in incommensurabilities between African American environmentalisms and Asian American environmentalisms related to differences in histories of enslavement and immigration, cultural influences, and U.S. racial formation. Similarly, indigenous cultures that inscribed their environmental ethics within vernacular culture might not be commensurate with the literary articulations of Chicanxs. Incommensurabilities also exist among the varieties of groups and individuals homogenized within any identity category. For example, the different histories and experiences of Chinese immigrants in the 1880s, Nisei with U.S. citizenship interned in U.S. concentration camps during World War II, and Vietnamese refugees entering the United States in the 1980s are gathered under a singular subject position (Asian American), problematically implying a common cultural heritage and historical experience in the United States. Moreover, and as Laura Pulido points out in the foreword to this volume, not all Latinxs agree with or ascribe to progressive environmental values. One need only look to lowriders or Latinx climate-change deniers to perceive that Latinx cultures are far from a monolithic environmental group. It thus bears repeating that as yet another panethnic identifier, Latinx is as complicated a subject identity as any. Rather than eliding these differences, we choose to highlight the uneven and sometimes incommensurate aspects of Latinx environmentalisms. We embrace Latinx as a politically efficacious category as well as a useful one for literary and cultural analysis given the ways we see aesthetic and formal choices as always and inherently political.[8]

Indeed, almost all of the essays engage with form and prioritize aesthetic questions. Yet they do so in ways that foreground social and historical contexts. In many of the essays we have included, form and context are coconstitutive. Such essays appear in their methodological approaches to refuse a dichotomy between surface and paranoid readings or between formalism and new historicism. As such, they fit broadly within the socio-formal reading methodology that Paula Moya outlines in *The Social Imperative: Race,*

Close Reading, and Contemporary Literary Criticism. As Moya explains her methodology, "I attend to the social dimensions of literary form by describing how the thematic and formal features of a text mediate the historically-situated cultural and political tensions expressed in a work of literature" (10). The scholarship included in this anthology is far less engaged with the social and cultural psychology that most shapes Moya's thinking. Yet many of our essays share an investment in the role of aesthetic form as mediating or navigating historical context and social condition.

The usefulness of Moya's framework for our project of Latinx environmental literary thought is perhaps unsurprising when seen in the context of two of Moya's major influences: the postpositivist realism of the Future of Minority Studies Project (which Moya cofounded) and new materialism and agential realism as detailed, for example, in the work of environmental humanities scholar Stacy Alaimo and philosopher and physicist Karen Barad. As Moya explains, postpositivist realism contends "that identities are better understood as socially significant and context-specific ideological constructs that refer in mediated but non-arbitrary ways to verifiable aspects of the social world" (28). New materialists view nature and matter itself as agents contributing to the construction of reality and see human bodies as permeable, incapable of being disentangled from larger flows of matter and energy. Both projects see a more-than-human world that stands aside and yet remains inseparable from the social construction of identity, culture, and even matter. Moya's *The Social Imperative* suggests the possibility of an alliance between cutting-edge approaches to identity within Latinx studies and innovative approaches to nature within ecocritical studies.

Moya's socio-formal reading methodology helps explain two other patterns that emerged in the essays solicited for this volume—the focus of the majority of the chapters on a single author or single text and thus on close reading as a primary methodology. We see the predominance of close reading, which often requires attending to a particular text for an extended number of pages, as an important contribution this volume makes, echoing the investment in formalism as part of Moya's socio-formal methodology. As Ralph E. Rodriguez has so brilliantly outlined in his recent *Latinx Literature Unbound: Undoing Ethnic Expectation*, the rise of new formalism (defined as attention to both the formal and generic qualities that constitute a text) during the past decade has enabled a different window into Latinx literature—one that both challenges our expectations of what texts "do" and helps us see how authors push against formal conventions in order to animate political possibilities.

Our contention in this volume is that forms of cultural representation matter. The stories that we tell to and about ourselves are key to how we understand and interpret the world. We hold that understanding the different environmental stories that Latinxs tell is crucial to developing decolonial environmental imaginaries. For us, the predominance of close reading is a critical strategy for understanding the formal, political, and sociological aspects of Latinx environmentalisms. As the essays included in this volume attest, close attention to textual form and analysis is a key strategy for understanding the innovative qualities of these complex environmental ideas.

Organization of the Book: Place, Justice, and the Decolonial

The foreword and afterword of this book speak to how this project intervenes in the two fields we are seeking to bring together in new ways: Latinx studies and the environmental humanities. Laura Pulido's foreword explores the contributions and remaining questions of *Latinx Environmentalism*'s intervention in Latinx studies, while Stacy Alaimo's afterword, "What Is Absent: Fields, Futures, and Latinx Environmentalisms," maps the book's extension of race and ethnic studies into the environmental humanities. In addition to a shared commitment to various forms of decolonial thought, the essays herein develop three persistent themes around which we organized the volume: racial capital and the production of place, an expansion of environmentalism around justice, and an engagement with alternative kinships and decolonial epistemologies.

The collection opens with a series of essays that engage the theme of place, specifically the role of racial capital in the production of place. These essays cumulatively expose the processes of racial capital (the idea that race is a structuring logic of capitalism), which produces the expendability of certain people and landscapes. In using the term *racial capital*, we draw from its original usage in Cedric Robinson's *Black Marxism: The Making of the Black Radical Tradition*, as well as ideas in the longer tradition of Black radical thought going back to W.E.B. DuBois that Robinson identifies. Racial capitalism is a phrase that marks the ways that racism infuses the social structures of capitalist development and is fundamental to the way that capitalism operates. As literary scholar Jodi Melamed explains, "Capital can only be capital when it is accumulating, and it can only accumulate by producing and moving through relations of severe inequality among human groups" (77). Racism produces the relations of inequality through which capital accumulation occurs. As Melamed highlights, these relations of inequality include facets of white supremacy such as slavery, genocide, incarceration, and exploitation of migrants as well as contemporary modes of multicultural liberalism and colorblind racism, which value some forms of humanity and devalue others.

The essays in this first section, following the work of Laura Pulido, echo the centrality of place and the environment to the workings of racial capitalism. Multiple essays return to Pulido's insight that "studying environmental racism is important for an additional reason: it helps us understand racism" ("Rethinking Environmental Racism" 12) and affirm her contention that environmental racism is "fundamental to contemporary racial capitalism" ("Geographies of Race and Ethnicity II" 525). The essays emphasize, moreover, the importance of literary and cultural approaches to environmental racism, using cultural critique to expose the ways neoliberalism or earlier forms of racial capitalism obscure the production of environmental privilege and environmental racism, often through narratives of individual attainment and multicultural inclusion.

In this section's first essay, "Greenwashing the White Savior: Cancer Clusters, Supercrips, and *McFarland, USA*," Julie A. Minich examines the erasure of environmental racism in the production of the Disney film *McFarland, USA* (2015). Minich is interested in "the narrative elements that permit stories about environmental racism to be told (or that facilitate their silencing)" (Minich). While, in Disney's narrative, McFarland is the story of a town where a white track coach leads a group of impoverished Latino track stars to victory, Latinx studies and environmental studies scholars may recognize McFarland as the site of cancer clusters featured in the United Farm Workers' film about pesticides, *The Wrath of Grapes* (1986), and fictionalized in Cherríe Moraga's play *Heroes and Saints* (1994). Minich, drawing on disability studies, argues that the film "discursively supplant[s] the McFarland children disabled by cancer" with the victorious bodies of the track team. Minich's essay reveals how neoliberal narratives of uplift and inclusion rely on a decontextualization, an erasure of history that obscures the disabling effects of racial capitalism and environmental racism. As Minich argues, *McFarland, USA* erases the structural inequalities that produce disability with an inspiring story of individual accomplishment and spectacular able-bodiedness, prioritizing emotional appeal over justice and substituting empathy for social change (Minich). Tropes of perseverance and hard work obscure the real landscapes of pesticides and prisons that present actual barriers to McFarland's residents.

Like Minich, Sarah D. Wald is concerned with the ways narratives of neoliberal multicultural inclusion erase longer histories of place. In "The National Park Foundation's 'American Latino Expedition': Consumer Citizenship as Pathway to Multicultural National Belonging," Wald examines a contest that granted Latinx bloggers all-expenses-paid outdoor adventures through the National Park Foundation and various sponsors including outdoor retailer REI and park concessionaire Aramark. Like Minich, Wald is interested in ways Latinx individuals are upheld when their achievements reinforce a neoliberal framework. According to Wald, a consumer citizenship is at work in the American Latino Expedition whereby the purchase of gear and participation in particular forms of outdoor adventure serve to write certain Latinx individuals into the nation while obscuring the claims of other less worthy (or less affluent) national subjects. The American Latino Expedition, Wald argues, fits into the new racial order that Jodi Melamed describes in which "official antiracism," as state project, replaces older modes of redistributive antiracism to further the expansion of global capitalism, creating new forms of environmental harms experienced by expendable groups unable or unwilling to be productive citizens within the global capitalist order.

In "'A Story Is a Physical Space': An Interview with Héctor Tobar," Shane Hall and Tobar explore how the physical environment and environmental thinking within the community are central to Tobar's work. The idea of functioning as a "paid witness" is crucial to his environmental imaginary. Part of what emerges from Tobar's conversation with Hall is that ideas about place and social belonging are intimately related to one's environment. As Hall points out, Tobar's work "stands out for vivifying how history and power relations forge environmental and social landscapes." This is apparent as Tobar describes his changing perceptions of Los Angeles in ways that illustrate that the various environments he captures in his writing are manifestations of capitalist inequality. The attention to environmental violence, individual experience, power, and privilege manifest as Tobar discusses his construction of the environment in *The Tattooed Soldier*, *The Barbarian Nurseries*, and *Deep Down Dark*. While Tobar does not use the term *racial capitalism*, his interview describes the ways in which his writing captures the negotiation of race, place, and power under capitalism.

Christopher Perreira builds on the theories of place forwarded by Minich, Wald, and Tobar, with a focus on how place can help reveal the ideological intersections of environmentalism and neoliberalism. In "Speculative Futurity and the Eco-cultural Politics of *Lunar Braceros: 2125–2148*," Perreira examines the relationship between waste management and population management through the unique genre of the "nanotext" invented by this novel. According to Perreira, *Lunar Braceros: 2125–2148* unearths the "layered story of colonialism and racial capitalism" that remains unseen in *McFarland, USA* and the American Latino Expedition. Telegraphing later chapters in this collection, Perreira scrutinizes the ways the novel "foregrounds revolutionary and radical forms of kinship that insist on imagining futures otherwise." The radical kinships in the novel allow the possibility of futurity in the novel's trajectory despite what Minich would call the disabling socioeconomic barriers of the landscapes neoliberalism created. Perreira's critique is that the greening of the nation-state produces enclosures of people and environments and, through the logic of neoliberalism, elides racial capitalism and the production of place. One solution, he concludes, is alternative kinship epistemologies, which are taken up further by essays in the last section.

A concern for the production of place and its contestation through art is also at the center of Jennifer Garcia Peacock's contribution to this volume, "Sun Ma(i)d: Art, Activism, and Environment in Ester Hernández's Central Valley." In this essay, Garcia Peacock examines Hernández's iconic *Sun Mad* poster and attends to the aesthetic and material context of Hernández's work, including the agricultural landscapes that Minich discusses and that haunt the depictions of labor in *Lunar Braceros: 2125–2148*. She is particularly interested in the ways Hernández's engagement with rural aesthetic traditions contrasts with "the rapidly industrializing countryside that was taking shape around her and her loved ones." The place-making at the heart of Hernández's aesthetic decisions contests the industrial capitalist territorialization taking place around her, a territorialization taken to speculative extremes in *Lunar Braceros*. In this way, Garcia Peacock recuperates *Sun Mad* from a decontextualizing or universalizing reading that renders its critique obvious without accounting for the ways it reflects the particularities of Hernández's lived experiences, including the landscapes she traversed.

Like the other authors in this section and in all of her creative works, Ana Castillo, interviewed here by Ybarra and Wald, seeks to expose the processes through which economic, gender, and racial exploitation occurs. Specifically, Castillo discusses her time as a student at the University of Chicago, where neoliberal economist Milton Friedman taught, and her critique of neoliberalism's effects, including environmental effects, on women of color globally. As Castillo asks, "Who is dispensable on this planet? The poor and needy who must work under whatever circumstances are available to them at whatever equally atrocious pay in order to keep their families alive. Apparently, according to the current administration," and, we would add, many previous administrations, "the planet is also dispensable." Castillo draws connections between the textual politics of her novels and this larger critique shared by Minich, Wald, Tobar, Perreira, and Garcia Peacock that foregrounds the processes through which the expendability and disposability of some communities and landscapes are obscured in prevalent popular narratives. Castillo offers an apt conclusion to this section on the production of place, as she articulates her positionality as one who consistently writes to expose the strategies of racial capital.

A second theme, justice, emerged in relation to two key questions that open this volume: What makes this work environmental, and why give these contributions this explicit label? One way the contributions to this volume seek to answer these questions is by accounting for the complex ways Latinx cultures are environmental but often don't assume the mantle of environmentalism. In considering this question, the essays in this section explore how Latinx environmentalisms intertwine critiques of capitalism, colonialism, and racism with environmental concerns. Within this framework, we argue that some forms of environmental thinking in Latinx literature and culture are misunderstood—or worse, overlooked—because they do not conform to what we have come to expect from environmentalism. Justice is often a core tenet in these forms of Latinx environmentalisms.

The essays and interviews in this section therefore trouble the borders of literature, culture, and environment in order to expand what counts as environmental thinking. For these scholars and authors, it is impossible to separate environmental struggles from other social justice concerns. They shift the terrain on which environmentalism takes place, emphasizing instead how racism, colonialism, and environmental racism are manifestations of a larger capitalist logic of power, or again, the "coloniality of power."

For example, Sarah Jaquette Ray's chapter dovetails with Castillo's interview in the previous section in its consideration of Castillo's novel *So Far from God*. Ray examines *So Far from God* in terms that expand the novel's reception as an environmental text. With the possible exception of Helena María Viramontes's novel *Under the Feet of Jesus*, perhaps no other Latinx or Chicanx novel has garnered as much attention from environmental studies and ecocritical scholars as *So Far from God*. Yet as Ray points out, Castillo's novel "indicts not only colonial-capitalist patriarchy but also environmentalism itself," clearing the way for a new understanding of the novel as demonstrating "how dominant environmentalism is *part of* the colonial-capitalist oppressive systems that environmental justice theory and activism challenge."

In an interview conducted by David J. Vázquez, Sarah D. Wald, and Paula M. L. Moya, Helena María Viramontes also expands the conventional parameters of "environmental." She acknowledges that environmental thinking has been a part of her work since she was a fifteen-year-old student at Garfield High School in East Los Angeles. While her conception of environmental thinking is inclusive of such traditional environmental figures as Rachel Carson and ideas such as "spaceship earth" (popularized by Buckminster Fuller in the 1960s), she also expands what it means to do environmental work by suggesting that "we carry our environments within ourselves." Viramontes's conception of embodied environmental knowledge shows how labor, culture, and materiality are fundamental to understanding the human-environment relationship.

Randy Ontiveros' essay, "'Between Water and Song': Maria Melendez and the Contours of Contemporary Latinx Ecopoetry," continues the thread of discerning environmental knowledges, specifically in the context of lyric poetry and the question of Latinx engagements with nature during a time of ecological crisis. His essay brings an engagement with genre to the discussion, adding to the robust subfield of eco-poetics to argue that the genre of poetry can be looked to for the ways it uniquely articulates a Latinx way of relating with the earth in the contexts of twenty-first century poetics and the social justice imperatives that operate within Latinx literary traditions. Ontiveros engages in close readings of several poems by the Chicana poet Maria Melendez in order to highlight "thematic and formal traditions vital to Latinx poetry" that Ontiveros argues move "Latinx poetry in new directions by imagining those traditions within the generic conventions of ecopoetry."

Complementing these perspectives are ideas offered by author Lucha Corpi, interviewed for this volume by Gabriela Nuñez. Corpi's poetry from the 1980s inspired other Chicana feminist writers, including Cherríe Moraga and Ana Castillo, who are also interviewed in this volume (Aldama). Her poetry from the 1980s gave way to an autobiographical novel in 1989, *Delia's Song*, and she now writes one of the most prolific detective series by a Chicana writer, the Gloria Damasco mysteries. Although Corpi rejects the idea that she is an "environmentalist," she acknowledges that in practice she shares environmental values, including the fact that she finds sustenance in the natural world: "Green makes me focus. If I see green, I feel not only calm, but I feel hopeful. It's sort of like knowing that the world will go on, even if I'm not in it anymore, that there is that possibility of constant renewal, as there is in nature, and that my children, my grandchildren, my great-grandchildren, will be able to enjoy that and have that sense of calm and focus also." This writer asserts her relation to life on Earth without recourse to the conventional environmentalist frameworks. In this way, Corpi participates in the various expansions of environmentalisms apparent in Ray's and Ontiveros's essays and Viramontes's interview.

The essays and interviews included in the final section of the volume build on the previous two sections by foregrounding various forms of decolonial environmental imaginaries. Latinx cultural production creates an awareness of how the history of colonization and the ongoing, present-day manifestations of colonialism materially impact any experience of the environment, as we have seen in our discussion of racial capitalism's production of place. The decolonial analytic also reenvisions what counts as environmentalism, or, in a broader sense, makes "environmentalism" a difficult idea for Latinx ecological thought. In addition to looking at how coloniality (the ongoing impacts of colonization) has shaped our past and present relation to the earth, what if we begin to imagine our future, taking seriously a range of alternative ways to define relations with one another and with the earth? Several of the essays in this collection envision decolonial alternatives to dominant ways of seeing our past in continuity with our present and future and propose counterframeworks of kinship that challenge the ways that neoliberalism, as yet another aspect of coloniality, underscores normative relationality.

It is important to see how the essays and interviews in this section do not necessarily conform to a linear chronology in their expectations for what is possible in human relations with the natural environment; they suggest instead that creative temporalities are key to decolonization and social justice. The contributions in this section push against traditional social relationships by refusing to conform to the categories or power relations of nuclear families or even extended family. Indeed, these essays advocate for reinventing kinship, importantly including the land as a relation. In some cases, they argue that Latinxs have always already been accomplishing these "new" models of relationships and community. Rather than considering these new relations as contradictions in terms, the contributions in this section assert that we attend to the ways that Latinx creativities pose a challenge to chronology and to false dichotomies such as indigenous wisdom versus Western knowledge. By acknowledging these false dichotomies, the contributions in this section collectively argue for recognizing how Latinx creativities have always already proposed a wide range of kinship structures. From this standpoint, antichronology itself is a strategy of resistance to modernity that declares the survival of pre-Columbian epistemologies evident in Latinx cultural expression. Thus, in the essays in this section, themes of temporality, futurity, and alternative epistemologies help address the question, "What does Latinx cultural production offer environmental thought?"

Vázquez opens this section by identifying decolonial themes in a contemporary urban context. He considers Ernesto Quiñonez's novel *Bodega Dreams* (2000) and its critique of gentrification, and he argues that the environmental nature of this critique is inseparable from its decolonial possibilities. The vector of this consideration of gentrification relies on the ways that Latinx communities (in this case the Puerto Rican community in New York's Spanish Harlem) lay claim to urban spaces by memorializing resistant histories. Vázquez thus suggests that "the novel offers an alternative ethos of preservation that memorializes the Puerto Rican Movement, especially the environmental activism of the Young Lords, and valorizes Latinx cultural and historical ties to Spanish Harlem." Taken together, these examples suggest the richness of Latinx environmental thought and the potential they hold for continuing to revise how we engage with environmental ideas.

Ylce Irizarry's essay, "Postcards from the Edges of Haiti: The Latinx Ecocriticism of Mayra Montero's *In the Palm of Darkness*," argues that Montero refuses to see ecological and social extinction in Haiti as purely a result of the Duvalier regimes and invokes an alternative sense of time to showcase colonial violence and neocolonial interference as examples of what Nixon calls "slow violence." Irizarry explicitly foregrounds the decolonial by arguing that the novel prefigures the "postcolonial, feminist, and decolonial ecocritical approaches" of contemporary ecocritical thought. She aligns Montero's novel with Ybarra's approach to decoloniality, specifically Montero's prioritization of nonhuman bodies and non-Western epistemologies.

The decolonial epistemology that Paula M. L. Moya's essay engages relates to lived experience and kinship. In "'Against the Sorrowful and Infinite Solitude': Environmental Consciousness and Streetwalker Theorizing in Helena María Viramontes's *Their Dogs Came with Them*," Moya reads the novel using a combination of Nixon's theory of slow violence and María Lugones's "streetwalker theory" to argue that an embodied, countergeographical (or even eco-phenomenological) philosophy of "streetwalking" demonstrates how an alliance of young women who inhabit a marginalized space together—East Los Angeles of the 1960s—gather more strength and resilience from one another than they do in relation to their nuclear families.

Through "streetwalking," they inhabit public space in a way that rejects the domesticity that Western modernity expects of women and develops a "decolonial imaginary" in response to the slow violence of infrastructure creep. This practice of public alliance invents an experience of the outdoors that operates far afield from conventional environmental expectations and enhances the complexity of Latinx decolonial environmentalism.

"Oedipal Wrecks: Queer Animal Ecologies in Justin Torres's *We the Animals*," by Richard T. Rodríguez, imagines alternative kinships in ways that center a decolonial vision. His reading of the novel integrates childhood, masculinity, filial relations, and human-animal identifications in order to argue for a language and sense of belonging required for environmental justice. The essay considers animal symbolism and sexual diversity as they complicate notions of nature and family bonds, which we see as extrapolating on the decolonial insight that the atomistic family unit is a product of empire. Rodríguez brings together posthumanism, queer theory, and ecocriticism to read this novel as offering an "alternative language of belonging that refuses the often interlocking heteronormative tenets of environment and kinship," which links it importantly to the decolonial Latinx environmentalisms that animate our volume.

This section ends with Priscilla Solis Ybarra's interview with Cherríe Moraga. In "The Body Knows and the Land Has Memory," Moraga elaborates on her long experience writing about colonization's disruption of the human relation with the natural environment. She sees humanity's relation with the earth as fundamental to achieving justice and thus challenges readers to recognize the body politics of knowledge and the way that a reciprocally respectful relation with land must include regard for land's memory—a memory that takes place outside of Western conceptions of time. As such, by looking to the past, Moraga suggests that we build toward a more just future. Together, these essays punctuate the volume by drawing together our focus on decolonial thinking, environmental justice, and Latinx cultural production in the service of imagining a future where social and environmental justice are in harmony with one another.

Why the Preponderance of Chicanx Texts?

As we gathered contributions for this anthology, we struggled with the overrepresentation of Chicanx texts. We aspired to a collection that would speak broadly to the category of Latinx literary and cultural traditions, balancing work from a variety of contexts including those of Caribbean, Central American, and South American Latinx migrants. Ultimately, only five of fifteen submissions attended to literature or cultural production outside of a Chicanx context. While we were (and are) disappointed that we did not recruit essays that spoke more evenly to the variety of Latinx literary expressions, we were delighted by the essays that came in, and we have come to make a certain sense of these results.

First, the essays we gathered reflect and represent the long history of scholarly engagement with place, space, and the environment within Chicanx literary and cultural studies. Pioneering scholars such as Pulido and Peña have exposed the crucial role that Chicanx activists and artists have played in environmental justice struggles and the role of decolonial struggles over land in the creation of a Chicanx environmental ethic. Moreover, Gloria Anzaldúa's *Borderlands/La Frontera* is not only a crucial work of Latinx scholarship and a transformative work of queer, women-of-color critique; it is also an impressive work of decolonial environmental imaginary with long-reaching implications for Chicanx literary and artistic production, as Ybarra discusses in *Writing the Goodlife* (115–117). Many of the pieces in this anthology are written in a scholarly tradition that includes Mary Pat Brady's examination of the ways Chicana literature and art have exposed the processural quality of space and Raúl Homero Villa's attention to Chicanx expressive culture's resistance to spatial oppression in *Barrio-Logos*.

Recently, Ybarra, Ontiveros, Wald, and Claudia Sadowski-Smith have each connected Chicanx literature and cultural productions to environmental thought in their various critical works. In *Writing the Goodlife*, Ybarra identifies a tradition of Mexican American environmental thought as decolonial with roots at least as early as the Mexican-American War. Ontiveros positions Chicano Movement cultural production from the art of Santa Barraza to the writings of Enriqueta Vasquez in *El Grito del Norte* as an environmentalism influenced by but distinct from the politics popularly captured in the environmentalism of the first Earth Day in 1970. In *The Nature of California*, Wald identifies a continuation of this artistic environmental thinking in what she reads as the queer ecology encapsulated in migrant butterfly art by cultural workers such as Favianna Rodriguez and Julio Salgado. Sadowski-Smith argues that civil rights struggles on the border as reflected in Chicanx literature have taken the form most recently of environmental justice. All four of these works make clear that a rich tradition of environmental thinking exists within Chicanx literature and cultural production that is distinct from environmentalism as it has been popularly conceived. This rich literary and scholarly tradition within Chicanx studies may make it easier to situate existing and forthcoming scholarship within rubrics of environmentalism, environmental justice, slow violence, and decolonial environmentalism.

Yet it is also worth noting that ecocriticism has had a longer-standing engagement with Chicanx literature than with Latinx literature more broadly defined. Ecocritics have pushed the boundaries of their own field and the genre of nature-writing by interpreting texts like Ana Castillo's *So Far from God*, Rudolfo Anaya's *Bless Me Ultima*, and Helena María Viramontes's *Under the Feet of Jesus*, among other texts. Such readings have often served to advance the scholarly conversation more within ecocriticism than within Chicanx or Latinx studies. Indeed, ecocritical studies rarely engage with those fields writ large.[9]

Environmentally attuned literary scholars' preliminary work on Chicanx texts could be interpreted as evidence that such environmental themes occurred earlier in these works than in Latinx literature more broadly. However, it seems more likely that the early ecocritical attention speaks to a U.S. West and antiurban bias that persists in ecocriticism. The Association for the Study of Literature and the Environment was founded, after all, at a meeting of the Western Literature Association. This makes it far less surprising that ecocritics would produce analyses of Castillo's and Anaya's fiction before picking up the writings of Piri Thomas, Judith Ortiz Cofer, Sylvia Sellers-García, and Sabrina Vourvoulias.[10] Clear evidence exists tying eastern, urban, and a wide variety of other Latinx authors outside of a Chicanx context to environmental justice concerns and situating them as producers of environmental imaginaries worthy of consideration. Much urban Latinx literature addresses the ways in which environmental racism operates as a form of oppression, with the environment acting as a key axis through which race is produced and racism experienced and enforced. The urban environmental justice struggles of the Puerto Rican Movement, such as the Garbage Offensive and free lead testing of the Young Lords, for example, certainly resonate within much Nuyorican literature. Additionally, the environment plays a crucial role in producing and resisting colonial discourses in much literature of U.S.-Caribbean migrants. It may be that the transnational contexts and anticolonial outlooks of much contemporary Latinx literature, including the work of Junot Díaz, Cristina García, and Nelly Rosario, require an environmental analysis only now appearing in scholarly works. Frameworks emerging from postcolonial ecocriticism, such as slow violence, thus combine with postcolonial studies discussions of diaspora and home to make the environmental imaginary of Caribbean literatures and their engagement with island ecosystems more legible within existing scholarly frameworks. The literary imagination here leads the way for the scholarship.

Latinx, Chicanx, and the Politics of Naming

Readers of this introduction have probably noticed our use of the terms *Latinx* and *Chicanx*, in place of other identifiers such as Latino, Chicano, Latina/o, Chicana/o, Latin@, or Chican@. Our use of the contested and still-in-formation terms *Latinx* and *Chicanx* is strategic. Although these identifiers are inchoate, we use the terms *Latinx* and *Chicanx* to signal our rejection of rigid gender and sexual binaries. We likewise signal our solidarity with LGBTQ and feminist scholarship and activism that we see at the cutting edge of both ecocriticism and Latinx studies. Frances Negrón-Muntaner explains that "Latinx is calling attention to issues of gender and LGBT exclusion and marginalization in a broad way," and that "the 'x' is also standing in for a critique of larger structures of power" (Armus). We concur with Negrón-Muntaner's assessment of the importance of Latinx and Chicanx as disruptive of gender and sexual normativity and point to these terms' potential utility for underscoring similar heteropatriarchal problematics that operate within ecocriticism and environmental studies.

It should be unsurprising that we see the use of *Latinx* as fundamentally intersectional: by refusing gender, sexual, ethnic, or racial binaries, the term seeks to encompass multiple aspects of identity and social justice. As a group of scholars committed to intersectional analysis—from racial, gender, and sexual analysis to environmental justice—we see this act of naming as a key aspect of the work this volume seeks to create and support. Another aspect of our embrace of the terms *Latinx* and *Chicanx* relates to the ways these terms reject the linguistic imperialism of both English and Spanish and the overwriting of indigenous languages and epistemologies. As Tanisha Love Ramírez and Zeba Blay observe, "the use of Latinx is also, as pointed out by writer Gabe Gonzalez, a way to reclaim identity, a form of rebellion against 'the language and legacy of European traditions that were imposed on the Americas.'" The term *Latinx* is thus a placeholder that acknowledges forms of indigenous knowledge and practice that colonization attempted to eradicate. While, as Mignolo has noted, we may never recover some of the forms of knowledge that were lost during the conquest, the "x" in Latinx serves as a poignant reminder that Eurocentric epistemologies—especially as they relate to environmental imaginaries—are not the only ways of the knowing the world. Moreover, it serves to remind us that indigenous forms of knowledge and practice thrive up to the present day throughout a myriad of powerful cultures, in defiance of ongoing epistemological and ontological assault.

Although as the editors of this volume we embrace the term *Latinx*, we also acknowledge that Latinx and Chicanx studies have not reached consensus on this terminology. Consequently, we encouraged our contributors to make their own scholarly and political decisions about how they signal their relationships to the terms *Latinx* and *Chicanx* and their variants. In addition to exploring the more obvious intersections of race, ethnicity, and environment that are apparent in the title of this volume, we also hope our use of and flexibility around these identifiers helps foster other intersectional conversations in the essays we include—perhaps even intersectional conversations that we have yet to imagine.

Conclusion

Our goal in this volume is to expand the consideration of environmental ideas within Latinx studies while also providing an engagement with critical race theory, the decolonial, new materialism, animal studies, disability studies, and queer theory as a desirable expansion of environmental justice studies. As author Cherríe Moraga notes in her conversation with Ybarra, "as long as you have a progressive movement that's a single-issue movement, it's never going to be an effective movement. If you can't deal with the impoverished conditions of the people who are living in the environment that you want to protect, it's not going to work." Apropos of this observation, we hope the essays and interviews included in this volume can serve as potential case studies or models for the types of theoretical and epistemological encounter Moraga urges us to consider. It is our desire that these essays and interviews serve as jumping-off points for other ecological and social justice conversations between Latinx studies, environmental studies, and other fields of race and ethnic studies. The strength and variety of the contributions to this volume show the ongoing rewards of continuing this endeavor.

NOTES

1. For data about Asian Americans, see Ramakrishnan and Shah, "Yes, President Trump," and Fahey, "Asian Americans." For data about Latinxs, see Anthony Leiserowitz, Matthew Cutler, and Seth Rosenthal's *Climate Change in the Latino Mind*. For data about African Americans, see Fahey, "Poll," and Leiserowitz and Akerlof, *Race, Ethnicity, and Public Responses to Climate Change*.

2. The category "mainstream environmentalism" deserves unpacking to avoid overdetermining the ideas and people associated with it. As scholars of environmentalism in the United States note, what we today know as environmentalism—movements, ideas, and groups that advocate for the preservation or conservation of natural resources, biodiversity, and ecosystems—has its roots in the Progressive Era. At that time, the debate between preservation (excluding humans from nature, as espoused most explicitly by John Muir, for example) and conservation (conserving resources for what Gifford Pinchot called "sustained yield," as espoused by Theodore Roosevelt, for example) divided the budding movement. Currently, both sets of values could be considered "mainstream" environmental ideas, and the division between such ideas is less pronounced than the division between mainstream environmentalism and environmental justice. What has resulted in the contemporary mainstream, then, is a more nuanced and fascinating history than we can cover in this book. We identify mainstream environmentalism as a set of ideologies, discourses, and policies that advocate for the preservation of nature, often without regard to—and sometimes even explicitly against—human security or questions of social justice.

3. Most commonly, scholars cite a 1982 protest against a hazardous waste landfill in Warren County, North Carolina, as the movement's origin point. Members of the predominantly African American community identified the environmental racism that contributed to the dump's location in their vicinity.

4. While this is the first volume dedicated to pan-Latinx literature and culture, it is important to acknowledge *Landscapes of Writing in Chicano Literature*, edited by Imelda Martín-Junquera, as well as path-breaking scholarship by Chicanx studies critics such as María Herrera-Sobek and Priscilla Ybarra, work by Latinx environmental justice scholars such as Robert Figueroa, and social science research by figures such as Laura Pulido and Devon Peña.

5. Entries from the *Keywords in Environmental Studies* (2016) volume help substantiate this brief discussion. In the "environmentalism(s)" entry, Joan Martinez-Alier observes that the largest branch of the environmental movement is motivated by its efforts to "to preserve pristine nature by setting aside natural areas from where humans would be excluded and the active protection of wildlife for its ecological and aesthetic values and not for any economic or human livelihood value" (97). Vermonja Alston, in her entry on "environment," concurs that the preservationist inclination in environmentalism correlates with the carceral paradigm inherent in colonization when she traces the etymology of "environment" and finds that it implies "the enclosure of bodies of land, water, people, plants and nonhuman animals in a colonial logic to export and appropriate biodiversity and indigenous knowledge" (94).

6. See, for example, Whyte, "Is It Colonial Deja Vu? Indigenous Peoples and Climate Injustice." In *Wastelanding*, Voyles suggests that some scholars who focus on decolonization are hesitant to see their work as advancing environmental justice because this framework has not fully grappled with colonization. Jaskiran Dhillon, as Ray describes in "Where Is Decolonialism in Environmental Justice? Jaskiran Dhillon's Critique," argues that many communities have been experiencing race-based environmental exploitation since long before environmental justice became an organizing strategy in the civil rights era.

7. By "cultural productions," we mean literary, visual, filmic, new media, or other creative texts. We consciously use the phrase *cultural productions* to imagine broad representational strategies across artistic, media, and cultural forms.

8. For more on Latinx as a literary or cultural category, see Rodriguez 1–21 and Caminero-Santangelo 1–35.

9. Notable exceptions include Platt's discussion of Castillo and Ybarra's and Wald's monographs, which situate the Chicanx environmental imaginary within the context of Chicanx or Latinx literary study at least equally to its position within ecocriticism. Laura Halperin's discussion of Ana Castillo in her monograph *Intersections of Harm: Narratives of Latina Deviance and Defiance* engages with ecocriticism to forward an argument primarily positioned within Latinx studies.

10. One exception is June Dwyer's application of ecocritical understandings of place in depictions of gentrification in Ernesto Quiñonez's writing.

WORKS CITED

Adamson, Joni. *American Indian Literature, Environmental Justice, and Ecocriticism: The Middle Place*. U of Arizona P, 2001.

Adamson, Joni, Mei Mei Evans, and Rachel Stein, editors. *The Environmental Justice Reader: Politics, Poetics, and Pedagogy*. U of Arizona P, 2002.

Alaimo, Stacy. *Bodily Matters: Science, Environment, and the Material Self*. Indiana UP, 2010.

Aldama, Frederick Luis. "Lucha Corpi." *Spilling the Beans in Chicanolandia: Conversations with Writers and Artists*. U of Texas P, 2006.

Alexander, Michelle. *The New Jim Crow: Mass Incarceration in the Age of Colorblindness*. New Press, 2010.

Alston, Vermonja. "Environment." *Keywords in Environmental Studies*, edited by Joni Adamson, William A. Gleason, and David N. Pellow, NYU Press, 2016, pp. 93–96.

Anaya, Rudolfo. *Bless Me Ultima*. Warner Books, 1994.

Anzaldúa, Gloria. *Borderlands/La Frontera: The New Mestiza*. 4th ed., Aunt Lute Books, 2012.

Armus, Teo. "Student Groups Shift toward Use of Latinx to Include All Gender Identities." *Columbia Daily Spectator*, 8 Oct. 2015, www.columbiaspectator.com/news/2015/10/07/latino-latinx/.
Barad, Karen. *Meeting the Universe Halfway: Quantum Physics and the Entanglement of Matter and Meaning*. Duke UP, 2017.
Bonilla-Silva, Eduardo. *Racism without Racists: Color-Blind Racism and the Persistence of Racial Inequality in America*. 3rd ed., Rowman and Littlefield, 2009.
Brady, Mary Pat. *Extinct Lands, Temporal Geographies: Chicana Literature and the Urgency of Space*. Duke UP, 2002.
Braun, Bruce. *The Intemperate Rainforest: Nature, Culture, and Power on Canada's West Coast*. U of Minnesota P, 2002.
Buell, Lawrence. *The Future of Environmental Criticism: Environmental Crisis and Literary Imagination*. Wiley-Blackwell, 2005.
Bullard, Robert. *Dumping in Dixie: Race, Class, and Environmental Quality*. 3rd ed., Westview Press, 2000.
———. "Environmental Justice in the Twenty-First Century." *The Quest for Environmental Justice: Human Rights and the Politics of Pollution*, edited by Robert Bullard, Sierra Club Books, 2005, pp. 19–42.
Cabeza de Baca, Fabiola. *The Good Life: New Mexico Traditions and Food*. 1949. Museum of New Mexico Press, 2005.
———. *We Fed Them Cactus*. 1954. U of New Mexico P, 1994.
Caminero-Santangelo, Marta. *On Latinidad: U.S. Latino Literature and the Construction of Ethnicity*. UP of Florida, 2007.
Chen, Mel Y. *Animacies: Biopolitics, Racial Mattering, and Queer Affect*. Duke UP, 2012.
Claborn, John. *Civil Rights and the Environment in African American Literature, 1895–1941*. Bloomsbury, 2017.
Cofer, Judith Ortiz. *The Line of the Sun*. Reprint ed., U of Georgia P, 1991.
Corpi, Lucha. *Delia's Song*. Arte Publico Press, 1989.
Cosgrove, Denis. "Habitable Earth: Wilderness, Empire, and Race in America." *Wild Ideas*, edited by D. Rothenberg, U of Minnesota P, 1995, pp. 27–41.
Crenshaw, Kimberlé. "Demarginalizing the Intersection of Race and Sex: A Black Feminist Critique of Anti-discrimination Doctrine, Feminist Theory, and Anti-Racist Politics." *University of Chicago Legal Forum*, vol. 1, 1989, pp. 139–167.
Davis, Angela. *Women, Race, and Class*. Vintage, 1983.
Dhillon, Jaskiran. "Introduction: Indigenous Resurgence, Decolonization, and Movements for Environmental Justice." *Environment and Society*, vol. 9, 2018, pp. 1–5.
Díaz, Junot. *The Brief Wondrous Life of Oscar Wao*. Riverhead Books, 2008.
———. "Monstro." *New Yorker*, May 2012, http://www.newyorker.com/magazine/2012/06/04/monstro.
Di Chiro, Giovanna. "Nature as Community: The Convergence of Environment and Social Justice." *Uncommon Ground: Rethinking the Human Place in Nature*, edited by William Cronon, Norton, 1996, pp. 298–320.
Dungy, Camille T. *Black Nature: Four Centuries of African American Nature Poetry*. U of Georgia P, 2009.
Dwyer, June. "Reimagining the Ethnic Enclave: Gentrification, Rooted Cosmopolitanism, and Ernesto Quiñonez's *Chango's Fire*." *MELUS*, vol. 34, no. 2, 2009, pp. 125–139.
Eze, Emmanuel. "The Color of Reason: The Idea of 'Race' in Kant's Anthropology." *Postcolonial African Philosophy: A Critical Reader*, Blackwell, 1997, pp. 103–131.

Fahey, Anna. "Asian Americans Lean Green." *Grist*, 26 July 2016, grist.org/climate-energy/asian-americans-lean-green/.
———. "Poll: African Americans Ahead on Climate Change." *Sightline Institute*, 29 Jan. 2016, www.sightline.org/2016/01/29/poll-african-americans-ahead-on-climate-change.
Fanon, Frantz. *The Wretched of the Earth*. Grove Press, 2004.
Figueroa, Robert. "Other Faces: Latinos and Environmental Justice." *Faces of Environmental Racism: Confronting Issues of Global Justice*, edited by Laura Westra and Bill E. Lawson, Rowman and Littlefield, 2001, pp. 167–186.
Finney, Carolyn. *Black Faces, White Spaces: Reimagining the Relationship of African Americans to the Great Outdoors*. U of North Carolina P, 2014.
Finseth, Ian Frederick. *Shades of Green: Visions of Nature in the Literature of American Slavery, 1770–1860*. U of Georgia P, 2013.
Fiskio, Janet. "Unsettling Ecocriticism: Rethinking Agrarianism, Place, and Citizenship." *American Literature*, vol. 84, no. 2, 2012, pp. 301–325.
Flores, Juan. *From Bomba to Hip-Hop: Puerto Rican Culture and Latino Identity*. Columbia UP, 2000.
Gaard, Greta. "Toward a Feminist Postcolonial Milk Studies." *American Quarterly: Special Issue on Race, Gender, Species*, vol. 65, no. 3, 2013, pp. 595–618.
Gamber, John. *Positive Pollutions and Cultural Toxins: Waste and Contamination in Contemporary U.S. Ethnic Literatures*. U of Nebraska P, 2012.
García, Cristina. *Dreaming in Cuban*. Ballantine Books, 1993.
González, Jovita Mireles. *Caballero: A Historical Novel*. 1st ed., Texas A&M UP, 1996.
———. *The Woman Who Lost Her Soul and Other Stories*. Edited by Sergio Reyna, Arte Público Press, 2000.
Gottlieb, Robert. *Forcing the Spring: The Transformation of the American Environmental Movement*. Revised ed., Island Press, 2005.
Halperin, Laura. *Intersections of Harm: Narratives of Latina Deviance and Defiance*. Rutgers UP, 2015.
Haraway, Donna J. *Staying with the Trouble: Making Kin in the Chthulucene*. Duke UP, 2016.
———. *When Species Meet*. U of Minnesota P, 2007.
Harris, Cheryl L. "Whiteness as Property." *Harvard Law Review*, vol. 106, no. 8, 1993, pp. 1707–1791.
Hayashi, Robert T. "Beyond Walden Pond: Asian American Literature and the Limits of Ecocriticism." *Coming into Contact: Explorations in Ecocritical Theory and Practice*, edited by Annie Merrill Ingram, Ian Marshall, Daniel J. Philippon, and Adam W. Sweeting, U of Georgia P, 2007, pp. 58–79.
Herrera-Sobek, María. "The Nature of Chicana Literature: Feminist Ecological Literary Criticism and Chicana Writers." *Revista Canaria de Estudios Ingleses*, vol. 37, 1998, pp. 89–100.
Hsu, Hsuan L. "Fatal Contiguities: Metonymy and Environmental Justice." *New Literary History*, vol. 42, no. 1, 2011, pp. 147–168.
Huggan, Graham, and Helen Tiffin. *Postcolonial Ecocriticism: Literature, Animals, Environment*. Routledge, 2015.
Iovino, Serenella, and Serpil Oppermann. *Material Ecocriticism*. Indiana UP, 2014.
James, Jennifer. "Ecomelancholia: Slavery, War, and Black Ecological Imaginings." *Environmental Criticism for the 21st Century*, edited by Stephanie LeMenager, Teresa Shewry, and Ken Hiltner, Routledge, 2011, pp. 163–178.

Kafer, Alison. *Feminist, Queer, Crip*. Indiana UP, 2013.
Kosek, Jake. *Understories: The Political Life of Forests in Northern New Mexico*. Duke UP, 2006.
Leiserowitz, Anthony, and Karen Akerlof. "Race, Ethnicity and Public Responses to Climate Change." Yale University and George Mason University, Yale Project on Climate Change, 2010, http://environment.yale.edu/climate-communication-OFF/files/Race_Ethnicity_and_Climate_Change_2.pdf.
Leiserowitz, Anthony, Matthew Cutler, and Seth Rosenthal. *Climate Change in the Latino Mind*. Yale University, Yale Program on Climate Change Communication, 2017.
Lipsitz, George. *The Possessive Investment in Whiteness: How White People Profit from Identity Politics*. Temple UP, 2006.
Love Ramírez, Tanisha, and Zeba Blay. "Why People Are Using the Term 'Latinx.'" *Huffington Post*, 5 July 2016.
Lowe, Lisa. *The Intimacies of Four Continents*. Duke UP, 2015.
Martinez-Alier, Joan. "Environmentalism(s)." *Keywords in Environmental Studies*, edited by Joni Adamson, William A. Gleason, and David N. Pellow, NYU Press, 2016, pp. 97–100.
Martín-Junquera, Imelda, editor. *Landscapes of Writing in Chicano Literature*. Palgrave MacMillan, 2013.
Melamed, Jodi. "Racial Capitalism." *Critical Ethnic Studies*, vol. 1, no. 1, 2015, pp. 76–85.
Mendoza, Mary E. "Treacherous Terrain: Racial Exclusion and Environmental Control at the U.S.-Mexico Border." *Environmental History*, vol. 23, no. 1, 2018, pp. 117–126.
Merchant, Carolyn. "Shades of Darkness: Race and Environmental History." *Environmental History*, vol. 8, no. 3, July 2003, pp. 380–394.
Mignolo, Walter. *Local Histories/Global Designs: Coloniality, Subaltern Knowledges, and Border Thinking*. Princeton UP, 2000.
Mignolo, Walter D., and Catherine E. Walsh. *On Decoloniality: Concepts, Analytics, Praxis*. Duke UP, 2018.
Mills, Charles. *The Racial Contract*. Cornell UP, 1997.
Minich, Julie Avril. Personal correspondence with editors. 13 June 2015. E-mail.
Molina, Natalia. *How Race Is Made in America: Immigration, Citizenship, and the Historical Power of Racial Scripts*. U of California P, 2014.
Monani, Salma. "Feeling and Healing Eco-social Catastrophe: The 'Horrific' Slipstream of Danis Goulet's *Wakening*." *Paradoxa*, vol. 28, 2016, pp. 192–213.
Moraga, Cherríe. *Heroes and Saints and Other Plays*. 1st ed., West End Press, 1994.
———. *Loving in the War Years: Lo Que Nunca Pasó Por Sus Labios*. South End Press, 1983.
Moreton-Robinson, Aileen. *The White Possessive: Property, Power, and Indigenous Sovereignty*. U of Minnesota P, 2015.
Mortimer-Sandilands, Catriona, and Bruce Erickson, editors. *Queer Ecologies: Sex, Nature, Politics, Desire*. Indiana UP, 2010.
Moya, Paula M. L. *The Social Imperative: Race, Close Reading, and Contemporary Literary Criticism*. Stanford UP, 2015.
Myers, Jeffrey. *Converging Stories: Race, Ecology, and Environmental Justice in American Literature*. U of Georgia P, 2005.
Niggli, Josefina. *Mexican Village*. U of New Mexico P, 1991.
Nixon, Rob. *Slow Violence and the Environmentalism of the Poor*. Harvard UP, 2013.
Omi, Michael, and Howard Winant. *Racial Formation in the United States*. 3rd ed., Routledge, 2014.

Ontiveros, Randy J. *In the Spirit of a New People: The Cultural Politics of the Chicano Movement*. New York UP, 2014.

Outka, Paul. *Race and Nature from Transcendentalism to the Harlem Renaissance*. Palgrave Macmillan, 2008.

Parlee, Lorena, et al. *The Wrath of Grapes*. United Farm Workers, 1986.

Peña, Devon. *Chicano Culture, Ecology, Politics: Subversive Kin*. U of Arizona P, 1999.

———. *Mexican Americans and the Environment: Tierra y Vida*. U of Arizona P, 2005.

Pezzullo, Phaedra, and Ronald Sandler. *Environmental Justice and Environmentalism: The Social Justice Challenge to the Environmental Movement*. The MIT Press, 2007.

Platt, Kamala. "Ecocritical Chicana Literature: Ana Castillo's 'Virtual Realism.'" *Ecofeminist Literary Criticism: Theory, Interpretation, Pedagogy*, edited by Greta Gaard and Patrick D. Murphy, U of Illinois P, 1998, pp. 139–157.

Pulido, Laura. *Environmentalism and Economic Justice: Two Chicano Struggles in the Southwest*. U of Arizona P, 1996.

———. "Geographies of Race and Ethnicity II: Environmental Racism, Racial Capitalism, and State-Sanctioned Violence." *Progress in Human Geography*, vol. 41, no. 4, 2016, pp. 524–533.

———. "Rethinking Environmental Racism: White Privilege and Urban Development in Southern California." *Annals of the Association of American Geographers*, vol. 90, no. 1, 2000, pp. 12–40.

Quijano, Aníbal. "Coloniality of Power and Eurocentrism in Latin America." *International Sociology*, vol. 15, no. 2, 2000, pp. 215–232.

Rahman, Shazia. "Karachi, Turtles, and the Materiality of Place: Pakistani Eco-cosmopolitanism in Uzma Aslam Khan's *Trespassing*." *Interdisciplinary Studies in Literature and Environment*, vol. 18, 2011, pp. 261–282.

Ramakrishnan, Karthick, and Sono Shah. "Yes, President Trump, Asian Americans Are Environmentalists." *AAPI Data*, http://aapidata.com/blog/trump-environment-asianam/.

Ray, Sarah Jaquette. *The Ecological Other: Environmental Exclusion in American Culture*. U of Arizona P, 2013.

———. "Where Is Decolonialism in Environmental Justice? Jaskiran Dhillon's Critique." *Writing at the End of the World*, 24 Oct. 2017, writingattheendoftheworld.blogspot.com/2017/10/where-is-decolonization-in.html.

Ray, Sarah Jaquette, and J. C. Sibara. *Disability Studies and the Environmental Humanities: Towards an Eco-crip Theory*. U of Nebraska P, 2017.

Reed, T. V. "Toward an Environmental Justice Ecocriticism." *The Environmental Justice Reader: Politics, Poetics, and Pedagogy*, edited by Joni Adamson, Mei Mei Evans, and Rachel Stein, U of Arizona P, 2002, pp. 145–162.

Robinson, Cedric. *Black Marxism: The Making of the Black Radical Tradition*. Zed Press, 1983.

Rodriguez, Ralph E. *Latinx Literature Unbound: Undoing Ethnic Expectation*. Fordham UP, 2018.

Roediger, David. *The Wages of Whiteness: Race and the Making of the American Working Class*. Verso, 2007.

Ruffin, Kimberly N. *Black on Earth: African American Eco-Literary Traditions*. U of Georgia P, 2010.

Ruiz de Burton, María Amparo. *The Squatter and the Don*. 2nd ed., Arte Público Press, 1997.

———. *Who Would Have Thought It?* 1872. Edited by Rosaura Sánchez and Beatrice Pita, Arte Público Press, 1995.
Sadowski-Smith, Claudia. *Border Fictions: Globalization, Empire, and Writing at the Boundaries of the United States.* U of Virginia P, 2008.
Said, Edward W. *Culture and Imperialism.* Vintage Books USA, 1994.
Salt, Karen. "Twilight Islands and Environmental Crises: Re-writing a History of the Caribbean and Pacific Regions through the Islands Existing in Their Shadows." *Humanities for the Environment: Integrating Knowledge, Forging New Constellations of Practices*, edited by Joni Adamson and Michael Davis, Routledge, 2017, pp. 57–69.
Sandoval, Chela. *Methodology of the Oppressed.* U of Minnesota P, 2000.
Schlosberg, David. *Environmental Justice and the New Pluralism: The Challenge of Difference for Environmentalism.* Oxford UP, 2002.
Sellers-Garcia, Sylvia. *When the Ground Turns in Its Sleep.* Riverhead Books, 2007.
Seymour, Nicole. *Strange Natures: Futurity, Empathy, and the Queer Ecological Imagination.* U of Illinois P, 2013.
Spence, Mark David. *Dispossessing the Wilderness: Indian Removal and the Making of the National Parks.* Oxford UP, 1999.
Stein, Rachel, editor. *New Perspectives on Environmental Justice: Gender, Sexuality, and Activism.* Rutgers UP, 2004.
———. *Shifting the Ground: American Women Writers' Revisions of Nature, Gender and Race.* UP of Virginia, 1997.
Sturgeon, Noël. *Environmentalism in Popular Culture: Gender, Race, Sexuality, and the Politics of the Natural.* U of Arizona P, 2008.
Sze, Julie. "From Environmental Justice Literature to Literature of Environmental Justice." *The Environmental Justice Reader: Politics, Poetics, and Pedagogy*, edited by Joni Adamson, Mei Mei Evans, and Rachel Stein, U of Arizona P, 2002, pp. 163–180.
Taylor, Dorceta. "The Challenge." *Green 2.0*, www.diversegreen.org/the-challenge/.
Thomas, Piri. *Down These Mean Streets.* Thirtieth anniversary ed., Vintage, 1997.
Tobar, Héctor. *The Tattooed Soldier.* Reprint ed., Picador, 2014.
Tuck, Eve, and K. Wang Yang. "Decolonization Is Not a Metaphor." *Decolonization: Indigeneity, Education and Society*, vol. 1, no. 1, 2012, pp. 1–40.
Vázquez, David J. "'Their Bones Kept Them Moving': Latina/o Studies, Helena María Viramontes's *Under the Feet of Jesus* and the Cross-Currents of U.S. Environmentalism." *Contemporary Literature*, vol. 58, no 3, 2017, pp. 361–391.
———. "'They Don't Understand Their Own Oppression': Complicating Preservation in John Rechy's *The Miraculous Day of Amalia Gómez*." *Transnational Cityscapes*, special issue of *Arizona Quarterly*, vol. 74, no. 1, 2018, pp. 17–43.
———. "Toxicity and the Politics of Narration: Imagining Social and Environmental Justice in Salvador Plascencia's *The People of Paper*." *Symbolism*, edited by Patricia Marie Garza and John Moran González, vol. 17, 2017, pp. 55–76.
Villa, Raúl Homero. *Barrio-Logos: Space and Place in Urban Chicano Literature.* U of Texas P, 2000.
Villarreal, José Antonio. *Pocho.* Reprint ed., Anchor, 1970.
Vourvoulias, Sabrina. *Ink.* Crossed Genres Publications, 2012.
Voyles, Traci Brynne. *Wastelanding: Legacies of Uranium Mining in Navajo Country.* U of Minnesota P, 2015.
Wald, Sarah D. *The Nature of California: Race, Citizenship and Farming since the Dust Bowl.* U of Washington P, 2016.

———. "'Refusing to Halt': Mobility and the Quest for Spatial Justice in Helena María Viramontes's *Their Dogs Came with Them* and Karen Tei Yamashita's *Tropic of Orange*." *Western American Literature*, vol. 48, nos. 1 and 2, 2013, pp. 70–89.

Whyte, Kyle Powys. "Is It Colonial Deja Vu? Indigenous Peoples and Climate Injustice." *Humanities for the Environment: Integrating Knowledges, Forging New Constellations of Practice*, edited by Joni Adamson and Michael Davis, Routledge, 2017.

Wolfe, Cary. *What Is Posthumanism?* U of Minnesota P, 2009.

Ybarra, Priscilla Solis. *Writing the Goodlife: Mexican American Literature and the Environment*. U of Arizona P, 2016.

Part I / Place

Racial Capital and the Production of Place

2

Greenwashing the White Savior

*Cancer Clusters, Supercrips,
and* McFarland, USA

JULIE AVRIL MINICH

In the late 1980s, regional and then national news outlets began reporting elevated rates of childhood cancers in McFarland, California, a predominantly Latinx agricultural town located in the San Joaquin Valley.[1] As news of the cancer cluster spread, McFarland was featured in the video *The Wrath of Grapes* (1986), a United Farm Workers documentary (produced by Lorena Parlee and Lenny Bourin) filmed to protest pesticide exposure, and fictionalized (as McLaughlin) in Cherríe Moraga's play *Heroes and Saints* (1994). As often occurs with cancer clusters, no definitive cause for McFarland's health crisis was ever identified. Eventually, stories about the McFarland cancer cluster simply stopped being featured in the media.

In 2015, McFarland returned to national headlines after the release of the Walt Disney Pictures film *McFarland, USA*, starring Kevin Costner as a white high school track coach who leads a Latino team to win the 1987 California state championship. Based on the story of Jim White, who coached the McFarland High School track team from 1980 to 2003 and won nine cross-country state championships, the film was a box office success. Yet Latinx critics, who objected to its white savior narrative, were skeptical; Domino Renee Perez wryly titled her review of the film "Dances with Mexicans." Although *McFarland, USA* appears to promote concern for Mexican American children and takes place as activists were bringing the cancer cluster to national attention, it never directly mentions the health concerns prevailing in McFarland at the time of its setting. By 2015, it seems, McFarland's health crisis had faded not only from headlines but also from public memory.

The discrepancy between Disney's representation of McFarland in the late 1980s and the experience of its residents in the same period prompts consideration of the narrative aspect of environmental injustice. In other words, what are the conditions under which stories of environmental racism can be told, heard, and remembered? And what kinds of narrative strategies are deployed to suppress these stories? This chapter engages a figure long critiqued by disability scholars—the *supercrip*—to elaborate how the able bodies of the *McFarland, USA* runners discursively supplant the McFarland children disabled by cancer. Supercrips, according to Eli Clare, "engage in activities as grand as walking 2,500 miles or as mundane as learning to drive"; they are disabled people deployed as "symbols of inspiration" for the nondisabled (2). Whereas disability scholars often dismiss supercrip narratives, Sami Schalk has argued recently that the supercrip figure merits more critical attention (84). This chapter answers Schalk's call, recruiting disability theory as a tool for Latinx ecocriticism, and argues that the *McFarland, USA* runners play the role of supercrips, triumphantly performing ability under profoundly disabling conditions. Of course, the elite runners of the film are not literally disabled, but their story follows the structure of a supercrip narrative, emphasizing "concepts of overcoming, heroism, inspiration, and the extraordinary" and focusing on "individual attitude, work, and perseverance rather than on social barriers" (Schalk 73). By treating the runners as inspirational individuals and ignoring the barriers (including an environmental health catastrophe) facing their community, *McFarland, USA* provides a case study for exploring how the supercrip can function not only as a figure of derision for disability activists but also as a narrative device used to conceal many forms of injustice, including environmental injustice.

At stake in this analysis is a claim for the importance of humanistic research in general (and cultural studies in particular) to producing knowledge about race, disability, and the environment. While environmental justice research is frequently understood to promote better policy, Laura Pulido argues that "studying environmental racism is important for an additional reason: it helps us understand racism" (12). Of course, literary and cultural criticism is rarely seen to impact policy. What cultural critique offers, though, is an account of the unjust social relations that shape policy and of the narrative processes that naturalize and reify systemic injustice. As Pulido notes, when understandings of racism are reduced to "individual, malicious acts," then "racial inequalities that cannot be attributed directly to a hostile, discriminatory act are not acknowledged as such" and the possibility for contesting them is limited (12–13). In arguing that *McFarland, USA* erases a racialized health crisis, my goal is not merely to criticize Disney for ignoring the cancer cluster (although I find this omission unethical) but rather to undertake a formal analysis of a narrative that occludes environmental racism and to elucidate more broadly the narrative techniques that reinforce unjust social relations. Rob Nixon defines environmental racism as a form of slow violence "that occurs gradually and out of sight, a violence of delayed destruction that is dispersed across time and space, an attritional violence that is typically not viewed as violence at all" and that poses particular "representational, narrative, and strategic challenges" (2). Nixon has famously illuminated the representational processes used to bring the slow violence of environmental racism to public awareness; in this essay, I take the opposite approach, examining narrative strategies that conceal slow violence and prevent it from being named as such.

The health crisis of McFarland was, from the beginning, also a crisis of narration. As soon as the cancer cluster was confirmed, a struggle began over how to report it. In 1988, for instance, as news reports on the cancer cluster intensified, Jack Early, president of the National Agricultural Chemicals Association, needed a story to absolve his industry; he wrote a letter to the editor of the *Washington Post* criticizing an article that posited a link between the elevated rates of cancer in McFarland and the use of pesticides in the surrounding fields:

> The industry does not view the abnormally high incidence of leukemia and cancer in that agricultural region any differently from the way anyone else does. It does not dispute for a moment that there is a serious problem.
>
> What we do dispute are a newspaperman's conclusions in a major newspaper with a large number of news service clients when the qualified scientific experts do not agree with those conclusions. ("The Mystery of McFarland, Calif.")

Early was not factually incorrect here; no scientists ever definitively named pesticides as the cause of McFarland's crisis. However, as Julie Sze points out, cancer clusters are rarely given official explanations, often owing not to a lack of evidence but rather to the biases that guide investigations: "While scientists often err on the side of rejecting environmental causation and seek to avoid a false positive, community residents . . . tend to err on the side of causation" (182). These biases are not difficult to understand: scientists, wary of challenges to their objectivity, avoid making politically controversial claims without absolute certainty, while affected communities seek to eliminate from local environments anything correlated to a problem. The point is not simply that the different stories scientists, industry executives, and community members tell about a health crisis have different motivations but that these stories give rise to different solutions.

In critiquing Disney's story of McFarland's supercrip runners, I seek what Alison Kafer calls "the possibility of a cripped environmentalism, one that looks to disabled bodies/minds as a resource in thinking about our future natures differently" (131). Kafer's *cripped environmentalism* redresses mainstream environmentalisms that typically present "illness and disability . . . almost exclusively as tragic mistakes caused by unnatural incursions into or disruptions of the natural body and the natural environment" (157–158). In response, Kafer advocates an approach that resists presenting disability as "a terrible unending tragedy" but claims "a difference between denying necessary health care, condoning dangerous working conditions, or ignoring public health concerns (thereby causing illness and impairment) and recognizing illness and impairment as part of what makes us human" (2, 4). As a scholar of Latinx disability studies *and* a guilty fan of cheesy, based-on-a-true-story sports movies, I feel urgently the difference between ignoring public health concerns and affirming disability, and I desire a narrative about the McFarland runners that neither consigns the children of McFarland to the realm of tragic victimhood nor exalts them as heroic overcomers.

I have elsewhere argued that the activist rendering of McFarland found in Moraga's *Heroes and Saints* avoids making disability a tragedy by portraying the children who were disabled by pesticide poisoning as privileged subjects of a Chicanx environmental justice movement (Minich, "'You Gotta Make Aztlán'"). The film *McFarland, USA* adds a new dimension to this conversation because it prompts analysis of the consequences of separating representations of 1980s McFarland into stories of environmental contamination (*The Wrath of Grapes, Heroes and Saints*) and stories of heroic athleticism (*McFarland, USA*). It is a matter of historical fact that the children experiencing leukemia and non-Hodgkin's lymphoma and those attending regional track meets lived in the same neighborhoods and attended the same schools, yet these children never appear together in the same representations. Remembering the track team and the cancer cluster together requires renarrating the history of McFarland not as one of exceptional victims and heroes but as the story of an environment that disables some while enabling others. It also requires dismantling the supercrip figures that continue to dominate stories about McFarland. To begin this dismantling, I interrogate how the following narrative elements of *McFarland, USA* reinforce the supercrip representation of the 1987 McFarland High School track team: the film's engagement with the physical and social landscapes of the San Joaquin Valley and the development of two characters (Coach White and Danny Díaz).

Pesticides and Prisons: *McFarland, USA* versus McFarland, CA

Directed by the acclaimed Niki Caro (of *Whale Rider* fame), *McFarland, USA* is shot primarily in Kern County, California, where McFarland is located. It features a mostly Latinx cast, a rarity for a major studio production, with some actors and most of the extras cast from the community. In an interview with the online film journal *The Credits*, Caro emphasizes the film's fidelity to McFarland and its history: "Here was a story that was true, based in a real community, based on real people. . . . Paradoxically, the way I work when it's not my own culture is I try to be very accurate and faithful to the way lives are lived and not impose my will" (Abrams). Clocking in at 128 minutes, a generous run time for a young adult film, *McFarland, USA* offers time for its audience to experience the beauty of the San Joaquin Valley landscape and to appreciate the actors' moving performances.

My analysis begins with an exploration of how the film's setting, which contributes to the appearance of authenticity that Caro emphasizes and to the film's emotional impact, also conceals the material conditions of life in McFarland. Like Early in his letter to the editor of the *Washington Post*, insisting that no scientist has identified a link between pesticides and cancer, *McFarland, USA* accurately portrays many facts about McFarland—namely, that it is a predominantly Latinx town whose local economy depends on agribusiness and the prison-industrial complex. However, the film treats these elements as innate features of the landscape rather than subjecting them to scrutiny and critique. Recalling Schalk's definition of a supercrip story as one that prioritizes individual achievement over structural barriers, it becomes apparent that the film's setting is crucial to its supercrip story: the setting works to depoliticize conditions of the runners' lives and to naturalize rather than interrogate the relationship between Latinx communities, prisons, and industrialized agriculture. In so doing, it makes the extraordinary dedication of the runners—and not the injustice of the social landscape they inhabit—the primary focus.

McFarland, USA's use of the agricultural setting to portray the physical effects of farm labor offers the most explicit evidence for my claim that its story of elite athletes functions as a supercrip narrative. The film portrays agricultural work as the reason for the runners' talent. They are shown waking at dawn to help their parents in the fields before school and returning to the fields when the school day ends. In a speech before the state championship match, Coach White rallies his team with the following comparison between the McFarland runners and the other teams: "They don't get up at dawn like you, go to work in the fields. They don't go to school all day, then go back to those same fields. That's what you do. And then you come out with me. . . . [Y]ou take on even more pain. . . . You guys are superhuman. . . . There's nothing you can't do with that kind of strength, with that kind of heart." Even *Variety* film critic Justin Chang, who is otherwise skeptical of the film's racial politics, takes at face value the presumption that McFarland teenagers would be "naturally fast and athletic" since "running daily from school to the fields to pick crops in scorching heat will do that to you" ("Film Review"). However, according to medical anthropologist Seth Holmes, what farm labor will actually "do to you" is offer a fatality rate five times that experienced by workers in nonagricultural sectors and elevated rates of "nonfatal injuries, musculoskeletal pain, heart disease, and many types of cancer" (101). There is a marked disparity between the film's depiction of farm labor and that offered in Chicanx expressive culture: from novels like Tomás Rivera's . . . *Y no se lo tragó la tierra* (. . . *And the earth did not devour him*, 1995) and Helena María Viramontes's *Under the Feet of Jesus* (1996) to paintings like Daniel Desiga's *Campesino* (1975) and murals like Juana Alicia's *Las lechugueras* (1983), farm labor is shown not only as exhausting but as harmful and dangerous. Holmes puts it in stark terms: "As a result of their dedication to the U.S. agricultural fields, [farmworkers'] bodies ache, decay, and are injured" (30). By positing farm labor as the reason for the runners' talent, the film obscures its disabling effects.

The film does, in one scene, *almost* appear to address the McFarland health crisis. When Coach White goes to his Latino principal hoping to start a track team, the principal dismisses him, stating that running is a "private-school sport" and that the kids who participate in it "breathe different air." This acknowledgment, however, is brushed aside when Coach White responds, "No, it's the same air." Here Coach White occupies a role analogous to one that Carrie Sandahl identifies in many supercrip stories: that of the "tough-love, able-bodied lover or assistant who shows the disabled person that his or her problems boil down to a bad attitude" (584). Like Sandahl's lover/assistant, Coach White in this scene willfully ignores the factors (environment, food access, leisure time, equipment) that make it possible for wealthy kids to become elite athletes, implying that the only necessity is a can-do spirit. Given the film's historical setting at a time when McFarland residents literally feared the air they were breathing, this line is exceptionally cruel. Here the film implies that the only thing children from towns like McFarland need to attain the same accomplishments as their private-school peers is a willingness to try, rather than the removal of health and economic barriers.

The agricultural industry disables not only bodies but also landscapes, a fact that is represented (but not explored) in the film through references to prison facilities. McFarland is currently home to three prisons (Central Valley Modified Community Correctional Facility, Golden State Modified Community Correctional Facility, and McFarland Community Correctional Facility) and located in what Ruth Wilson Gilmore calls California's "prison alley," a 375-mile rural stretch dotted with towns whose defining characteristics include majority Latinx populations, high unemployment and poverty, and abundant surplus land that was once irrigated cropland (129). According to Gilmore, these towns courted prisons to remedy declines in agricultural wages but have, over time, fared worse than towns without prisons (247). To be clear, the prisons are not presented positively in *McFarland, USA*. A concerned fellow teacher, hoping to recruit Coach White to become involved in advocacy efforts for the students, points to a prison from a classroom window and says, "These kids are invisible; they're expendable. They come from the fields, and they go back to the fields unless the prisons get them first." Later, however, the prisons become an element of the background as the runners are shown running past barbed wire fencing. This juxtaposition of the moving, muscled bodies of the McFarland runners against the prison fences highlights the runners' heroic achievements against the failures of those (absent) subjects who have failed to persevere, minimizing the role of incarceration in actively constructing what Michelle Alexander calls a contemporary racial caste system. Prisons do not naturally occur in the San Joaquin Valley; they result from political choices that, as Gilmore notes, leave behind a residue of "devalued labor, land made toxic, shuttered retail businesses" that secures the exclusion of entire populations from economic advancement and state protection (179). The prison, then, is a key component of the runners' disabled and disabling social environment, but because this environment is naturalized rather than treated as a political construct, the narrative emphasis is placed not on the obstacles the runners face but on the heroism with which they overcome them.

Not all of the historical McFarland runners were able to overcome the disabling effects of agricultural industrialization and prison construction in their local environment. A scene entitled "The Real McFarland," which takes place just before the final credit sequence, replaces the actors portraying Coach White and the runners featured in the film with contemporary footage of the people on whom each character is based, accompanied by text explaining how each person's life has unfolded since 1987. Most of the runners still live in McFarland or in central California and now work in middle-class occupations (teachers, coaches, police detectives); one is enlisted in the U.S. military. However, one runner, Victor Puentes, spent two years at California Polytechnic State University before dropping out and eventually serving a sentence at a state penitentiary. The film's inclusion of Puentes among the runners featured in the final sequence highlights the success of the others, suggesting that most of the runners who worked with Coach White escaped the prevailing fate of their town, securing middle-class employment. News coverage of the film reinforces this emphasis on individual accomplishment and is particularly noticeable in stories featuring Puentes. For instance, a *Runner's World* feature on Puentes suggests that the film gave him a "new lease on life" and inspired him to begin "cleaning up his act" (Wade). The feature mentions that Puentes was forced to drop out of college because of his mother's illness but largely frames his incarceration as the result of his own poor decision-making, with a quote from Puentes about his need to "rethink the choices that I've made in the past," another from teammate Danny Díaz about how Puentes has overcome his "bad choices," and reassurances from the article's author, Allison Wade, that Puentes now "takes full responsibility" for his addiction (Wade). Wade neglects to pose any questions about the effects of growing up in a town where prisons and agricultural work comprise the majority of available employment, about the fairness of a system that would force a young man to choose between securing health care for his parent and a college education for himself, or about the consequences of addressing the public health problem of addiction by incarcerating those it affects. Treating its setting as background rather than an object of critique, *McFarland, USA* foments narratives that presume the irrelevance of the social environment and human-altered landscape to peoples' lives and life chances.

McFarland, USA's interpretation of life in McFarland is also detrimental to struggles for environmental justice, not merely because it fails to acknowledge the health crisis but more importantly because it treats the landscape of the San Joaquin Valley—an environment created by human dependence on unsustainable agricultural practices and mass incarceration—as natural and even beneficial to the lives of the children who grow up there. Structural inequities appear in the film to highlight the accomplishments of the runners who overcome them, not as objects of analysis in their own right. Furthermore, as I demonstrate in the following sections, the film's portrayals of heroic characters contain factual inaccuracies that further prevent the film from offering a meaningful representation of life in McFarland during the late 1980s. While any fictional narrative based on a true story will certainly deviate in some ways from the historical record, it is instructive to examine the particular deviations of *McFarland, USA*, since the elements that Caro and Disney understood to create a compelling storyline are precisely those that render invisible the slow violence of life in McFarland and reinforce the supercrip status of the runners. To elaborate this point, I now turn to the character narratives of Jim White and Danny Díaz, focusing on the representation of whiteness in Coach White's story and fatness in Danny's.

Coaching Whiteness

McFarland, USA is arguably just as much a story about the restoration of Coach White's white dominance and patriarchal authority as it is a story about the 1987 California track and field championship. In fact, the centrality of Coach White's redemption to the film's plot is the primary reason that the film's director claims to avoid telling a "white savior" story. Costner's fame for portraying white saviors notwithstanding, Caro asserts her desire to avoid such a narrative with *McFarland, USA*: "We were very conscious of not making a white savior movie, and you could have with the material, but it was really important for us that he be a flawed guy who was ultimately redeemed by the community. You see him become a better coach, a better father and a better man through his interaction with this place and these people" (Abrams).[2] For some critics, however, this emphasis on the redemption of Coach White results in a preferential depiction of whiteness. As Chang writes,

"What's really at stake throughout this movie is how Jim White and his family feel about it all: their discomfort at being forced to relocate to a low-income Hispanic neighborhood, followed by their gradual realization that, hey, these folks aren't so bad after all, with their quinceaneras [sic] and low-riding Chevys and free-range chickens."

I posit that beyond merely centering whiteness, as Chang suggests, the film depicts white patriarchy under threat (through scenes illustrating Coach White's personal and professional failures) and ultimately restored to dominance (as when Coach White is reestablished as the proper head of his own household and the metaphorical father of his team). In this reading, Coach White's redemption story does not preclude a white savior narrative but reinforces it. Coach White is depicted early in the film as volatile, losing his temper with students in Idaho (and thus losing his job as a football coach). Being forced to relocate to McFarland represents the loss of his patriarchal authority, a loss that is further exacerbated by the fact that the stress of starting over causes him to neglect his children; he becomes so focused on coaching (which he sees as his path to a better job) that he forgets his daughter's fifteenth birthday. After agreeing to help the Díaz family in the fields (hoping to convince Mr. Díaz to allow his sons to stay on the team), he finds that he is an incompetent farmworker. For each of these failures, the Latinx residents of McFarland consistently redeem him, most memorably by throwing a surprise quinceañera for his daughter to compensate for the ruined family celebration, and thus help him regain his patriarchal authority and white savior status.

Although Coach White is, as Caro points out, a "flawed guy" whose parenting skills need brushing up, the effects of his flaws are minor when compared to those of the other parents in the film. Unlike the parents of the runners he coaches, Coach White is presented as having natural parenting abilities that he simply needs to recover rather than being in need of basic instruction in how to parent. While Coach White is late for his daughter's birthday dinner, Mr. and Mrs. Díaz (parents of runners David, Damacio, and Danny) force their children to quit the team because they are needed in the fields. Meanwhile, the alcoholic father of star runner Thomas Valles turns abusive when he discovers that Thomas's sister is pregnant. In response, Coach White lectures Mr. and Mrs. Díaz about the benefits of extracurricular activities and convinces Thomas not to jump off a bridge. Thus, despite Coach White's imperfect parenting, he is still shown as a more suitable patriarch than the runners' parents, who are at best shortsighted (failing to see team sports as a path to upward mobility) and at worst violent. An apparently more trivial but nonetheless significant example occurs after Mrs. Díaz changes her mind about allowing her sons to run and decides to raise money for new team uniforms, which she emblazons with the word C-O-U-G-E-R-S; one of her sons in this scene orders Coach White not to tell her that she has misspelled the name of the school mascot (the Cougars). In fact, the historical Coach White has said in interviews that the team did have misspelled uniforms but presents the spelling error as his.³ These representations not only undermine the runners' parents but also accentuate the runners' supercrip status by portraying their home lives as intellectually disabling.

Coach White's whiteness is further accentuated in the film through a misrepresentation of McFarland's demographics. McFarland has had a majority Latinx population only since the 1980s, and the percentage of Latinx residents has steadily increased since then, suggesting that Latinx residents were forced to remain in the town while others left it as the local quality of life deteriorated.⁴ The film shows Coach White moving to McFarland in 1987, the year the McFarland team won its first state championship; the historical Coach White was a longtime community resident who began teaching at McFarland High School in 1964, when the town was still predominantly white (and who neither coached in Idaho nor was ever fired from a job there). By changing this historical detail, *McFarland, USA* highlights an inspirational aspect of the McFarland track team's story: the cross-cultural collaboration between Coach White and his runners, who surmount racial tensions to achieve victory. To further highlight the poignant story of interracial collaboration, the film exaggerates Coach White's outsider status. One scene, intended as humorous, shows Coach White taking his family out for dinner on their first night in McFarland; the family tries to order burgers at the local taquería only to be told their options consist of "tacos, tortas, tostadas, burritos, and quesadillas" with "asada, al pastor, chorizo, cabeza, lengua." The attempted humor of this scene comes at a price. First, the depiction of Coach White as a McFarland outsider reinforces the idea that McFarland needs help from white outsiders to solve its problems, a suggestion belied both by the fact that Coach White was a McFarland resident and by local Latinx activism against environmental hazards. Second, by neglecting to show that McFarland was actually becoming more (not less) racially homogenous during the time of the events depicted, the film ignores an opportunity to explore the racial barriers facing McFarland residents that are not so easily resolved by an individual track coach, no matter how charismatic or inspirational.

The representation of the parents in *McFarland, USA* not only functions to affirm the patriarchal authority of Coach White; it also presents a sharp contrast with the McFarland parents whose children were diagnosed with cancer and who brought the community's health crisis to national attention. The best-known of these parents is Connie Rosales, whose fourteen-year-old son, Randy, was diagnosed with non-Hodgkin's lymphoma in 1983. She began to notice other families affected by childhood cancer in her neighborhood, and, as she told the *Washington Post* in 1988, "I knew then there's something definitely wrong here. . . . At the time we had nothing but little kids running around the neighborhood with bald heads and dark circles under their eyes" (Weisskopf). Rosales took the issue to the Kern County Health Department and began organizing other parents to write the California legislature. Because of her efforts, public hearings were held in 1985, and reporters from national media (beginning with the *Los Angeles Times*) began covering the story and interviewing her.[5] The work of Connie Rosales is not unique or exceptional, nor is it confined to the past. For a more contemporary example, the website *Voices from the Valley* serves as a moving record of local community members' ongoing efforts throughout the San Joaquin Valley to document the effects of environmental toxins and to challenge the environmental conditions in which they live.[6] The stories of Rosales and *Voices from the Valley* stand in contrast to a supercrip narrative: rather than being exceptional or heroic, they are stories of everyday resistance to the everyday work of slow violence.

According to Pulido, white privilege "thrives in highly racialized societies that espouse racial equality, but in which whites will not tolerate either being inconvenienced in order to achieve racial equality, . . . or denied the full benefits of their whiteness" (15). Coach White's character narrative similarly espouses racial equality without denying his character the representational benefits of whiteness; in other words, the film invests Coach White with ideals of racial equality while also maintaining the privileged status of whiteness by portraying him in ways that highlight his patriarchal status by emphasizing his superior intelligence, compassion, and ability to offer the runners a better future. Moreover, as Pulido notes, it is "impossible to privilege one group without disadvantaging another" (16). The positive portrayal of Coach White occurs at the expense of the Latinx parents depicted in the film, who appear by comparison to be shortsighted, ignorant, and unable to provide for their children's futures.

I began this essay critiquing the film's omission of the McFarland health crisis. The omission of the health crisis also gives rise to the unflattering portrayal of McFarland's Latinx parents, whose history of advocacy for McFarland children is erased. In the final section, I discuss the function of fatness in Danny Díaz's story, which links health to personal responsibility and further deflects narrative attention from the environmental determinants of health.

Overcoming Obesity: Danny Díaz

Danny Díaz gives *McFarland, USA* one of the great stock characters of the based-on-a-true-story sports movie: the uncoordinated, athletically disinclined character who, in a crucial plot twist, delivers an against-all-odds victory to his team. Furthermore, despite being based on events three decades in the past, Danny's story gives the film a contemporary feel by linking it to current concerns about obesity, for Danny is visibly the fattest runner on the team. Coach White tells Danny during the team's first practice that he needs to lose weight and recruits him to join the team only because he wants Danny's faster brothers (David and Damacio); other characters address Danny as "panzón";[7] and Danny is the team's slowest runner. Nonetheless, in the final state championship match, it is Danny who leads his team to victory when another runner starts too fast and can't finish. Danny easily qualifies as *the* inspirational character of the film on the merits of this story alone, but the moving performance of unknown actor Ramiro Rodríguez (a McFarland High School student) accentuates the effect.

All the details about Díaz's story as shown in the film are true, except one. He really was the slowest runner on the team, recruited only because Coach White wanted his brothers to run, and he really did save the day in the 1987 state championship meet. *Yet Díaz was not fat as a teenager.* As a result, the Danny Díaz story as presented in the film reinforces an argument by Julie Guthman about obesity discourse: that the framing of "obesity epidemic" rhetoric often excludes "other possible explanations of both obesity's causes and its effects" and that "some of the consequences of these explanations and proposed solutions work against social justice" (23). Fatness is commonly understood as a consequence of personal choices (excessive caloric intake, insufficient exercise), and yet, as Guthman points out, it is often better explained by environmental factors (including environments that discourage exercise and environmental contaminants that affect metabolism). Like Coach White's comment about McFarland students breathing the "same air" as private-school athletes, the Danny Díaz storyline in *McFarland, USA* works to present the community's public health problems as the result of individual choices and behaviors. In other words, Danny Díaz in the film becomes a microcosm for McFarland itself: the film implies that just as Danny became a thinner, faster runner through hard work and perseverance, so too can the community of McFarland become a healthier place.

As people in the United States grow undeniably bigger (taller as well as wider), both medical experts and media pundits have directed increasing attention toward a so-called obesity epidemic. The term itself is an engine of panic, as Amy Erdman Farrell observes: "With its connotations of disease, contagion, and proliferation, the choice of the term 'epidemic' is deliberately alarmist, suggesting imminent danger and sure catastrophe. . . . Such thinking not only clouds judgment, it also induces a moral panic about the 'guilt' of the one who 'causes' such a catastrophe, often leading to extraordinary and discriminatory actions on the basis of 'health' and 'well-being'" (9). Furthermore, because the so-called problem of obesity tends to be more concentrated among Black and Latinx populations, discourses that ascribe stigma to fat people overlap heavily with racial stigmas, as evident from anti-immigration groups' responses to a 2013 report from the United Nations Food and Agriculture Association that Mexico's obesity rate has now surpassed that of the United States. For instance, the right-wing blog *FrontPage Magazine*, run by the David Horowitz Freedom Center, ran a piece shortly after the report came out (which has since been removed from the site) by writer Daniel Greenfield under the disturbing headline "Will Amnesty for Illegal Aliens Make America the World's Fattest Country?"

The discourse in Greenfield's provocative question is not limited to right-wing bloggers, however, as Sarah D. Wald has observed. Wald critiques a neoliberal model of personal health that she finds in both conservative anti-immigrant discourses and liberal sustainable food movements: "Citizen health is not the state's responsibility. Rather, it is the responsibility of the informed, educated, moral citizen making proper choices and exercising self-control and self-discipline.... In claiming that eating sustainably, locally, and with justice in mind is also healthier, the food movement unintentionally aligns itself with neoliberal cultural values" (198). The story of Danny Díaz as it is told in *McFarland, USA* similarly aligns with cultural values that promote extreme public divestment in communities like McFarland, visible not only in the disproportionate exposure of its residents to diseases linked to environmental contaminants but also in its dependence on the prison system to compensate for depressed agricultural wages. *McFarland, USA* does not merely include a character who overcomes the limitations of his fat body for the good of his team but prominently features that character, making its thrilling conclusion depend on his individual supercrip story of exceptional personal achievement. In this way, the film reinforces its message that "willpower, self-control, discipline, and personal responsibility" are the keys to success for a community like McFarland, thus downplaying the more urgent need for public investment and social change (Wald 198).

The fact that *McFarland, USA* avoids addressing the cancer cluster while inventing an inspirational fat-kid-turned-track-star story to include among its portfolio of supercrips has important consequences for broader understandings of health risk and responsibility. Sze critiques the way scientific investigations of environmental health risks often rely on a model that avoids assigning responsibility to those producing environmental toxins: "The traditional scientific method that underlies environmental risk assessment is based on an idealized model of risk systems best practiced under laboratory conditions" that "tends to produce knowledge that does not address where risk exposures are from and ignores questions such as who is producing the risk, who benefits from this production of risk, and why certain groups and not others are exposed" (181). To understand why the film's specific telling of McFarland history is so harmful, it is important to pair Sze's critique of the way polluters like large agricultural corporations *avoid* blame with a critique of the ways in which racialized health disparities are often explained in ways that *assign* blame to populations at greater risk of experiencing health problems. In other words, *McFarland, USA* simultaneously occludes a structural threat to the health of the children it portrays and emphasizes a supercrip story that reinforces the idea that health is solely a matter of making the right choices. And as Jonathan M. Metzl and Dorothy E. Roberts argue, "an ideological framework centered on 'individual choice' and 'individual responsibility' often makes attempts to improve health infrastructures or health/race/wealth inequities more difficult" (683).

While the fears about obesity were not quite so pervasive at the time that the McFarland cancer cluster occupied national headlines, discourses borrowed from the most alarmist aspects of obesity panic have made their way into stories about how the crisis has been remembered. In a 1998 retrospective about the health crisis published by the *San Francisco Chronicle*, just as concerns about the growing girth of U.S. Americans began to surface in news outlets, McFarland city manager Gary M. Johnson expresses regret for the negative press that McFarland received because of the cancer cluster. Johnson staunchly rejects the possibility that pesticides were to blame for the health crisis and proposes different causes. One of these is the food eaten by the families affected. Johnson states: "Preferred diets could also be part of the problem. Our population is 94 percent Hispanic, mostly from Mexico. A lot of folks have kept to a traditional diet, and that involves plenty of lard—you see them lined up at the store for it. A diet that high in animal fat has tremendous health risks, including cancer" (Martin). Johnson's characterization of the "traditional Mexican diet" as leading to elevated cancer risk is, of course, highly misinformed; as Holmes reminds us, there is "a strong focus in public health on what is often called the healthy Latino paradox," indicating "that there are certain health conditions for which Latino populations overall fare better than other ethnicities despite having relatively lower socioeconomic status" (873). More important than the ignorance of Johnson's comments, however, is their discursive effect: implying that those who bear the brunt of environmental injustice are responsible for their own poor health. The story of Danny Díaz as presented in *McFarland, USA* lacks the overt racism of Johnson's comments, but by similarly removing consideration of the social environment while emphasizing personal triumph, it ultimately creates the same effect.

Conclusion

McFarland, USA is, on the surface, a film about individual triumph over adversity. An early sequence—taken from the scene depicting the team's first major race at the 1987 Palo Alto Invitational—encapsulates its argument. Runner Thomas Valles is gaining momentum as he approaches two white runners from opposing teams. These runners, hearing Thomas behind them, attempt to physically push him back, even moving their bodies together in order to block him from passing. Thomas, however, squeezes his body between those of the runners and triumphantly moves ahead of them. Thomas's brown body, first held back and then victoriously springing forward, serves as a perfect visual microcosm of the film itself: portraying injustice as an individualized problem (of individual people literally holding others back) with an individualized solution (of other individuals moving forward) rather than as a political problem requiring collective and systemic solutions.

An interpretation of the film that pays closer attention to the historical forces that have affected the town of McFarland, however, reveals that *McFarland, USA* is also (unintentionally) a film about how human-altered landscapes and social environments work to enable some while disabling others. In this chapter, I have sought to critically interrogate the film's portrayal of individual triumph in landscapes that are both socially and physically disabling to show how these stories of individual achievement efface the ways in which we are all, collectively but differentially, affected by human-altered environments. Indeed, even saying that "we are all affected" by our social environments requires acknowledging that some are affected positively by social systems that disadvantage others. The stories we tell about those affected by pollution and contamination, by the prison-industrial complex, and by other forms of inequality have important implications for the kinds of solutions we can offer for these concerns. Stories of tragedy and stories of inspiration, which have dominated the narratives about McFarland, *both* work to sustain the idea that social failures are individual, personal failures. Critically engaging with these stories, interrogating their reliance on tropes like the supercrip or the white savior, allows us not only to better recognize injustice but also to better respond to it. Instead of demanding that the Thomas Valleses (and the Danny Díazes and the Victor Punteses) of the world overcome the circumstances of their lives, a critical reading of an apparently innocuous feel-good film like *McFarland, USA* can prompt viewers to identify and hold accountable those who benefit from others' oppression.

NOTES

1. Reported figures for the McFarland cancer cluster vary, depending on how far back a given news report goes and whether the report includes people not living in McFarland at the time of their diagnosis. In all of the news reports I consulted for this essay, the occurrence of childhood cancer in McFarland is estimated at three to four times the national average. The most recent report I consulted, a 1998 *San Francisco Chronicle* retrospective report, gives the following statistics: "From 1975 to 1996, 21 cancers of various kinds were reported in McFarland children ranging in age from under two to 19. That's about three times the expected rate for a town of its size. About 8,000 people live in the community, virtually all of them Latinos" (Martin).

2. Other films for which Costner has been critiqued for playing a white savior role include *Dances with Wolves* (1990) and *Black or White* (2014).

3. In an interview for the blog *SportsLetter*, produced by the LA84 youth sports foundation, White states, "There's a scene in the movie where our name was misspelled on the hats: 'Cougars' was spelled with '-ers.' That actually happened, but it was on our sweats, not the hats. The athletic director said, 'Jim, you need to learn how to spell.' I said, 'I told you to order some sweats. It's October, [and] we're just now getting the sweats. Do not send them back. We'll use them'" (LA84 Foundation).

4. By 2010, the U.S. Census found that more than 91 percent of the McFarland population was Latinx. (See CensusViewer.)

5. See Scott; Warren.

6. See http://www.voicesfromthevalley.org.

7. Derived from the word *panza* (Spanish for "belly"), the moniker "panzón" refers to people with large midsections.

WORKS CITED

Abrams, Bryan. "Director Niki Caro Finds Her Place in *McFarland, USA*." *The Credits*, 23 Feb. 2015, http://www.wheretowatch.com/2015/02/director-niki-caro-finds-her-place-in-mcfarland-usa/. Accessed 14 Mar. 2016.

Alexander, Michelle. *The New Jim Crow: Mass Incarceration in the Age of Colorblindness*. New Press, 2010.

Caro, Niki, director. *McFarland, USA*. Walt Disney Studios Home Entertainment, 2015.

CensusViewer. "McFarland, California Population: Census 2010 and 2000 Interactive Map, Demographics, Statistics, Quick Facts." *Census Viewer*, 2011–2012, http://censusviewer.com/city/CA/McFarland. Accessed 14 Apr. 2019.

Chang, Justin. "Film Review: *McFarland, USA*." *Variety*, 4 Feb. 2015, http://variety.com/2015/film/reviews/film-review-mcfarland-usa-1201423326/. Accessed 14 Mar. 2016.

Clare, Eli. *Exile and Pride: Disability, Queerness, and Liberation*. 3rd ed., Duke UP, 2015.

Early, Jack D. "The Mystery of McFarland, Calif." *Washington Post*, 16 Sept. 1988, https://www.washingtonpost.com/archive/opinions/1988/09/16/the-mystery-of-mcfarland-calif/008336c2-4109-4879-a93d-c2a24772e4c5/. Accessed 2 Feb. 2016.

Farrell, Amy Erdman. *Fat Shame: Stigma and the Fat Body in American Culture*. New York UP, 2011.

Gilmore, Ruth Wilson. *Golden Gulag: Prisons, Surplus, Crisis, and Opposition in Globalizing California*. U of California P, 2007.

Greenfield, Daniel. "Will Amnesty for Illegal Aliens Make America the World's Fattest Country?" *FrontPage Magazine*, 10 July 2013, http://www.frontpagemag.com/point/196425/will-amnesty-illegal-aliens-make-america-worlds-daniel-greenfield. Accessed 20 Aug. 2015.

Guthman, Julie. *Weighing In: Obesity, Food Justice, and the Limits of Capitalism*. U of California P, 2011.

Holmes, Seth M. *Fresh Fruit, Broken Bodies: Migrant Farmworkers in the United States*. U of California P, 2013.

Kafer, Alison. *Feminist, Queer, Crip*. Indiana UP, 2013.

LA84 Foundation. "SL Interview: McFarland, USA's Coach Jim White." *SportsLetter: A Youth Sports Blog*, 26 Mar. 2015, http://www.la84.org/sportsletter/sl-interview-mcfarland-usas-coach-jim-white/. Accessed 29 Mar. 2016.

Martin, Glen. "Cluster: Random or Environmental?" *San Francisco Chronicle*, 4 Oct. 1998, http://www.sfgate.com/education/article/Cluster-Random-or-Environmental-The-small-2987351.php. Accessed 9 Mar. 2016.

Metzl, Jonathan M., and Dorothy E. Roberts. "Structural Competency Meets Structural Racism: Race, Politics, and the Structure of Medical Knowledge." *Virtual Mentor*, vol. 16, no. 9, 2014, pp. 674–690.

Minich, Julie Avril. "'You Gotta Make Aztlán Any Way You Can': Disability in Cherríe Moraga's *Heroes and Saints*." *Disability and Mothering: Liminal Spaces of Embodied Knowledge*, edited by Cynthia Lewiecki-Wilson and Jen Cellio, Syracuse UP, 2011, pp. 260–274.

Moraga, Cherríe. *Heroes and Saints and Other Plays*. West End Press, 1994.

Nixon, Rob. *Slow Violence and the Environmentalism of the Poor*. Harvard UP, 2011.

Parlee, Lorena, and Lenny Bourin, producers. *The Wrath of Grapes*. United Farmworkers, 1986.

Perez, Domino Renee. "Dances with Mexicans: Disney's *McFarland, USA*." *Huffington Post*, 8 Mar. 2015, http://www.huffingtonpost.com/domino-renee-perez/dances-with-mexicans-disn_b_6809962.html. Accessed 3 Feb. 2016.

Pulido, Laura. "Rethinking Environmental Racism: White Privilege and Urban Development in Southern California." *Annals of the Association of American Geographers*, vol. 90, no. 1, 2000, pp. 12–40.

Rivera, Tomás. . . . *Y no se lo tragó la tierra* [. . . And the earth did not devour him]. Arte Público, 1995.

Sandahl, Carrie. "Black Man, Blind Man: Disability Identity Politics and Performance." *Theatre Journal*, vol. 56, no. 4, 2004, pp. 579–602.

Schalk, Sami. "Reevaluating the Supercrip." *Journal of Literary and Cultural Disability Studies*, vol. 10, no. 1, 2016, pp. 71–86.

Scott, Janny. "McFarland Cases: Child Cancer Cluster Poses Puzzle." *Los Angeles Times*, 21 Sept. 1988, http://articles.latimes.com/1988-09-21/news/mn-2231_1_cancer-cluster. Accessed 2 Feb. 2016.

Sze, Julie. *Noxious New York: The Racial Politics of Urban Health and Environmental Justice*. The MIT Press, 2006.

Viramontes, Helena María. *Under the Feet of Jesus*. Plume, 1996.

Wade, Alison. "'McFarland' Movie Helps One of Original Runners Get Back on Track." *Runner's World*, 26 Feb. 2015, http://www.runnersworld.com/newswire/mcfarland-movie-helps-one-of-original-runners-get-back-on-track. Accessed 26 Nov. 2016.

Wald, Sarah D. *The Nature of California: Race, Citizenship, and Farming since the Dust Bowl*. U of Washington P, 2016.

Warren, Jennifer. "Mysterious Cancer Clusters Leave Anxiety in 3 Towns." *Los Angeles Times*, 12 July 1992 http://articles.latimes.com/1992-07-12/news/mn-4269_1_cancer-cluster. Accessed 23 Aug. 2018.

Weisskopf, Michael. "Pesticides and Death amid Plenty." *Washington Post*, 30 Aug. 1988, https://www.washingtonpost.com/archive/politics/1988/08/30/pesticides-and-death-amid-plenty/57bdfbce-6fcd-4c3a-b732-8f680566b630/. Accessed 15 Mar. 2016.

3

The National Park Foundation's "American Latino Expedition"

Consumer Citizenship as Pathway to Multicultural National Belonging

Sarah D. Wald

In the summer of 2013, Kathy Cano-Murillo, founder of the blog CraftyChica.com, concluded her final day at Glen Canyon National Recreation Area by posting to her trip blog, "If you've never experienced an outdoor adventure, I really suggest you do. I never had any desire to hike or swim in a lake, etc. I didn't know what I was missing" ("15 Tips").[1] Cano-Murillo is a member of Latina Blogstars, one of three teams of Latinx bloggers selected to participate in the inaugural year of the American Latino Expedition, a project of the American Latino Heritage Fund (ALHF) of the National Park Foundation.[2] In 2013 and 2014, the American Latino Expedition (ALEX), an innovative social media campaign, sent Latinx bloggers on all-expenses paid trips to U.S. national parks, outfitting them with gear provided by outdoor retailer REI and clothing manufacturer Columbia Sportswear. The contest, whose sponsors also included national park concessionaire Aramark (also known for their food services and prison contracts), aimed to increase Latinx national park visitation by helping Latinx social media influencers see themselves recreating at national parks and encouraging them to promote outdoor recreation to their followers.[3]

Latinxs are significantly underrepresented as national park visitors. A study commissioned by the National Park Service in 2011 found that only one in ten national park visitors identify as Hispanic (the study's term), as compared to 16.3 percent of the total U.S. population in the 2010 Census (Taylor, Grandjean, and Gradmann; 2010 Census). Additionally, Latinx peoples are underrepresented in the historical narratives presented at national park and national monument sites. Only 4 percent of national parks and monuments focus on Latinx histories, according to the Center for American Progress (Johnson; Goad et al.). ALEX was one of many projects that arose within and outside the federal government during the Obama administration (2009–2017) to address inequities in federal public lands' narratives about and visitation by Black people, Latinxs, Asian Americans and Pacific Islanders, and Alaska Natives and Native Americans. Within the federal government, President Obama emphasized the creation of national monuments that told stories of historically marginalized groups such as the César E. Chávez National Monument (2012), the Pullman National Monument (2015), and the Stonewall National Monument (2016). According to the National Park Service, 70 percent of national landmarks established in 2011 and 2012 "reflect and tell complex stories regarding the diversity of the American experience" (Goad et al.). Under the leadership of Jonathan B Jarvis, who served as the director of the National Park Service from 2009 to 2017, the National Park Service also prioritized efforts to diversify national park employees and visitors (Szremski).

Grassroots efforts, including the creation of a significant number of new organizations focused on increasing underrepresented groups' engagement in conservation and recreation, complemented and encouraged such equity, diversity, and inclusion (EDI) efforts by the federal government. For example, Rue Mapp founded Outdoor Afro in 2009, and José González founded Latino Outdoors in 2013. In 2016, the National Park Service's centennial year, Latino Outdoors and Outdoor Afro joined dozens of other groups from the NAACP to the Japanese Americans Citizens League (JACL) to advance a public lands diversity agenda as the Next 100 Coalition. Shortly before leaving office, President Obama issued a presidential memorandum, "Promoting Diversity and Inclusion in Our National Parks, National Forests, and Other Public Lands and Waters" (January 12, 2017), that echoed the Next 100 Coalition's vision statement in several key regards (Next 100 Coalition). Numerous recreation-oriented corporations played a significant role in public and private sector diversity efforts, with REI serving as one of the most visible and consistent funders across organizations.[4]

There is a long history in the United States of positioning national parks as central to national identity. Historically, this tying of the national park system to American exceptionalism has occurred in exclusionary ways. That is, narratives about national parks and wilderness adventures have justified a settler-colonial logic by erasing indigenous claims to those very lands. The National Park Service's current tagline is "Discover Your America." As scholars like William Cronon, Paul Outka, Carolyn Finney, and Jake Kosek have argued, visions of a sublime and romantic wilderness have served narratives of white supremacy that promote a right and wrong way of engaging with nature. Moreover, backpacking and adventure culture have fed a frontier mythology built on white heteronormative masculinity and a eugenicist investment in able white bodies, as scholars from Gail Bederman to Mei Mei Evans,

Sarah Jaquette Ray, and Alexandra Stern have shown. This history provides an essential context for national park diversity efforts.

It also raises a number of questions about ALEX: First, what cultural work occurs when social media posts depict the traditional proving ground for white heteronormative masculinity and ideal citizenship as Latinx leisure space? How does ALEX reshape ideas about national identity and national belonging? How does it rework ideas about what nature is and who it is for? Second, how does ALEX understand and represent contemporary U.S. Latinx identity? That is, what does "Latino" in American Latino Expedition mean, and how does that identity relate to ALEX's production of national identity? Finally, how should we understand the central role that public-private partnerships (like REI and Aramark's sponsorship) play in ALEX and other national park diversity efforts?

Cano-Murrillo's blog post is similar to others in ALEX as it presents national park visitation as "outdoor adventures," where one can find personal wellness and aesthetic appreciation. As Cano-Murillo continues, "It really does clear your mind and makes you appreciate your body and nature in general. Connect with some friends and find local places with nice scenery and at least go for a walk. Better yet, visit your local REI store to see what hiking trails they are featuring! They also have lessons and workshops you can attend" ("15 Tips"). Cano-Murillo's post is representative of ALEX as a whole in positioning REI as a venue for successful outdoor experiences. Cano-Murillo contends that REI's importance is not only in its gear but also in its consumer education in the gear's proper place of use ("see what hiking trails they are featuring!"). As Cano-Murillo's writing indicates and as I argue throughout this essay, ALEX participants repeatedly offer consumption as the proper way for Latinxs to gain access to both nature and the nation. This pattern results from the ALHF's organizational logic, the contest's structure, and the selection of ALEX participants.

Indeed, ALEX produces a particular form of Latinx identity that situates consumer citizenship as the proper mode of national belonging for Latinxs. Under such a model, the purchase of recreation gear allows for particular types of outdoor adventures that in turn produce particular types of reactions to nature that have been long seen as markers of ideal U.S. citizenship. ALEX blogs often represent nature as a commodity and outdoor recreation gear as a vector to allowing nature's consumption. In doing so, ALEX produces a particular vision of Latinx identity within a U.S. national context and positions the recreation industry as an essential actor in EDI implementation within government. In the cultural logic ALEX puts forth, REI both allows the production of a Latinx outdoor recreation identity and positions Latinx holders of that identity as proper citizens of the nation. The model for national belonging that ALEX offers thus sits at the intersection of a multicultural liberalism that promotes incorporation and inclusion and a neoliberalism that relies on individual consumption as the key to proper citizenship.

Yet, as my attention to ALEX blogs shows, ALEX not only incorporates Latinxs into the nation as new outdoor recreationists; it also celebrates the future of national parks, and implicitly the future of the nation, as Latinx. In this way, it moves beyond typical official U.S. antiracisms to transform hegemonic understandings of nature and nation. Moreover, while the majority of the blog posts fit into a nationally dominant narrative of REI-purchased gear leading to self-improvement through solitude and sublime vistas, some blog posts offer counternarratives that align with longer histories of Latinx environmental thought. Such posts challenge a model of knowing nature primarily through consumption and recreation to incorporate modes of knowledge through family, community, history, and labor. These posts, I argue, participate in the tradition of what literary scholar Priscilla Solis Ybarra terms "goodlife writing" by envisioning a relationship with nature that transcends possession and instead focuses on "simplicity, sustenance, dignity, and respect" (Ybarra 7). Taken as a whole, I argue, ALEX as a neoliberal multiculturalist project (a term I define below, drawing on Jodi Melamed) is ambiguous and incomplete. It suggests the ways in which emergent Latinx outdoor identities may fit into narratives of U.S. exceptionalism and U.S. colonialism and simultaneously offer models to resist their confines.

The American Latino Heritage Fund (ALHF) and the American Latino Expedition (ALEX)

In order to understand the possibilities and limits of the ALHF and ALEX, some context about both is in order. The ALHF is a project of the National Park Foundation, the official charity of the National Park Service. The National Park Foundation, which Congress chartered in 1967, brings in money from both individuals and corporate donors. To suggest the extent of corporate money that flows into the National Park Foundation, the following is a partial list of corporations that donate a minimum of $1 million annually: American Express, Budweiser, the Coca-Cola Company, Coleman, Disney, Hallmark Channel, Hanes Brands, Humana, REI, and Subaru of America. In addition to raising funds for popular programs like "Every Kid in a Park," the National Park Foundation eases the way for private land donations. As such, it is not only essential to national park programming but also responsible for much of the national park system's expansion in the second half of the twentieth century (National Park Foundation).

The ALHF is one of several National Park Foundation programs, such as the African American Experience Fund, that seek to connect a broader and more diverse range of U.S. Americans with national parks. It emerged alongside of and in support of the National Park Service's American Latino Heritage Initiative, which Secretary of the Interior Ken Salazar announced in 2011. The ALHF offers direct financial support to the American Latino Heritage Initiative. For example, it funded the theme study, "American Latinos and the Making of the United States," which incorporates seventeen scholarly essays by noted Latinx historians on topics such as arts, education, immigration, law, and military. It also provided funding toward the establishment and operations of the César E. Chávez National Monument and the Casa Dra. Concha Meléndez Ramírez National Historic Landmark in Puerto Rico (National Park Foundation).[5]

The ALHF was most active from 2011 to 2014 under the leadership of its founding director, Midy Aponte, a second-generation Cuban American (her parents were immigrants) who has described herself as a "bicultural and bilingual communications and business strategist" (LinkedIn). Before her tenure at ALHF, Aponte served as the president and founder of the Sanchez-Ricardo Agency, which Aponte described on LinkedIn as a "boutique communications firm providing strategic social media and public relations counsel to businesses and non-profit organizations developing outreach efforts to the Hispanic Market." Aponte specializes in "content curation strategies for reaching Hispanic audiences through social media," a strength she brought to ALHF (Spitfire Strategies). During her time at ALHF, Aponte shifted her focus from marketing to more socially engaged work. When she left the ALHF in May 2015, she became vice president at Spitfire Strategies. In 2016, she joined the board of directors of Latino Outdoors. By November 2017, Aponte described herself as having a "career [that] spans the public and private sector and has often intersected with pressing policy and social issues affecting societal systems" (LinkedIn).

Perhaps unsurprisingly, given her background, Aponte's time at the ALHF was marked by inventive use of social media to inform and engage U.S. Latinxs about national parks and the role of national parks in telling Latinx histories. One of the key ways that Aponte achieved this was through two years of ALEX (on social media as #ALEX13, #ALEX14). REI, Columbia Sportswear, and Aramark, among others, sponsored the contest, which the ALHF referred to as one of its "marquee programs." In its first year, three teams of bloggers went on separate adventures to Glen Canyon Dam, Olympic National Park, and Mesa Verde National Park. In its second year, eight social media influencers traveled together to Grand Teton National Park.

ALEX as Nation-Building Project

The ALHF positions its work to increase Latinx engagement with national parks as part of a nation-building project, producing a particular form of

Latinx identity that aligns with existing narratives of the nation-state.[6] The ALHF recognizes the National Park Service as a key location for the preservation and celebration of U.S. heritage. In expanding Latinx-focused historical sites within the National Park Service, the program seeks to integrate Latinx populations more fully into the nation. However, for ALHF, incorporating Latinxs into the national narrative does not always involve challenging that national narrative. Judging from the ALHF's social media feeds, the nation does not necessarily look different from a Latinx perspective. Neither does nature. In other words, the ALHF's depiction of nation and nature in its Twitter and Facebook feeds, as well as in the ALEX blogs, reflects the historical white, colonialist, romantic view.

In ALHF's Twitter and Facebook feeds (both of which ceased activity in 2015), pictures of dehumanized vistas dominate. The images of national parks that ALHF uses could be taken from the Sierra Club's website. One post encourages users to learn about national parks through an iPad application drawn from Ken Burns's documentary *The National Parks: America's Best Idea*, a film that reinforces discourses of American exceptionalism and romantic visions of nature (Jacoby, "Ken Burns Gone Wild"). ALHF social media feeds encourage followers to understand nature as sublime and spiritually uplifting. The few photos of national parks with people in them show one individual dwarfed by the landscape, a common sublime aesthetic. Such representations of national parks recall environmental historian William Cronon's arguments in his famous essay, "The Trouble with Wilderness." Cronon argues that in romanticizing a particular representation of nature as separate from humans and ignoring the historically and socially constructed nature of wilderness, we neglect the nature that is closer to home. We prioritize protecting large swaths of land rather than recognizing the complex interplay of humans and nonhumans that is integral to both ecosystem and human health. Through its visual storytelling, ALHF reinforces such an oversimplified and romantic construction of U.S. landscapes, neglecting the environmental justice constructions of nature as places of community, where we live, play, and work (Di Chiro).

This is also the vision of nature that predominates in ALEX posts. The blogs showcase a traditional preservationist relationship to nature that focuses on aesthetic beauty and personal transformation. As scholars have acknowledged for decades, wilderness preservation is a discourse about purity and pollution that emerged because of racial anxieties in the late nineteenth and early twentieth centuries. As geographer Jake Kosek explains, "racial and class fears surrounding purity and degradation became a primary means through which wilderness and environment became discernable" (155). Wilderness, moreover, serves as a location of individual subject formation. The wilderness experience of untarnished nature cleanses the individual from the corrupting and degrading ills of modernity. According to Kosek, "Nature's external purity became a catalyst for internal purity" (157). Variations of this transformation through outdoor adventure recur in Frederick Jackson Turner's frontier thesis and John Muir's odes to Yosemite, both of which speak to the United States' national identity. As geographer Bruce Braun states, "Nature, then, served as a place where purification occurred, a place where people became white" (197). How do we understand the replication of this narrative when it centers not on the white U.S. citizen-subject but on an emergent Latinx outdoor recreationist? To what extent does the wilderness experience perpetuate its ideological work when the ethnic background of its citizen-subject shifts?

ALEX blogs repeatedly recount moments of individual transformation through the aesthetic beauty of nature, often with an emphasis on the same sublimity celebrated by the United States' original national park advocates. For example, Yvette Marquez-Sharpnack writes, "The highlight of my trip was seeing the geysers of Yellowstone and the Grand Canyon of Yellowstone. I didn't expect the emotional reaction I had when I saw the Grand Canyon. I just broke down in tears. I was in shock. I didn't know that kind of natural beauty existed in our world" ("Proud"). Denise Cortes writes, "Perhaps it was the time away from the constant din of work and family that gave me some clarity. Maybe it was the red rocks in the distance that I woke up to every morning—they made my problems feel small. Maybe it was the cool, peaceful lake that refreshed my stressed out soul" ("One Year Later"). In blog after blog, participants highlighted such reactions to national landscapes. Joy, awe, tranquility, and renewed sense of perspective are repeated themes.

Certainly, Latinxs can have such transformative experiences. It is not surprising to read the kinds of emotional responses that are common in white recreationists. How do we account, though, for the ways in which such descriptions replicate the very tropes that ethnic studies and environmental justice scholars have criticized for so long?[7] Are the tropes less problematic because the recreationists are Latinx? Does the discourse of racial purity at work in outdoor adventure shift because the individual who experiences the cleansing power of nature is not white? Is the nationalism less problematic because it is less racially exclusive?

Significantly, not all ALEX blogs suggest that Latinxs are transforming into conventional national park users. A subset of ALEX blogs claim the future of national parks and the future of the nation as Latinx. They seek through engagement with national parks to rewrite the identity of the nation. Take, for example, the blog entry "Dear Ranger, You Inspire Me," by Chelle Roberts. The blog begins with a description, taken from Burns's documentary, of the types of park rangers that Stephen Mather, the first director of the National Park Service, sought to hire. While Roberts finds Mather's description of "a team of saints" improbable upon viewing the documentary, her mind is changed after meeting with six rangers on her trip. She profiles each ranger, emphasizing "the spirit of Mather's rangers has never faded." The profiles emphasize this connection to the past and to the history of the National Park Service, except for the one profile of a Latina, Ranger Danielle Archuleta. Of Archuleta, Roberts writes, "This young Latina has a master's degree in Public History, an insatiable thirst for knowledge, a deep love for nature, and an easy spirit. It's clear that she's the future of the park service!" Roberts positions Archuleta as both the continuation of Mather's vision and a Latinx reinhabitation of it. The future of the National Park Service, and the future of the nation, Roberts implies, is Latina.

Melanie Mendez-Gonzales makes this argument as well, and, more surprisingly, rejects a reading that places Latinxs into national park history. She explains:

> Queridos, as I got myself ready for #ALEX14, I anticipated learning some secret history of how Latinos contributed to something really special at Grand Teton National Park. There is no secret history. So, what did I learn? . . . Latino leaders in the National Park Service like Superintendent Vela and park rangers like Millie and Ricardo, and the ALEX13 and ALEX14 (and future) bloggers ARE writing the Latino heritage of the national parks. ("Latino Heritage")

None of the ALEX blogs depicts national parks as particularly important Latinx historic sites. No participants describe learning Latinx history from their visits to national parks. This is surprising because there is a long Latinx engagement with public lands in the United States (as discussed later in this chapter), and because exposing this history was supposedly an explicit aim of ALEX. Yet Mendez-Gonzales explicitly rejects such a narrative by declaring, "There is no secret history." Rather, participants like Chelle Roberts and Mendez-Gonzales position the future of national parks as the future for Latinx environmental thought. In this way, they position Latinxs at the center of the United States' future. Thus, even as participants contribute to the ALHF's nation-building project, they often do so in ways that lay claim to the nation as a site of Latinx futures. It is in this context that Latinx claims to national parks seems least troubling and most promising for transforming, rather than replicating, problematic discourses of the nation based on racial purity and settler-colonial logics. Explicit engagement with the complexity of Latinx histories, however, would enrich such a futurity project.

Liberal Multiculturalism and Neoliberal Citizenship

Moreover, the radical potential for the nation-state's Latinx futures posed by some ALEX participants remain tempered by ALEX's very understanding of nation and citizenship. That is, the particularities of ALEX's production of nation and national identity are a product of the cultural and economic circumstances of the early twenty-first-century United States. As such, ALEX exists at the juncture of liberal multiculturalism and neoliberal governmentality and citizenship. It embraces and participates in the incorporation of antiracism into official state policy. Its reliance on private corporate sponsorships and its emphasis on nature as a commodity to consume and the importance of commodity consumption, such as proper gear purchases, as central to the national park experience, speak to neoliberal notions of consumer citizenship and the privatization of government services.

According to literary critic Jodi Melamed, a significant break occurred in the U.S. racial order after World War II in which the system of racial capitalism and colonialism built around white supremacy was replaced by a system in which the global expansion of U.S.-led global capitalism officially incorporated particular forms of antiracism. As Melamed writes, "Whereas in the 1940s political economic critiques of racism made race appear as an index for the inequalities of capitalist modernity, after the racial break official antiracisms have not only suppressed this reference but also lent antiracist codes to the pursuit of new forms of capitalist development" (10). Melamed contends that the incorporation of official antiracism into U.S.-led global capitalism has led to the erasure of antiracist material and redistributive demands, "deflected criticisms of US global power," and "compel[led] antiracist discourses to validate culturally powerful notions of the U.S. nation" (10). ALEX is in some ways a poster child for this incorporation of official antiracism in global capitalism, participating in market creation through the extended commodification of land, identity, and experiences.

ALEX, much like other federal lands and outdoor recreation EDI projects, positions outdoor recreation and public lands engagement within the discourse of federal civil rights, often relying on the language of equal opportunity and equal access. The desire for national parks to tell more inclusive stories and include broader histories of the nation-state and national belonging speaks to the expansive notions of national belonging advanced by ideologies of liberal multiculturalism. The efforts of the organizers of and participants with ALEX are certainly laudable in their desire to open up greater access for Latinxs to participate in outdoor recreation, enshrine Latinx histories as influential shapers of U.S. history, and create celebratory spaces of leisure and recreation for Latinx peoples in the United States. This representational work is important, and, as seen in Chelle Roberts's and Mendez-Gonzales's counternarratives discussed above, potentially transformational.

Yet ALEX also resonates with Melamed's critiques, as it works against the material and redistributive demands of earlier forms of antiracism, validates certain forms of U.S. nationalism, erases ongoing indigenous presence, and embraces property ownership and forms of individualism and consumer power that are central to capitalism and colonialism.[8] Specifically, ALEX is representative of the liberal antiracism that, as Melamed explains, "defined antiracism as the extension of property rights and of possessive individualism to people of color" (148). The National Park Foundation presents the ALHF and its ALEX program as actively incorporating Latinx peoples into the "We" that owns public land. In doing so, even as it performs an important gesture of inclusion in the imagined nation of the United States, it simultaneously imbricates Latinxs into the settler-colonial nation-building project to which national parks stand as testament. As historians Mark Spence and Karl Jacoby (*Crimes against Nature*) have shown, national park creation went hand-in-hand with indigenous dispossession and the creation of the reservation system. The National Park Foundation explains, "After all, the national parks belong to every American—past, present and future" ("Programs That Connect"). Through this settler-colonial logic, the narrative about equal access to national parks furthers the commodification of nature. If national parks are property that belongs to all Americans, including Latinxs, then outdoor adventure or recreation becomes an experience that all Americans, including Latinxs, can purchase with just the right gear.

Popular narratives about U.S. demographic change help explain the emphasis on marketing national parks to Latinxs that occurs in the ALHF, including why a marketing strategist was hired as its founding director. Anxieties about U.S. demographic changes underlie a significant amount of the EDI work undertaken by the National Park Foundation, the National Park Service, and their allied corporate partners. It is common among these organizations to cite demographic changes that will grant the United States a majority people of color population by 2050. Previous generations of conservationists often responded to demographic change with racially exclusionary rhetoric and a defense of whiteness. These responses range from Theodore Roosevelt's concern with white suicide to the environmental nativism of the Federation for American Immigration Reform (FAIR), which is an organization that uses racially coded rhetoric to blame environmental destruction on increased immigration (see Bederman; Kosek; Park and Pellow; Ray). Today's conservationists have more often chosen a less xenophobic path, seeking instead to incorporate and include new demographic groups into their fold. Rather than position people of color as pollutants threatening the purity of U.S. nature, contemporary U.S. conservation leadership has often sought to position people of color as the future of conservation. This position opens up radical possibilities for twenty-first-century environmentalism.

Yet the lack of diversity in public lands usage also speaks to an anxiety about the future of public lands advocacy. In its opening paragraph, the vision statement for the Next 100 Coalition explains that public lands' failure to reflect "our country's demographic and ethnic diversity" is becoming "more urgent because the future of our public lands will depend upon public support from all people." There is widespread concern among public lands professionals and public lands advocates that the lack of visitation by people of color will result in declining federal support for public lands. This concern is based on the assumption that public land support ties directly to recreation use. However, studies repeatedly show that people of color, including Latinxs, are more likely to support environmental initiatives than white populations. Low rates of public lands visitation by people of color have not resulted in lower levels of support for public lands compared to white populations.[9] As Ybarra discusses, white mainstream progressives in the United States continue to find Latinx political support for environmental issues confusing because of narrow views about what environmentalism is and who environmentalists are.

The Next 100 Coalition's appeal capitalizes on white mainstream confusion about Latinx environmentalisms. It addresses the self-interest of white conservationists who may be more motivated by the urgency of land preservation than the morality of social justice. In doing so, it reflects a form of what Sarah Jaquette Ray terms "strategic environmentalism" rather than deeply entrenched beliefs among the Next 100 Coalition's membership (see Ray, this volume). Drawing from the work of Laura Pulido and Soenke Zehle, Ray is interested in the ways in which communities perform an essentialized environmental identity in order to gain access to what Pulido terms "ecological legitimacy." By appealing to white conservationists' self-interests and their problematic assumptions about the relationship between recreation and public lands advocacy, the Next 100 Coalition gains access to resources and ecological legitimacy for demographic groups often excluded from the conservation table.

Yet, as a result of this choice to emphasize use and visitation as an indicator of public lands support, groups like the Next 100 Coalition and the ALHF position public land as a consumable good. Consumer citizenship is the logic at work here as value (and thus political support) is presumed to derive primarily from use. In contrast, research from scholars like Ybarra suggests that much Latinx concern for the environment manifests outside the consumer structure. In the context of this problematic assumption (use leads to value leads to political support), the choice to use marketing strategies makes sense. It emphasizes the commodification of nature required for its preservation in late capitalism. Nature as a commodity must be sold to the rising Latinx consumer to ensure its continued existence. If they are to be preserved, national parks must retain relevance as sites of use and as vectors for capitalist consumption.[10]

Corporate endorsers of these programs repeat this narrative. As the white population in the United States shrinks and Latinxs and other people of color become dominant demographically, the market share of outdoor recreation companies presumably shrinks as well. Expanding Latinx interest in shopping at outdoor retailers, then, is good business. Scott Welch, a spokesman for Columbia Sportswear, told the *New York Times*, in an article about ALEX, "The future is diverse. If you want to be a brand for the future, you've got to embrace that" (Johnson). For such businesses, supporting expanded recreation opportunities for Latinx communities creates a market for outdoor gear among Latinx populations.

It is sensible that these companies would identify expanded visitation rates to national parks and other public lands as a key avenue for creating more Latinx outdoor recreationists. Enhancing Latinx public land visitation is a key strategy for creating a Latinx outdoor recreation identity. According to outdoor retailer Patagonia, "Public lands host 71 percent of climbers, 70 percent of hikers, and 43 percent of paddlers in America, and they also contain nearly 200,000 miles of hiking trails and 13,000 miles of mountain biking trails." Public lands provide the site at which the equipment and clothing purchased through companies like REI, Patagonia, and Columbia Sportswear are most likely to be used. In such marketing logic, encouraging Latinx usage of public lands creates the market that these companies see as necessary for future profit.

In ALEX's social media marketing strategies, the narrative of national inclusion relies on consumer citizenship. The ideal twenty-first-century Latinx citizen in ALEX materials is a consumer of both public lands and recreation gear. According to ALEX, national inclusion requires equitable access to nature as commodity and outdoor recreation opportunities at national parks. The purchasing and use of gear marks the incorporation of Latinx peoples into the United States as proper citizens. This is even as the purchasing and use of gear is sold as a project to support the telling of Latinx histories and the writing of Latinx presence into the United States. In the consumer citizenship that emerges at the nexus of neoliberalism and multiculturalism, national inclusion and purchasing power cannot be separated.

First-Timers in Nature?

ALEX emphasizes the selection of bloggers and social media influencers who are first-timers in "outdoor adventures" and in doing so positions Latinxs as "new citizens," whose ability to access national parks coincides with their ability to access national inclusion. As Cano-Murillo details, her team, the Latina Blogstars, consisted of "a craft blogger, a fashion blogger, a mom blogger and a food blogger. Hiking boots didn't exactly fit in to our daily routine" ("Eee Gads"). Entries like Cano-Murillo's "15 Tips for First-Timers" emphasize how few participants had hiked, kayaked, or visited national parks before their ALEX trip. In "Proud of Myself and Proud to Be an American," Marquez-Sharpnack explained that ALEX taught her that "you do not have to be an athlete or in amazing shape to visit a national park." Latinxs in ALEX blogs frequently appear as a blank slate, learning about nature for the first time and learning how to access nature through their purchasing power rather than as peoples defined by their histories of struggle over land and environment.

For the most part, ALEX materials ignore what might be identified as the existing environmental ethics of U.S. Latinx populations, such as the tradition of goodlife writing Ybarra identifies. They also ignore disputes over land grants that have marked Mexican American relationships to U.S. federally claimed land (Pulido, *Environmentalism and Economic Justice*; Peña; Kosek). Erasing the history of land disputes renders invisible the critique of federal agencies' claim on Mexican land and the environmental ethics that emerges from those claims. It dehistoricizes Latinx relationships to federal public lands, ignoring the specific types of claims to land that different Latinx groups have made. It ignores a long history of existing Latinx land use in the United States from urban gardening to fishing and sheep grazing (Pulido, *Environmentalism and Economic Justice*; Peña; Kosek). It also ignores one of the primary Latinx encounters with public lands—through labor. Many Latinxs in the Pacific Northwest, for example, work in the forestry and restoration industries and are heavily engaged in special forest products, often as independent contractors to supplement income from farm labor (Sifuentez; Green; Hansis). Engaging Latinx relationships to public lands through labor would trouble the recreation focus of ALEX. National parks exist in ALEX blogs as places of possession, consumption, and individual transformation, not as active locations of struggle, labor, and conflict.

It is not just Latinx history that ALEX neglects. ALEX also ignores the problematic foundation of the National Park Service, a troublesome history of removing Native Americans and indigenous Mexicans made clear in the work of environmental historians like Karl Jacoby and Mark Spence. In most ALEX blog posts, indigenous claims to federal public lands appear as ancient history. For example, Chelle Roberts, in "Dear Ranger, You Inspire Me," writes, "I keep imagining what it would be like to travel back in time to meet the indigenous men and women of the Olympic Peninsula." The one exception appears in Ana Serafin's "Rich History of the Makahs." Serafin emphasizes both the past and presence of Makah and their relationship to Latinxs. She points out that the Makah weave baskets like the indigenous people of Latin America. She also "learned that the ladies within the Makah tribe are very similar to us Latinas... they always like to be pampered and looking beautiful at all hours of the day." Her Makah dinner companion, William, describes his mother, who used to sing with Louis Armstrong and Bing Crosby and won't be seen outside "without makeup on, her nails perfect." This description pushes back against stereotypical conceptions of native dress. It implicitly contests relegations of native peoples to distant pasts even as it emphasizes the beauty, fashion, and consumer concerns that dominate many other ALEX blog posts.

While the ALHF urges recognition of national historic sites that privilege Latinx history as a key part of U.S. history, ALEX social media and blog posts rarely acknowledge the history of U.S. imperialism or struggles in the Southwest over landownership. They do not recognize the way racialized and contingent membership of undocumented Latinxs renders them a particularly exploitable labor class, nor do they explore what that relationship means for

Latinx engagement with nature. ALEX's repeated idea that Latinx are "first-timers" in engaging the landscape erases the long history of the relationship between the U.S. landscape and Latinx communities. It privileges a relationship based on particular types of leisure and consumption over relationships of production and community. Moreover, ALEX generally relegates native peoples to prehistory, such as with the Condes family's visit to the Mesa Verde caves, participating in the settler colonialism necessary to U.S. nationalist narratives.

Out of over forty blog entries, there were only two that explicitly challenge the narrative of Latinx as first-timers in nature. Staci Salazar refutes the first-timer narrative by emphasizing continuity with her childhood experiences. She writes, "Having spent most of my childhood in Ouachita National Forest with my cousins, the smell of Grand Teton National Park alone brought back a flood of memories. The pine trees and animals running wild reminded me of days past. I remembered walking through the forest in bright colors while singing loudly so that both hunters and animals alike would know we were near" ("How to Free"). This passage not only points out Salazar's experience but also highlights the environmental knowledge she gained from this experience.

Carol Cain similarly employs nostalgia as a means to understand her national park experiences. Walking on Second Beach, in Olympic National Park, Cain writes, "The boulders blocking the crash of the waves from the shore reminded me of my days as a little girl walking the shore of Puerto Rico, where my mother's family is from. I couldn't help but immediately feel nostalgic" ("Exploring the Seashore"). A section of her blog is worth quoting extensively:

> A place that couldn't be any further from the Caribbean shores of my childhood, yet it felt so familiar to me. I didn't want to leave as I recalled the sunsets on the beach sitting by a fire as my uncles brought buckets of crabs they had just caught. I remember the fear and fascination I had as I watched them try to escape the bucket, the sounds of their claws scrapping against the smooth sides of their tin trap. I remember how one of my uncles explained their purpose to me, of how we would feast with them and how nothing would go to waste because whatever we didn't consume we would return to the ocean, which in turn would feed another. I recall how the satisfaction with this idea made it easier for me to try them, then like them, and try them again.
>
> My happiest memories were created in places like these, wild and untamed, raw and beautiful. It was hard not to feel a sense of home. And as I sat there reconnecting with my youth, I developed an urgent sense to want to share it with those whom I love the most. I wondered how my family would feel visiting a place such as this, so different and yet so familiar. How insane it would be if we ventured back during whale season. How my boys would go nuts climbing the beach

logs and wet boulders ahead. I envisioned them collecting rocks and being in awe of the little snails clinging on to them. ("Exploring the Seashore")

Cain establishes national parks as a home. They connect the author's Puerto Rican roots with her family's mainland future. She moves in the piece from a recollection of her uncles on a Puerto Rican beach to a vision of her sons on a Pacific Northwest beach. In this entry, Cain offers an explicit and reverberating rejection of narratives of Latinx as unlikely hikers and first-timers in nature. She establishes nature as home for both previous generations and future ones. She uses nature and national parks to stake a claim in the nation, albeit one complicated by Puerto Rico's status of colony of the United States and Puerto Ricans as both U.S. citizens and colonial subjects. She emphasizes as well an environmental knowledge and sustainability ethos that comes not from the education offered by park rangers but from the lessons taught by uncles on the beach. Additionally, Cain in referencing her identity as a Puerto Rican offers one of the only posts to draw on a more specific identity than "Latino" or "Latina." In contrast to Cain's post, national heritage of the majority of bloggers (be that Mexican, Guatemalan, Chilean, etc.) remains unmentioned, contributing to the panethnic production of the "American Latino," and positioning that identity category as itself part of U.S. exceptionalism.[11] Significantly, there is no mention of gear and no marketing plug for REI, Columbia, or other company embedded in Cain's post, unlike so many other ALEX blogs.

The Travelistas in Nature, of which Cain was a part, was a group particularly notable for the ways they credited Latinx heritage and culture for shaping their experiences. In her final blog post for ALEX13, Cain ascribes the specialness of her experience to being among women of color, a category that, for her, emerges from "Black and Latino culture," which she positions as distinct from "New World practices," a framing that I read as an implicit embrace of Afro-Latinidad in Cain's writings. Cain explains, "The ability to support and encourage each other is the strength of who we are as women of color" ("Connecting with Your True Self"). According to Cain, national parks provided time for the women to connect to each other in "material, sisterly, and friendly relationships" disallowed by the hustle and bustle of daily life in the United States. In counter to the many blog posts that emphasize the internal transformation and inspiration of solitude, Cain's posts repeatedly return to a Latinx community that emerges in national parks, whether that is through sisterhood or through nostalgic memories of family. Cain and Salazar in their blog posts thus challenge the dominant narrative of first-timers in nature. Their writings enrich the claims to Latinx futures made by Mendez-Gonzales and Chelle Roberts by emphasizing these connections to various Latinx histories. As such, they complicate any reading of the ideological and material work of the ALEX project as simply extending capitalist commodification of nature to new markets.

The U.S. Latinx Consumer

ALEX participants were instructed not only in the proper use of national parks but also in the proper use of recreation gear. Their first well-documented stop was REI. REI gear became the key vector through which the bloggers experienced national parks. Repeatedly participants described wearing high-end outdoor fashions as a pleasurable and luxurious experience. Relishing the proper gear was as much a part of outdoor recreation as enjoying nature. ALEX establishes consumption as the appropriate avenue through which Latinxs take their place in the nation. It also produces a particular kind of Latina as a new kind of citizen, useful to U.S. global capitalist expansion under neoliberalism.

Visits to REI and references to REI gear reinforced ALEX narratives about "first-timers." The information that first-timers need to know is almost always about gear. As Ramon Gonzalez reported, "I learned why I couldn't go on a hike that lasted three hours in my street wear and jeans. Pants that converted into shorts were a lifesaver" ("Well-Equipped"). At least two bloggers provided packing lists for first-timers focused on REI and Columbia gear (Salazar, "Day Hiking Check List"; Marquez-Sharpnack, "Why Layers"). Participants repeatedly established an REI shopping spree as the necessary first step for any successful national park adventure. As Crystal Roberts describes, "There was a moment when I had my gear on and stepped out of the dressing room at the REI store, I felt so ready for the trip that I wish I could have been magically dropped into Olympic National Park at that very moment" (Serafin, "Travelistas in Nature").

ALEX participants expressed the same trepidation and excitement about their first visits to REI as about their inaugural visits to national parks. As Cano-Murillo states, "I was so nervous about going into REI for my gear. . . . I'm used to shopping for yarn and glitter, not hydration reservoirs!" ("Latina Blogstars Visit REI"). Monique Frausto reports, "You're all going to laugh, but I've never been inside of a REI store before. It was like a whole new world and unchartered territory," a comment that emphasizes the ways REI situates itself within the settler-colonial logic of outdoor adventure (Cano-Murillo, "Latina Blogstars Visit REI").

In contrast to their subject position as inexperienced hikers, participants tended to present themselves as fashion experts and savvy shoppers. As Daily Baez explained, "The REI clothing sections (for the whole family) are definitely high quality and totally fashionable, coming from a girl who NEEDS fashion in her life" ("Where to Get the Gear"). While some participants mentioned the technology behind the gear, describing it as "Very

MacGyver-esque" and as if "made by some NASA designer," more often participants highlighted its stylishness (Cano-Murillo, "Latina Blogstars Visit REI"). Yvonne Condes explained, "They have the cutest clothes," while Nicole Presley proclaimed, "Who knew sportswear looked so good? I guess I need to get outdoors more!" ("Condes Campers Visit REI"; Cano-Murillo, "Latina Blogstars Visit REI"). Fit was as important as fashion. As Monique Frausto stated, "Us curvy girls love the outdoors too!" Denise Cortes shared, "Being a plus-size woman, I wasn't sure if the clothes would be comfortable" (Cano-Murillo, "Latina Blogstars Visit REI"). Chelle Roberts concurred, "I have to admit, I didn't expect to find so many stylish options to fit my curvy frame" (Serafin, "Travelistas in Nature"). The emphasis from Latina bloggers on REI's size range is striking given that REI continues to face criticism online for its lack of offerings for women, particularly its size range.[12] These blog posts construct REI as a friendly and welcoming site for Latinas and REI clothing as comfortable and stylish in and out of the woods.

ALEX not only depicts a particular type of Latinx relationship to land; it also constructs a particular type of Latino, or really a particular type of Latina. In *Latinos, Inc.* Arlene Davila examines the attempts by television stations Univision and Telemundo to create a pan–Latin American identity where Latin America operates as a signifier of authenticity and identity. Such texts emphasize the use of a standard upper-class Mexican Spanish and depict the use of standard English as ancillary to U.S. Latino identities. Code-switching, Spanglish, and indigenous language use are ignored. In contrast, ALEX promotes a female construction of U.S. Latinidad, a centrality the Latina gains through her empowered shopping. Spanish use is almost nonexistent on the site. The website constructs a Latina consumer who is modern, savvy, and sophisticated, and whose bilingualism is a strength. Whereas the marketing agencies Davila studies often focus on Latinos as new immigrant populations, the ALHF posits Latinas as transcendent of borders in their identities as sophisticated global travelers and new consumers.

The choice of winners of the #ALEX13 contest is particularly suggestive of this reading of U.S. Latina identity as standard English speaking and nonimmigrant. Two of the groups were women whose style derived from mainstream U.S. fashion, such as designer labels, manicures, and brand name accessories. The first group, who call themselves the Travelistas in Nature, are self-styled world travelers. They represent themselves as modern, well-off, sophisticated urbanites. Their blogs suggest a global U.S.-based traveler discovering the wonders of national parks. Through their adventures, a narrative of global sisterhood and female empowerment emerges. As Crystal Roberts writes, "At the peak of the trail, I felt free and inspired to be!! It seems we all felt that way, as we stood with our arms in the air, ready to take flight" ("Hiking Big Meadow Trail"). The second group, Latina Blogstars, emphasize shopping, eating, sisterhood, and self-pride of individual attainment in their posts. Hiking together forms bonds of strength and sisterhood. In "We'll Always Have Lake Powell," Denise Cortes explains, "It's one thing to hang out with your girlfriends for an afternoon of lunch and shopping. It's quite another to place yourself in a foreign landscape, overcome fears and challenges together, and immerse yourself in the moment." The use of "foreign" in Cortes's description accentuates these women as adventurers and travelers. As Cortes writes, "The things we experienced, the sights we saw, the emotions we felt, the challenges we overcame—it made us more than fellow bloggers."

All three groups selected for ALEX13 represented an upper-middle-class English-speaking vision of Latinidad. Spanish words were used only a handful of times over dozens of blog posts. Such images contrast with what Davila identified as advertisers' construction of Latinidad as new immigrants, Spanish speaking, conservative, working class, and culturally conservative. This suggests the way advertisers have adjusted their ideals of the "Hispanic market" since the 1990s. Instead, ALEX constructs U.S. Latinidad as the primary site of a new U.S. identity. Consumption and leisure become the primary ways in which these Latinx subjects explore not only their position in the nation but also the United States' position in the world.

This analysis is in keeping with the kind of global consumer that Melamed argues is promoted under neoliberal global capitalist conditions, in which a certain level of class and particular forms of cultural identity offer access to some forms of privilege through an identity as a multicultural global consumer (169). Specifically, Melamed argues that "neoliberal multiculturalism has created new privileged subjects, racializing the beneficiaries of neoliberalism as worthy multicultural citizens and racializing the losers as unworthy and excludable" (xxi). ALEX performs the conditions under which Latinx consumers are offered access to privileged subject status through their identification with the linked projects of capitalism, consumerism, settler colonialism, and nationalism. ALEX participants are presented with access to leisure, luxury, and adventure while being assured their experiences constitute an active form of antiracism. Yet the continued ruptures and counternarratives within ALEX that I have highlighted reveal the contradictions of such a project and its inability to fully erase alternative forms of Latinx environmental engagement.

Interrupted by Trump, or Toward a Conclusion

When I first encountered ALEX, I was excited. After nearly two decades studying the ways that U.S. conservation has manifested as a racial project, it was invigorating to see efforts underway by both the National Park Service and the National Park Foundation to transform the racial discourse around public lands in the United States. I was hopeful that projects such as ALEX might address the environmental justice movement's ongoing critique of the mainstream environmental movement. Could projects like ALEX contribute to a transformation of the problematic colonialist, capitalist, and racial foundations of the U.S. conservation movement?

Yet the more I read about ALEX, the more cynical I became. ALEX seemed less interested in transforming traditional environmentalism by incorporating alternative ways of imagining the relationship between humans and the more-than-human world and appeared more as a savvy marketing campaign. I began to ask myself if ALEX was merely extending environmental privilege to a new group rather than trying to dismantle the ideological systems that contribute to environmental privilege's production. If so, was that necessarily a problem? White people have transformational experiences in sublime landscapes while wearing expensive backpacking gear all the time. Is there anything inherently wrong with ensuring that such experiences are not racially or ethnically exclusive?

Ultimately, I have concluded that while such efforts as ALEX are in and of themselves laudable, they also have significant limitations and pose possible dangers. ALEX is not a racial justice or environmental justice project, despite the counternarratives participants and organizers put forth within its framework. It reinforces settler colonialism while replicating dominant relationships of economic power and a problematic human-nature binary based in wilderness worship. Its danger lies in the potential that its call for diverse and inclusive "outdoor adventures" may override calls for global environmental justice, further legitimize settler colonialism, or justify the extension of racial capitalism across the earth through the further production of forms of global consumer citizenship.

In many ways, ALEX is a neoliberal project interested in niche market creation. That niche market creation relies on the production of a Latinx identity, the "American Latino" of "American Latino Expedition." The pan-Latinx identity that ALEX produces relies on consumption as a pathway to inclusion. It incorporates certain Latinx individuals who have the economic means to purchase particular types of "outdoor adventure," an inclusion that is based on the implicit exclusion of others. ALEX's forms of incorporation continue to render Latinx individuals who lack economic means as excludable, expendable, and invisible while ignoring forms of Latinx environmentalisms that exist outside of consumption, possession, and leisure. As Melamed points out, it produces good and bad neoliberal subjects.

ALEX has not existed since Aponte left the American Latino Heritage Fund in 2014. ALHF social media sites have been silent since 2015. Under the Trump administration, moreover, many of the diversity initiatives that marked the Obama administration have been removed or are under threat of removal. Nearly all members of the National Park Advisory Board, including historian Stephen Pitti and geographer Carolyn Finney, resigned together in January 2018, after the Department of the Interior's unwillingness to meet or otherwise engage with them (Neuman and Dwyer; Knowles). The multicultural neoliberalism of the Obama era has been replaced by the "transgressive racism" of the Trump administration (Pulido et al., "Environmental Deregulation"). Antiracism is no longer official state policy. When Mexicans are rendered rapists by the Trump administration, Latinx incorporation by consumer citizenship is no longer an option. Whereas the Obama administration's neoliberal multiculturalism rendered national parks as a desirable consumer good, the Trump administration threatens the very existence of the national park system, seeking privatization and environmental deregulation that privileges extractive economies over recreation economies (Pulido et al. "Environmental Deregulation").

David N. Pellow, in outlining his vision of Critical Environmental Justice, is skeptical of political efforts that primarily seek redress from the state. In his third pillar of Critical Environmental Justice, Pellow argues that seeking remedies for environmental injustices from the state, often the perpetrator of environmental harms, does not alter and may reinforce the power structures responsible for creating the inequality (17). Likewise, Laura Pulido advises environmental justice advocates to position the state as an adversary, contending that environmental racism is constitutive of contemporary racial capitalism and thus a form of state-sanctioned racial violence ("Geographies of Race and Ethnicity II"). Under the Obama administration, multicultural neoliberalism provided a framework through which the state appeared to offer access to certain forms of "environmental privilege" (Park and Pellow's term) to some formerly excluded groups (Park and Pellow 3). The explicit racism and neoliberal environmental policies of the Trump administration render such access unviable. It remains to be seen how the movement for equity, diversity, and inclusion in federal public lands and outdoor recreation will respond in the face of the environmental threats, explicit xenophobia, and mobilized racism of the Trump era.

NOTES

1. This essay was improved by thoughtful comments from David J. Vázquez, Priscilla Solis Ybarra, Sarah Ray, Alaí Reyes-Santos, Laura Pulido, Gabriela Martinez, Catalina de Onis, Geraldo Sandoval, and the attendees of the Environmental Justice, Race, and Public Lands symposium at University of Oregon.

2. Throughout this essay, I cite blog posts from the American Latino Expedition. I include the original links to the blogs. These links stopped working since I began writing this piece. They currently take the user back to the main page of the American Latino Heritage Fund.

3. Throughout this essay, I use Latinx as pan-ethnic marker for the reasons outlined in the volume's introduction. However, I use Hispanic, Latino, or Latina in direct reference to a text or author who uses that particular term (such as in reference to American Latino Expedition).

4. For organizations receiving funding from REI since 2017, see www.rei.com/stewardship/creating-access.

5. The accents on Chavez's name are in accordance with the monument's official National Park Service name.

6. Latinx/Latina/o/Latin@ is a multifaceted category without inherent meaning combining diverse heritages and experiences. In this essay, I do not take Latinx/Latino/a/Latin@ as a self-evident term, but rather I am interested in how projects like the American Latino Expedition produce a particular understanding of Latinx/Latino/a/Latina@ identity. For more on the uses and limitations of Latina/o/Latinx in literary and cultural studies, see Caminero-Santangelo 1–35 and Rodriguez 1–20.

7. For examples, see Cronon; Di Chiro; Evans; Finney; Jacoby, "Ken Burns Gone Wild"; Gottlieb; Outka; Peña; Pulido, *Environmentalism and Economic Justice*; Ray; Spence; White.

8. For more on the role of property ownership and possession as central to the production of white supremacy and justification for colonialism, see Harris; Moreton-Robinson.

9. For example, see the poll of voters of color commissioned by New American Media and the Next 100 Coalition, which found that 92 percent of voters of color approved of the Obama administration's steps to protect public lands.

10. My thinking here was influenced by the work of Jennifer Price and Susan Davis.

11. One exception is Melanie Mendez-Gonzales, who repeatedly refers to herself as Tejana.

12. For REI's response to this criticism, see Parris.

WORKS CITED

Aponte, Midy. LinkedIn profile. www.linkedin.com/in/midyaponte/.

Baez, Daily. "Where to Get the Gear You Need." *American Latino Heritage Fund*, ALHF.org/ALEX-blog/where-get-gear-you-need.

Bederman, Gail. *Manliness and Civilization: A Cultural History of Gender and Race in the United States, 1880–1917*. U of Chicago P, 1996.

Braun, Bruce. "On the Raggedy Edge of Risk: Articulations of Race and Nature after Biology." *Race, Nature, and the Politics of Difference*, edited by Donald S. Moore, Jake Kosek, and Anand Pandian, Duke UP, 2003, pp. 175–203.

Cain, Carol. "Connecting with Your True Self and Heritage in Nature." *American Latino Heritage Fund*, ALHF.org/ALEX-blog/connecting-your-true-self-heritage-nature.

———. "Exploring the Seashore and Feeling Nostalgia." *American Latino Heritage Fund*, ALHF.org/ALEX-blog/exploring-seashore-feeling-nostalgic.

Caminero-Santangelo, Marta. *On Latinidad: U.S. Latino Literature and the Construction of Ethnicity*. U of Florida P, 2017.

Cano-Murillo, Kathy. "15 Tips for First Timers." *American Latino Heritage Fund*, ALHF.org/ALEX-blog/15-tips-first-timers.

———. "Eee Gads, I'm Going to Kayak!" *Crafty Chica*, Aug. 2013, www.craftychica.com/2013/08/eee-gads-im-going-to-kayak/.

———. "Latina Blogstars Visit REI." *American Latino Heritage Fund*. ALHF.org/ALEX-blog/latina-blogstars-visit-REI.

Condes, Yvonne. "Condes Campers Visit REI." *American Latino Heritage Fund*. ALHF.org/ALEX-blog/condes-campers-visit-rei.

Cortes, Denise. "One Year Later: Reminiscing on My ALEX13 Adventure." *American Latino Heritage Fund*. alhf.org/ALEX-blog/one-year-later-reminiscing-my-ALEX13-adventure.

———. "We'll Always Have Lake Powell." *American Latino Heritage Fund*. alhf.org/alex-blog/well-always-have-lake-powell.

Cronon, William. "The Trouble with Wilderness." *Uncommon Ground: Rethinking the Human Place in Nature*, edited by William Cronon, Norton, 1995, pp. 69–90.
Davila, Arlene. *Latinos, Inc.: The Marketing and Making of a People*. U of California P, 2001.
Davis, Susan. *Spectacular Nature: Corporate Culture and the Sea World Experience*. U of California P, 1997.
Di Chiro, Giovanna. "Nature as Community: The Convergence of Environment and Social Justice." *Uncommon Ground: Rethinking the Human Place in Nature*, edited by William Cronon, Norton, 1996, pp. 298–320.
Evans, Mei Mei. "'Nature' and Environmental Justice." *The Environmental Justice Reader: Politics, Poetics, and Pedagogy*, edited by Joni Adamson, Mei Mei Evans, and Rachel Stein, U of Arizona P, 2002, pp. 181–193.
Finney, Carolyn. *Black Faces, White Spaces: Reimagining the Relationship of African Americans to the Great Outdoors*. U of North Carolina P, 2014.
Goad, Jessica, Matt Lee-Ashley, and Farah Z. Ahmad. "Better Reflecting Our Country's Growing Diversity." *Center for American Progress*, 9 Feb. 2014, www.americanprogress.org/issues/green/reports/2014/02/19/84191/better-reflecting-our-countrys-growing-diversity/.
Gonzalez, Ramon. "Well-Equipped and Ready to Go." *American Latino Heritage Fund*, ALHF.org/ALEX-blog/well-equipped-and-ready-go.
Gottlieb, Robert. *Forcing the Spring: The Transformation of the American Environmental Movement*. Revised ed., Island Press, 2005.
Green, Emily. "Timber's Fallen: The Plight of Immigrant Forestry Workers." *Street Roots*, 5 Feb. 2016, news.streetroots.org/2016/02/05/timber-s-fallen-plight-immigrant-forestry-workers.
Hansis, Richard. "Latinos/Hispanics and Federal Lands in the Interior Columbia River Basin." Interior Columbia Basin Ecosystem Management Project, www.fs.fed.us/r6/icbemp/science/hansisrichard_10pg.pdf.
Harris, Cheryl L. "Whiteness as Property." *Harvard Law Review*, vol. 106, no. 8, 1993, pp. 1707–1791.
Jacoby, Karl. *Crimes against Nature: Squatters, Poachers, Thieves, and the Hidden History of American Conservation*. U of California P, 2001.
———. "Ken Burns Gone Wild: Naturalizing the Nation in *The National Parks: America's Best Idea*." *Public Historian*, vol. 33, no. 2, 2011, pp. 19–23.
Johnson, Kirk. "National Parks Try to Appeal to Minorities." *New York Times*, 5 Sept. 2013, www.nytimes.com/2013/09/06/us/national-parks-try-to-appeal-to-minorities.html?pagewanted=all&_r=0.
Knowles, Tony. "Letter of Resignation from Members of the National Park System Advisory Board." *Washington Post*, 15 Jan. 2018, apps.washingtonpost.com/g/documents/national/letter-of-resignation-from-members-of-the-national-park-system-advisory-board/2711/.
Kosek, Jake. *Understories: The Political Life of Forests in Northern New Mexico*. Duke UP, 2006.
Marquez-Sharpnack, Yvette. "Proud of Myself and Proud to Be an American." *American Latino Heritage Fund*. ALHF.org/ALEX-blog/ proud-myself-and-proud-be-american.
———. "Why 'Layers, Layers, Layers' Is Good Advice." *American Latino Heritage Fund*. ALHF.org/ALEX-blog/layers-layers-layers-good-advice.
Melamed, Jodi. *Represent and Destroy: Rationalizing Violence in the New Racial Capitalism*. U of Minnesota P, 2011.

Mendez-Gonzalez, Melanie. "Latino Heritage in Our National Parks." *American Latino Heritage Fund*. ALHF.org/ALEX-blog/latino-heritage-our-national-parks.

Moreton-Robinson, Aileen. *The White Possessive: Property, Power, and Indigenous Sovereignty*. U of Minnesota P, 2015.

Muir, John. *My First Summer in the Sierra*. Penguin Books, 2003.

National Park Foundation. "Programs That Connect." www.nationalparks.org/our-work/programs/programs-connect.

National Park Service Advisory Board. "American Latinos and the Making of the United States: A Theme Study." National Park Service, 28 Feb. 2013, www.nps.gov/heritage initiatives/latino/latinothemestudy/index.htm.

Neuman, Scott, and Colin Dwyer. "Majority of National Park Service Board Resigns, Citing Administration Indifference." *NPR*, 18 Jan. 2018.

New American Media, Next 100 Coalition, and Bendixen and Amandi International. "An Untapped Natural Resource: Our National Public Lands and the New America." media.namx.org/images/editorial/2016/08/0822/pub_land_div_poll.pdf.

Next 100 Coalition. "Our Public Lands: An Inclusive Vision for the Next 100 Years." drive.google.com/file/d/134wxq5M9gN-ZrZM8PpfunSVDWG0Q-NEm/view.

Obama, Barack. "Promoting Diversity and Inclusion in Our National Parks, National Forests, and Other Public Lands and Waters." Presidential memorandum, the White House, 12 Jan. 2017, obamawhitehouse.archives.gov/the-press-office/2017/01/12/presidential-memorandum-promoting-diversity-and-inclusion-our-national.

Outka, Paul. *Race and Nature from Transcendentalism to the Harlem Renaissance*. Palgrave Macmillan, 2008.

Park, Lisa, and David Naguib Pellow. *The Slums of Aspen: Immigrants vs. the Environment in America's Eden*. New York UP, 2011.

Parris, Aer. "REI Extended Sizes Update: More Sizes, More Women, Right Now." 14 Sept. 2017, www.rei.com/blog/news/rei-extended-sizing-update-more-sizes-more-women-right-now.

Patagonia. "The President Stole Your Land." www.patagonia.com/protect-public-lands.html.

Pellow, David Naguib. *What Is Critical Environmental Justice?* Polity Press, 2018.

Peña, Devon G. *Mexican Americans and the Environment: Tierra y Vida*. U of Arizona P, 2005.

Price, Jennifer. "Looking for Nature at the Mall: A Field Guide to the Nature Company." *Uncommon Ground: Rethinking the Human Place in Nature*, edited by William Cronon, W. W. Norton, 1996, pp. 186–203.

Pulido, Laura. *Environmentalism and Economic Justice: Two Chicano Struggles in the Southwest*. U of Arizona P, 1996.

———. "Geographies of Race and Ethnicity II: Environmental Racism, Racial Capitalism, and State-Sanctioned Violence." *Progress in Human Geography*, vol. 41, no. 4, 2016, pp. 524–533.

Pulido, Laura, Tianna Bruno, Cristina Faiver-Serna, and Cassandra Gallentine. "Environmental Deregulation, Spectacular Racism and White Nationalism in the Trump Era." *Annals of the American Association of Geographers*, March 2019. Forthcoming.

Ray, Sarah Jaquette. *The Ecological Other: Environmental Exclusion in American Culture*. U of Arizona P, 2013.

REI. "Creating Access." www.rei.com/stewardship/creating-access.

Roberts, Chelle. "Dear Ranger, You Inspire Me." *American Latino Heritage Fund*. ALHF.org/ALEX-blog/dear-ranger-you-inspire-me.

Roberts, Crystal. "Hiking Big Meadow Trail and Sunrise Peak." *American Latino Heritage Fund*. alhf.org/alex-blog/hiking-big-meadow-trail-sunrise-peak.

Rodriguez, Ralph E. *Latinx Literature Unbound: Undoing Ethnic Expectation*. Fordham UP, 2018.

Salazar, Staci. "Day Hiking Check List." *American Latino Heritage Fund*. ALHF.org/ALEX-blog/day-hiking-checklist.

———. "How to Free Your Mind in National Parks." *American Latino Heritage Fund*. alhf.org/alex-blog/how-free-your-mind-national-parks.

Serafin, Ana. "Rich History of the Makahs." *American Latino Heritage Fund*. alhf.org/alex-blog/rich-history-makahs.

———. "Travelistas in Nature Visit REI." *American Latino Heritage Fund*. alhf.org/alex-blog/travelistas-nature-visit-rei.

Sifuentez, Mario Jimenez. *Of Forests and Fields: Mexican Labor in the Pacific Northwest*. Rutgers UP, 2016.

Spence, Mark David. *Dispossessing the Wilderness: Indian Removal and the Making of the National Parks*. Oxford UP, 1999.

Spitfire Strategies. "Get to Know Our Team: Midy Aponte." *Spitfire Strategies*. www.spitfirestrategies.com/team/midy-aponte/.

Stern, Alexandra Minna. *Eugenic Nation: Faults and Frontiers of Better Breeding in Modern America*. U of California P, 2005.

Szremski, Kristin. "Diversity and Inclusiveness Goals for Next 100 Years of National Park Service." National Press Club, 1 Aug. 2016, www.press.org/news-multimedia/news/diversity-and-inclusiveness-goals-next-100-years-national-park-service.

Taylor, Patricia A., Burke D. Grandjean, and James H. Gradmann. "National Park Service Comprehensive Survey of the American Public, 2008–2009: Racial and Ethnic Diversity of National Park Service Visitors and Non-Visitors." Natural Resource Report NPS/NRSS/SSD/NRR—2011/432. Wyoming Survey and Analysis Center, University of Wyoming, July 2011.

Turner, Frederick Jackson. *The Significance of the Frontier in American History*. Forgotten Books, 2017.

U.S. Census Bureau. "American Fact Finder." Race and Hispanic or Latino Origins: 2010. 2010 Census. https://factfinder.census.gov.

White, Richard. "Are You an Environmentalist or Do You Work for a Living?" *Uncommon Ground: Rethinking the Human Place in Nature*, edited by William Cronon, W. W. Norton, 1996, pp. 171–185.

Ybarra, Priscilla Solis. *Writing the Goodlife: Mexican American Literature and the Environment*. U of Arizona P, 2016.

4

"A Story Is a Physical Space"

An Interview with Héctor Tobar

SHANE HALL

The scholarship in this collection curates a broad archive of Latinx literary texts that foreground environmental concerns within their enacting of antiracist struggles. In such an archive, the literature of Héctor Tobar stands out for vivifying how history and power relations forge environmental and social landscapes. A war in the tropical periphery of U.S. empire where germs kill as many as do bullets. A gated LA community where a couple outsources parenting to an undocumented caretaker. The hot, fetid darkness of a collapsed mineshaft where thirty-three men struggle to survive. A mosaic nation of movement and migration. These are the settings that Héctor Tobar makes into worlds of prose in his literary writing. These worlds emerge from the interplay between concrete specificity—of character, identity, emotion, and environment—and the broader social forces of history and politics. This interview, the first of five included in this volume, highlights how Tobar's work is attuned to the way capital shapes the environments he engages and puts him into conversation with the other chapters in this section on "Place."

His writing is prolific—both terms in fact doing little justice to the scope of his achievements. He has published hundreds of pieces as a journalist, and while he has edited and contributed to the *LA Weekly*, *El Tecolote*, and the *New York Times*, he worked for his hometown newspaper, the *Los Angeles Times*, for over two decades. While working for the *LA Times*, he was part of a team that won the Pulitzer Prize for reporting the 1992 LA riots and later served as bureau chief for the *Times* in Mexico City and Buenos Aires. Tobar earned a creative writing MFA from the University of California, Irvine, and has published four books: two novels, *The Tattooed Soldier* (1998) and *The*

Barbarian Nurseries (2011), and two works of creative nonfiction, *Translation Nation* (2005) and *Deep Down Dark: The Untold Stories of 33 Men Buried in a Chilean Mine, and the Miracle That Set Them Free* (2014).

Of Tobar's books, *The Tattooed Soldier* has garnered the most scholarship surrounding its articulation of environmental racism, and deservedly so. *The Tattooed Soldier* indexes the ecologies of violence that U.S. imperialism produces and reproduces at both the periphery and core of its empire: in the Guatemalan Civil War funded by the United States and in Los Angeles. One of the central ways Tobar links these two spaces and the characters that inhabit them is by mirroring the descriptions of environmental degradation in both locations. The environmental hazards of "hydrocarbon winds" in LA and "germ warfare" in rural Guatemala are tools inextricable from the repressive state forces that produce and maintain social inequality in the novel. For readers, *The Tattooed Soldier* is a text wherein students and scholars can take up Rob Nixon's call for environmental literary studies to tackle "the environmental fallout of U.S. foreign policy head on" by tracing the ways in which U.S. imperialism produces different kinds of environmental violence (Nixon 34).

While *The Tattooed Soldier* centers environmental justice struggles within racist oppression, Tobar's work often traces the importance of place, history, and political economy to Latinx characters' lives. This is true even in *Deep Down Dark*, a story not of environmental conflict but rather of the human and technological heroism that liberated the thirty-three Chilean miners trapped 2,300 feet below the surface of the Atacama Desert. In the opening pages of *Deep Down Dark*, Tobar traces how the men and minerals of the mine have, for centuries, been exploited in service of global economic forces. The narrative establishes the cyclical elation of exploitative "boom" and the violence of "bust," of poverty and the death of rivers. This pattern sets up the precarity of the miners who are sent deeper and deeper into the aging mine for the latest economic boom—$1,200-an-ounce gold.

I had the opportunity to sit down with Tobar to discuss his writing and teaching for *Latinx Environmentalisms* in October 2015.[1] I conducted the interview over two hour-long sessions spanning two days in Tobar's office at the University of Oregon, where he taught in the School of Journalism. Tobar currently teaches Chicano/Latino Studies and English-Literary Journalism at UC Irvine. I have lightly edited and abridged the transcript in service of clarity and concision.

SH: *What attunes you to environments—did you have any early experiences that made you pay attention to environmental issues?*
HT: Well, I'm a city kid. I grew up in Los Angeles, and I grew up in a section of East Hollywood that is today known as Little Armenia. In the early 1970s, I was a fourth, fifth, and sixth grader at Grant Elementary in Hollywood. My fourth-grade teacher, Mrs. Feldman, was an environmental-

ist, and she brought in all these things to educate us on the environment. I remember drawing that famous green flag with the yellow "E" in the canton of the American flag and green stripes.[2] And she had this kit that she had brought to teach us basic lessons about the environment. We did this one experiment where we tested the quality of the air. She put some Vaseline on a paper in our classroom, and she put one by the window, outside the window, taped it to the window, and one inside our classroom. Our school was, and still is, less than a block from the Hollywood Freeway. Within days, the Vaseline was covered with dirt, and soon the experiment showed us how much dirtier the air was outside because of the exposure to the freeway. She also had us design and build a planter box around the school flagpole. We planted a bunch of marigolds around the flagpole. It was a very powerful symbolic act, because the American flag was at the top of that pole, and every time I drove by for the next twenty to thirty years, it was still there. It was a redwood box that we put around the flagpole in this very urban area.

SH: *Did you keep that sort of environmental consciousness in your early reporting?*

HT: No. By the time I became a professional journalist, the environment was just one of many issues that were on my plate. I had a big palette in terms of social justice. As an undergraduate, I went to UC Santa Cruz and became aware of capitalism and inequality. But yes, living in Santa Cruz, you can't be ignorant of the environment when you live in a redwood forest and you have living things around you. I also thought about imperialism a lot and about Guatemala, where my parents are from. By that time, I had a whole education on the history of Latin America in the twentieth century especially, the history of coups and repression and dictatorships.

But I would say that for me, then, as a writer, the environment and the natural world became two issues. There was the issue of the degradation of the environment—obviously you can't live in a city like LA and not see the way the physical world is degraded by urbanization. But also, when you create real and fictional worlds on a page, you need to place a story in a physical space. And the way you make a physical space come alive is by learning about the environment. I'm very ignorant. I'm very uninformed, uneducated about the physical world. So when I was a reporter, I would often ask . . . "Well, excuse me, sir, what kind of trees are these?" And so, my whole life has been in this process of acquiring knowledge about the physical world in order to create the world on the page.

I think that awareness of the environment begins with knowing your own environment. When you're living in a place where the natural space has been degraded in some way, you need to gain perspective.

That's really important. You have to acquire the knowledge of the "privileged," in quotes. For me that was going to UC Santa Cruz.

SH: *In what ways did this change in perspective change how you read your hometown?*
HT: I remember growing up, thinking that I was growing up in this jewel of a city. This space-age city. My father had come to LA from Gualán, a little town in the department of Zacapa, in Guatemala. He grew up telling me stories of this village that had a river that went around it and how they would play in the river growing up. How when his mother kidnapped him to take him away from his father and evil stepmother, they dragged the river with nets to see if they could find his body because they thought he had drowned in the river. So this man from this village is transported to LA when the freeways are being built. I remember driving to the end of the Pomona freeway, which we now call the 60, but in those days it was called the Pomona freeway. And it was cutting through these orange groves—the orange groves of the San Gabriel Valley—and headed towards Arizona. My first vision of LA was this place of just incredible modernity and opportunity. You know, aerospace is huge in LA. My father was fascinated with the Jet Propulsion Laboratory, which is in La Cañada, Flintridge, not far from downtown LA, and he always talked to me about space travel, and I had this sense that I was in the place where space travel was born. So to me, that was a really powerful vision of what LA was.

And then when I returned to Los Angeles after going to college and living in Northern California for a decade, I saw LA as this place that was getting older, wearing down. Plus, I had this education in political economy, and I just saw the city as this place where the capitalist model had exhausted itself. This was the LA that was being deindustrialized, in the late 1980s. Only now is the city beginning to become aware collectively of the damage that was done to the environment and how it can be repaired. Now, for example, there's a huge movement in LA towards native plants. I have native plants in my home in LA. I have California sagebrush growing, two big native California sagebrush, which I planted after interviewing a naturalist at the Audubon Center who pointed out to me that there was California sagebrush growing in the Arroyo Seco that runs along the Pasadena freeway.

SH: *Does that changed perspective come across in the way your characters interact with LA in your books?*
HT: In the late 80s, I was fascinated by these open fields that were just west of the financial district in downtown Los Angeles, an area that I wrote about a few times; the neighborhood was known to the city planners as Temple

Beaudry. I found out that the people who used to live there called it Diamond Street; it was the name of a street there and also of a gang. Now it's part of what's called Pico Union. When I was there, in the late eighties, there were these open fields. It looked like a war zone, like ancient ruins; in the movie *Falling Down*, there was this scene that's shot in this area, and this is where the Michael Douglas character fights these two guys. I wrote an article about this neighborhood for the *LA Times*. It was a little allegory about capitalism and inequality, and it was about how these homeless people were living in the ruins of a Victorian neighborhood there. To me that was an extremely compelling image of Los Angeles— that you could be looking over the busiest stretch of freeway in the United States while standing in these open fields where there's homeless camps! And then to discover there's a tunnel underneath this place that was built during the early twentieth century, was a tunnel for the famous red cars, the Pacific Railway. And now there were wild grasses growing there, this invasive grass from Eurasia. It was a symbol of emptiness and of the wounded characters who live in LA, an imperial city. I always thought LA as an imperial city; it's a capital of this empire that is fighting this war by proxy in Guatemala and El Salvador, and here, in the heart of the empire, there's this empty space. To me, that was an extremely compelling setting for a story. And it really matched the themes of the story, which became my novel *The Tattooed Soldier*. Now, with Araceli in *The Barbarian Nurseries*, I drew from my experiences many years later, when I was getting my MFA at UC Irvine. My wife and I would drive down to Newport Beach to have dinner, and we'd drive by the grasslands, the old ranchlands of south Orange County. To me it was beautiful and, at the same time, kind of empty. The best real estate was being transformed into gated communities. I set my novel there, and the characters travel from this bucolic place into the heart of Los Angeles. The characters take a train that follows the LA River, which is, of course, an important place in LA history. And they see these homeless camps along the river, and then the physical space of the city is just, for me, it's this fantastic place. And it's not just the environment; it's the people there, and there's so many elements of myth and folklore in the way I sort of came to understand what LA is.

SH: *What made you move from journalism to fiction?*
HT: I had been a *LA Times* reporter for five years, in 1993, and I was successful, I think, within the newspaper, but I found it less satisfying as a writer because I didn't feel that I was being allowed the full expression of my voice as a writer within the boundaries of daily journalism. I was one of the younger reporters on the staff, so I wasn't always given the best assignments, and there were key events in the history of the city, which I

wanted to write about—specifically the LA riots—and I was not really allowed to write those kinds of stories.

I remember the moment that I decided that I really needed to study... that I wanted, seriously, to study fiction. I was at this now defunct bookstore in Santa Monica called Midnight Special. I read a novel by an LA writer that began in East LA. It had a portrayal of a neighborhood that I did not recognize and that seemed incredibly stereotyped and exploitative. And it made me really angry because I loved to read! I was reading, at that time, more than I probably had in my life. I was just reading a novel a week and going to the bookstore and reading very widely and just loving especially Italo Calvino and Nadine Gordimer and J. M. Coetzee... the South African writers were really important to me. And then to see a novel about my own city that was so shallow and still published and in this bookstore, and I thought, "I have to do something. I mean, I can do something better than this." So I started taking creative writing classes. I took a creative writing class at UCLA extension, and I took one at a poetry center that still exists called Beyond Baroque. And I started writing my short stories and getting my application together for MFA programs. It was mostly just wanting to embrace the fact that I had a voice as a writer, that I could be an artist, something that only recently I've allowed to call myself. But that's when I knew that's what I wanted to be. I felt I had more stories to tell; I felt I had stories to tell that didn't fit within the columns of a newspaper.

At the same time, I think that for me the idea of what a writer can be and the way a writer should work is deeply influenced by journalism because I was, for much of my career, a paid witness. I'd be sent into places, almost always places I had never been before, whether it be a courthouse, a jail, a neighborhood, a country, to see hurricanes, earthquakes, rebellions, officer-involved shootings. What that experience teaches you is that the world has a lot to show you and you can go and find things for the world to show you. And it teaches you that anything that you could imagine will probably pale in comparison to what the world has to offer if you go out and explore. That's now my writerly practice—to use my imagination and my love of language to create worlds in prose, at the same time that I am using my reporting skills to interrogate the world and investigate and probe the world.

SH: *You talk about how your theory of writing is informed by your experience as a journalist. Do you feel you gain from flipping back and forth between different genres while writing?*
HT: Definitely. Writing journalism you learn the importance of precision, and you learn how to assemble facts into a narrative. You also learn the importance of character. Character is extremely important in writing journalism because people want to read stories about other people. And in

journalism, you have to go out and find them and then talk to them, and they have to be real—you can't make them up. Some people try to make them up, but they always get caught! If you're a sensitive person, you become more aware of the variety of the human condition and of human experience. Then, when you write fiction, you take that knowledge of the world, and you enter into deeper emotional spaces. Fiction, in order to work, has to be more real than nonfiction because it has to go deeper into the human experience. So, for example, in a newspaper account, I can write about someone who has undergone a tragedy, and it has power because you know it's true; so you can write a nonfiction account, and it can have less emotional textures than a work of fiction does. A work of fiction has to have more emotional textures to it. If you were to write a fictional account of a family that loses a child drowning in a stream, and you wrote it the way the average newspaper or magazine story approaches the subject, it would seem kind of empty. It wouldn't seem quite as full because in fiction we go deeper—and the reader expects this—the reader expects us to go deeper into loss, anger, joy, all these things. So that's what I learned as I became a fiction writer. You can tell when you read a work of fiction that isn't emotionally intelligent or emotionally attuned; it doesn't really work as art. After I'd written a couple of novels, I learned that I can bring deep emotions into journalism; I realized that you if approach a group of real people with the respect that you have for a fictional character, then they become more alive on the page. In my last book, in *Deep Down Dark*, I really wanted to have the thirty-three Chilean miners feel like characters in a novel . . . but I couldn't write anything that wasn't true because they would read about it! Interviewing them required me to think like a novelist. When someone tells you a story about their family, you go into the complexity of it; you're not afraid of the complexity of it. All the ambiguity in it. You're not afraid, as a writer, of the things that make the story more complicated, whereas in journalism, if there's something that makes the story complicated, it's trouble for you because you just need to get through the story, and the story really cannot linger—it's not allowed to linger in complexities and ambiguities too much. So in this book about the miners, I think I allowed myself to have things not be resolved all the time. You don't have to explain everything in fiction. You can allow a mystery to linger. To me, that's what fiction writing has taught me about journalism. Now I'm writing a novel again. Thanks to the experience of my last book, a work of nonfiction, I have more discipline in the sense of plot and character and pacing of the story. Going between these two forms of storytelling has really enriched both of them for me.

    I am very research-centered and just because that's the fun part, for me, of being a writer. Because when you make yourself into a professional witness, you very often are becoming informed about human experiences that are unlike your own; you are becoming aware of social relationships; you're becoming aware of suffering, of how people retain a sense of power in a world that tries to make them feel powerless.

SH: *In addition to the precision you bring to your writing—of identities, of specific natural environments, and of emotions—could you comment on how you approach society and social forces?*

HT: My first iteration as a writer was history geek. I have an eleven-year-old daughter, and she's a history geek. It's just wonderful to see! And now, the word *geek* isn't even an insult; it's sort of a badge of honor. I was the kid who read almanacs and memorized state capitals and stuff like that! My reptilian writer brain is the History Geek. Any good work of history will present you with some truth that you didn't know. I was a sociology major, basically studied political economy at UC Santa Cruz—Latin American studies major, too. Latin American history. So, to me, that is just another element in storytelling... and it works in several ways. History has left all these artifacts for us to look at, and whether it be an old sagging house or a river made of concrete. History is also our myths and our self-image. I am the grandson of a peasant—that tells you a little bit about who I am. Araceli in *The Barbarian Nurseries* is, I like to say, an intellectual trapped in the body of a servant. I say that because that's basically me: an intellectual trapped in the body of a servant. I'm Guatemalan. And up until recently, Guatemalan was synonymous in LA with "hired help." If you say, "I got five Guatemalan guys in my house," it means that they're there to do some work for you.

My father is from Guatemala, and he's a total history geek. When I was growing up, he was taking classes to get his AA degree at LA City College. He had a U.S. history textbook; it was beautiful! All of United States history in one book! Crimson bound, hardcover, binding—and I loved reading this book and looking through it. The photographs, the graphics, the maps—and this goes deep, because my father had to quit school at age eleven because his mother kidnapped him and took him away from the village, and she had to go work in Guatemala City, and he wasn't able to go back to school. So he told me that from the time that he was eleven until he came to the United States when he was twenty, he didn't go to school, and the only education he really had was that he had a copy of a book called *History of the Roman Empire*, and that was his education. For a big chunk of his life, he was reading and rereading this book on the Roman Empire. And he, to this day—he is in his seventies—he is a Roman history geek.

SH: *Is "geek" really a badge of honor these days?*

HT: Well, you know, for a time I was on the board of California Humanities, and the reason I agreed to join the board was because I have belief that there is a hunger in working-class California and the working-class United States for education in the humanities. In this hyper test-driven academic, education culture that we have, very often creative thought and creative writing, literature, and even history get placed on the back burner. I have spoken at high schools and junior high schools in Southern California many times. And I'm invited to speak because I'm a Latino writer, and these are schools that are ninety percent Latino, and several times I've gone to speak at a school like that, and, at the end, a few kids linger . . . and they're the literati of the school. You know, the kids who keep journals at home and love to write and love to read and sort of feel almost like they're outcasts because of it. That, to me, is totally tragic and disgusting. That we live in a society where the high schools that these kids go to are like the high schools that I went to. I went to a high school in South Whittier, California, an unincorporated community that was, at that moment, fifty percent Latino, fifty percent white—now it's eighty percent Latino. It was a community with a strong anti-intellectual streak. I didn't have teachers who encouraged me—very few—who ever encouraged me to be a writer. Very few teachers who ever awakened in me a love of literature, the love that I have of literature today. And so, I just think that there are many young people in high schools like that, places where creative endeavors are not encouraged, and where kids are not taught to appreciate the beauty of language for its own sake—as opposed to the uses of language in passing a test.

SH: *What is it that you say when "the school's literati" hang around after your talk? What do they want to know from you?*

HT: They want to know that it's okay to be a writer. They want to talk to someone who is as passionate about writing and ideas as they are. They want to just tell someone that they like words and books. And one particular student—I remember this young woman—and she told me, "I don't even. . . . I don't tell anybody about it, not even my parents, and I just feel so lonely." And I said, "Well, look, your job is just to hang on here for two more years at this school and go to college, and then you're going to be surrounded by people like you, and you're going to meet a community of people who are like you. You'll be in a circle of people who value that in you—who value your curiosity and value your bookishness and your word-nerdiness." That's what I tell them. I think part of my job when I speak to a high school class is to demystify what a writer is. Part of my job is to say, "Well, look, I've written books, and they're the product of a lot of effort, suffering, and a lot of humility." I think that what makes you a writer is just to be a book nerd who goes off and studies and then writes for twenty-five years until you finally become an author. I try to communicate the humility of my own circumstances—the illiteracy in my family, the lack of education because of social circumstances. I try to show them that it's not a journey that they can't undertake. That, in fact, they've already taken a few steps of that journey along the way just by reading and by being curious. That's the beginning of what makes a writer, and that there really isn't much of a difference between who they are and who authors are. I love, for example, this biography of William Shakespeare called *Will in the World*. Shakespeare, like many writers, is a person from public schools, son of a glover, a middle-class provincial. When he goes to London, his rivals in the playwriting and poetry scene are very jealous of him because he didn't go to Oxford. He's from someplace called Stratford that no one's ever heard of. He is an outsider. Many times I tell students that the things that you have that make you feel like an outsider, that make you feel like you don't belong, are a source of strength for you as a writer; they give you a vision and knowledge other people don't have. Very often, when I talk to high school students, I say, "Look, those of you, when you go to college, you're going to be around people who are from much better-off families than you. And you're going to realize that there are many things about the world that they don't know that you know. You're going to see how innocent they are next to you, because you've seen the things your family has struggled through to get you the opportunities you have. You've seen things that happen in your neighborhood. And so those things are a real source of strength for you."

My father, growing up, never told me I could be a writer because I don't think he ever knew that that was a profession that existed, that was within our range—but he loved to read. When I was a little kid, he was taking night-school classes to get his AA degree; once he took a photography class, and he would take pictures of me surrounded by books. I found out later that his own mother was illiterate. My grandmother was illiterate. And so, I realized why words had become so important in my life and why they were so important to my father. "The book" was always a symbol of knowledge, a symbol of authority, a symbol of power. I grew up with this idea of books and words being important. And so my own, as we say in Spanish, trayectoria as a writer, my own journey as a writer, is to search for the power of language and believe that I have a right to write books. A lot of people can write really well but don't really believe they're writers. I see this now when I teach, where people are very, very articulate, great writers, but they don't really feel like writers . . . they've had the idea that they could be writers beaten out of them by the education system. I value the idea that you can fight your way into becoming a writer.

NOTES

1. A note to readers: My discussions with Tobar occurred before Trump's election. As Tobar himself has noted, "Trumpism hangs over everything Latino," as "the accomplishments of our valedictorians, our mayors, and our veterans are weighed against the

crimes that Donald Trump and Bill O'Reilly attribute to our 'alien' fathers and sons." But while Trumpism may hang over "everything Latino," Tobar himself has been all over Trump, offering up some of the sharpest criticism of the Trump administration in opinion pieces and essays in the *New York Times* and the *New Yorker*, as well as short fiction in *Slate* imagining the short- and long-term effects of Trump's anti-immigration policies. See Tobar, "Latinos Feel the Sting of Trump's Presidency."

2. Tobar refers to the "Ecology Flag," created by cartoonist Ron Cobb in 1969 and adopted by American environmentalists throughout the 1970s.

WORKS CITED

Falling Down. Directed by Joel Schumacher, Warner Home Video, 2009.

Greenblatt, Stephen. *Will in the World: How Shakespeare Became Shakespeare*. W. W. Norton, 2004.

Nixon, Rob. *Slow Violence and the Environmentalism of the Poor*. Harvard UP, 2011.

Tobar, Héctor. *The Barbarian Nurseries*. Farrar, Straus and Giroux, 2011.

———. *Deep Down Dark: The Untold Stories of 33 Men Buried in a Chilean Mine, and the Miracle That Set Them Free*. Farrar, Straus and Giroux, 2014.

———. "Latinos Feel the Sting of Trump's Presidency." *The New Yorker*, Mar. 2017, www.newyorker.com/news/news-desk/latinos-feel-the-sting-of-trumps-presidency.

———. *The Tattooed Soldier*. Penguin Books, 2000.

———. *Translation Nation: Defining a New American Identity in the Spanish-Speaking United States*. Riverhead, 2005.

5

Speculative Futurity and the Eco-cultural Politics of *Lunar Braceros: 2125–2148*

CHRISTOPHER PERREIRA

Waste management, population management, it was all part of the same thing in the end for the state.
  We all know that the universe has many histories . . . that it undergoes many changes and faces many possible turns . . .
—ROSAURA SÁNCHEZ AND BEATRICE PITA,
Lunar Braceros: 2125–2148[1]

Global warming is at once a metaphor for catastrophic degradation of the environment and for the understanding that greed and self-interest are entirely inadequate for the creation of a global ethic that might adequately address or adjudicate the means for collective human survival.
—LISA LOWE, "Metaphors of Globalization"[2]

In 2013, residents of Barrio Logan organized large-scale counterefforts to shipping and naval industries attempting to acquire neighborhood blocks to expand the industries' production. Those neighborhood blocks, located in a historically working-class Mexican American waterfront community in San Diego, California, had served for decades as a kind of "buffer zone" between the residential areas and the high levels of pollutants produced by multiple maritime industries distributing and receiving goods, people, and supplies out of the local port—including those produced through tuna canning and the navy, which relied heavily on Mexican and Mexican American workers since the early twentieth century. Well-known as the San Diego neighborhood that challenged and halted the city's initiative to build a new California Highway Patrol substation in Logan in the 1970s, building instead what became known as Chicano Park,[3] residents in the twenty-first century now framed new mobilizations as part of an ongoing struggle for environmental justice—one wrapped up in a complex history of "mixed use" (residential, industrial, and commercial) space and community life. These blocks, historically situated and contested for decades, mark the convergence of environment, belonging, resistance, and emergent social identities as they evolve within multiple processes of globalization. As Raúl Homero Villa argues, what produces the meaning of such contested spaces is barrio residents' "resistive tactics . . . to secure and preserve the integrity of their cultural place-identity within and against the often hostile space regulation of dominant urbanism" (5). Forty-three years after the creation of Chicano Park, the residents of Logan, along with groups such as San Diego's Environmental Health Coalition, engage in a cultural politics of organizing art exhibits and new murals, publishing in newspapers, and protesting the long-standing high levels of toxins in the area.[4]

A "second city" emerges in this example, multiform creative practices that "materially reconstitute and expressively represent place of community well-being against the degradations to which those places have been subject" (Villa 157). Neighborhoods, city management, and the environmental sociality of life in Barrio Logan, read against the production of toxic waste, point to an environmental discourse anchored in spatial and temporal landscapes that move beyond progress narratives of the nation-state, militarism, security, and public health. That the question of toxicity in this residential area has not registered as an environmental concern, but rather as one foregrounding industry and labor concerns, prompted a response that sought to reframe the discussion as centrally about a complex discourse of environmental justice. As noted in the 2013 city document "Barrio Logan: Community Plan and Local Coastal Program," "while some properties transitioned into industrial uses, many of the residential uses that pre-dated the rezone remained, and commercial and community amenities developed to serve the residential population" (iii). Acknowledging conflicts between industry and residents, the "mixed pattern of land uses" became a given factor in what defined the space: "Barrio Logan is primarily a neighborhood with uses mixed side-by-side that provides interest, variety, and identity to the area." As a site of tension, Barrio Logan is working out creative environmental futures while responding to a toxic worlding[5] with narratives of modernity, reshaping the kinds of questions we ask about stories of globalization and imagining futures within and beyond them.[6] What futures, in other words, can speculate on the many histories of human collective survival?

The 2009 science fiction novel *Lunar Braceros: 2125–2148*, co-written by Rosaura Sánchez and Beatrice Pita, recasts such questions to reflect on what an environmental imaginary about contested space—land space as well as outer space—might reveal as mid-twenty-second-century global history. The novel spans centuries, mapping a layered story of colonialism and racial capitalism through "nanotexts"—epistolary-style, often fragmented electronic messages sent by the novel's protagonist, Lydia, to her son Pedro. Those messages lay a foundation for Pedro to understand social and political formations across the Americas in the twenty-second century, intended to both educate him and situate him within it. Lydia's nanotexts depict corporations controlling and disciplining Earth's land and life, managing waste and people as "all part of the same thing." Political reconfigurations of nation-states amplify racial and class inequalities in order to maintain an endless supply of "reslifers"—coerced and indentured laborers forced to live on new "Reservations" or prison camps. The plot follows those laborers into space as they carry out the dangerous work of storing toxic waste in the colonial waste stations on the moon.

While the novel outlines far-off and distant futures filled with internment and exploitation, it at the same time foregrounds revolutionary and radical forms of kinship that insist on imagining futures otherwise. The fragmented metanarratives in *Lunar Braceros*, presented as a series of unanswered correspondence, add to what some readers of speculative work have described as critical conceptions of time, space, and displacement that resist "the nihilist impulse of most postmodernist narratives" (Olguín 129–130).[7] For many readers, the novel does the imaginative work of speculating on future histories and their emergent possibilities, allowing Sánchez and Pita to explore the legacies of capitalism as an ongoing, contested continuum of colonial modernity.[8] Building on such work and drawing on discussions in critical environmental justice, I read *Lunar Braceros* as speculative fiction that envisions new kinships and environmental imaginaries, using the nanotext to read against the grain of dominant narratives in history, policy, and publics, and to reimagine those relationships to people and land across time, space, and memory.

Lydia's accounts, for example, frame political and ecological transformations of Earth to trouble official narratives of those changes—such as "The Great Political Restructuring"—and describe other roles that impact the geopolitical realignments that create a new corporate nation-state named "Cali-Texas." The Northern Mexican states, the U.S. Southwest, Alaska, Hawaiʻi, and other territories and peoples shaped by intersecting colonial histories are consolidated under Cali-Texas, controlled by "transnational agri-business corporations and the four big biotechs." These powers, Lydia tells Pedro, manage the technological developments that govern and discipline life, including "technology transfer, informatics, and any kind of power generation, bio-fuel, nuclear or otherwise" (Sánchez and Pita 6–7). Lydia explains further:

> The splitting-off of half its territory led to the definitive weakening of the U.S. Not even the return of civilian government was able to lead to any meaningful recovery. Attempts were made to bring Cali-Texas back into the fold, but they all failed, and after a few years, the U.S., Canada and Mexico had no other option but to become part of the Cali-Texas commonwealth, autonomous regions but economically linked to and dependent on the hegemonic power. While those old nation states, as well as the rest of Latin America, remained suppos-

edly politically independent, they were economically tied to Cali-Texas to an extent previously unseen. And Cali-Texas, let's not forget, was allied with China. The rapid spread of a variety of high-tech industries, on the one hand, and mining, oil and natural gas industries, on the other, throughout every Latin American nation led to greater contamination of the soil, the water and the air. Ecologically, as you know, the planet is one enormous haz-mat zone. (12–13)

While Lydia narrates the novel's historical backdrop as a dystopic world yet to come, a familiar story unfolds around geopolitical violence produced by nation-states and transnational circulations of capital and its industrial waste. The "splitting-off" of half of the United States' territories, for example, ironically recalls the U.S.-Mexico War and the 1848 Treaty of Guadalupe Hidalgo, marking the novel's closing date (2148) as the three-hundred-year anniversary of the imperial project that resulted in the U.S. annexation of half of Mexico's territories. The formation of the United States at the mid-nineteenth century shapes future colonial imaginaries about Mexico and Latin America more broadly, narrated as at once "empty" and valuable spaces simultaneously ready for removal, dispossession, resettlement, and land/labor extraction.[9] In *Lunar Braceros*, those twenty-first-century "empty" spaces take on a dystopic form of haunting when they become the ideal dumping sites for toxic waste—a state of reality carried out to extreme levels by the time Pedro is born in the mid-twenty-second century.

Yet something else surfaces at the end of the above nanotext passage, which reframes the narrative as an ecological one. Referring to Earth as a "haz-mat zone," the narrative remembers the conditions that make life livable or not. Widespread toxicity is the backdrop of this world, operating continuously as the logical conclusion to what scholars have examined as the global wastes of colonial modernity.[10] Lydia's return to pasts, particularly *failed* pasts—the failed "return of civilian government," the inability to achieve any type of "meaningful recovery," or the impossibility of bringing "Cali-Texas back into the fold"—is tempered by Lydia's imperative to "not forget" and to instead remember what they know too well about the ecological state of the planet. To remember that the planet has become one "enormous haz-mat zone" puts the hegemonic imperialist worldview of the novel into question, as this lethal environmental condition has become the lived experience of most of the world's population. The nanotext grounds its story in how those realities are the political, cultural, and economic contexts for resisting forms of violence in a dystopian expression of racial capitalism.

Such tensions exist not only in *Lunar Braceros* but also in speculative films such as Alex Rivera's 2009 *Sleep Dealer* and in cultural production in communities like Barrio Logan, which make visible other discourses within environmentalism. *Lunar Braceros* in particular carves out significant space for rethinking the conceptual frameworks of the nation and racial capitalism, borders and walls, and how an understanding of the environment has shaped and is shaped by them. It does this while negotiating contradictions that define kinship and resistance, unsettling paradigms of modernity and racialized labor, land, and resistance through hemispheric, interplanetary environmentalisms. In dialogue with other science fiction narratives thinking about political ecologies, what surfaces from *Lunar Braceros* is an ecocultural critique that questions neoliberal frameworks as central to the logics of (rather than perceive them as apart from) what is understood as natural. The novel asks how those political structures prioritize profit-driven models for dealing with both environment and people, conditions that prompt connections that redirect definitions of "environment" away from human/nonhuman binaries long associated with framing nature and wilderness. In doing so, it focuses on ecologies that include racial and social hierarchies and wrestles with Lydia's insight that, historically, waste management and population management have been at their core one and the same.

Speculative Environmentalisms

Lunar Braceros imagines large-scale and radical forms of hope under these speculative dystopian futures. The plot, which spans centuries of interplanetary history in only 120 pages, unfolds in the twenty-second century under the shadow of a corporate-state consolidation, where corporations control the planet's resources and the political reconfiguration of nation-states across the globe amplifies racial and class inequalities. Poor people cannot attain work, and as a result they are quarantined on "Reservations." Lydia describes the Reservations of Cali-Texas as barrios produced by the state to contain unemployed, racialized "surplus" populations—"Latinos ... blacks, Asians, Native Americans, and poor whites" (30). The Reservations work like "a panoptic prison" to hold an unlimited labor pool for the state (35). To support families, "reslifers" give their coerced consent to work jobs under the most precarious conditions, such as waste management and mining for minerals in space. The promises made by corporations and the state, such as assurances that workers' wages will be sent to family members, are regularly broken.

Lydia narrates these details in her nanotexts, providing a long history for Pedro's education. She describes how the space project designed to colonize the moon was conceived as a Cold War–type response to major pollution and depletion of resources on Earth. Nation-states across the globe scrambled to establish lunar stations in order to capitalize profits and political power, building water stations and fuel sources. While initial attempts focused on sending robotic labor into space, the high costs motivated corporate funding of technology development that would instead manage human workers, or "Tecos," easily found in Reservation camps. As Lydia outlines political reconfigurations and human "purges" to tell how she was first imprisoned as a political organizer, she couples those stories with fragmented narratives of global social movements and organized resistance. The anarcho-guerilla group with whom Lydia and Pedro's brother, Frank, protested, for example, target the "NIO global corporate offices" (34), an event that leads to their arrest and eventual forced involvement with the space program. Once on the moon, Lydia discovers that the previous teams of lunar braceros were mysteriously killed instead of transported home, prompting the crew to organize a takeover of the station to ensure a safe return to Earth; however, not long after they return to Earth, Lydia and Frank disappear. We read Pedro's only nanotext at the end of the novel, explaining his decision to leave the Chinganaza collective (the Amazonian commune in which he was raised) to search for his disappeared family and continue the struggle for liberation.

As a narrative, *Lunar Braceros* taps into many of the tropes of speculative work engaging with decolonial and critical dystopian frameworks, what critics have described as a move in Latina/o/x fiction and cultural production to speculate on futures and possibilities. For example, in the 2017 anthology *Altermundos: Latin@ Speculative Literature, Film, and Popular Culture*, Cathryn Josefina Merla-Watson and B. V. Olguín describe the turn to theorize speculative cultural production as always already working at these critical intersections. These collective futures, they write, are often imagined as reckoning with "the hoary ghosts of colonialism and modernity that continue to exert force through globalization and neoliberal capitalism" (Merla-Watson and Olguín 4). Such creative work engages the notion of other worlds to imagine otherwise, while at the same time grounding those futures in the "concrete realities" of the "decolonial and the utopian" (Merla-Watson 355). Catherine Ramírez further argues that the speculative in Chicanafuturism has often prompted recognition and the rethinking of the status quo, depicting those alternative worlds, distant futures, and especially "revised pasts" as contested narratives. The speculative "re-presents the present or past," Ramírez observes, and "tweaks what we take to be reality or history and in doing so exposes its constructedness" (186). Under such conceptions of the speculative, good science fiction is good precisely because it offers up those critiques of things taken for granted—"tradition, history, or the norm"—but also because it dwells on horizons and possibilities (190). Shelley Streeby, in *Imagining the Future of Climate Change*, suggests that critical dystopias can also productively distort the present to produce the conditions for conjuring up a different future (100), while Aimee Bahng draws on Ramón Saldívar's conceptions of a transnational imaginary to frame "migrant futures"—the collective cultural work of Afrofuturist, Chicanafuturist, Asian futurist, and more—as a "counter-poetics to the predatory speculations of global capitalism" (8).

Through the lens of critical speculation, then, we might read the "enormous haz-mat zone" that Lydia depicts as an extension of theories on waste, toxicity, and disposability. These discourses in the novel tend to operate as ecological frames for understanding a politics of environmental justice—to read political entities as emergent from conditions that are fought over and contested and to see how displacement functions through an analytic of excess and waste. Critical environmental and race studies scholar David Naguib Pellow, for example, has argued that the "toxic nature of late modernity" is one central lens through which to understand how waste management, transnational capital, and social movements can help situate longer histories of race, gender, class, and nation (4–8).[11] Locating Africa as the historical site of coeval global North/South narratives of extractions, exploitation, waste, and resources, Pellow notes that the past half millennium demonstrates how "Africa has served as the world's primary colony for precious natural resources and slave labor" (13). Pellow draws lines that show how these discourses traverse time and space to connect historical narratives to contemporary environmental logics. Toxic waste dumping from the global North to the global South reflects the ongoing attempts by corporate capitalists to find the most profitable and exploitative ventures with the least protections, and consequently those with the least resistance. The line "from slavery to colonialism and toxic waste dumping" (13) maps a continuum, finding new expressions in narratives of environmental waste.

Ethnic studies scholar Curtis Marez develops similar frameworks that focus on the speculative work of California farmworkers and how they counter the dominant narratives that justified their regular exposure to pesticides and corporate big farming industry technologies. Marez finds that turning attention to such histories probes the "blind spots in corporate imaginary" and highlights overlooked farmworker vantage points, ultimately disrupting the privileged agribusiness perspectives that have dominated the stories of migrant farmers (8).[12] The "visual field" of agribusiness and farmworkers highlights corporate farm owners' rationalizations, and in many cases their celebrations, of the uses of pesticides known to kill laborers, reproducing and circulating racist views of migrant farmworkers—particularly Filipino, Yemeni, and Mexican—"as uniquely abject and naturally well suited to their status as mere means of production, without a meaningful past or future beyond the fields" (84).[13]

Framing *Lunar Braceros* through these lenses, and as a radical history concerned most with power, centers multiple moments of resistance to such dominant narratives as they manifest across space and over time. The novel itself grounds the presumption that platforms for posing environmental questions are necessarily global, and those radical redefinitions of the environment desire expansive frameworks to account for the dynamic conversations that occur within them. It is within these frames that I wish to situate the nanotext, the novel's primary narrative form, as important for navigating radical environmental futures in their articulation of collective memory and kinship.

Eco-cultural Politics and the Future Histories of *Lunar Braceros: 2125–2148*

How does the nanotext as a form of representation reveal something about kinship formations? And what does it mean to situate layered memory—via Lydia remembering her own team of workers, the crews before them, or the longer histories of corporate accumulation through dispossession—as the frame for understanding waste management? In depicting the ecological ruin of the planet through the nanotext, what work is done to revalue memory and kinship? The authors present this revolutionary praxis as historical memory, weaving together the pasts and futures of people and land. The opening of the novel, for example, begins with Lydia recounting early memories as a lunar bracero:

> There were seven of us. Our particular lunar transport landed late in 2125. We were the fourth crew of lunar braceros sent to the Moon to work on the waste and toxic landfills sent up from Earth. Sometimes we called ourselves the Tecos or the "techs," and sometimes, for good reason, "the motley crew"—you'll see why. Down here on Earth they'd long since exceeded the capacity to store waste products, so when they couldn't find any more places in the Periphery to warehouse the stuff, plans were made to ship it to the Moon. The plan was to develop sublunar deposit sites, similar to the ones they had carved out in the Arizona and Sonoran deserts. (6)

The layers of these events braid together what Lydia describes throughout the novel as the radical potential of collectives and their specific conditions produced under racial capitalism. Setting the scene in 2125 places one formation (the emergence of the "Tecos" that eventually revolt against the corporations exploiting them) within and as part of the centuries-long ecological narration of the excess waste on Earth. Lydia directly connects this history to the toxic dumping stations on the moon. The nanotext allows for the crisis of "the waste trade" (and its management by an emergent corporate state) to be understood as the very conditions of possibility for a motley crew of lunar braceros to come into existence. The nanotext tells that story through memory and unsettles the space and times of official history. Subverting the story of how these things happened—disposable workers disposing of the excess of corporate state waste and toxicity—turns over that version of history to instead explore a different kind of value: the nanotext in opposition to what the novel identifies as excess, waste, and toxicity. Moreover, this nanotext provides a memory about kinship by linking not only the unidirectional conversation between Pedro and Lydia, and even the motley crew of seven workers, but also the crews of workers before it and the ongoing acts of resistance coterminously taking place on Earth. Pedro's access to Lydia through collective memory is what makes possible a sense of what is under threat, as well as what is being fought for: people and places that connect and make possible other forms of kinship grounded in interdependence across time and space.

When understood through this layered lens of collective memory, Lydia's conceptions of the environment present Earth as land overwhelmed by toxicity and on the brink of ecological collapse. That it has "exceeded capacity" gestures toward an environmental frame that depicts the planet as both quantifiable and limited. And its relation to humanity is further understood through what it can or cannot offer as an accumulation of land, laborers, and capital, or as human survival from those toxic discourses that a capitalist worldview produces. Yet the nanotext, as a form that we can interpret as palimpsestic, resists reading collapse apart from collective memories of kinship that bind people and place. Arizona and Sonoran deserts recall the centuries-long project of colonialism in what came to be the U.S. Southwest, but they also disrupt the framing of those histories through binary structures. As a flashpoint for thinking about historical pasts—what became the borderlands of two nation-states in the U.S. Southwest and Northern Mexico—these deserts also stand as a kind of palimpsest for a new moment of off-world colonization. The layers of future histories that Pedro (and readers) must confront are, at once, the temporally unfixed emerging police-states, the legacies and futures of the "Reservation," settler colonialism, and the management of global capitalism and its byproducts. While much of the novel focuses on the interplanetary management of waste—again, the impetus for aggressive lunar colonization—the attention to historical memory here shifts our understanding of relations as continuous, enduring, and structuring, even as it locates what is erased or forgotten as the thing making that "imperfectly erased scripting" possible (Gordon 146). The play with futurity, then, allows the novel to locate memory as collective—the same idea that allows readers to see interdependencies in socialist projects and nonnormative kinships.

References to "Arizona and Sonoran deserts" as precedents for later forms of colonization and environmental abuse significantly rework the nature of "futures." Sonora's deserts and land in the U.S. Southwest are layered with settler meaning—from Spanish empire to Indian displacement and dispossession, the U.S.-Mexico War, Japanese American internment, and the militarization of the border. Mary Pat Brady has noted that the folding of northern Sonora into U.S. territory and the ensuing subjection of its population should be understood as intimately tied to "the 150-year effort of the U.S. government to solidify its southern border in both material and discursive terms" (11).[14] Priscilla Solis Ybarra further observes that a more nuanced reading of land and Mexican American life disrupts this narrative as memoirists complexly chart place and experience in the Southwest through a lens of generations of Spanish-era land grants.[15] Attentive to settler histories, the passage above resists cultural amnesia by connecting those longer narratives to environmentalism; "sublunar deposit sites," in other words, recall U.S. militarized border-making, effectively situating environmental and racialized subaltern subjects as part of the same genealogy. Links between storing and containing toxic waste and managing "reslifers" on reservations are explicit, challenging a discourse that erases Indigenous people and people of color from the land.[16]

The emphasis on collective forms of memory as counternarrative imagines the environment both outside and within the futures of capitalism. Importantly, Sánchez and Pita identify this class struggle—made up primarily of poor and marginalized people of color across Earth—as an environmental struggle, narrating a future where poor people are imprisoned, work as an indentured laboring class for state projects, and even become the materials used in scientific laboratories that harvest organs. As Lydia elaborates:

> The Reservations were and are a type of population control camp mechanism. They were started to keep the homeless and the unemployed off the streets and off welfare. In the Reservation we were required to work at assigned tasks; some had jobs in nuclear weapon industries, chemical labs, and more routine industries. The skill-less were made to maintain the streets. Unemployed teachers were required to teach in the Reservation schools. Unemployed nurses and doctors were required to work in the Reservation clinics. The Reservations are really a type of prison, surrounded by a razor wire fence that could easily be cut or jumped. But rarely does anyone try. We knew as kids that beyond a clearing there were patrols and that if you were caught trying to run away you could be killed on the spot. (13–14)

Workers are represented as a multiethnic population looking to avoid or escape the Reservations and prison, but the conditions resemble what Gabriela Nuñez interprets as a more familiar barrio experience. Trash-tech work provides a way out of corporate-managed Reservations, "organized by housing projects, and complex systems of surveillance cameras, panoptic-style architecture, and razor wire [to] confine the 'reslifers' to their neighborhoods" (240). Yet these sites of the Reservation in *Lunar Braceros*, like barrios, are where collective memories and shared struggles find new forms of seeing, thinking, and being.[17] Near the end of the novel, for example, Lydia describes the collective nature of the growing resistance: "It became clear in our discussions at night in Chinganaza that change had to come through struggles within Cholo Reservations. Several of us in the group, both ex-techs and ex-miners came from reservation backgrounds" (Sánchez and Pita 118). With the spread of Reservations across the former United States, from Texas to California and Washington, in Chihuahua and Nuevo Leon, discussions about how to establish contact across these sites as a network sets the way forward. Lydia points to continued efforts, remembering that over the years there have been

> a few meetings in Coahuila and Baja with delegates from the Reservations, that is, with residents of the Res'es that have had trusty positions and could go in and out without any problems. . . . Plans have been set in motion and we are now eager to return and become involved. This is not merely a personal thing, not an individual battle, although I have much to resent. It will be a collective struggle, a class struggle. . . . Our struggle will be the beginning of a different world. (118)

Along with oppressive systems, Sánchez and Pita's futures represent abuses to humans and land alike, including destroyed rainforests, polluted waters, and corporate waste. The narrative refuses to read "natural," however, as pastoral, again shifting the paradigm of what has traditionally constituted environmental concerns to include human conditions at many levels. Depicting disposable workers, excess populations, and throwaway medical subjects used to develop and harvest human organs through medical experimentation, it shows discursive connections between a disposable population and a disposable planet, both of which are easily used and discarded without explanation or notice. Lydia's deep history outlines the development of the Reservation to trace lines between land and racialized labor:

> The Reservations, both domestic in the Cali-Texas Confederation and in Europe, were first created around 2090 and had become fully functional by 2100 as sites for the housing of the unemployed and homeless that had been essentially squatting by taking over streets in several sectors of metropolitan areas, especially commercial sectors, and in the slums. The number of people in these Reservations grew tremendously, year by year, not because of any spike in the birthrate but because of massive unemployment and world-wide migrations. These new "vagrants" or "migros," as they were called back then, were forced into the Reservations, located throughout the Southwest, where they became, like I said, a wage-less labor pool, almost like slave labor, to be used in a variety of areas as needed and determined by corporate interests managing the Reservations. (15).

Lydia notes that the transient population, the "squatter problem," emerged "at just about the same time that waste deposits for radioactive materials became scarce and the need to corral Migros and others and herd us into controlled populations sites became critical" (15). Enclosures serve as a function of the nation-state via new, reconfigured political entities and as the Reservations, the attention to enclosures for both people and waste surface throughout the text and link waste control and population control as part of the same discussion for the new state capitalism of the twenty-second century. The various hierarchies maintaining class and economic inequalities allow for implicit and explicit blaming of poor communities as the source of social, moral, and environmental problems, while at the same time praising the wealthy for solving those problems. That Lydia's account narrates them as surfacing at the same time follows a familiar logic, what Pellow cites as the toxic logic of capitalism: "If the domination of nature is part of a broader project of class domination inherent in capitalism, then environmental inequality is the logical result" (98). Lydia's telling echoes Pellow's reading of the historical (and current) framing of immigrants, Indigenous peoples, and people of color by "policymakers, politicians, and ecologists as a source of environmental contamination" (98). The most fitting place for toxic waste, such logic rationalizes, are those "spaces these populations occupy"—and equally so those populations would be the most fitting to manage and be exposed to toxicity.[18]

The dystopic imagery narrated here draws on histories and policies anchored in the exclusionary flashpoints of the United States, policies that recall the strange-yet-familiar narratives of the Chinese Exclusion Act of 1882, Mexican deportations during the first half of the twentieth century, Executive Order 9066 creating Japanese internment camps, the militarization of borders, and the general environmental degradation of the last century. The representation of these historical examples in *Lunar Braceros* calls to mind contemporary activism in Barrio Logan that insists on framing its most recent struggle as an environmental one, showing that the toxic logic of late capitalism holds a particular sway in the present. The spokesperson hired by the San Diego shipyard, Chris Wahl (also president of a public relations firm nationally recognized for nullifying community resistance against industry clients), made visible the naturalized assumption that industries matter more than the people who maintain and live near them. The health of Barrio Logan residents, Wahl noted at a press conference, "cannot be at the expense of the shipyard and its future."[19] Expressing frustration when dealing with Logan residents' unwillingness to imagine and value industry futures over their own, he continued, "It's hard to believe that it's come down—after five years and two million dollars—to two blocks, but it has, and I think it's a principle issue. I think the fact of the matter is that the shipyard and maritime industry believes that the city would rather have homes than the shipyard industry there."

Utopia and dystopia, as cultural forces in *Lunar Braceros*, invite even deeper critical analysis of contemporary contradictions at national and global levels. The current U.S. administration's return to xenophobic, nativist, and racist policies, tactics, and fantasies indeed calls for other kinds of analyses and responses.[20] President Trump's proposal for a solar-powered, militarized wall at the U.S.-Mexico border, as just one example, consolidates these imaginaries against what are constructed as threats of invasion continuously coming from Mexico and Latin America. A solar wall that "pays for itself"—the border understood as a greenwashed capitalist project, as opposed to one destructively at odds with numerous actual environments and ecologies—is a logical outcome to the anti-immigrant narratives that amplified existing platforms of racism and xenophobia.[21] While abhorrent, this vision of the future is not new and, within its own logic, not even abhorrent. It draws, in other words, on the familiar figure of an enemy of the nativist nation yet creates the conditions of nation building, opening bids for construction and attracting businesses to imagine a future of a new green police-state. The toxic logic, then, reproduces the contradictory notion that capitalism stands to fix the crises it produces, to save the world from its own destructive system.

As U.S. government environmental agencies such as the Environmental Protection Agency are under attack and dismantled, looking to the ways *Lunar Braceros* imagines otherwise offers an explicit narrative against the template of green capitalist fantasies. When confronted with the work of fighting for a better world, Lydia concludes with the pressing question that reworks the intimate notion that the personal is not only political but also as much about histories as about futures: "How do you make sense of your life, those moments that are so like a distant past and yet not so different from what is going on today. Chingones and Chingados, but on a totally different scale. I can't answer these questions; perhaps in the telling, in the writing, in the recollection of people, through memory, dialogues and scenes, it'll all make some sense . . . , fragmented though it may be" (58). *Lunar Braceros* presents official histories critically, not only by playing with history-making tropes that narrate life through the authoritatively linear, event-focused grand narratives of the past, such as "The Great Political Restructuring" noted at the beginning of this essay. The novel also unsettles the progress narratives of national histories and benevolent states by linking the conditions of racial capitalism and the global waste trade to common but unevenly distributed vulnerabilities. The archive of nanotexts that makes up the novel centers those who have been displaced, subjected to mass incarceration, and sent into space as expendable laborers managing the toxic waste of corporations. By doing so, the nanotexts challenge the naturalization of nation-states as the singular framework through which to imagine justice and a livable life. A future history, in this formation, tells us something about the environment as imagined through capital and therein offers a cultural response to those eco-dreams and desires continually being reworked and contested.

NOTES

Over years, locations, and environments this essay lived many lives through conversations with friends, comrades, and colleagues. My special thanks to Joo Ok Kim, Curtis Marez, Shelley Streeby, Josephine Talamantez, Marissa López, Cécile Accilien, and the community at UCLA's Chicano Studies Research Center. I am grateful to Ben Chappell,

Yumi Pak, and Emma Stapely for organizing interdisciplinary seminars on the cultures and arts of the present, and for their invitations to develop this project with them. My ongoing appreciation goes to the editors of this collection, Sarah Wald, David Vázquez, Priscilla Solís Ybarra, and Sarah Jaquette Ray, for their generous engagements and collective work.

1. Sánchez and Pita 14, 37.
2. Lowe, "Metaphors of Globalization" 50.
3. Raúl Homero Villa frames the emergence of Chicano Park as a green space, discussed in *Barrio-Logos: Space and Place in Urban Chicano Literature and Culture*, created when, on April 22, 1970, Chicana/o residents of Logan Heights and supporters from throughout San Diego County "drew their line in the sand and mobilized to stop bulldozers." The building of an Interstate 5 freeway ramp leading to the new Coronado Bridge cut a line directly through the neighborhood. The City of San Diego promised to build a community park for residents; however, instead the City began working up plans for a new California Highway Patrol substation. Residents blocked that plan and created Chicano Park. Artist Salvador Torres, one of the planners of the park murals, described the general sentiment: "They sent this freeway down the heart of our community and nearly killed it. We did not want it. We hated the bridge [and the columns]. . . . But now that we have them, we have to deal with them creatively" (Villa 176).
4. See CalEnviroScreen, a website that maps California's neighborhood pollution levels, public health conditions, and environmental quality. The website shows Barrio Logan at the very highest pollution. See also "Clean Air and Safe Streets: A Truck Ordinance for Barrio Logan" and "Local Students to Develop New Mural for Barrio Logan," *Environmental Health Coalition* website.
5. See Chen, *Animacies*. Chen explores the "queer reach for toxicity's 'worlding'" (194) as it challenges and, at the same time, alters narratives of capitalism.
6. See Lowe, "Metaphors of Globalization." Lowe frames persistent contradictions of "a future guaranteed by social progress" as a central problem of globalization, marking the limits of positivist analysis and disciplinary knowledge production. This presumption of progress is continuously troubled, however, by the uninterrupted experiences of surviving world wars, poverty, and displacement. Rather than returning to nationalisms, nation-states, and militarism to imagine a future within globalization—frameworks that have "pressed the empirical social sciences to its epistemological limits"—Lowe argues for a more sustained, interdisciplinary engagement with culture (52).
7. See also Hester Williams.
8. See Chabram-Dernersesian; Marez; Millán; Nuñez; Rivera; Irizarry.
9. For a diverse body of scholarship examining this historical moment and its afterlives, see Brady; Gómez; Huizar-Hernández; Kim; Saldaña-Portillo; Sánchez, *Telling Identities*; Streeby, *American Sensations*; Ybarra.
10. See Gamber; Kinney; Mignolo; Pellow; Sisavath.
11. Specifically, Pellow focuses on the nearly three million tons of hazardous waste produced in Europe, the United States, Japan, and other industrialized nations, as well as its dumping and disposal in Latin America, the Caribbean, South and Southeast Asia, and Africa.
12. See also Pulido 13–16. Laura Pulido's critique of environmentalism foregrounds the subaltern and emergent social movements within the context of the United States.
13. See also Gamber; Kinney; Sisavath. Recent scholarship on waste, ruin, and toxicity in the fields of empire, ecocritical, ethnic, race, and refugee studies has reframed conversations to complicate the key term *waste* as it has been produced through empire,

militarism, and deindustrialization, as well as how communities use, refuse, and reuse narratives of waste.

14. The processes used to "produce Arizona," Brady further notes, were ultimately the same that were "fired up again to produce a militarized border." See also Huizar-Hernández.

15. Ybarra notes that such writing resituates the vast space of the Southwest region—in which people like Fabiola Cabeza de Baca and Eva Wilbur-Cruce reflect on their own lives in farming, ranching, and living over generations—and brings about a conception of natural space as both desolate and deeply meaningful, as "the beginning and end of [their] most vital experiences" (Kindle edition).

16. See, for example, O'Brien; Ramírez. O'Brien discusses "firsting" and "lasting"—the formations of that settler modernity that depended on the construction and reproduction of histories in which "Indian peoples became ancient—mired in the static of the past" (4), while Ramírez has described the process as narrating racialized land and people as out of modern time, "fixed in a primitive and racialized past" (188).

17. See Avila 118; Moya (this volume).

18. Drawing on philosophers Charles W. Mills and Robert Higgins, Pellow notes that the forms of racialization that have identified Indigenous and poor people of color across the globe as social pollutants have been at the center of rationalizing garbage dumping and trashing the planet.

19. See "Debate over Zoning Puts Barrio Logan at Center of Turf War," *KPBS News*.

20. Recent examples are Executive Order 13769 ("Protecting the Nation from Foreign Terrorist Entry into the United States") and rescinding the Deferred Action for Childhood Arrivals (DACA) program, efforts to fortify, militarize, and increase the carceral capacities of U.S. borders by targeting Latinx and Muslim communities.

21. See Ryan. During a June 21, 2017, rally, thousands cheered as President Trump announced his plan for securing an eco-friendly border wall, where the profit-making potential of solar energy, job creation, and U.S. border tourism framed the project to overwrite a progressive association with environmental work.

WORKS CITED

Avila, Eric. *The Folklore of the Freeway: Race and Revolt in the Modernist City*. U of Minnesota P, 2014.

Bahng, Aimee. *Migrant Futures: Decolonizing Speculation in Financial Times*. Duke UP, 2018.

"Barrio Logan: Community Plan and Local Coastal Program." City of San Diego Planning Department, 17 Sept. 2013, www.sandiego.gov/sites/default/files/legacy/planning/community/cpu/barriologan/pdf/bl_cpu_full_w_historic_res_091913.pdf. Accessed 28 Oct. 2018.

Brady, Mary Pat. *Extinct Lands, Temporal Geographies: Chicana Literature and the Urgency of Space*. Duke UP, 2002.

"CalEnviroScreen." *CalEnviroScreen 3.0 (June 2018)*, Office of Environmental Health Hazard Assessment, http://oehha.maps.arcgis.com/apps/webappviewer/index.html?id=4560cfbce7c745c299b2d0cbb07044f5. Accessed 4 Nov. 2018.

Chabram-Dernersesian, Angie. "Bucking Tradition: Sci Fi with a Chicana/o Latina/o Twist." *Confluencia*, vol. 26, no. 1, 2010, pp. 192–194.

Chen, Mel Y. *Animacies: Biopolitics, Racial Mattering, and Queer Affect*. Duke UP, 2012.

"Clean Air and Safe Streets: A Truck Ordinance for Barrio Logan." *Environmental Health Coalition*, 16 Apr. 2018, www.environmentalhealth.org/index.php/en/media-center

/blog-for-environmental-justice/127-toxic-free-neighborhoods/686-clean-air-and-safe-streets-a-truck-ordinance-for-barrio-logan. Accessed 4 Nov. 2018.

Dirks, Sandhya. "Debate over Zoning Puts Barrio Logan at Center of Turf War." *KPBS News*, 17 Sept. 2013, https://www.kpbs.org/news/2013/sep/17/battle-barrio-logan/.

Gamber, John. *Positive Pollutions and Cultural Toxins: Waste and Contamination in Contemporary U.S. Ethnic Literatures*. U of Nebraska P, 2012.

Gómez, Laura. *Manifest Destinies: The Making of the Mexican American Race*. 2008. New York UP, 2018.

Gordon, Avery. *Ghostly Matters: Haunting and the Sociological Imagination*. U of Minnesota P, 2008.

Hester Williams, Kim D. "Earthseeds of Change: Postapocalyptic Mythmaking, Race, and Ecology in *The Book of Eli* and Octavia Butler's Womanist Parables." *Racial Ecologies*, edited by Leilani Nishime and Kim D. Hester Williams, U of Washington P, 2018, pp. 234–249.

Huizar-Hernández, Anita. *Forging Arizona: A History of the Peralta Land Grant and Racial Identity in the West*. Rutgers UP, 2019.

Irizarry, Ylce. *Chicana/o and Latina/o Fiction: The New Memory of Latinidad*. U of Illinois P, 2016.

Kim, Joo Ok. "'Training Guatemalan Campesinos to Work Like Korean Peasants': Taxonomies and Temporalities of East Asian Labor Management in Latin America." *Verge: Studies in Global Asias*, vol. 3, no. 2, 2017, pp. 195–216.

Kinney, Rebecca. *Beautiful Wasteland: The Rise of Detroit as America's Postindustrial Frontier*. U of Minnesota P, 2016.

"Local Students to Develop New Mural for Barrio Logan." *Environmental Health Coalition*, 14 Nov. 2017, www.environmentalhealth.org/index.php/en/media-center/press-releases/653-local-students-to-develop-new-mural-for-barrio-logan. Accessed 4 Nov. 2018.

Lowe, Lisa. "Metaphors of Globalization." *Interdisciplinarity and Social Justice*, edited by Joe Parker et al., SUNY Press, 2010, pp. 37–62.

Marez, Curtis. *Farm Worker Futurism: Speculative Technologies of Resistance*. U of Minnesota P, 2016.

Merla-Watson, Cathryn Josefina. "(Trans)Mission Possible: The Coloniality of Gender, Speculative Rasquachismo, and Altermundos in Luis Valderas's Chican@futurist Visual Art." *Altermundos: Latin@ Speculative Literature, Film, and Popular Culture*, edited by Cathryn Josefina Merla-Watson and B. V. Olguín, UCLA Chicano Studies Research Center Press, 2017, pp. 352–370.

Merla-Watson, Cathryn Josefina, and B. V. Olguín, editors. *Altermundos: Latin@ Speculative Literature, Film, and Popular Culture*. UCLA Chicano Studies Research Center Press, 2017.

———. "Introduction: Altermundos: Reassessing the Past, Present, and Future of the Chican@ and Latin@ Speculative Arts." *Altermundos: Latin@ Speculative Literature, Film, and Popular Culture*, edited by Cathryn Josefina Merla-Watson and B. V. Olguín, UCLA Chicano Studies Research Center Press, 2017, pp. 1–36.

Mignolo, Walter D. *The Darker Side of Western Modernity: Global Futures, Decolonial Options*. Duke UP, 2011.

Millán, Isabel. "Engineering Afro-Latina and Mexican Immigrant Heroines: Biopolitics in Borderlands Speculative Literature and Film." *Aztlán: A Journal of Chicano Studies*, vol. 40, no. 2, 2015, pp. 167–185.

Nuñez, Gabriela. "The Future of Food? Indigenous Knowledge and Sustainable Food Systems in Latin@ Speculative Fiction." *Altermundos: Latin@ Speculative Literature, Film, and Popular Culture*, edited by Cathryn Josefina Merla-Watson and B. V. Olguín, UCLA Chicano Studies Research Center Press, 2017, pp. 235–248.

O'Brien, Jean M. *Firsting and Lasting: Writing Indians out of Existence in New England*. U of Minnesota P, 2010.

Olguín, B. V. "Contrapuntal Cyborgs? The Ideological Limits and Revolutionary Potential of Latin@ Science Fiction." *Altermundos: Latin@ Speculative Literature, Film, and Popular Culture*, edited by Cathryn Josefina Merla-Watson and B. V. Olguín, UCLA Chicano Studies Research Center Press, 2017, pp. 128–144.

Pellow, David Naguib. *Resisting Global Toxics: Transnational Movements for Environmental Justice*. The MIT Press, 2007.

Pulido, Laura. *Environmentalism and Economic Justice: Two Chicano Struggles in the Southwest*. U of Arizona P, 1996.

Ramírez, Catherine. "Afrofuturism/Chicanafuturism: Fictive Kin." *Aztlán: A Journal of Chicano Studies*, vol. 33, no. 1, 2008, pp. 185–194.

Rivera, Lysa. "Future Histories and Cyborg Labor: Reading Borderlands Science Fiction after NAFTA." *Science Fiction Studies*, vol. 39, no. 3, 2012, pp. 415–436.

Ryan, Joe. "Panel Makers Surge after Trump Proposes Solar on Border Wall." *Bloomberg*, 21 June 2017, www.bloomberg.com/news/articles/2017-06-22/solar-companies-surge-after-trump-proposes-panels-on-border-wall.

Saldaña-Portillo, María Josefina. *Indian Given: Racial Geographies across Mexico and the United States*. Duke UP, 2016.

Sánchez, Rosuara. *Telling Identities: The California testimonios*. U of Minnesota P, 1995.

Sánchez, Rosaura, and Beatrice Pita. *Lunar Braceros: 2125–2148*. Calaca Press, 2009.

Sisavath, Davorn. "The US Secret War in Laos: Constructing an Archive from Military Waste." *Radical History Review*, vol. 133, 2019, pp. 103–116.

Streeby, Shelley. *American Sensations: Class, Empire, and the Production of Popular Culture*. U of California P, 2002.

———. *Imagining the Future of Climate Change: World-Making through Science Fiction and Activism*. U of California P, 2018.

Villa, Raúl Homero. *Barrio-Logos: Space and Place in Urban Chicano Literature and Culture*. U of Texas P, 2000.

Ybarra, Priscilla Solis. *Writing the Goodlife: Mexican American Literature and the Environment*. U of Arizona P, 2016.

6

Sun Ma(i)d

*Art, Activism, and Environment in
Ester Hernández's Central Valley*

JENNIFER GARCIA PEACOCK

A Poster, 1982

Completed in 1982, Ester Hernández's *Sun Mad* (Figure 6.1) stands as one of the most widely circulated—and most iconic—images in Chicanx art. The familiarity of its imagery (a reworking of the Sun Maid raisin logo in the spirit of Mexican Revolution era printmaker Jose Guadalupe Posada) and its central message (a pointed critique of pesticide use in the agricultural industry) make the piece both instantly recognizable and resonant, a kind of shorthand for expressing the high cost of cheap food in America during the late twentieth century.

This move—a searing fact, simply expressed—is a defining characteristic of Hernández's visual language and can be seen across the large body of work she has steadily produced during the last several decades. From the early drawings she contributed to campus publications as a student at the University of California, Berkeley, during the 1970s,[1] through her ongoing work in printmaking, pastel-based portraiture, drawings, and installations (including numerous collaborations with filmmakers, writers, and activists), Hernández's style might be imagined as equal parts wit and grit, a straightforward and incisive homage to the everyday experiences of the people, landscapes, politics, and histories that surround her.

The architecture of *Sun Mad* engages the viewer with a kind of generous and frank efficiency: a quick tour around its focal points provides swift, ample, and unequivocal commentary on issues related to labor rights, environmental justice, ecofeminism, and agribusiness. A large yellow circle is set just above center, establishing both a line into the image through the figure set in its

Figure 6.1 *Sun Mad* (1982). Illustration by Ester Hernández.

center and a diffused set of lines out through the pointed edges of the small triangles that surround it. The sun and its bright rays place emphasis on the smartly dressed woman set within it. With an oversized red bonnet and broad basket (handmade from dried grapevines), the skeletal face draws attention to the inconsistencies—or disinformation—that the agricultural industry drew on in its advertising in twentieth-century California to create the perception of health to promote its products. Hernández's image—through a Posada-like use of satire in the Mexican graphic arts tradition that flourished during the Mexican Revolution—*Sun Mad* offers a counterpoint by emphasizing the toxicity of grapes, noting that they are "unnaturally grown" through the aggressive use of pesticides including insecticides, miticides, herbicides, and fungicides. Held at womb level, their placement also brings subtle attention to the disproportionate effects for female farmworkers, particularly on their reproductive systems.[2]

The basket is also important because it brings attention to the rural aesthetic practices that repurpose materials such as dried vines into vernacular domestic arts such as baskets and wreaths. This kind of decorative basket is better suited for home display than heavy use in the harvest, obscuring the harsh scale of industrial grape production. In reality, the eighteen-pound cartons used in the industry are stacked high and with swift precision, requiring not a gentle touch suggested here by the pastoral basket but instead a more rugged engagement that requires the use of gloves, long-sleeve shirts, and sturdy hats to protect from the hundred-degree heat typical in the region during the harvest season.

Scholars have shrewdly recognized the semiotic power of the image, and it has enjoyed broad use across a number of disciplines. Most recently, scholarship has emphasized its landmark status in Chicanx aesthetic and political discourse with scholars such as Randy Ontiveros highlighting the significance of Hernández's "confrontational approach" (65) in the larger body of environmentally themed Chicanx visual culture and Maylei Blackwell noting the important ways Hernández "grounds social commentary with lived experience" (147), a kind of place-based aesthetic resistance that aims to honor both the spirit of the Chicanx movement and the women who helped shape its cultural landscape through their art, activism, domestic work, and community building.[3]

The sheer volume of its use also attests to its facility—and utility—in communicating these complex social and environmental concerns to diverse audiences. Passionate, precise, and presented in an accessible format, the image has a familiarity that has gained wide favor in museums, galleries, and among the general public.[4] In other words, even if a viewer has not seen the image previously, any familiarity with its thematics, aesthetics, landscape, or the cultural heritage it references produces a sense of intimacy: it *feels* like you have seen it before or *should* have seen it all along.

In fact, perhaps this is the enduring gift of the image, a gift that simultaneously haunts it: because many of its central messages and lessons are self-evident, *Sun Mad* has become as ubiquitous as the agricultural advertising and calavera imagery it references—but it has yet to enjoy the depth of treatment that works of its cultural significance tend to receive. A closer look at the critical attention the piece has received—while impressive in its breadth—reveals a dearth of historical analysis, particularly in relation to the traditional formalist readings so important to understanding the aesthetic and cultural significance of the piece. In this chapter, I build on these scholarly and popular engagements with *Sun Mad* to explore how and why this image helps illuminate critical dimensions of twentieth-century Chicanx environmental history that are curiously, and simultaneously, out of view and in plain sight. More specifically, I take what architectural historian and cultural critic John Brinckerhoff Jackson refers to as the "vernacular landscape"—the everyday, mundane features of the built environment such as roads, houses, irrigation canals, gardens, and bridges—as a tool to bring the homegrown messages found within Hernández's print into clear view.

To look more closely at *Sun Mad* in this mode, then, brings attention to parts of the cultural landscape that are not often explored in architectural studies or environmental history yet are vitally important to understanding rural Latinx environmental experience: the back roads of raisin country, a landscape that came alive with startling speed in California during the twentieth century through a series of massive public and private investments required to transform a desert landscape into a lush, productive garden.[5] I argue that Hernández's artistic style and political voice took shape amid the everyday sights and sounds of the raisin industry and through the larger set of historical forces that shaped it. I show through close readings of key features of Hernández's childhood home that this rich cultural landscape nurtured a politicized view of the environment, not one merely of dissent but of deep respect for nature and the diverse people that brought the vineyards (and garden) that surrounded her home to life. By stepping inside the houses, gardens, and yards of the Hernández family—across generations—we can touch what often remains elusive in the history and cultural production of the Central Valley (but where *Sun Mad* is so instructive): how women of Mexican heritage have improved the cultural life of the Central Valley through their attentiveness to long-standing visual and place-making traditions. In what follows, I trace four elements central to the aesthetics of place-making in the valley: the nonhuman environment, the rise of an industrial raisin industry in Central Valley towns like Dinuba, the aesthetics and commercial imagery that sought to represent the valley and its grape landscapes, and the vernacular histories and aesthetics that inspired artists like Hernández to bundle their children and return home.

A Journey Home, November 1980

A young mother wakes her five-year-old son from sleep, quietly lifting him out of his pajamas and into jeans and a light sweater. Pulling away from their small house in Oakland, California, they travel west, across a still sleeping city, and merge onto the southbound lane. A thick mist hangs above the Eastside Freeway, the portion of Interstate 80 that edges the San Francisco Bay and serves as the hub of the Bay Area transportation network. As the sun breaks above the eastern horizon line, its light cuts across the sky, moving up and over this maze of concrete and pavement, where it stretches west across an estuary dotted with small islands and large cargo ships and fades into the bright mouth of the Pacific Ocean. Here, at the cool edge of the morning, the Golden Gate Bridge peeks through the fog, vividly marking the confluence of river and maritime ecosystems, the point where fresh water from the Sacramento and San Joaquin Rivers completes the long journey from their headwaters, meets the rough saline tide, and is pulled into to the sea.

Heading to her childhood home, this young mother's journey follows a similarly long and winding path, across the set of paved roads that flow southeast from the Bay Area to the lower San Joaquin Valley. Just south of the town of Tracy, she merges onto Interstate 5—known locally as the Westside Highway—the wide and fast-moving corridor linking San Francisco and Los Angeles. This road, set in thick, black pavement, stretches long and smooth across the sparsely populated western edge of the Central Valley. Miles and miles of grassland define the view, flat and matte gold from seasonal rain. Turning east onto Highway 152, mother and child pass through Los Banos, or Los Baños del Arroyo, the site of a natural spring or bath visited by the Spanish during their exploration of the valley in the early nineteenth century and used frequently by clergy from the nearby Mission San Juan Bautista (Gudde; Hoover and Kyle). This coarse pavement is typical of the roads found along the rural interior of the state, both narrower in their composition and with fewer safety features than the larger state and federal roads that they connect. The safety features present on the more traveled byways (speed bumps, rumble strips, medians, and roadside pullouts and shoulders) are not merely decorative elements—a fact the driver knows well. She slows her speed as a precaution when she encounters a second cloud of morning fog on her journey. Driving along this thin layer of faded pavement, it is difficult to see the faintly marked metallic yellow line dividing the lanes—or the cars and farm equipment traveling within them. Covering the valley floor from November through March, the Tule fog creates a dangerous seasonal beauty across this rural landscape.

By late morning, when she turns south onto Highway 99, the primary route for local traffic, the fog has cleared, exposing the growing city of Fresno, with its malls, sprawling residential neighborhoods, and surrounding network of farmworker towns. Following the eastern the edge of the Sierra Nevada foothills from Red Bluff to Bakersfield, Highway 99 serves as one of the primary axes in this rural landscape. Rich soil washed down from the mountains, sitting atop what was once the ocean floor, has made this part of the Central Valley particularly fertile. Looking west from Highway 99 shows the major differences in the natural and built environments: a bit out of range from these small but important benefits of mountain erosion, the view to the right of the car window shows a drier and less fertile landscape, a sparse patchwork of old ranches and fields.

As the young boy awakens in the late morning light, he and his mother pass through the towns south of Fresno, where they soon head east on the J-40 between Selma and Kingsburg, a county road also known as El Monte Way. As its name suggests, its view is a delight for sleepy eyes: long lines of orchards, fields, and vineyards stretch east to the mountain's edge, climbing first through a dense collection of California black oak and chaparral and then up through thick forests of mixed conifers and across cascading slabs of smooth granite that reach into the bright blue sky that stretches above this part of the Sierra Nevada.

On this final leg of the journey home, the mother and young child cross the Kings River, a major tributary of the San Joaquin River named by Spanish explorers during their brief exploration of the region during the Mission Era. As the woman approaches her hometown, Dinuba, she passes the Tulare County Courthouse, set ahead of an irrigation canal just along the upper edge of her old neighborhood. Pulling her car to a stop at the curb in front of 141 South P Street, she unbuckles Jacobo from his car seat and walks up the driveway. Twenty feet of pale gray concrete leads to a handmade stone pathway lined with yellow and orange marigolds. Together, the mother and son have traversed a series of roads, moving steadily from national superhighways—Interstates 80 and 5—to regional corridors such as State Highway 99, to county roads and local streets, to the smallest scales possible—driveways and stone paths. At the end of this path are four wooden steps, leading up to a small porch. Beams made from the local wood (and material salvaged from the surrounding vineyards) support the roof above, which is in the shape of an inverted V and set with thin sheets of aluminum. The door is set between two square windows with dark green trim, and with Jacobo in her left arm, she turns the clear plastic knob with her right hand and enters her mother's house. Ester Hernández is home (Hernández, "Personal Interview 1").

Two Views of the San Joaquin Valley

Standing at 14,494 feet above sea level, Mount Whitney is the highest point in the continental United States and the focal point in the alpine landscape that looms above the San Joaquin Valley. Mount Whitney is set within the Sierra Crest, a five-hundred-mile long ridgeline that forms the thick spine of the Sierra Nevada range. It is neighbor to four other peaks that top 13,000 feet—the links in this part of the mountain chain are particularly formidable.[6]

Like all rocks, the granite of the Sierra Crest is an aggregate of minerals, bound together during moments of intense heat, pressure, and movement. But its long cooling process has given its minerals a relatively long time to crystalize, creating a hard, tough texture. Pale in color, granite tends to have an unassuming neutral shade of white, gray, or rose. But when examined closely, the crystallization process of this particular mineral composition imbues the rocks with intricate patterns and a delicate sheen. Embedded with tiny pieces of translucent quartz and glittery mica crystals, dotted with dark grains of opaque hornblende, and bound by the neutral matte shades of feldspar, it takes on a subtle shimmer in the light that has inspired a wide range of artists and observers (Hill).

In 1869, for example, naturalist John Muir arrived in San Francisco and immediately set out on the first of the many walks that would take him from the San Francisco Bay and Sacramento-San Joaquin Delta across the Central Valley and to the canyons and peaks of the Sierra Nevada near Mount Whitney. These journeys, in these mountains—"the most beautiful as I have ever beheld" (5)—would form a cornerstone in the aestheticized imaginary of the modern environmental movement. Muir recorded the view during one of these early journeys, giving us both an urtext of American environmentalism and a small glimpse into the region's landscape before large-scale agricultural production:

> Looking eastward from the summit of Pacheco Pass one shining morning, a landscape was displayed that after all my wanderings still appears as the most beautiful as I have ever beheld. At my feet lay the Great Central Valley of California, level and flowery, like a lake of pure sunshine, forty or fifty miles wide, five hundred miles long, one rich furred garden of yellow Compositae. And from the eastern boundary of this vast flower-bed rose the mighty Sierra, miles in height, and so gloriously colored and so radiant, it seemed to me that the Sierra should be called, not the Nevada or Snowy Range, but the Range of Light. And after ten years of wandering and wondering in the heart of it, rejoicing in its glorious foods of light, the white beams of the morning streaming through the passes, the noonday radiance on the crystal rocks, the flush of the alpenglow, and the irised spray of countless waterfalls, it still seems above all other the Range of Light. (5)

At the end of the nineteenth century, when Muir began traveling extensively in the Sierra Nevada, the Central Valley would have been realizing the fruits of its first generation of large-scale agricultural production. In this location, the lower San Joaquin Valley, wheat and cotton were being grown on land that was in the process of conversion from Spanish- and Mexican-era use for livestock grazing. Muir was well acquainted with the American agricultural story of the Central Valley and Bay Area, first as a sheepherder in the Yosemite foothills east of the city of Merced and later as caretaker of his wife's family's orchard estate in Martinez. Agricultural labor, however, as historian Donald Worster notes, was merely a means to fund his writing and time in observation of Sierra Nevada natural history, and nearly all of Muir's writings focus on his journeys in California's wilderness and not its fields, pastures, range, or gardens.

Muir's line of vision, then, standing at Pacheco Pass, moved east across the fertile Central Valley, up the foothills lightly dotted with California oak, up the thick stands of conifers, through the majestic sequoia forests, and rested on the sharp granite peaks thick with snow cover. His line is valuable to our understanding of this landscape because it thoroughly and thoughtfully covers several ecological zones and over two hundred million years of geologic history. And, at sunrise, it is truly a lovely garden framing a grand mountain range, backlit along the eastern horizon. However, his naturalist aesthetic kept him from commenting on other aspects of the scene that are essential to this story: the then-tiny village of Los Banos, the nascent raisin and citrus industry, and just to the south, to his right, the town of Dinuba.

Muir has handed down to us his sense of the real picture: his beloved Mount Whitney, set within the towering peaks of the Sierra Crest and the Great Western Divide. These mountains—not the valley itself—comprised "the Range of Light." Indeed, the valley itself was the Muirian equivalent of "flyover country"—pretty enough, but something through which to pass on his way to a destination that mattered, the majestic mountains.

When Hernández made the turn from Interstate 5 to Highway 152, she occupied the same point of view—but she saw it quite differently. She took the Central Valley not as frame but as the picture itself, the real thing that mattered. The glittering range of light was part of her visual vocabulary, of course, but it was qualified by the industrial grape fields, the small harvest and processing towns, and the experiences and memories clustered around her own hometown of Dinuba. Muir saw—and experienced firsthand—but did not remark on the beginnings of that landscape, though he came over the course of his career to understand the challenges, paradoxes, and cruel realities that faced the state during its rapid expansion, with its resource extraction, factories, dams, canals, and fields, all of which sustained an ever-growing population with the necessities and luxuries its climate, soil, and other natural resources provided: food, municipal water, electricity, flood management, jobs, and recreation.[7]

Hernández and other Chicanx cultural producers have seen different forms of light in the Sierra's granite: not Muir's diffuse and heavenly glow but the fragmented glitter of the granitic crystalline forms themselves, sharp facets that might become the faux jewels on a pair of jeans or the diamond dust look of a painting on velvet. Muir, who transmuted Calvinism into a gentle religion of nature, was always looking toward the heavens. Hernández looked down from Pacheco Pass toward a vision of labor, houses, roads, and water, for Dinuba sits directly below Mount Whitney; one might as easily choose to emphasize not the peak but the town, noting its vaulted position in the valley. Surrounding it is a working landscape, a translation of the nonhuman environment into an agro-industrial social and cultural place based on the raisin.

A House, 1950

At sunrise in Dinuba, sunlight entered the street side of the house through three small windows and spread across the surfaces of the front room. Back then, the night sky was dark, an inky blue dotted with white-yellow stars, distinct constellations above. Around this time—Hernández's childhood—an increasing number of neon-lit structures would rise from below, dimming the light above and recentering it along the packing-houses, warehouses, and truck yards that would come to define the valley during the second half of the twentieth century. Like all light, this industrial form illuminated more than the structures themselves. Their architectural features—the chutes, ladders, pipes, staircases, and electrical wire—also serve as an archive of important clues that inform the viewer of these larger processes that were underway in rural America during the mid-twentieth century. Large and efficient, they speak to the relation between artificial and natural light in these landscapes. The sun provides the energy to bring these crops to life, and hydroelectric power plants harvest the electricity needed to light these sorting, packing, and shipment facilities.[8]

As Hernández recalls ("Personal Interview 2"), the house at 141 South P Street (Figure 6.2) was not part of a formal factory or mill town, but its architecture might suggest otherwise. Like the other modest farmworker houses in this neighborhood, the floor plan was designed along a simple rectangle plan, divided into three wide rooms. Each morning, when the day would break over Mount Whitney, soft light was cast down the western slope of the Sierra Nevada and across the valley floor, touching the thin glass of the square windowpanes along the east-facing wall of the Hernándezes' childhood home. Filtering through the ivory lace curtains, the early morning light would then travel across the front room of the house, gently touching the objects in its path. Moving across the armchair, the fine rays of the first sun would then cross the floor, up and over the rollaway bed and sofa bed where Hernández and her sisters slept, finally coming to a rest on the altar and television against the west-facing wall. The glassy surfaces of the television screen, picture frames, candles, and figurines thus created a multidirectional flow of light, reflecting it back over the rollaway bed, where it diffused into the dimly lit room. The floral patterns of the lace curtains created shadows on the small beds, forming delicate patterns atop the brightly colored quilts and pillows.[9]

As the sunlight intensified, clearing the Sierra Crest and rising high and hot above the valley, three little girls, arrayed in their beds in this single room, would wake (Figure 6.3). Their mother, Luz, had risen from her bed in the adjoining room long before, moving quietly in the kitchen as she prepared their lunches for school. Later in the morning, Hernández and her sisters would board the bus on their own, long after their mother had checked into her shift down the road at the packinghouse.

A Young Artist's Home

Born in 1944, Hernández developed a special interest in the cultural landscape around her home through working as a young girl in the fields with her parents during summer breaks. Limiting her work in the fields to summer allowed her valuable time to earn her education, a benefit not always available to children growing up in the agricultural industry. Growing up in one house during her entire childhood—and not a series of temporary migratory dwellings—permitted her to cultivate her interests in art and the natural world that she would first develop through helping her mother in the

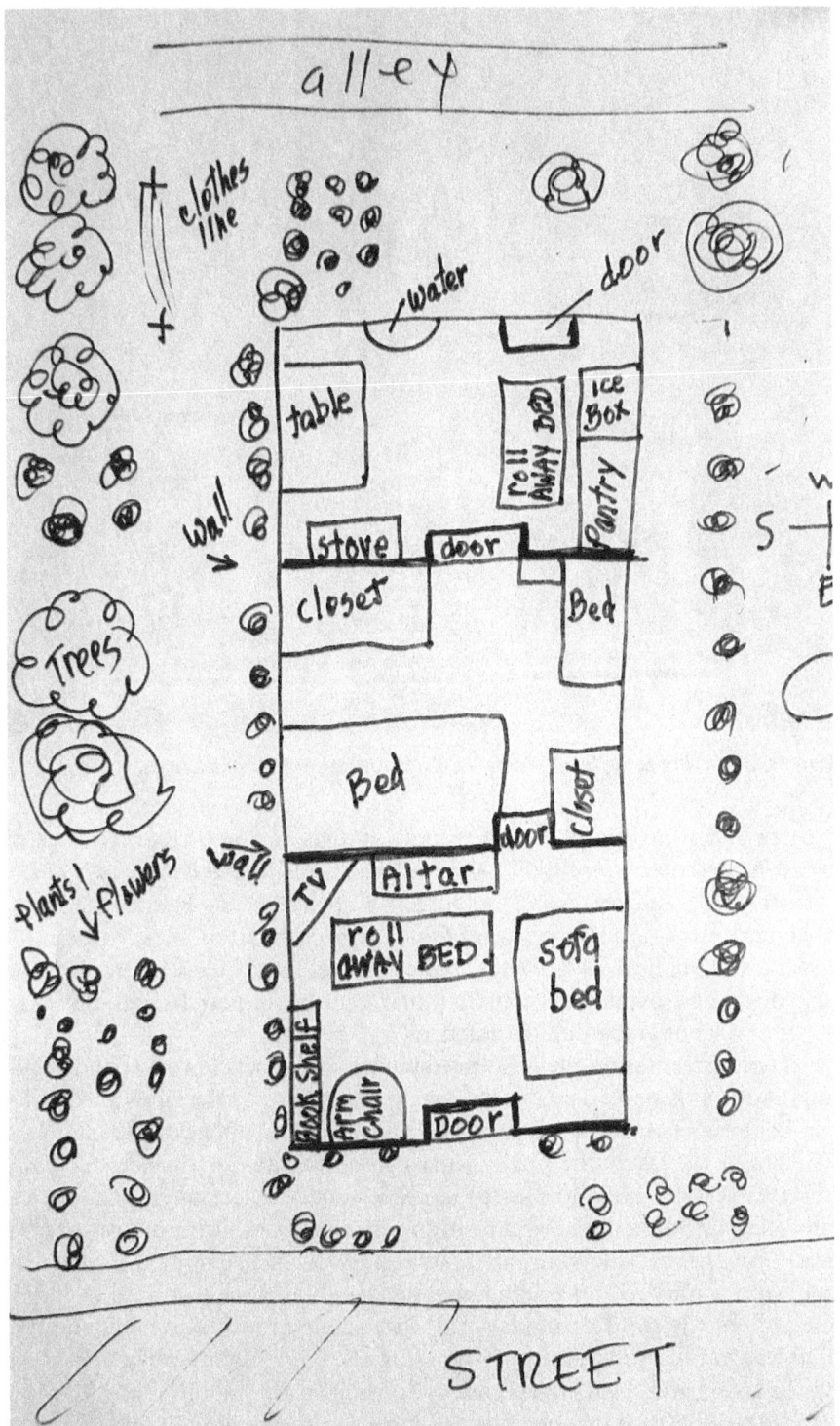

Figure 6.2 *141 S P Street* (2014). Illustration by Ester Hernández.

Figure 6.3 The altar at the Dinuba house (c. 1970). Courtesy of Ester Hernández.

garden and amid the thick, leafy vineyard rows during the harvest. In her artist statement to *Chicana Voices and Visions: A National Exhibit of Women Artists* (1983)—the first major exhibit to feature *Sun Mad*—Hernández states that her "images are always those of *la mujer chicana* (the Chicana woman)" (Social and Public Arts Resource Center Venice) in its fullest form, a kind of tribute to these overlooked contributions made by women through their agricultural labor and domestic practices.

Hernández was deeply influenced by her time as a fieldworker and packinghouse worker and developed a strong attachment to the fields and farmworker towns of the San Joaquin Valley. She played in ditches and canals as a young girl, the last of the small owner-driven irrigation network that would soon give way to federal and state watershed management systems. The streets and alley outside her family home in Dinuba were rich with animal and plant life during her childhood in the 1940s and 1950s. Tucked away at the edge of the main county road through town, the J-40, the house was both secluded enough for the children to play and close enough to town, school, and the highway to feel a sense of connection (Figure 6.4). Hernández was absorbed in the colors and spent endless hours drawing in the smooth dirt, a clay- or sand-like substance that created awe-inspiring shapes and textures: "It was smooth, like sand, because millions of years ago it was once at the bottom of

Figure 6.4 Ester Hernández (right) with sister Esperanza at the Dinuba house (c. 1949). Courtesy of Ester Hernández.

the ocean" ("Personal Interview 1"). She fell in the mud when she was three or four years old, and the experience shaped her early view as an artist: "amazed by its plasticity," she was fascinated when she "saw [her] movements captured in it" ("Personal Interview 1") and changed to hard dirt the next day.

The Central Valley was not the only landscape that shaped her young artistic sensibility; the nearby Sierra Nevada foothills were also formative in shaping her appreciation for art and the environment. Most weekends her family would journey to the lower edge of the Sierra Nevada into the Sequoia National Park and Forest near Porterville, one of the larger farmworker towns near Dinuba. She was deeply influenced by her father, a carpenter by training, a farmworker seasonally by necessity, and an amateur photographer and naturalist by instinct. He was curious about the natural world and in capturing it on film, and the family possesses a rich archive of snapshots like these (see figures 6.3 and 6.4) taken in and around their home in Dinuba. These experiences, "born and raised on the western slope of the Sierra Nevada in the central San Joaquin Valley of California, an area paradoxically known for its natural beauty and ongoing farmworker struggle," helped cultivate an interest in that place—much like Dinuba itself—between nature and culture, a "beauty" that she likens to "the seed that uplifts our spirit and nourishes our souls" ("Artist's Statement").

Ultimately, the time spent in her parents' home in Dinuba cultivated a strong appreciation for the Mexican American cultural landscape, a place that was at once a product of its time and place in the mid-twentieth Central Valley and alive with the memories and traditions her parents and grandpar-

Figure 6.5 Mother Luz Medina Hernández and family in the Sierra Nevada foothills. Courtesy of Ester Hernández.

ents had brought from Mexico (Figure 6.5). In her childhood home, Hernández found other visual and sensual vocabularies. The lace curtains told stories of Mexican lacemaking, domestic practices with a long history; the shadows cast on the bed offered tutorials in complex patterns. Visible from the front door, the altar (see Figure 6.3) offered constant reminders of La Virgen and the Santos and a long tradition of images and practices that carried Catholic Mexican faith communities back to a baroque sensibility. Next to the altar stood a television, a conduit into the popular culture of advertising and the political news of the world. On that TV, she could have seen the projection of a flourishing postwar American economy and the hints of the culturally based political upheavals that were to follow. Outside, her mother's garden bespoke a long Mexican and Mexican American tradition of aesthetic management of exterior space, of domestic plant nurture that offered solace and company to the industrial agricultural work taking place only a few blocks away. On the wall, Hernández would have seen classic forms of Mexican art. The calavera images—satirical skeletons crafted by Jose Posada—became part of her vocabulary here, as did the extensive use of Mexican heritage textiles, pottery, and clothing, often homemade (or modified) by her mother, aunts, and grandmother. And every morning, the light shone through the mountains—not John Muir's light, in her experience—and through her windows, casting a distinct kind of glow on her time and place.

Place-making, at its root, is about the materiality of belonging. Subjects form attachments to their material objects, produced in specific times and places, and these allow them to move through the past, present, and future. In the Dinuba house, belonging was made for Hernández through the domestic practices learned from Luz's mother, Tomasa Medina, and the life she built and rebuilt along her journey from the mountains of Guanajuato to her husband's world in Aguascalientes and their path through El Paso, Los Angeles, and into the lower San Joaquin Valley. These kinds of cultural influences, across time and place for three generations of the Medina-Hernández family, are in some ways difficult to document. Very few records remain of their move from Mexico to the United States. The route they traveled along the primary railroad lines in central Mexico and the southwest United States was typical of that generation of migrants, generating only a few photographs and stories. This modest archive creates challenges in measuring the changes they experienced over the course of their lives, offering only a few slivers of evidence. But we can say a few things.

Tomasa Medina ended up in a house on Nebraska Street in Selma, California, as a young mother from Aguascalientes. There, they had once lived on the town square where her husband had a carpentry school (Figure 6.6). They built a nice house where they began their family. She was from the mountains and was an excellent gardener and seamstress. But the Mexican Revolution was raging, and Aguascalientes was an important strategic center. So she, her husband, and their three kids packed up and left in the middle of the night. Tomasa hid everything in a dress she had sewn. They came by train through El Paso—like most families in that day—and they continued on to Los Angeles. But they found the space too urban—even back then—and sought a more rural setting to raise their family (Figure 6.7). They found a little piece of land in Selma, on Nebraska Street, and built a beautiful home and small workshop and guesthouse in the back. Tomasa slept in the main house with the children, and her husband slept in the smaller house, often with a few of his brothers and nephews as they made their journey north. Eventually the workshop trained other men in carpentry, while Tomasa and her daughters built a glorious garden and a multigenerational home that centered a small community ("Personal Interview 1").

The Selma cultural landscape—Grandma's house—can be seen in subtle detail across Hernández's visual production. In *Mis Madres*, Tomasa is seen cupping the earth in her left palm as her right hand touches the shawl that drapes long across her shoulders and stretches down her right side (Figure 6.8). Stars twinkle in bursts, creating blots of light in the deep blue sky. Stylized as Mother Earth, she presents a sturdy and wise presence caring for a troubled world. Much like the photographs taken of the young Tomasa as a young mother en route to what would become her new home in the Central

Figure 6.6 Grandmother Tomasa and mother Lucy in Aguascalientes, Mexico, house (c. 1912). Courtesy of Ester Hernández.

Figure 6.7 Grandmother Tomasa, mother Lucy, and uncle Hilario in El Paso house (c. 1916). Courtesy of Ester Hernández.

Figure 6.8 *Mis Madres* (1986). Illustration by Ester Hernández.

Figure 6.9 *Cosmic Cruise* (1990). Illustration by Ester Hernández.

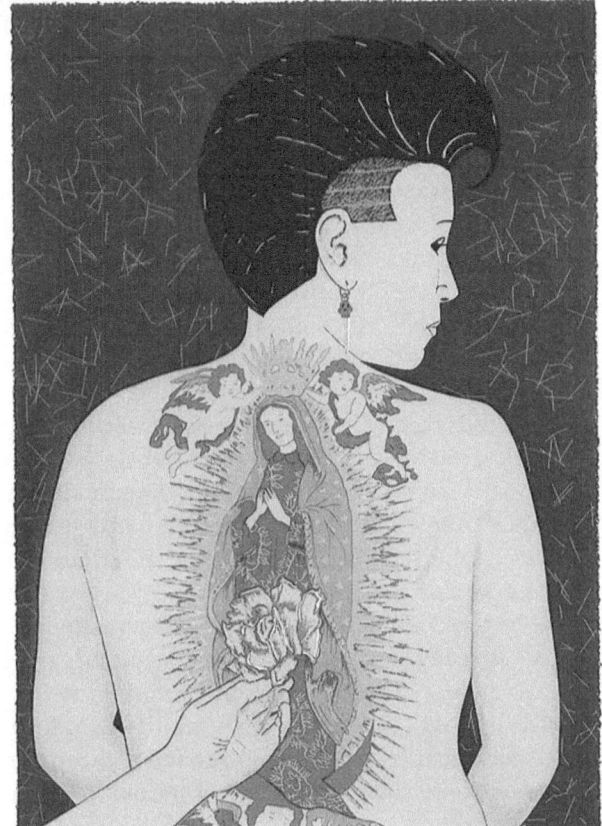

Figure 6.10 *La Ofrenda* (1988). Illustration by Ester Hernández.

Valley, Hernández's print also presents a stoic figure here, a woman who evokes a sense of otherworldly strength expressed through her seamless integration into the starlight and Earth's glow.[10]

The use of oversized blots of starlight—micro explosions of light found deep in the cosmos—can be found in high use in *Cosmic Cruise*, an homage to the road trips Hernández would enjoy with her mother and sisters along the small rural roads of their homeland (Figure 6.9). Here, we see La Virgen de Guadalupe at the wheel, with Tomasa riding by her side and Hernández in the back seat with her mother, Luz. The starlight suggests a joyride, as large, inky light spills across the sky. As Hernández notes, "The theme is our interconnectedness with each other and the universe. The car represents movement in space, and time is represented by the images of the women. 'La Virgen de Guadalupe' (the driver) the Mexican-Indian grandmother, the modern Chicana mother and child. The Aztec moon goddess-Coyolxauqui signifies our link with the past. The print is part of my ongoing tribute to la Mujer Chicana" (*The Cosmic Cruise*). Riding with these women, on this journey, speaks to the explosion of cultural and aesthetic beauty a young child must surely feel riding that high, that fast, and in such esteemed company, a path ablaze in bright pink and red tones.

The night sky also features prominently in a third piece, depicting a tattoo-like body painting Hernández did on the back of filmmaker Renee Moreno, capturing the image in two editions of *La Ofrenda* (Figure 6.10). Here, in this version, the night sky is rendered in similar deep blue shades, but the stars themselves are more in constellation form, a kind of crosshatching or etching that echoes the thin lines of paint used to detail the figure of La Virgen. The picture was inspired by Hernández and Moreno's attendance at an arts festival held in Golden Gate Park in the early 1980s. The transposition of the Central Valley sky into the Bay Area cultural landscape speaks to the ways in which this deep memory traveled with Hernández and continued to shape her experience in her new home far away from the long, deep blue hues of the rural night sky of her childhood.

The deep blue hues of the night sky would not be the only childhood influence Hernández would carry forward from her childhood into her artwork. Her mother, Luz, took a strong interest in the dancing traditions brought from their homeland in Aguascalientes and participated in local dance troupes with other Mexican-heritage women in the Selma area (Figures 6.11 and 6.12). The buildings and grounds at Tomasa and Luis's house were comfortable, owing to her facility in the garden and in domestic arts like sewing and his training as a carpenter, making their central lawn a community gathering space of sorts during weekends and holidays. As historian Vicki Ruiz notes, "Mexican women's community activism is not limited to city streets" (143); rather, it takes a multitude of forms including environmental justice organizing, economic development, and arts and culture activities like the dance recitals and rehearsals hosted in the family garden at Selma.[11]

Figure 6.11 Mother Lucy (top left). Courtesy of Ester Hernández.

The rural woman's dress would also find its way into Hernández's work through an installation piece that focuses on the domestic elements of her grandmother's journey from Mexico and the life she would remake in Selma. Set with fine-grain sand, evoking the rich clay soil of Tomasa's garden, the work layers up and across the floor, a neatly set circle of marigolds framing the scene. A heavy chest filled with embroidered textiles—like the ones Hernández would learn to make with these women in the Selma garden—is stacked next to the now-vintage Singer sewing machine used to make the dresses in the photograph and the installation. The large orange circles of the marigolds create complementary patterns with the small silver coins inlaid in the dress, an offset centerpiece to this composition that serves to distribute or achieve a sense of balance between the value of the process of domestic work—the sewing machine, "grown" in rich soil—and the product: a shimmering, sheer tribute to the migrant woman's journey.[12]

For Hernández, these family houses—and the childhood she would enjoy in Dinuba—offer an alternative view of the rapidly industrializing countryside that was taking shape around her and her loved ones. The Selma house would be demolished in 1964 as part of the regional transportation plan, a large-scale infrastructure project that would see the expansion of Highway 99 into multiple lanes. While this work would allow for a more efficient flow of traffic, relocating part of the highway from its original site in downtown Selma to an area just at the edge of town, it also destroyed the homes along Nebraska Street. Also lost in this moment of rural infrastructure "improvements" were many

Figure 6.12 Mother Lucy. Courtesy of Ester Hernández.

of the small alleys, canals, and pathways that adjoined the Selma and Dinuba houses, sites where a young artist's creativity and imagination flourished amid the mud, stones, and plant and animal life she would see in her adventures. As seen in *California Special* (1988)—and the accompanying photograph taken outside the Dinuba house—the aesthetics of commercial industry would merge with these vernacular histories in the form of a child's dress repurposed from a cloth sack from the market in Fresno where Hernández and her mother would drive to together (Figures 6.13 and 6.14). These engagements with popular culture, family story, Mexican imagery, and the vernacular world of the garden and the ditch all circled round and round the raisin industry—which, thanks to the marketing tradition inaugurated by Martin Kearney, had its own visuality. It is to that body of images we now turn.

By the 1960s—just as Cesar Chavez was challenging the industry around labor issues—new revelations about the dangers of chemical technology and a heightened ecological consciousness posed another set of challenges. Rachel Carson's 1962 book *Silent Spring* offered a particularly salient rallying cry for

Figure 6.13 (*top*) Ester at the Dinuba house (c. 1950). Courtesy of Ester Hernández.

Figure 6.14 (*bottom*) *California Special* (1988). Illustration by Ester Hernández.

questioning pesticide use—which had become pervasive in the valley's grape fields and continued throughout the 1970s. It was at this long moment of turmoil—labor organizing in the fields, Chicana/o art and activism in the cities, the stirrings of the environmental movement—that Hernández made one of those journeys from the Bay Area back to Dinuba with her son in 1980.

Walking in the door of the little house at 141 South P Street, she found her mother, Luz, standing at the stove boiling water. "I thought that was kind of strange," she recalled, given how hot the valley is that time of year. Her mother showed Hernández a notice from the city notifying residents that the city's wells were polluted ("City of Dinuba Notice"). They talked for a long time about health and justice, the first time they had ever done so. Dinuba had been contaminated with pesticides for twenty-five to thirty years, and she realized that she and her family "had drunk and bathed in this water." "It kind of stayed with me, it bothered me," remembered Hernández ("City of Dinuba Notice"). Though there was perhaps the urge to just go back to the city and forget about it, she did not. For two years it haunted her, keeping her up at night.

Eager to understand the extent to which Dinuba groundwater was polluted, Hernández began researching the issue. After talking with city and state public health officials, she learned that on November 1, 1980, the City of Dinuba, California, had issued a public notice to "All Consumers of the City of Dinuba Water System" announcing that "with the advent of cool weather, it [was] no longer necessary for the City to use the four contaminated wells" ("City of Dinuba Notice"). Further research revealed that the closing of the four polluted wells had come after months of pressure by local activists and UC Berkeley environmental scientists who were concerned that the California Department of Health Services (CDHS) was not doing enough to address the larger problem of groundwater contamination in the Central Valley. These advocates argued that the CDHS water rationing program implemented with the four remaining "clean" wells, encouraging residents to purchase bottled water or boil their tap water, obscured a significant fact: Dinuba, "Raisinland, USA," a predominately Chicana/o community in the Central Valley, had been drinking polluted water for over twenty-five years (Hernández, "Information Regarding Dinuba, CA").

Hernández knew she wanted to do a piece on the issue of pollution and the raisin industry, particularly its effects on Mexican American women, but she didn't know what. Then, she recalls, "one day I was driving back to see my mom, driving down the little country road . . . and, oh my God! There it is: The Sun Maid raisin signs at the edge of each vineyard. What is it? How can I unmask it? What can I say?" It bothered her that "they claimed to be natural but they're not" ("Personal Interview 1"). It did not take her long to recall Posada's calaveras from the revolution era, and as she researched them, Hernández became intrigued by how alive they were amid such death and destruction. Not surprisingly, she was also always touched by Posada's origins in her own town of Aguascalientes, the politically engaged and artistically inclined city in the interior that was important during the revolution as a strategic organizing site—so much so that her family lost their carpentry workshop near the town square. "I always fantasize [that Posada] made a poster for my grandfather's school!" ("Personal Interview 1").

Her family helped her assemble local news clippings about the raisin industry, Sun Maid, and water pollution issues as she developed the piece ("Personal Interview 1"). Research with UC Berkeley helped her learn more about the water table issues, and their researchers confirmed that the city had long known about the pollution but had not notified residents. Her political motivation came from her early work as a UC Berkeley student, and one might draw a direct line back to the first piece she contributed to student newspapers, an etching-style drawing that depicted a pollution dispute regarding mercury poisoning among First Nations people in Canada. It was the first time she had heard the term "environmental racism," and she started to feel a responsibility to pass this kind of information on to viewers.

A Poster, 1982

Sun Mad, then, is as much about a critique of pesticide use—and its harmful effects on the people and places that make up the Latinx cultural landscape—as it is about the aesthetics of place, work, and memory. It came together around Hernández's political coming-to-consciousness around both Chicana/o and environmental politics, a nostalgic engagement with the traditions of Mexican political art in the form of Posada's calaveras, and a strong awareness of the local environments—her house and garden and her town. The red bonnet called to mind the Okies she worked with in the fields as a young girl. The dress has a strong resemblance to the ones her mother wore as a young woman in Selma as part of the Mexican dance troupes popular during the day, which Hernández would later turn into an installation piece. Most of all, it was the fields and factories of Dinuba that generated the impetus for *Sun Mad*. In those fields, Mexican-heritage workers labored while chemical pollution seeped into their groundwater. Dinuba and Sun Maid leaders knew this and were willing to sacrifice the land, the people, and the town. Was this not enough to drive one "sun mad"?

Hernández hand-lettered the first edition without the support of a computer or advanced drafting tools: "It was horrible, I went nuts!" ("Personal Interview 1"). And the initial response was no response at all. She at first thought that she had made a mistake. But historian and curator Shifra Goldman included it in a national exhibit and featured it in her writings, helping create a buzz and an engaged critical reception. It felt to Hernández like it was ten years or so before the image really caught on in shows and publications. Her sense was that it was too edgy, too direct. Once it caught, though, *Sun Mad* rapidly became

Figure 6.15 Ester and Luz Hernández in the Dinuba garden (c. 1975). Courtesy of Ester Hernández.

canonical. By the 1990s, it was almost a free-floating signifier, mobilized as both a Chicana/o arts object and an astute environmental critique.

While it is revelatory on all these counts, *Sun Mad*'s historical contexts—family history, intimate landscapes, and aesthetic vocabularies—help explain the work as a particular thing: a piece of art that reveals the Chicana/o vernacular rural landscape as aesthetic ground, inspiration, and memory. Even in the case of a cosmopolitan urbane Bay Area artist like Hernández, the rural vernacular anchors her politics and artistry—and indeed offers a powerful way of seeing the connections between the two. When Hernández walked out of her mother's kitchen, left behind Luz's boiling water, and stepped into the garden (Figure 6.15); when she drove into and out of Dinuba; when she descended from Pacheco Pass—in each case, Sun Maid structured her life. The factory loomed above the house. The storage sheds and service roads surrounded the town. The fields stretched out below her. In a very real sense, only Hernández could have made *Sun Mad*, an important environmental text that helps document and preserve how the mid-twentieth-century rural Chicanx landscape changed over time in California's Great Central Valley.

NOTES

1. See, for example, *La Virgen de Guadalupe Defendiendo Los Derechos de Los Xicanos*.

2. For examples of critics who detail these environmental justice and ecofeminist concerns, see Bullard and Doyle; Pardo.

3. See also Marez; Hutchison; Gaspar de Alba.

4. *Sun Mad* has enjoyed display at a wide number of national and regional museums, including the Legion of Honor (San Francisco), the Smithsonian American Art Museum (Washington, DC), the Crocker Museum (Sacramento), the National Museum of Mexican Art (Chicago), the Autry National Center (Los Angeles), the Oakland Museum of California (Oakland), the California Historical Society (San Francisco), El Museo del Barrio (New York City), Galeria de la Raza (San Francisco), the National Hispanic Cultural Center (Albuquerque), and the Los Angeles County Museum of Art (LACMA). *Sun Mad* has also been included in several major permanent collections, including the Museum of Contemporary Native Art, Institute of American Indian Arts (Santa Fe, NM); the Victoria and Albert Museum (London); the University of California Los Angeles, UCLA Chicano Art Collection (Los Angeles); the Oakland Museum of California (Oakland); the Library of Congress, Permanent Collection, Prints and Photographs (Washington, DC); Cheech Marin, Chicano/a Collection (Santa Monica, CA); the National Museum of Art—Smithsonian Institute (Washington, DC); Museo Casa Estudio Diego Rivera and Frida Kahlo, Permanent Collection (Mexico City); the Bronx Museum of the Arts (New York City); the Mexican Museum (San Francisco); the San Francisco Museum of Modern Art (San Francisco); Museo del Barrio (New York City); and the National Museum of Mexican Art (Chicago).

5. For an overview, see Stoll. For a specific account of how the grape industry took hold among early growers in the Fresno area, see Eisen.

6. For more on the geology of the Sierra Nevada, see Farquhar.

7. For more on Central Valley development, especially as it relates to water infrastructure, see Bull; Page and LeBlanc.

8. In *Artificial Love: A Story of Machines and Architecture*, Paul Shepheard argues that the sculptural qualities of these buildings and machines—and the relation their workers and neighbors develop with them—provide important clues into individual and community values and desire. For more on how these relationships shaped an earlier generation of industry, or how "the mill resembles a meeting house" in New England, see Stilgoe, especially pp. 324–333.

9. Hernández further explains that an item missing from the drawing is a small "rasquache" shed built by her father Simon to store his tools and his wife Luz's gardening supplies ("Personal Interview 2"). Following critic Tomas Ybarra-Frausto's Chicana/o aesthetic sensibility, rasquachismo, or a "something out of nothing" quality (Barnet-Sanchez), this informal feature of their everyday built environment—which was remembered fondly by Hernández—might be imagined as an example of Chicana/o place-making, where something as simple as the memory of a tiny shed placed behind a small farmworker's house several decades in the past could evoke a deeply held set of cultural memories about what it felt like to be in that backyard, during that time and place.

10. For discussion of her early connections to the lower San Joaquin Valley landscape, particularly the night sky, see Hernández's "Keynote Address" to the Daughters of the Shaking Earth: Bay Area Latina Artists and the Environment Symposium.

11. For an overview of this wider effort to bring the everyday stories of Mexican-heritage women into wider view, see also Ruiz, *From Out of the Shadows: Mexican Women in Twentieth-Century America*. For an account of how Mexican-heritage gardens and yards had shaped migrant vernacular landscapes, see Hondagneu-Sotelo. For a comprehensive overview of garden aesthetics, architecture, and cultural practices, see Francis and Hester; Leslie and Hunt.

12. For more on the spiritual dimensions of this installation, see Pérez, especially p. 57. For an account of how this piece fits into the larger tradition of Chicana home altars, see Mesa-Bains.

WORKS CITED

Barnet-Sanchez, Holly. "Tomás Ybarra-Frausto and Amalia Mesa-Bains: A Critical Discourse from Within." *Art Journal*, vol. 64, no. 4, 2005, pp. 91–93.

Blackwell, Maylei. "Women Who Make Their Own Worlds: The Life and Work of Ester Hernández." *Chicana Movidas: New Narratives of Activism and Feminism in the Movement Era*, edited by Dionne Espinoza et al., U of Texas P, 2018, pp. 138–158.

Bull, William B. "Alluvial Fans and Near-Surface Subsidence in Western Fresno County, California." USGS Professional Paper, 1964.

Bullard, Robert D., editor. *Unequal Protection: Environmental Justice and Communities of Color*. Sierra Club Books, 1994.

Carson, Rachel. *Silent Spring*. Boston, MA: Houghton Mifflin Harcourt, 2002.

The Cosmic Cruise. Online Archive of California, https://oac.cdlib.org/ark:/13030/hb1d5nb1x5/?brand=oac4&layout=metadata. Accessed 20 Nov. 2018.

Eisen, Gustavus A. *The Raisin Industry: A Practical Treatise on the Raisin Grapes, Their History, Culture and Curing*. H. S. Crocker, 1890.

Farquhar, Francis Peloubet. *History of the Sierra Nevada*. U of California P, 1966.

Francis, Mark, and Randolph T. Hester, editors. *The Meaning of Gardens: Idea, Place, and Action*. The MIT Press, 1990.
Gaspar de Alba, Alicia. *Chicano Art Inside/Outside the Master's House: Cultural Politics and the CARA Exhibition*. U of Texas P, 1998.
Gudde, Erwin Gustav. *1,000 California Place Names: Their Origin and Meaning. Based on California Place Names, a Geographic Dictionary*. U of California P, 1947.
Hernández, Ester. "Artist's Statement." 1998. Ester Hernández Papers, Stanford Special Collections, Box 71, Folder 9.
———. "City of Dinuba Notice." Ester Hernández Papers, Stanford Special Collections, Series 4, Box 45, Folder 10.
———. *Cosmic Cruise*. 1990. Ester Hernández Papers, Stanford Special Collections, Map Folder 13.
———. "Information Regarding Dinuba, CA: News Articles, Slides, Etc." Ester Hernández Papers, Stanford Special Collections, Series 4, Box 43, Folder 8.
———. "Keynote Address." Daughters of the Shaking Earth: Bay Area Latina Artists and the Environment Symposium, 12 May 2012.
———. *La Ofrenda*. 1988. Ester Hernández Papers, Stanford Special Collections, Map Folder 12.
———. "Personal Interview 1." San Francisco, California, 21 Nov. 2010.
———. "Personal Interview 2." San Francisco, California, 28 Sept. 2014.
———. *Sun Mad*. 1982. Ester Hernández Papers, Stanford Special Collections, Flat Box 10.
Hill, Mary. *Geology of the Sierra Nevada*. U of California P, 2006.
Hondagneu-Sotelo, Pierrette. *Paradise Transplanted: Migration and the Making of California Gardens*. U of California P, 2014.
Hoover, Mildred Brooke, and Douglas E. Kyle. *Historic Spots in California*. 4th ed., Stanford UP, 1990.
Hutchison, Sharla. "Recoding Consumer Culture: Ester Hernández, Helena María Viramontes, and the Farmworker Cause." *Journal of Popular Culture*, vol. 46, no. 5, 2013, pp. 973–990.
Leslie, Michael, and John Dixon Hunt. *A Cultural History of Gardens*. Bloomsbury, 2013.
Marez, Curtis. *Farm Worker Futurism: Speculative Technologies of Resistance*. U of Minnesota P, 2016.
Mesa-Bains, Amalia. "Exhibit Statement" in *Imagenes E Historias/Images and Histories: Chicana Altar-Inspired Art*, Catalogue, Constance Cortez, ed. Tufts University, Medford, MA, 1999.
Muir, John. *The Yosemite*. Century, 1912.
Ontiveros, Randy J. *In the Spirit of a New People: The Cultural Politics of the Chicano Movement*. New York UP, 2013.
Page, Roland W., and R. A. LeBlanc. "Geology, Hydrology, and Water Quality in the Fresno Area, California." U.S. Geological Survey, https://ngmdb.usgs.gov/Prodesc/proddesc_53766.htm. Accessed 18 Nov. 2018.
Pardo, Mary S. *Mexican American Women Activists: Identity and Resistance in Two Los Angeles Communities*. Temple UP, 1998.
Pérez, Laura Elisa. *Chicana Art: The Politics of Spiritual and Aesthetic Altarities*. Duke UP, 2007.
Ruiz, Vicki, editor. "Claiming Public Space at Work, Church, and Neighborhood." *Las Obreras: Chicana Politics of Work and Family*, UCLA Chicano Studies Research Center, 2000, pp. 13–39.

———. *From Out of the Shadows: Mexican Women in Twentieth-Century America*. Oxford UP, 1998.
Shepheard, Paul. *Artificial Love: A Story of Machines and Architecture*. The MIT Press, 2003.
Social and Public Arts Resource Center Venice, Los Angeles. *Chicana Voices and Visions: A National Exhibit of Women Artists: 27 Artists from Arizona, California, Colorado, Michigan, New Mexico, and Texas*. Social and Public Arts Resource Center, Venice, California, 3 Dec. 1983 to 21 Jan. 1984.
Stilgoe, John R. *Common Landscape of America, 1580 to 1845*. Yale UP, 1982.
Stoll, Steven. *The Fruits of Natural Advantage: Making the Industrial Countryside in California*. U of California P, 1998.
Worster, Donald. *A Passion for Nature: The Life of John Muir*. Oxford UP, 2008.

7

"An Organic Being in the Middle of Chicago"

An Interview with Ana Castillo

Priscilla Solis Ybarra
and Sarah D. Wald

Ana Castillo (1953–present) was born and raised in Chicago, Illinois. Primarily known as a writer, she originally trained as a visual artist, and she has recently returned to drawing and painting (see book cover). Her writings summon images as vibrant as her visual art works. Her written language is often beautiful, sometimes shocking, and always compelling. Her breadth of genre—from poetry to the academic essay to drawing and painting—reveal her commitment to constant creativity. But it is her novels that stand out most to critics and fans alike. Her work was among the earliest of Latinx literature to catch the attention of ecocritics, namely her novel *So Far from God* and its portrayal of toxic contamination and environmental injustice. Her work consistently engages with Latinx culture's integration with and respect for the natural environment. In this interview we discuss the influence of her paternal grandmother's curanderismo, the limits of conventional gender roles, and prospects for change in consumerist and exploitative practices. The second of five interviews with writers included in this volume, this conversation fits well within the theme of "Place" explored in this section's chapters, as Castillo directly discusses her sensitivity to neoliberalism's power to shape lived experiences, including one's relation to the local and the global.

We spoke in Chicago in November 2017 on the day before a beautiful snowfall covered the city. She was visiting the city to moderate a panel about her work at the American Studies Association convention and to spend time with her family. She now resides in both New York City and eastern New Mexico. It was an honor to speak with her in her hometown. Sometimes it felt the city was feeding her memories through the high-rise hotel windows we sat next to during our conversation. Her recent memoir, *Black Dove: Mamá, Mi'jo and Me*, offers an intimate view of this influential and foundational Chicana writer. In this interview, we explore some details she shared in that book and discuss her many contributions to literature and cultural studies.

PY: *You write in your memoir,* Black Dove, *that you remain skeptical about organized religion but that you gain solace from your spirituality. You say that "one aspect" of your "spirituality comes from nature, my environment, and people whose priority it is to respect life on the planet" (183). How did this develop for you? Was it something that you remember since your childhood, was it something that developed gradually over time, or was it something that came to you later in life?*

AC: I was a young Latina-identified aspiring artist, writer, and poet of my generation when there was nothing that came before. With regards to us in the U.S. media or in textbooks to serve as examples, it was blank. At a certain point in my midtwenties, I was very disillusioned with the sexism, misogyny, and homophobia that were present amongst Latino activists. I had burnt out, and I had to step back to evaluate for myself what happened. They were struggling toward something in society that would bring us all together, but I realized that in terms of gender and sexuality, we were being separated. It was a time when the Left subscribed to some form of Marxism. Feminism, for working-class women of color, was considered a luxury.

It was one of those moments where you decide either to go this way or go that way. I decided that rather than to say, "I'm no longer going to care anything about the whole Latino movement or the Chicano movement because I have had terrible experiences (with men)," I decided to ask myself, who believed she was as hardworking as anyone to make things happen, "What's the variable?" The variable was quite often—in whatever context I considered—that I was a woman; I was a female. Sometimes I was the only woman at the meeting. Sometimes I was the only woman, *and* I was the one writing the grants. It was only men that were taking the credit. It was also the fact that when you're a young woman in your twenties, probably every single one of those men (who is not gay) in your activist group is hitting on you. They were crossing boundaries at a time in which those things weren't recognized as dead wrong, not just inappropriate in work spaces. Although there are laws now, we still live in those times.

The experience made me step back and think about myself as a human being. Since I was viewed on the surface as an indigenous, working-class woman, I reflected on what I came with into this world. Biologically speaking, I came into this world with a reproductive system. This basic view made me start thinking about my body. I became this organic being in the middle of Chicago. I wasn't out on a farm helping cows give birth or having some connection with nature and knowing what happens with the harvest [laughter]. I was in an asphalt environment. But I still made that connection for myself. I was asking, intellectually, "What happened that the human woman is not allowed to participate fully and fairly in society? Where did this go so wrong?"

I was raised a Catholic. My parents were not devout; they rarely went to church. But they were Catholic for cultural reasons and brought that to their children. So that's the only religious background that I had. I read the Bible since I was a child mostly for its storytelling. What's the prominent theme there? It's the patriarchs. As a young intellectual, I began to make connections with women's roles versus the males. The men saw themselves as superior to women and justified it in their writings and laws and sealed it with making it their God's word. The difference, for me, however, was the fact that women were able to procreate and men could not. What men could do was build up, reach for the heavens, and destroy what was on Earth. So they built obelisks and high rises. Everything that went into the ground, that existed deep in the ocean, was seen as negative, but which is everything that we eat and that goes back into the earth to continue to sustain us. Lo and behold! Women, the procreator of the species, was associated with negativity. There's more to this analysis, economics related, but we are talking here about spirituality.

In those days, I was thinking about my connection with everything that nourished our world. We have to ask ourselves, are we destroying more than we are creating? And when I think even now about destruction, I'm thinking about patriarchy because patriarchy went in the direction of military might and greed. When you exploit your resources, then you're destroying the rest of us who are not satisfied with accumulating material power and exercising greed, and we end up being part of the collateral damage. We're being destroyed along with everything else that's being pushed aside, people of color, women, children, animals, species of all kinds—we're part of that because we haven't joined the patriarchy.

PY: *It sounds like you created a spirituality that's alternative to anything that was presented to you. You had to come up with your own vision. What experiences helped shape that spirituality?*

AC: Although I was born and raised in Chicago, when I graduated from college, I got on a bus and went to join Cesar Chavez and the United Farm Workers in California and became a "Chicana." And they thought, "Oh, a Chicana from Chicago?" [laughter] What could I possibly know about the fields? I come from a very humble family. From very early on, I had family members, including my siblings, who worked in the fields out here in Indiana in the summer. My mother didn't send them, may she rest in peace, to summer camp. She sent them out to work in the fields to pick tomatoes. I was much younger than they were, so I got away with not going out there, too. But I did visit the labor camps.

The other experience that impacted me was my grandmother's vocation as a curandera [spiritual healer]. My paternal abuelita that raised me, may she rest in peace, and to whom I attribute teaching me how to love unconditionally, was a curandera here in Chicago. She was also a leader in her community. When she passed away it was announced on the radio—"Doña Jovita passed away"—so that all the people knew. They came to our modest flat in the back building where she made tortillas and frijoles every day, y sobaba. Era, entre otras cosas, una sobadora [She was, among other things, a masseuse.]

One of my memories is her growing herbs in coffee cans in our flat. Growing up very poor in Texas and in California, you still had a yard; you knew what a horse looked like [laughter]. I didn't know anything like that at all where I was living. But my grandmother brought those ideas with her. She was like the old woman in *One Hundred Years of Solitude*. I don't know how old she was. She was very old. I don't think she was my biological grandmother. I think she may have been my great-grandmother. She was also a midwife. Perhaps she brought my father into the world and kept the baby if the mother, for whatever reason, had been unable to do so. My abuelita came from the days of Pancho Villa; she had these really old ways. She grew todas las hierbas [all the herbs] she needed for her healing and for tea. Children are given chamomile and spearmint teas for settling their tummies. I was given that, for sure. But I was given coffee as a daily beverage. Go figure. Those of us who have had the privilege to be inducted as healers and curanderas into our communities understand that children are often assistants to our medicine people because of their pure hearts. As a small child, my grandmother had me next to her, helping her with healing. I have very powerful memories of that time in my early childhood.

I also understand that there was a connection between her work setting bones and the taking in of children that were abandoned. I think my father was one of them, actually. She would take in other children during the time I was growing up. All of that caring. I understood that this is part of a tradition; this is how it's done among our people who come from the campos [fields], who often must fend for themselves. It was embedded into me in Chicago as a child.

Years later, fast-forward, I moved to New Mexico by myself for the first time and wrote *So Far from God*, which I did very soon after I moved there. I wrote it in a matter of months. Later on when I moved to southern New Mexico, I wrote *The Guardians*. It's not just Ana Castillo, this Chicana from Chicago, who puts these stories together, out of her imagination. I'm connected to a big picture. The big picture is our big history as Mexicans, as Latinos, as mestizos, as indigenous people who have been crossing back and forth in North America for centuries. We have a long history here, and it didn't start two hundred years ago. Our families, our stories that we've passed on, our ways of using language, English, Spanish, and many indigenous languages, have been shared amongst each other for many generations. It's a testimony to our fortitude that we haven't forgotten our roots. Although I was born and raised in Chicago and I went to school in Chicago, our cultural legacies are not totally unfamiliar to me.

PY: *I love that sense of connection between the garden of hierbas [herbs] in the windowsill in Chicago and the desert in New Mexico.*
AC: I think that sometimes people wonder, "Well, how can she be from Chicago and write about New Mexico?" The way I see it is that the people that move to the North, that come to Chicago, to Michigan, to Kansas, the Midwest, to Washington state and so on . . . we're all part of one family that's been migrating over and over again. Some stayed, some came and went, and new ones came. And it's layering of generations communicating with each other. That's what I speak to when I talk in my narratives, in my stories, through one character. I always think of her as many of us. She brings many of our stories together. And they are, for the record, fictitious characters.

PY: *I'm also intrigued with what you said about getting on a bus and going to join Cesar Chavez. Can you say more about that experience?*
AC: Well, I went to two years of community college and, with great determination, transferred to a university in the city of Chicago. I was working while going to school. Every year of my life since I was sixteen years old, I became more politically aware of who I was as a brown woman. By the time I graduated from college, I just couldn't wait to go and join my people. I mean, there were Latinos in Chicago. But I felt that the root of the Chicano movement, the heart of it, was in California. I started doing some volunteer work with the United Farm Workers while I was still in college here. I participated in protests, passed out leaflets, and did the boycotts. That was really important, but I thought, "I've just got to get over there and check it out." I didn't even go to my graduation. My parents weren't very acknowledging of my whole college experience anyway or anything. I just thought, "It's time for me to go and do what I have to do."

PY: *What happened when you got there? Did you reach out to the United Farm Workers?*
AC: I didn't so much reach out as it was happening all around me. I actually did get to meet Cesar Chavez—one of many volunteers who met him. I

traveled all over Northern California. Keep in mind, those were also hitchhiking days, so I hitchhiked constantly by myself from there to San Francisco and back every weekend. I went all over the place, and it was in that context with other Chicano organizers and activists that I began to solidify my identity as a Chicana. There was an older woman who was working out in the fields as an organizer. I was going to give a reading somewhere, and she introduced me at the event as "this Chicana from Chicago." It was the first time that somebody introduced me as a Chicana. I was so surprised—"I'm a Chicana?" Yes, okay. It was a very embracing time.

PY: *What an amazing historical moment to experience. Did you meet Dolores Huerta too?*

AC: I met Dolores personally a few years later. We're good friends now, and I'm friends with a couple of her daughters. The very first time that I met her, we were on a panel together for MALCS [Mujeres Activas En Letras y Cambios Sociales]. By then, I was a single mom, and I had this three-year-old running around. I had to get off the panel to run and go catch up to him, and she said, "That's okay. I'm so used to that with my child" [laughter]. At that time, I didn't know she had eleven children. Todos mis respetos [I have total respect] for everything she has done. Her youngest is my son's age. I would say that Dolores, from the mid-1980s onward to the present, and certainly with her daughters, began to see what was developing in terms of Chicana feminism. Before that, with her generation, it was more of a socialist agenda. I cannot even begin to imagine how difficult it was for her in that environment with union organizing. There wasn't anything talking about women in a special context. Now we have a different way of looking at and thinking about our social justice organizing, whereas before, it was about the material things that we needed, and that's all you could really talk about.

SW: *Speaking of social justice and intersectionality, how do you feel about the way ecocritics and environmentalists have taken up your work? Priscilla and I were both at the Association for the Study of Literature and Environment's 2005 conference in Eugene and saw you give this wonderful keynote address there. We're interested in how you feel about your work being taken up as "environmental" by environmentalists.*

AC: I am absolutely honored, and I feel very glad in my heart that other people in other disciplines see value in the stories that I have told. Moving up to the end of 2017 and the times that we are living in right now, I think that it is even more critical that we remind people of the dangerous moment that we are in. We are at a critical time in terms of clean air and water, fracking, toxic waste, how you live your daily life, and many other areas. I feel privileged and honored that people who devote their lives to these issues would find value in the stories that I've told.

Did I tell those stories intentionally with regards to environmentalism and other social issues? Yes, I did. Because again, as a woman, and as a woman of color, and as a Mexican Chicana who has ancestral history on both sides of the border, I'm proud and I'm cognizant of the work that my ancestors have done, that my parents, that my grandparents did to contribute to the continuance of nurturing our society and our culture. We're doing it now.

PY: *You've spoken in these past couple of responses about your mestiza identity. You have referred to two aspects of that identity—your connection to indigeneity and your connection to land. But there is a colonial history with that connection to the land that conflicts with our indigenous roots as mestizas, too. How do you confront that particular tension within mestiza identity?*

AC: Speaking about northern New Mexico and *So Far from God*, I had to step back. By the time I moved to New Mexico, I absolutely identified as a Chicana. I was thirty-nine when I wrote *So Far from God*. In terms of identity, this is where that part of my history separates from northern New Mexico history. The Hispano families that I knew were very proud of their Spanish heritage to the extent that they did not readily acknowledge that they had any indigenous blood at all—even after hundreds of years of being there, even though they're right there with indigenous people. I respect the history of that area. That's their history.

Having said that, they are also part of the Chicano experience now. They are definitely not Anglo. They know they're not Anglo. They're not Black. They have the tradition of being looked at as Mexicans later on, or as Hispanos, and they speak Spanish, and we share that as Chicano/as. In that sense, there is commonality in culture. Also, they are colonized people. Spaniards came here. Then they got kicked out when Mexico declared its independence from Spain. And then the United States came, the Anglos from New England, and took over. For a long time, the Nuevo Mejicanos had land, and they were able to keep up a lot of their heritage. But then they were bamboozled considerably by the Anglos.

We share that history of colonization and understand that we're not part of mainstream or dominant culture. The Anglo took over. We have that in common along with any other colonized people. Filipinos came to work; Chinese came to work out in the fields—they're also part of that history of working agriculture and working the railroads. There's a lot of overlap with people of color and with poor people, for that matter. Our ethnicities and cultures may vary, but we share a class history here. We share prejudices against our communities.

PY: *So, what you really identify with in the mestizo identity is the experience of colonization?*

AC: Exactly. And of womanhood—the ways that in the process of colonization you are seen as a woman with a womb, whether or not it works. I'm thinking about Puerto Rico and the Taino Indians that were invaded and the stories I have read about the women committing suicide and eating dirt rather than continuing to exist under those conditions. That's how women are looked at: as a procreator and not for the intellectual contributions we make to society, at least historically speaking. I think in my midtwenties when I made those connections, I made them far and wide all the time, and I see so many more connections with people than I see differences because of that.

PY: *Speaking of identity—do you identify as an environmentalist?*

AC: I'm not an environmentalist in the sense of joining environmental organizations. I definitely live my life with the hope and ambition of reducing my own personal carbon footprint and, in every way that I can, to be cognizant of the world that I live in. I do that every day. I do a whole range of things on an everyday basis like not wasting food to using well water at my ranchito, to recycling and composting. The ranchito, a spread of desert in fact, where nothing grows but cactus, is a lifestyle that I created for myself. I think it is a luxury to be able to recycle that way. I made it my home many years ago, giving up a steady job in a city. Consequently, I don't have things that a lot of other people have—like a pension, for example. I don't have a regular income. I create an income by public speaking, offering writing workshops and such. I've managed from month to month for a long time.

So if you want to say being an environmentalist is how you live your life versus it being your profession, I am one. We are living in a country and time when it may be said that the federal government has declared an all-out war against conservation and preservation on air, land, and sea, nature, and humanity. Anything and everything one does in favor of our resources is important.

We may also refer to environmentalism to do with social issues. We may point to all levels of society and see how our environmental injustice affects our daily lives. Cancer (I am a breast cancer survivor) is rampant. What groups does cancer affect in some cases at suspiciously high rates? I raised a young man of color in the city of Chicago. One of the issues we experienced was when he was beaten up by the police as a late teen. The rage, stress, pain, and confusion—these experiences affect the victim, a young, brown man, and his family (in this case, his single mother, me) go largely unrecognized. Issues like racism and its effects are connected with our environment. Communities of the poor are often ridden with toxic waste dumping, toxic emissions, contaminated water, et cetera. To advocate against social injustice, in my view, is also a kind of environmentalism.

Spiritually speaking, on that small patch of desert land where I've made my home, I also constructed an adobe chapel for meditation and gatherings with like-minded Xicanas, medicine people, et cetera. I see my life and spirituality as connected with environmental issues.

As a lifestyle, I cannot see things going to waste or of abusing anything in our environment, whatever it might be, in any context. I won't say that I never take a fly swatter in my house and use it [laughter]. I wouldn't go that far. I think that I'm an environmentalist in practice and consciousness. I will always bring the issues that I think represent a grave injustice to the planet and to humanity into my stories.

SW: *It's apparent in your work all of the ways that food comes up and particularly the ways it overlaps with this concern we have now about farming and healthy eating, but also food justice and toxicity in the food chain. I'd love to hear you talk more about the ways you think about food from consumption to production in your work.*

AC: The presence of food in my books has been pointed out to me, and I think, "That's true." I'm always talking about food in *So Far from God*. In that story about a culture and tradition, it is tied to the land and the economic stability once based on ranching and farming. In *Give It To Me*, a contemporary novel about a middle-aged woman moving around the U.S., somebody was saying the character was anorexic because she's throwing up. I thought, "Really?" Instead, I suggest, it may have to do with the crisis and philosophical turmoil she goes through. *Give It To Me* is about a character who is displaced in almost every way. The Dalai Lama speaks to her at one point to advise her on life's meaning. Perhaps then, the relationship with food and our connections to the earth, place, community is key in my writing.

When you think about it, food is the base of all life. In *So Far from God*, Sophia was a butcher. It's a small community. She doesn't have one hundred thousand acres to maintain to make billions of dollars so she can go and do other gross and greedy things for herself and her family while contaminating the air and the land with all this livestock. In that context, the unfortunate livestock are having a horrible quality of life, and the food that we are eating is making our children go into puberty at seven and eight years old. Ammonia emissions from livestock contribute to air pollution. Finally, spiritually we may also reflect on the cruelty of raising livestock for the sole pleasure of people's tastes and not for survival. It's a whole cycle of sustainability, our own and the earth's.

Although these issues are critical to me, in everyday life I'm not a self-righteous, preachy person. How you live your life and your choices are not my business. I don't like people to tell me how to live, either. But in my writing and in my storytelling, poetry, and in my thinking, I can put out those ideas. People can take away from it what they want. For me, food—which is associated with culture, tradition, history, with memories, with sensuality—all of those things—is very much who we are. But today, in a globalized economy, how we produce food is also part of the society that we are creating. I wonder why are we making certain choices over other choices? Invariably, it's always about the monetary profit for very few people, not for the consumers and not for the benefit of the planet.

SW: Contamination and toxicity are also constant themes in your novels from the death of Fe in So Far from God *to the asthma suffered by Miguel's son in* The Guardians. *How do you understand issues of contamination and pollution? Why foreground them, for example, in a novel like* The Guardians *that more directly is focusing on immigration and the humanity of people without papers? What relationship do you see between issues of immigration and migration and these issues of environmental contamination?*

AC: If we don't have a planet, theoretically or ideologically, where do we go from there? If we don't have healthy people, where do we as a society go from there? We cannot talk about any kind of change in democracy if we don't have decent food, clean air, and soil growing uncontaminated produce. These are all things that are becoming too rare. . . . Where do you go from there when you don't have those fundamental things to sustain a healthy society? Where do you migrate to when you're going to migrate to a country for "a better life" in which your children are going to become sick?

I think so much about interconnectedness. It has to do with Mother Earth and my early identification with being female and who could procreate or at least was looked to for that purpose. If procreating wasn't for me, then what else would I give? What might I create? What would I produce? I didn't think the opposite, which would be, "What am I going to destroy? What am I going to take away from others or the planet and, for my own selfish gain, exploit?"

Regarding your question about toxic waste and toxic poisoning, women working in the field are exposed to the possibility of giving birth to children with birth defects, but also, many poor communities are susceptible to toxic exposure through land and waste water dumping. Their children may be born without arms and legs, cancer, et cetera. Throughout all my work as a Chicana, I'm asking, "Who does that happen to?" It didn't happen to Melania Trump or her son. It happens time and time again to poor women! Today we still have the same statistic that we had when I first wrote *Massacre of the Dreamers* in the late 1980s. Eighty percent of the world's impoverished workforce are women of color and children of color.

They work in the Trump factories in Mexico. Who is dispensable on this planet? The poor and needy who must work under whatever circumstances are available to them at whatever equally atrocious pay in order to keep their families alive. Apparently, according to the current administration, the planet is also dispensable.

I see those connections without trying to fall into some cliché or even mythological way of thinking that associates all that is feminine to be with "Mother Earth." The world that we live in denigrates and dismisses all that is feminine inasmuch as its true power and value are always diminished; this is also associated with the earth. This is the reality that I feel that we live in and how I experience it.

PY: *We have been talking about environmentalism and social justice. The two go hand-in-hand. Every time we ask you about one, the other one comes up. Do you find that environmentalism is fundamentally about social justice or that justice is fundamentally about our relationship with the planet?*

AC: Environmentalism has to come under the struggle of social justice because if it doesn't, we won't do anything about it. Those of us who have some consciousness and are striving towards some form of democracy need to look to not just human rights but to the rights of all living things on this planet. We know that, as we speak, those values are being left by the wayside intentionally in favor of greed, might, and profit. We have to make it a political issue. It cannot be any other way. When it isn't, it always remains a question of exploitation and profit for very few, and that exploitation includes of the planet. What I try to do is level criticism at the status quo, a very old status quo of elite. That's how I see what I'm doing also when I talk about the exploitation of our natural resources, which has been going on for a long time.

PY: *What role do you see for Chicana/o/x cultural production in this historical or political moment that we're in right now? And I have a quote of yours from a past interview, from 1997, so I'll read that out to you. You said in regard to Latina identity, "My projection of our future is that it's not so much for us to assimilate and be accepted by society, but for us to bring society to the fold, bring the dominant society, bring men of all backgrounds to our way of thinking because we have in our psyches and in our bodies and in our memories and in our histories everything possible to make a different world" (Saeta).*

AC: I'm glad that past self said that to me right now because more than ever I believe that those of us with consciousness and with heart, as difficult as it is, we still have it in our bodies, and in our psyches, and our memories to turn this around, to be able to turn around the enormous amount of damage that we are doing to the earth—to the ocean and the air, everything. Those people who have consciousness, who are humble people, who aren't wanting glory and power for themselves, can still make a difference. I think about what I'd be willing to do to turn things in the opposite direction. I have found it enormously distressing and tragic that we are continuing to move in the other direction in these last twenty years since that statement. In my worst nightmare, I would not have wanted to reach this place where we are right now.

I'm glad to hear that voice from twenty years ago because I still believe that statement would be the truth if we had been able to make some of it come to pass. Toward that end I think that our job is bigger and more critical right now. I don't know that we can, but I hold to that idea, and I wish it to be right.

PY: *Are there particular leaders or writers or social movements that, when you're feeling despair, you look to as a direction for hope?*

AC: Between November and January, I felt an enormous amount of despair. If I feel any ray of hope and light, it is in the enormous amount of people who go out every day and do things: the intellectuals who are publishing books as fast as they can, the people who join marches all over this country and in this world, the activists who are working very specifically on critical matters. That's the thing that I always suggest: pick the social issue you are most passionate about and work on it, whether it's on immigration, Black Lives Matter, or the Me Too movement, or specific issues, such as local problems, police abuses, education, homelessness, et cetera. I have an enormous amount of respect and love for every single one of them. When I hear certain people speak who are writing, thinking, and evaluating what is currently happening, I'm grateful to my core for their courage and their clarity.

Dr. Gloria I. Joseph edited *The Wind Is Spirit: The Life, Love and Legacy of Audre Lorde*, a biography/anthology that tells of Audre Lorde's life. Lorde is a writer who speaks to us beyond her own lifetime. She speaks about maintaining true to your integrity as a woman, a person of color, a human being connected to all humanity. I reread Naomi Klein's *The Shock Doctrine* in January [2017]. Her new book, *No Is Not Enough: Resisting Trump's Shock Politics and Winning the World We Need*, which came out months after the inauguration, continued the dialogue of the earlier book. In it she made suggestions about local organizing, and I think that that's very important.

PY: *What is it about Klein's analysis that really hit home for you?*

AC: In one sense, it felt personal. I was one of the first two graduates from the Latin American and Caribbean Studies Program at the University of Chicago in 1979. Milton Friedman was one of our professors. He was a consultant with Pinochet. At that time there were dictatorships throughout Latin America. Let me make clear that in that program we were not persuaded toward one way of political thinking but encouraged at all times to come to our own conclusions.

I was in this program with about twelve other people, and some of the most outstanding professors of Latin America at that time were my professors. In Naomi Klein's *The Shock Doctrine*, she's talking about the Chicago School. One of my classmates asked Milton Friedman about Pinochet, about Chile, and Friedman's reply was, "Economics has nothing to do with people." Friedmanite economics is a reverse philosophy from Marxism. Naomi Klein's book exposed that history.

At this time, I thought about going to law school. I was given a fellowship at the University of Chicago to stay and to pursue that or a Ph.D. I thought about studying international relations. I was in my midtwenties. I wrote and published poetry. But remember, it was a time when there were no U.S. Latinas being published in the mainstream. It was a time when your mere Spanish surname was enough to keep you out of publishing in this country, with the exception of the new small Latinos presses. The idea of a "career" in writing didn't occur to me as even a possibility.

In *The Shock Doctrine*, Klein is writing about that particular time, but what's particularly horrifying for us right now is that the Chicago School or Friedmanite economics agenda stayed on track until they came to rest in the belly of the beast. It is where we are right now in the Trump era. It is why I just said that anybody who speaks up right now is a hero of mine because *maybe* they—Trump team—preempted themselves. Maybe they thought the U.S. as a country would tolerate its economic takeover. Just maybe they came in a little too soon, and there are still some of us (according to polls, maybe 66 percent, and too many of us perhaps) that are not going to allow them to take this country that easily. They were able to take many throughout this world. Maybe they just thought, "Well, now we'll go for the big prize and take over the United States." They don't like the browning of America. But above all, I believe such powers that be are motivated by greed. We, the majority of the people, are not ready to give in. Having the history of that nefarious agenda laid out in that book resonated so much for me.

There are days where I think, "Maybe whatever we say and do won't be enough," but not every day. I'm just hanging on right now with the hopes of "Could be. Let's try. It won't hurt." If you're in a burning building and you're on the third, or fourth, or even fifth floor and there's maybe a couple guys out there trying to put out the fire, what choice do you have but fight for your life, too? I feel like, "What choice do we have but to fight back right now?" We've got very little to lose in speaking out and, of course, always the aspiration of something to be gained.

When I started to speak out in January on social media, a couple of people sent me messages and they said things like, "Well, *they* do read what you write." And I said, "I'm very well aware of the fact that for a dictatorship no enemy is too small." What choice do you have but to speak out when you see injustice? If you have a conscience and you're going to stay on this earth, you have to stand by your convictions.

WORKS CITED
Castillo, Ana. *Black Dove: Mamá, Mi'jo, and Me*. Feminist Press at CUNY, 2016.
———. *Give It To Me*. Feminist Press, 2014.
———. *The Guardians*. Random House, 2008.
———. *Massacre of the Dreamers: Essays on Xicanisma*. 20th anniversary updated ed., U of New Mexico P, 2014.
———. *So Far from God*. W. W. Norton, 2005.
García Márquez, Gabriel. *One Hundred Years of Solitude*. Pan Books, 1978.
Joseph, Gloria I., editor. *The Wind Is Spirit: The Life, Love and Legacy of Audre Lorde*. Villarosa Media, 2016.
Klein, Naomi. *No Is Not Enough: Resisting Trump's Shock Politics and Winning the World We Need*. Haymarket, 2017.
———. *The Shock Doctrine: The Rise of Disaster Capitalism*. Picador, 2008.
Saeta, Elsa. "A *MELUS* Interview: Ana Castillo." *MELUS*, vol. 22, no. 3, 1997, pp. 133–149.

Part II / Justice

Expanding Environmentalism

8

Environmental Justice and the Ecological Other in Ana Castillo's *So Far from God*

SARAH JAQUETTE RAY

Latinx cultural texts are important not only for their keen articulation of environmental theories and sensibilities, as so many of the essays in this volume showcase, but also because they often in the process powerfully outline the colonialist and exclusionary tendencies of mainstream environmentalism. Ana Castillo's novel *So Far from God* is exemplary in that it both recovers a distinctly Chicanx environmentalism and points to the hypocrisies and problems with dominant environmental discourse.

As Priscilla Solis Ybarra and Sarah D. Wald's interview with Ana Castillo in this volume illustrates, the novel has, since its publication in 1993, been canonized in environmental justice scholarship. Ecocritical reception of the novel confirms Castillo's description of her intentions as described in the interview: the novel shows the interconnections between how colonial-capitalist patriarchy treats people it conceives as "disposable" or expendable the same as it treats the environment. The novel connects social injustice and environmental degradation and exposes their mutually shared roots in colonialism and patriarchy. As Kamala Platt has shown, *So Far from God* is squarely situated in what ecocritics such as Greg Garrard, Cheryll Glotfelty and Harold Fromm, and Joni Adamson and Scott Slovic have called the "second wave" of environmental literary production. This wave is characterized by nondominant perspectives joining the environmental turn by centering concerns of environmental justice—toxicity, unequal distribution of environmental benefits and burdens, and the interconnectedness of various forms of both social and environmental oppression. As Laura Halperin explains: "the environmental critique that Castillo provides cannot be separated from her portrayal of racialized, ethnicized, classed, gendered, and sexualized harm" (125).

The novel challenges many forms of dominant ways of thinking, inviting readers to interrogate their values and assumptions, thereby narrating the ecofeminist insight that different forms of oppression are linked. It also draws causal, material connections between disparate events and places, exhibiting what geographer Doreen Massey has called a "global sense of place," a theory that reveals how local events are connected to spaces and places elsewhere. These theories help illustrate even more ways that the novel argues for an environmental justice epistemology rooted in what Gloria Anzaldúa in *Borderlands/La Frontera* calls a "*mestiza* consciousness."

As powerful as the novel is at promoting environmental justice orientations, its critique of environmentalism has earned less scholarly attention. In this essay, I seek to push the environmental justice and ecofeminist analysis to show how the novel indicts not only colonial-capitalist patriarchy but also environmentalism itself. I read the novel as doing even more environmental justice and ecofeminist work than has been described thus far. By scrutinizing the ways that the environmental themes are not just interconnected to but also paradoxically *belie* the justice dimensions, I hope to intensify the extant environmental justice and ecofeminist appreciation of the novel by arguing that Castillo shows how dominant environmentalism is *part of* the colonial-capitalist oppressive systems that environmental justice theory and activism challenge. Ecocritical interpretations of the novel that fail to recognize its challenge to environmental ideas risk sanitizing it for white audiences, or worse, appropriating the parts that reinforce ecocritical values while selectively ignoring the novel's call for environmentalism—not just colonial-capitalism—to change. I want to focus on this aspect of Castillo's intervention because the novel holds the promise not just to bring a particular kind of epistemology emerging from indigenous Mexican or Mexican American positionality, or mestiza consciousness, to the environmental table but to change the very form of the table itself.

To briefly summarize the novel, *So Far from God* takes places in the fictional town of Tome, New Mexico. Castillo's magical realist novel's protagonist, Sofi, spends most of her life tending to her four daughters and trying to keep her family together. Her husband, Domingo, is addicted to gambling and comes and goes from the house as his winnings dictate. Sofi is the matriarch of the house. The central narrative focuses on Sofi's four daughters, Esperanza, Caridad, Fe, and La Loca, all of whom die young, even as they remain present in the story. The story opens with the miraculous resurrection of La Loca, the youngest daughter, who died as a baby but whose resurrected spirit stays at home with Sofi until the end of the novel, afflicted with epilepsy, a special connection to animals, and a phobia of people. At the novel's end, La Loca dies a second time, this time of AIDS, which she contracted inexplicably. Esperanza majors in Chicano studies and receives an M.A. in communications. She has a short-lived, dangerous career as a journalist covering the Gulf War. She disappears while in the Middle East, presumably taken hostage and killed. Her ghost visits her friends and family in Tome. Beautiful Caridad is brutally and sexually attacked in the first chapter and goes on to become a clairvoyant and curandera, finally falling in love with a woman, with whom she jumps off the Acoma Pueblo to enter a next world. Fe attempts to live the American dream of getting married, working hard, and raising a family. But the American dream proves to be false and lethal. Fe's first fiancé leaves her, causing Fe to scream for years until she earns the title La Gritona. With her speech impaired, the only job she can land is at a weapon factory, Acme International, where exposure to chemicals gives her a terrible cancer that kills her. In the midst of all of this tragedy and the comings and goings of her husband and her daughters (or their spirits), Sofi runs for mayor of Tome and slowly helps recover the struggling town by creating a series of cooperatives and an organization of mothers called M.O.M.A.S. (Mothers of Martyrs and Saints).

So Far from God as an Environmental Justice Text

In many ways, the novel advances a distinctly environmental justice, even ecofeminist, set of values. As Platt argues, *So Far from God* centers "images of environmental injustice and resistance" within "the larger fields of race, class, and gender justice" (139). For example, the cooperative that emerges at the novel's end and the centrality of the family unit throughout the novel privilege community-based forms of support and political organization (as opposed to the solitary communion between heroic male individual and wilderness). The specific problems facing this particular community are loss of access to and rights of land and resource use, pressure to find employment in dangerous jobs, victimization and exploitation by men (even men who are central figures in the community, such as the priests), the removal of members of the community for wars abroad, and the interrelation of these environmental, economic, military, and patriarchal forces. The novel shows the community's integrity under attack by interrelated external and internal forces.

Fe best embodies the tangle of external and internal forces. Her job at a weapon-manufacturing plant exposes her to toxic chemicals, which kill her. As a mestiza with a speech-impairment, Fe is portrayed as triply disempowered, which creates the conditions that force her to take such a dangerous job. Counter to the individualist-capitalist logic that attributes individuals' economic and physical mobility to the strength of their will and merit, Castillo outlines the structural inequity caused by extraction. Playing on New Mexico's nickname as the "Land of Enchantment," Castillo writes, "Unlike their abuelos and vis-abuelos who thought that although life was hard in the

'Land of Enchantment' it had its rewards, the reality was that everyone was now caught in what had become: The Land of Entrapment" (172). New Mexico may be "enchanting" to some, but it is a trap for others. The line between them is about relative access to colonial-capitalist power, and, importantly, that power shapes how different people view the environment in this place. For some, the environment is beautiful and transcendent, but for others it is deadly and inescapable. The novel demands that we recognize the unevenness of these experiences of "nature" and space.

And although "it was the job that killed" Fe (171), "most of the people that surrounded Fe didn't understand what was slowly killing them, too." The incidents of "dead cows in the pasture, or sick sheep, and that one week late in winter when people woke up each morning to find it raining starlings" (172) evince Rachel Carson's argument in *Silent Spring* about how systemic poisoning reveals nature-human interdependence, down to the "raining starlings" that silence spring, as well as Rob Nixon's theory of "slow violence." Acme International, which "subcontract[s] jobs from larger companies with direct contracts with the Pentagon" (180), is the source of this systemic poisoning, which binds ecosystems, military campaigns, and individual bodies in one "power geometry"—a notion that helps us see the layering of and causes between seemingly disparate events across geography, space, and even time (if we also consider Nixon's focus on temporality)—to use Massey's language. Acme benefits on multiple levels from U.S. military campaigns. That is, Acme extracts Fe's labor and the very means of her labor (her body) as it makes money from war (the killing of people for geopolitical aims), all by externalizing across space and time the costs of the damage it causes.

In addition to being supported by the labor of "dead bodies," a form of exploitation that David Harvey explores in his theory of "the body as an accumulation strategy," Acme's viability is underwritten by the sacrifice of ecosystems that help displace Acme's impact onto poor communities. Acme instructs Fe to "dump the chemical down the drain," where it contaminates the community. Castillo presents Acme's actions as simultaneously supporting war in a distant part of the world on the one hand and supported by the sacrifice of humans and ecosystems in the village of Tome, New Mexico, whose specificity Castillo captures by evoking the chemical contamination of such personal items as "septic tanks, vegetable gardens," and "sun-made tea" (188). Here, Castillo uses pollution not only to draw attention to the shared trashing of nature and human bodies but also to materially link the seemingly innocuous, low-risk, relaxing pleasure of drinking sun tea to the violent war happening overseas. This is an example of how the novel does more than just promote an environmental justice orientation to show that human oppression and the exploitation of nature are interconnected. The novel takes an "eco-cosmopolitan" approach, to use a term Ursula Heise proposed in *Sense of Place, Sense of Planet,* to describe what otherwise might be called a fourth wave of environmental works. That is, as Nixon aptly describes it, such an approach allows us to recognize "local materiality," such as the sewages and sun-made tea of Tome, while exposing "the web of transnational forces that permeate and shape the local" (52), such as Acme's investment in overseas military operations. Put another way, Acme's product—weapons—are intimately linked to its byproduct—chemical waste. Through Acme International, Castillo reiterates a structural critique of the military-industrial complex, showing the interrelations of issues of environment, labor, gender, and international conflict, as well as how these connections materialize in a particular local community, an analysis that Halperin details in her chapter on *So Far from God* in *Intersections of Harm: Narratives of Latina Deviance and Defiance*.

The novel also advances this new materialist, eco-cosmopolitan critique through the themes of health and medicine. Representing the dominant medical model, the nurse at Acme International tells Fe that her cancer symptoms are caused by "pre-menopause and the dropping of estrogen levels in women over thirty," and that her symptoms were "just about being a woman and had nothing to do with working with chemicals" (178). Here, the medical model is both sexist and exploitative in terms of labor. The nurse works for Acme and yet represents objective "medicine." The same capitalist system that benefits from exposing the community to ailments in the first place is also the source of its medical treatment. Indeed, Fe is entrapped in this system, finally coming to see the treatment she receives at the hospital as "torture" (186).

Fe's illness exemplifies how the novel challenges the binary between the dominant medical model and traditional healing paradigms and forwards what Halperin, drawing on Theresa Delgadillo, calls a "hybrid practice" that combines scientific and traditional healing models. Castillo dramatizes these hybrid practices through the character of La Loca, whose spirit provides a healing source, and through Caridad's training as a curandera. Caridad's mentor, Doña Felicia, tells us that "everything we need for healing is found in our natural surroundings" (62). This view opposes the dominant medical model, which posits standardized, Western medicine as the only legitimate source of healing, locates the ailment in the individual patient, rejects structural or holistic approaches to healing as "backward" and unscientific, and is invested in industry, which puts capital growth ahead of health.

So Far from God shows that these interconnections between social injustice and environmental degradation are yoked together in the cultural logic of colonialism. The text challenges colonialism's appropriation of indigenous and Mexican lands in the Southwest and directly addresses the U.S. government's disregard of land grants. Sofi explains the ongoing effects of colonialism on her family: "First the gringos took most of our land away when they took over the territory from Mexico—right after Mexico had taken it from Spain and like my vis-abuelo used to say, 'Ni no' habiamo' dado cuenta,' it all happened so fast! Then, little by little, my familia had to give it up 'cause they couldn't afford it no more, losing business on their churros and cattle" (217). The novel scrutinizes the continued structures of capitalist dominance, and it does so in a distinctly feminist way—that is, by focusing on the environmental and lived experiences of colonialism of the women in Sofi's family, it demonstrates that the "personal is political." Sofi's choice to run for mayor is based on her experience as a mother and on the fact that the mothers of her community disproportionately suffer environmental costs and burdens, which I elaborate below in my discussion of the novel's end. And the novel shows that colonialism's violence continues in distinctly sexist ways, as La Loca points out; she sees "healing her sisters from the traumas and injustices they were dealt by society" (27) as her purpose. Thus, continued colonial relations create the conditions in which women and their environments become externalities of economic and military hegemony.

The novel's central concerns are those of land grants and claims, healing and knowledge, the military-capitalist exploitation of poor communities (specifically their bodies, through the sacrifice of their environments), and the patriarchal dimension of these issues. The novel's vision of justice is thus a feminist one but also a specifically Chicanx feminist one, as Castillo rejects "white women's self-help books" (47) as supporting, if not part of, the problem. In contrast to the (white) liberal feminist model that seeks the same kinds and spheres of power that white men have, the unit of power in the novel is the family (not the bread-earner whose power operates in the public sphere), and the sphere of power is "private"—the home. We see this in the chapter describing Doña Felicia's remedies, in which she equates the spiritual health of the individual to the cleanliness of the home. Spiritual cleansings of the individual are linked to the spiritual energy and health of the home; use of salt, turpentine, incense, onion, garlic, ammonia, and other cleansers are meant for use in the home to treat a person's spiritual ailments.

Of course, the novel challenges this binary as well; the home, the community, and "the political" are one and the same, as Sofi's final role as mayor illustrates. In the following passage, Castillo powerfully blurs the line between seemingly trite domestic problems and broader "structural" issues such as injustice and the military-industrial complex. In referring to Esperanza's passion for politics, Sofia comments:

> Our 'jita, Esperanza, always tried to tell me about how we needed to go out and fight for our rights. She always talked about things like working to change the "system." I never paid no attention to her then, always worried about the carnecería, the house, the girls. . . . But now I see her point for the first time. I don't really know how to explain myself right yet, but I see that the only way things are going

to get better around here, is if we, all of us together, try to do something about it. (142)

Here, readers might expect she will go on to list ways we typically imagine "fight[ing] for our rights" and "chang[ing] the system," such as political activism and organizing. Instead, she says, "The washing machine, the screen door, the stall for the horses, one of the freezers at the carnecería has been out for months." Her comadre adds, obviously fully grasping this theory of the domestic-as-political, "Your sewing machine . . . " Domingo doesn't get it. He challenges her: "Sounds like you're going to run for mayor of this house, not of Tome" (142). By using Domingo as the foil to set up this binary, Castillo challenges readers to imagine a world where these two spaces—the home and the public sphere of politics—are interconnected. One might read Sofia's list of things to fix as a metaphor for broader political structures or, in line with the Chicanx-feminist ways that the novel challenges so many binaries, as a claim that fixing the sewing machine is in fact the first step toward challenging the system, especially in contrast to the patriarchal view of the home that Domingo represents. Halperin puts it another way—each of the characters' individual problems "acts as a microcosm for a larger sociopolitical and geopolitical commentary" (91). Here, the scale of the individual, the home, or the microcosm serves to highlight "an integral connection between individual and collective harm" (91). Indeed, as Halperin argues, Castillo "shows how social activism can happen on an individual and everyday basis" (118).

These examples confirm Platt's view that the novel articulates an environmental justice epistemology, especially in its rejection of the binaries of personal/political, private/public, female/male, domestic/global. Sofi "engages in a U.S. Third World feminist praxis" because she "showcases how the personal is political," "relies on her personal knowledge and intuition," and reveals that "the individual cannot be separated from the collective" (Halperin 119). Through Massey's and Heise's lenses, the novel could therefore be understood as eco-cosmopolitan, espousing a "global sense of place." Alternatively, one might see it as reflecting an indigenous cosmology because it connects events and processes across time and space and attributes the cause of these material and mutual layers of exploitation to colonial-capitalist patriarchy.

Mainstream Environmentalism as Socially Oppressive

However, the novel does not simply articulate this alternative to the dominant model of first wave environmental texts, as I have been outlining thus far. It even focuses *blame* on the dominant model as invested in the very colonial-capitalism that, paradoxically, degrades the environment. That is, the novel does not just add an environmental justice lens; it indicts dominant environmentalism for socially oppressive values and discourses. In what follows, I show how Castillo is much more critical of environmentalism's ties to colonial-capitalism than ecocritics have recognized thus far, and I argue that the evidence for this is in her ironic use of dominant environmental modes against themselves. While ecocritics like that the novel validates many traditional environmental ends as a means of social justice, such as attacking capitalism, I argue that the text also indicts environmentalism for having worked against social justice historically and for being tied to colonizing practices.

This criticism of environmental ideas in the novel gets overshadowed by ecocritical praise of the novel, which I worry whitewashes, sanitizes, and even appropriates the novel for purposes that may work against what the novel otherwise achieves. Castillo's condemnation of mainstream environmentalism is as important as her contributions to environmental justice and ecofeminism; or, put another way, a truly environmental-justice and ecofeminist reading of the novel must recognize its critique of the mainstream. Such an examination holds a mirror up to mainstream environmentalism's hypocrisies and demands it continue to reflect on its own "hidden attachments," as Denis Cosgrove calls them, to colonialism and racial hierarchy. Because I believe environmentalists and the discipline of environmental studies need to continue to undertake this self-reflection, it is especially important for environmentalist readings of the novel to grasp Castillo's critique. In registering her call for such reflection—rather than myopically reading the novel as evidence that Chicanxs are finally coming around to loving nature—readers can help break the divisions between social justice and environmental interests.

One particular scene powerfully captures this criticism of environmentalism. At the end of the novel, the members of the community, including members of M.O.M.A.S. and the cooperative, participate in the Way of the Cross Procession. The procession is "not in the least religious in nature but about workers and women strikers and things like that." Participants "carried photographs of their loved ones who died due to toxic exposure hung around the necks like scapulars" (241). This procession serves the purpose of witnessing and mourning environmental injustice, not supporting the Catholic tradition, which the text treats as an extension of colonialism. The novel's syncretistic revision of the Catholic ceremony is key to its environmental justice message: "At each station along their route, the crowd stopped and prayed and people spoke on the so many things that were killing their land and turning those lands into an endangered species" (241–242). By using the Catholic ceremony as an opportunity to vocalize their concerns, Castillo reveals the power of using what Audre Lorde might call the "master's tools" to expose the relationship between labor and environment.

The Subaltern Discourse of Endangerment

In the middle of this event, which makes environmental injustice a spiritual matter even as it highlights the Catholic Church's complicity in these injustices, a participant critiques mainstream environmentalism for failing to address environmental injustices:

> We hear about what environmentalists care about out there. We live on dry land but we care about saving the whales and the rainforests too. Our people have always known about the interconnectedness of things, the responsibility we have to "our mother" and to seven generations after our own. But we, as a people, are being eliminated from the ecosystem, like the dolphins, like the eagle. We are trying very hard now to save ourselves before it's too late. Don't anybody care about that? (242)

In this passage, the marginalized Chicanx community asks for inclusion in an "ecosystem" view of society and frames itself as an endangered species within a global environmental model, as suggested in the language of "interconnectedness" and responsibility to "mother earth." The community is directly speaking to mainstream environmentalists, for whom the preservation of charismatic megafauna in exotic corners of the planet takes precedence over concerns of social justice or racial inequality. The speaker presents the community as in need of saving, as having been deprived of basic human rights that even the dolphins are granted (in the eyes of mainstream environmentalists). Mainstream environmentalists are thus positioned as having greater relative power and are even framed in a paternalistic role, relative to the community. The passage exposes the privilege of the mainstream environmental community and the disparity between its "endangered species" model and the Chicanx community's environmental concerns.

The community's claims to the rights of animal-hood echo and yet crucially revise the civil rights movement's claims to personhood. That is, when an oppressed community asks for more rights (such as the right to vote) on the grounds that its members have humanity—as in the civil rights mantra, "I am a man"—they are implicitly asking not to be treated as that which is less than human: animals. It is fascinating that the community of Tome in the novel makes the opposite move, asking that they be treated not humanely, as social justice movements, from civil rights to suffrage and now even the animal rights movement, have always done, but as an endangered animal species, which ostensibly receives more protection and care than some human communities. In other words, only in a post–Endangered Species Act moment can we imagine that some human communities are treated worse than animals. The claim to the rights of animal-hood challenges the dominant humanist perception that humans are separate from and better than animals; in a humanist ontology, nobody would rather be a whale than a human.

But the real critique is in how this reversal of rhetoric exposes the "inhumanity" of dominant environmentalists—those most likely to reject that humanist conceit by really loving animals—as packaging their hidden attachment to white supremacy in animal love. When the community asks for the status that dolphins enjoy, it is asking environmentalism to care about the mistreatment of oppressed human groups as much as it cares about the mistreatment of charismatic megafauna. Such a rhetorical shift draws on a recent tradition of people-of-color social movements that tap into anxieties about extinction that are directed by dominant groups at biodiversity loss and animals. These claims expose what George Lipsitz would call "the possessive investment in whiteness" of environmentalists who care about the fate of animals more than they do the fate of (some) humans, while hypocritically peddling this concern as a politics of care rather than a politics of white supremacy.[1]

Giovanna Di Chiro has examined this discourse of endangerment in the environmental justice movement: "The question of what (and who) counts as an endangered species is," she writes, "a crucial aspect of the environmental justice movement's reconceptualization of the relationships between nonhuman and human nature and the emergence of new ideas of nature and new forms of environmentalism. Activists use the highly potent and provocative signifier 'endangered species' in strategic ways" (315). Thus, in the novel when "the people spoke on the so many things that were killing their land and turning the people of those lands into an endangered species" (Castillo 241–242), they are "reinvent[ing]" the term's "limited use by mainstream environmentalists" and expose how "mainstream environmentalists miss or obscure the many other related problems that contribute to environmental deterioration for all species, including people" (De Chiro 317). Claims of endangerment by environmental justice communities and activists serve to broaden what environmentalists perceive to be the victims of degradation to include human communities. And more important, I contend, these claims demand that the environmental movement account for its internal inconsistencies and arguably racist values.

This passage about the endangerment of the community of Tome marks a departure from the much more explicit ways in which the novel criticizes and rejects dominant society as patriarchal, racist, individualistic, and capitalist. While the novel otherwise works against the animalizing of nonwhites and women (even Sofi's form of livelihood changes from butcher-shop owner to mayor of Tome, demonstrating an ecofeminist vision of empowerment and raised consciousness about structural violence against animals), and while it rejects Anglo romanticization of natives or racial "others" as "closer to nature," it also turns to dominant environmentalism as contributing to these forms of oppression. The claims to endangerment reinforce Anglo stereotypes about Chicanx and indigenous communities being closer to nature in a nostalgic, mythologized past. They reinforce imperialist nostalgia and the "ecological Indian" identity, despite important distinctions between Mexican and indigenous colonial relations in Southwest, about which Castillo is undoubtedly aware. On the surface, then, the procession in the novel seems to undermine the liberatory work that it has achieved thus far. Why, after all the novel does to dismantle white assumptions about the Spanish-Mexican-indigenous communities in the Southwest (Sofi's heritage is mestiza), does it then turn to reifying such troubling stereotypes?

We might draw on geographer Laura Pulido's insights to better understand this scene in the novel. In her article "Ecological Legitimacy and Cultural Essentialism: Hispano Grazing in the Southwest," Pulido examines how the community on which the community in *So Far from God* is modeled made similar claims as the character in the novel to gain ecological legitimacy. Pulido observes that the Hispano community of Los Ojos, New Mexico, enlisted a similar argument in order to prove to state resource managers and mainstream environmentalists that they are good stewards of land. Los Ojos and the cooperative that emerged out of this tension—Ganados del Valle— can be seen as the real-world equivalent of what happens in the novel, as even Castillo seems to credit: "Sofi's vecinos finally embarked on an ambitious project, which was to start a sheep-grazing wool-weaving enterprise, 'Los Ganados y Lana Cooperative,' modeled after the one started by the group up north that had also saved its community from destitution" (146). Ganados del Valle (and its fictional counterpart, Ganados y Lana) accomplished this by constructing a narrative of having a heritage that was "close to nature."

In an interview with Pulido, one community activist made such a claim to legitimacy in a way that echoes the character's claims in Castillo's novel: "Elk and deer are not endangered in northern New Mexico. But the survival of New Mexico's Hispanic pastoral culture is endangered. Our proposal to graze the wildlife refuges is an opportunity to strengthen one of the United States' richest cultures, improve the wildlife habitat, and raise the standard of living in one of the nation's poorest rural counties" (53). While the passage insists on the possibility that certain human cultural traditions are pro-ecological, preservationism maintains that nature must be protected from human activities—especially those of the poor. In this case, officials saw the community a threat to nature because they "overgraze," a contested term that carries assumptions about what constitutes ideal levels of grazing and whose ideals about "nature" get to shape policy. Rather than seeing the Hispanos' environmental behavior within the broad structural conditions of capitalism and colonialism, officials saw the community as "ecologically other" (to use a concept I describe in *The Ecological Other*) and, in the name of "preservation" (of the wildlife refuge), ignored the community's history of environmental management. Pulido thus theorizes that "ecological legitimacy"—the power to make environmental decisions—"often eludes poor rural populations because officialdom has long assumed that landless and land poor groups do not care about protecting their environments" (37). I would add that ecological illegitimacy, like ecological otherhood, is a way for those in power to maintain power, using preservation of "nature" as an excuse for social control.

Pulido interprets this moment as an empowering moment of "cultural essentialism." This concept draws on Gayatri Spivak's notion of "strategic essentialism," which refers to women's performance of feminine stereotypes, such as being "inherently" maternal, to gain political power in the public sphere, qua women. Similarly, the Hispano community countered to their perceived ecological illegitimacy by claiming an essential, inherent closeness to the land—what Pulido registers as a kind of "cultural essentialism." This allowed them to gain standing comparable to the wildlife that the environmentalists were attempting to preserve.

Within this framework, it could be argued that the community in *So Far from God* deploys essentialism not because it sees itself as being close to nature, necessarily, since, after all, that stereotype has served to oppress, but rather for strategic, political purposes. That is, if we applied Pulido's interpretation of the Los Ojos example to the similar moment in *So Far from God*, we could see the passage as an example of strategic environmentalism, or, even more specifically, in Soenke Zehle's words, "ecological essentialism," which Zehle describes in this way: "Performances of ecological essentialism can turn out to be (strategically) useful, when images of sustainability and ecospiritual integrity are appropriated and mobilized by indigenous peoples themselves, precisely because they resonate with supporters in the environmental mainstream and can contribute to the affirmation and protection of native communities along with their own ecological traditions" (335). In other words, even when an "environmental subaltern" (to use Pulido's term) speaks in the master's language in order to "resonate with supporters in the environmental mainstream," they gain "the affirmation and protection of native communities along with their own ecological traditions," or, in other words, they gain ecological legitimacy.

This strategic environmentalist moment in the text is important not just because it earns the community ecological legitimacy. It is important precisely because it shows the problems of the very *terms* of this legitimacy. By playing the role of the ecological Indian—or worse, by equating themselves to a species of charismatic megafauna—the community reinforces assumptions that Chicanxs are close to nature in ways that justify their management, not in ways that grant them agency. Gaining equal status to wildlife may achieve some short-term leverage, but it does not challenge the environmental paradigms that create the disparity of power between those who do the protecting and those who are protected in the first place. The result of such a reading as merely strategic means that the Chicanx community's "power" is not based on their own authority or land ethic. A "closeness to nature" gained through cultural essentialism is not the same as having agency to make environmental claims. By reading this moment as simply "strategic," these issues of ecological authority, paternalism, and racism implicit in equating a community with a species go uncorrected; the community might now be worthy of protection, but the environmental norms on which this logic rests still stand. This may be ecological legitimacy, but it is not ecological self-determination.

Rather than being just politically strategic, which it certainly is, I see Castillo's move as a literary use of irony to expose the faults in the mainstream. Environmentalism makes the conditions within which communities must negotiate ecological legitimacy impossible, which helps explain why many groups do not see their concerns as "environmental" in the first place. Regina Austin and Michael H. Schill thus argue that the "narrowness of the mainstream movement, which appears to be more interested in endangered animals (non-human) species and pristine undeveloped land than at-risk humans . . . makes poor minority people think that their concerns are not 'environmental'" (qtd. in Pulido, *Environmentalism* 25). Environmentalism is thereby exclusionary not only in terms of how it draws lines around who is included and who is not. By defining "environmental" issues in ways that hide the environmental nature of many communities' problems, the mainstream hides the very presence of environmental injustice.

Pulido argues that the use of essentialism was the only way for the real-life Los Ojos community to gain ecological legitimacy, but I would argue that her interpretation does not quite account for implicit eco-imperialist underpinnings of these stereotypes and how they are, seemingly paradoxically, used to marginalize communities. That is, if we read this moment in the novel as strategic environmentalism, we must assume that Castillo intends to leave the dominant environmental model intact. This reading misses the novel's revisionary potential. The novel goes further to critique the mainstream model than Pulido's theory of cultural essentialism allows. Rather, even more than it is a claim to legitimacy, Castillo's character's performance of support for mainstream environmental values is in fact an ironic *challenge* to and mockery of the mainstream. This moment is inconsistent with the rest of the novel's messages, and so if we fail to read the novel as a whole, we miss the possibility that the character's claims undermine rather than reinforce the mainstream model. Rather than seeing this gesture in the novel as only a self-degrading rhetorical strategy to gain favor in the eyes of an environmentalist audience, following this line of argument, we might also see it as a performance of ecological essentialism that challenges dominant environmentalists to recognize the hypocrisy of romanticizing animals and indigenous ethics while not approving of a mestiza community because they seem to not fit the white environmentalist framework.

Castillo's use of this performance of "endangerment" as a critique of the mainstream is further illustrated by her use of scare quotes around "mother earth"; the quotes signal Castillo's understanding that the term has multiple connotations and that the speaker uses the term disingenuously. It signals a strategic use of the term as essentialist. Castillo's explicit use of "mother earth" as someone else's words mocks white environmentalists' appropriation of indigenous values. Without quotation marks, we could read the appeal to Mother Earth on its own terms rather than as a rhetorical strategy used by the speaker to register value within her audience's framework. Further, Castillo's reference to the community's attempts to "save ourselves" reveals the audience's complicity in the environmental injustices that have all along been occurring in "someone else's backyard." It suggests that the community is not ecologically other, unwilling to be good environmental stewards, and criticizes the mainstream environmentalists as NIMBY-ist, complicit in displacing injustices to times and places that are out of sight and out of mind for them.

In these senses, then, I would argue that this seemingly inconsistent move at the novel's end directly attacks mainstream environmentalists for their complicity in colonial-capitalism, for their use of the ecological Indian stereotype to ironically limit the Hispano-mestiza community's ecological legitimacy, and for their hypocrisy of wanting to protect "nature" from the very communities they claim were once "close to nature." Thus, this passage exemplifies the power of using the master's tools, but only when read in the context of the whole novel. On its own, as a gesture of cultural essentialism, it reinforces mainstream values that the novel as a whole subverts. Rather than celebrating the strategic move as a sign of the community's ability to speak the right language, as Pulido argues about the community in Los Ojos, this passage signals a fissure in mainstream environmentalism to be exploited and exposed, an "opening" that Castillo's character and her novel reveal. Read as a whole, the novel presents a picture of the community's environmental concerns that may be outside conventional notions of "the environment." If we look only at the "culturally essentialist" moment at the novel's end, we miss the point: while we have been reading, an entirely different environmental positionality has taken shape, one that is not just strategic but one that revises the very terms of ecological legitimacy.

Conclusion

Too often, discussions about how to diversify mainstream environmentalism center on the question of how to persuade underrepresented groups to get involved in protecting and enjoying "nature" and fail to acknowledge the ways in which those groups are already engaged in those and other environmental efforts. As that argument goes, if the environmental movement could convince more people of the value of nature and the beauty of the great outdoors, they would pursue both lifestyle and political avenues to protect the environment. It becomes a campaign of missionary zeal for traditionally white environmental groups, and all the more righteous, when new members are "diverse." Yet the failure to challenge status quo notions of environmental aesthetics and values has prevented environmental thought and environmental studies more specifically from imagining an environmentalism that not only includes but is designed by a wide variety of interests and cultures. This insight is the central argument of Priscilla Solis Ybarra's book *Writing the Goodlife: Mexican American Literature and the Environment*, in which Ybarra asks, "Do Chicanas/os appear in an environmental context only as victims of exploitation, or can they also be a source of knowledge and alternative approaches?" (20). She argues that we are missing the point if we see only conventionally defined environmental themes in Mexican American literature: "One of the most significant things that environmentalism can learn from the decolonial writings of Chicanas and Chicanos (among other peoples of color) is the fact that we never needed to become environmentalists in the first place, and we therefore have an array of strategies at our disposal for how to live well with Earth" (28). In other words, it is simply not enough to canonize *So Far from God* as environmental without registering its critiques of mainstream environmentalism. The latter opens the possibility for recognizing the ways in which Chicanxs have been thinking about environmental issues in non-Anglo ways for generations, instead of just delighting in the growing diversity of the dominant forms of the environmental movement.

The passage I analyzed above is exemplary of how resistance discourse within this context might leverage environmentalism's assumptions about communities of color, while pushing environmentalism to broaden its notion of what counts as worthy of saving or what counts as "environmental" at all. Indeed, my reading of the passage suggests that it posits the environmental movement as not just exclusionary or limited in its politics, but worse: it is actively invested in Anglo privilege. Although the novel does provide an alternative to the mainstream, it does so by explicitly calling out the mainstream for its exclusionary practices. But it is also troubling in its deployment of essentializing qualities of the mestizo community. "Performances" of mainstream environmental identity as evidenced in this particular passage indict environmentalism for its investment in various forms of hegemony while also prescribing how an excluded group might articulate its own concerns within those dominant frameworks.

Reception of the novel that counts it as seminal to the environmental justice canon often fails to see its critique of mainstream environmentalism. The community of Tome is not just battling against colonial-capitalism. They also have to resist dominant environmentalist expectations of "ecological Indians" and to rewrite narratives that frame the community as ill-equipped to make ecological claims on their own terms, as in the paternalistic "environment-poverty" paradigm the political ecologists reject. The novel's contribution is not simply that it outlines environmental justice and ecofeminist concerns. In my view, more important is its call for mainstream environmentalist discourse to do two things it has thus far failed to do: (1) reflect on the ways it works against social justice, even as it is increasingly willing to recognize interconnections between social and environmental degradation, and (2) stop appropriating ecological Indianness as it simultaneously and hypocritically discredits actual indigenous people and their claims. These ideals, outlined over twenty-five years ago in *So Far from God*, remain to be realized, making the novel just as relevant and urgent today.

NOTE

1. Animal studies scholars further challenge the assumption that we need to choose between the liberation of oppressed humans and the liberation of oppressed animals. The preference for one relies on the assumption of the other as not as worthy of moral consideration. If, as Ursula Heise argues in *Imagining Extinction*, "speciesism and racism are systematically connected in the cultural logic of colonialism," the answer is not to leverage the inferiority of one to improve the conditions of the other. That is, drawing on Cary Wolfe, Heise explains, "it is the category of the animal, understood as another that does not have the same claim to moral consideration as a human and can therefore be killed or let die with impunity, that opens up the possibility of relegating other humans legally, ethically, and politically to that category" (165). Animal studies scholars, such as Claire Jean Kim, offer alternatives that reconcile this tension, a review of which is beyond the scope of this chapter.

WORKS CITED

Adamson, Joni, and Scott Slovic. "Guest Editors' Introduction: The Shoulders We Stand On: An Introduction to Ethnicity and Ecocriticism." *MELUS: Multi-Ethnic Literatures of the United States*, vol. 34, no. 2, 2009.

Anzaldúa, Gloria. *Borderlands/La Frontera*. Aunt Lute Books, 1987.

Carson, Rachel. *Silent Spring*. Houghton Mifflin, 1962.

Castillo, Ana. *So Far from God*. W. W. Norton, 2005.

Cosgrove, Denis. "Habitable Earth: Wilderness, Empire, and Race in America." *Wild Ideas*, edited by David Rothenberg, U of Minnesota P, 1995, pp. 27–41.

Di Chiro, Giovanna. "Nature as Community: The Convergence of Environment and Social Justice." *Uncommon Ground: Rethinking the Human Place in Nature*, edited by William Cronon, Norton, 1995, pp. 298–320.

Garrard, Greg. *Ecocriticism*. 2nd ed., Routledge, 2011.

Glotfelty, Cheryll, and Harold Fromm, editors. *The Ecocriticism Reader: Landmarks in Literary Ecology*. U of Georgia P, 1996.

Halperin, Laura. *Intersections of Harm: Narratives of Latina Deviance and Defiance*. Rutgers UP, 2015.

Harvey, David. "The Body as an Accumulation Strategy." *Environment and Planning D: Society and Space*, vol. 16, no. 4, 1998, pp. 401–421.

Heise, Ursula. *Imagining Extinction: The Cultural Meanings of Endangered Species*. U of Chicago P, 2016.

———. *Sense of Place, Sense of Planet: The Environmental Imagination of the Global*. Oxford UP, 2009.

Kim, Claire Jean. *Dangerous Crossings: Race, Species, and Nature in a Multicultural Age.* Cambridge UP, 2015.

Lipsitz, George. *The Possessive Investment in Whiteness: How White People Profit from Identity Politics.* Temple UP, 1998.

Massey, Doreen. "A Global Sense of Place." *Space, Place, and Gender,* U of Minnesota P, 1994, pp. 146–156.

Nixon, Rob. *Slow Violence and the Environmentalism of the Poor.* Harvard UP, 2013.

Platt, Kamala. "Ecocritical Chicana Literature: Ana Castillo's 'Virtual Realism.'" *ISLE: Interdisciplinary Studies in Literature and Environment,* vol. 3, no. 1, 1996.

Pulido, Laura. "Ecological Legitimacy and Cultural Essentialism: Hispano Grazing in the Southwest." *Capitalism Nature Socialism* vol. 7, no. 4, 1996, pp. 37–38.

———. *Environmentalism and Economic Justice: Two Chicano Struggles in the Southwest.* U of Arizona P, 1996.

Ray, Sarah Jaquette. *The Ecological Other: Environmental Exclusion in American Culture.* U of Arizona P, 2013.

Spivak, Gayatri. "Can the Subaltern Speak?" *Marxism and the Interpretation of Culture,* edited by Cary Nelson and Lawrence Grossberg, Macmillan, 1998, pp. 271–313.

Ybarra, Priscilla Solis. *Writing the Goodlife: Mexican American Writing and the Environment.* U of Arizona P, 2016.

Zehle, Soenke. "Notes on Cross-Border Environmental Justice Education." *The Environmental Justice Reader: Politics, Poetics, and Pedagogy,* edited by Joni Adamson, Mei Mei Evans, and Rachel Stein, U of Arizona P, 2002, pp. 331–349.

9

"We Carry Our Environments within Ourselves"

An Interview with Helena María Viramontes

DAVID J. VÁZQUEZ, SARAH D. WALD,
AND PAULA M. L. MOYA

Without question, Helena María Viramontes is among the most important Latinx authors of the past forty years. Her novels *Under the Feet of Jesus* (1995) and *Their Dogs Came with Them* (2007) and her short story collection *The Moths and Other Stories* (1985) are standard reading in Chicanx and Latinx literature, ethnic studies, and feminist studies courses. Viramontes's body of work is celebrated for its expressions of Chicana feminism, farmworker justice, and decolonial politics. Less appreciated, however, are Viramontes's robust and consistent engagements with environmental ideas. Ranging from nature appreciation, environmental awareness, toxic exposure, and food justice in *Under the Feet of Jesus* to environmental agency, transportation accessibility, and contestations of gentrification in *Their Dogs Came with Them*, Viramontes often engages ideas that are central to environmental justice, ecocriticism, and the environmental humanities, and she articulates Chicanx environmental concerns that have been under-addressed in those fields. The third of five interviews with writers in this volume, this conversation reveals Viramontes's long-standing engagement with environmental issues as a social justice concern, which participates in the focus of other chapters in this section on "Justice."

Ecocritics have turned to Viramontes's novels as touchstone texts representing issues related to environmental justice. With the possible exceptions of Ana Castillo's novel *So Far from God* and Cherríe Moraga's play *Heroes and Saints*,[1] no Chicanx or Latinx text has garnered as much attention from ecocritics as *Under the Feet of Jesus*. Despite this attention, ecocritical readings trend toward food justice, setting, place, and the novel's problematizing of the agrarian ideal, sometimes overlooking the ways *Under the Feet of Jesus* foregrounds decolonial and feminist issues.[2] In fact, despite rich representations related to urban space, environmental justice, and gentrification, ecocritics have only rarely taken up Viramontes's novel *Their Dogs Came with Them* or her short stories.

A similar lacuna exists within Latinx studies, as critics have considered a broader cross section of Viramontes's work (particularly her short story "The Cariboo Café") but tend to focus on her representations of feminism, farmworker justice, citizenship, and solidarity with social justice struggles in the developing world in isolation from her environmental engagements.[3] More recently, a growing body of Latinx and environmental studies critics have sought to bring Viramontes's social justice concerns into conversation with her environmental engagements, as is apparent in the decolonial environmental framework Paula Moya brings to Viramontes's fiction in her essay in this volume.[4]

We sat down with Viramontes to discuss the environmental aspects of her work to include in this volume in June 2015. Viramontes spoke with us on the telephone from her sister's home in East Los Angeles. Much to our surprise, Viramontes told us that this was the first time she had been asked to discuss her environmental engagements and her history of environmental activism. Over the course of about ninety minutes, Vázquez and Wald talked with Viramontes about issues of farmworker rights, pesticide use, climate change, and transportation justice as they are represented in her work. Paula M. L. Moya provided valuable editorial assistance in preparing the manuscript, which was edited for clarity.

DV: *We really appreciate you taking the time to speak with us. I think understanding how environmental ideas work in literary texts is an important issue. Among many Chicana/o and Latina/o artists, your work seems to be so self-conscious about engaging environmental issues that I think it's a shame that no one has talked with you about these issues before. Can you share with us some of the critical particulars of your relationship to environmental ideas?*

HV: My work has been engaged with the environment for a long time—at least since I was fifteen or sixteen years old. I am a graduate of Garfield High School in East LA and had just arrived there when the Walkouts happened—so that would have been 1968. The school was in huge academic trouble at the time. But in 1969 a young, idealistic teacher by the name of Tom Woessner pushed to have the first ecology class taught in the rough half of the school district. It was a class where we read, for example, *Silent Spring* and talked about issues of pollution. One of our class projects was to organize an event, and so I organized with some other students a recycling drive where we collected information, made video-graphs, and talked with people about Rachel Carson and "spaceship Earth"—the idea that we have precious resources that we all share. We carried our videograph around the neighborhood because, while I had been witness to the coming of the freeways and it seemed that there was always room to put another scrap yard around where we lived, there weren't a lot of images of nature. It was Mr. Woessner's class that gave me the language with which to speak about all these issues. You have to remember that we were talking about environmental issues in the barrio! No one else there was talking about these issues at the time. To this day Mr. Woessner has never forgotten the work we did. So, it was in 1969, in that class, that my interest in looking at our environment really began.

I've always thought that we carry our environments within ourselves: you can take the person out of the barrio, but you can't take the barrio out of the person—that's me! Right now, I'm staying at my sister's house—where I grew up. Even as we speak, I can hear the drone of the freeway in the background. And it reminds me that the freeways really did affect me, even when I wasn't aware of it. I never consciously thought about writing about the freeways until after Raúl Homero Villa did an analysis of my short story "Neighbors." When I read his analysis, I thought "oh!" When he pointed out how the freeways operate in that story, I thought, "Wow, it's there; it really is. I need to explore this!" That was when I began thinking about *Their Dogs Came with Them*.

DV: *That's wonderful! I think Sarah wanted to ask you about* Under the Feet of Jesus.

SW: *Recently, I taught an environmental literature class in which we read* Thoreau and Edward Abbey and a bunch of other canonical nature writers and ended it with Under the Feet of Jesus. *The novel is often read as prioritizing the knowledge of those working at the bottom of the food system. But critics such as myself who want to complicate the modern environmental movement are looking at* Under the Feet of Jesus *in terms of food justice and environmental harm; this is what we were doing in that class. How do you think about the environmental knowledge your characters have? What kinds of knowledges do Alejo and Estrella have that those active in the alternative food movement might not have because they are not actually working to produce food?*

HV: I think Alejo's and Estrella's environmental knowledge comes from their experiences with handling the fruit and vegetables that people eat every day. They truly understand, in an embodied way, how incredibly difficult and hard farmworking is. I don't think most people understand how truly back-breaking it is to be a farmworker—to the point that it limits the lifespan of a sharecropper or farmworker. It reminds me of a line in the novel I'm currently writing: "our intestines are loaded with complaining want." The characters in *Under the Feet of Jesus* work around a huge abundance of food that simply is not available to them to eat. It's not, you know. They can't afford to buy the organic produce they harvest. People will pay incredibly high prices for produce that's grown without using pesticides, that comes from clean soil. How can farmworkers afford seven dollars for organic kale? It's impossible! What they know comes from their work and from their bodies. This is how I understand the relationship of the characters to their environment.

Think about Estrella. She is an incredible individual because she doesn't have book smarts. But she has a sensitivity to her environment that allows her to think about things—she's a thinker. If Estrella had been born in different circumstances—if she had had upper-middle-class, professor parents—she would be gangbusters! Not that she isn't going to be gangbusters after the book ends, but her opportunities are incredibly limited. Her limitations force her to concentrate on her immediate environment; she doesn't have the imagination or the wherewithal to think outside of it. But she's somebody who can look at things and understand how they are unfair. Consider the scene with the baseball game. When Estrella sees the baseball game, she feels incredible exhaustion. My family and I worked in the fields when I was a young person. It's exhausting—beyond exhausting. You can barely move at the end of the day. So when she decides that she wants to watch a baseball game, it becomes clear that her childhood was rough and that her brothers and the twins are going to be robbed of their childhoods if something is not done. In writing that scene, I picked baseball because it's the American pastime, especially during the summer. What could be more natural than to watch a baseball game and see the kids and the enjoyment of parents on a summer day? But what happens? The lights go up, and she gets stunned like a deer. She understands that beyond her limited knowledge is complete and total danger. That's why she runs and runs. She can't imagine herself outside her current environment. To even think about leaving her environment is dangerous. She's afraid for herself and her family.

You know, people always ask me whether Estrella's in love with Alejo. I'm not sure she's "in love" with him, but I'm confident that she does love him. One reason she loves him is because he brings to her something from outside her environment. He brings to her another world that she knows is out there but that she both desires and fears as dangerous. For him, that world is all about dreams and accomplishments. But Estrella has never thought in terms of dreams and accomplishments, and they're beautiful to her. In my mind, Alejo becomes her best friend—something she's never really had. She had tried with Maxine, but in these migratory rounds it's horrific. Children never learn to be a part of a community! As a result, the family becomes very insular.

If you move and move and move around, you can depend only on your family. So the family becomes your main protector but also—especially for mujeres—your main suffocator. I do have one section that takes place in LA. The family is in Los Angeles when the father abandons them. The mother has a nervous breakdown and is incapable of caring for them. Again there's danger—something is not right—and Estrella knows that she has to take care of the kids; there's no food, and it's a crime. That's why that scene with the "full of empty Quaker man" is one of the most powerful scenes in the novel for me. The image of the Quaker man takes me back to LA and to my childhood. We had oatmeal for breakfast every morning. I always thought that Quaker man was so significant to our existence. That knowledge began my awareness about our dependence on agriculture.

But even though my family was aware of our environment, and we carried it with us in our bodies always, we also lacked a certain kind of knowledge about it. My family could always say when they were spraying pesticides, but it never dawned on us that the pesticides could harm us. Even though we knew that people became sick, we didn't connect their illnesses to the poison of the pesticides. It wasn't until much later that I made the connection. My husband and I were driving to Vancouver when we passed through Fresno and I smelled that agricultural smell and said, "Oh man, I miss that smell; it smells like ocean." And he turned to me and said, "Helena, that's the pesticides." That's what killed me! The scent of pesticides permeated our lives! It was a constant. Then I realized, "Wow, man, how much we have all been dosed by that?" But as workers we didn't think about it. It was pretty devastating to me to realize our lack of knowledge about the pesticides that had been poisoning us.

DV: *May I ask you a question about the centrality of pesticides in the novel? I'm wondering about the crop dusting and how you think about Alejo's poisoning in the novel. More broadly, what for you is the role of fiction in bringing awareness to pesticide use and exposure? As you said, driving through the Central Valley of California you see the crop dusters, you smell the pesticides. There have been a number of campaigns in the public designed to bring awareness to these issues, and yet it seems like we're not able to get our heads collectively around environmental danger. Is a novel like* Under the Feet of Jesus *doing a different kind of work than other forms of media and culture?*

HV: Well, that's a very good point. Because of my experience working in the fields, I saw the injustice and the dangers faced by farmworkers. So I became a United Farm Worker[s] supporter immediately upon going to college. I remember we held clothes drives and went up to Delano for the first health clinic opening. One thing I learned early on during the Safeway boycotts is that I had been very naive about people's ultimate goodness. I thought that I could just stand there and talk to them about the Safeway boycott, that I could just explain to them the issues farmworkers were facing, and that would move them to turn around and say, "Yeah, you're right" and help us out. I came to realize that this wasn't the case at all. It isn't until people are themselves directly affected by an issue that they are willing to pay attention. If, as farmworkers, we say that it isn't fair that we are getting poisoned by pesticides, not that many people will listen. But if we say instead that everyone gets poisoned by pesticides, then they will listen. Cesar Chavez's brilliant idea to promote the boycott was to point out that pesticides were poisoning everybody. That's when people became interested. So for me it was difficult: I felt bad that farmworkers were experiencing cancer clusters and dying. But then I had to accept that most people didn't care about pesticide poisoning until they felt themselves to be in danger. Only then did they care about these issues! This made me realize how insignificant farmworkers are and how utterly cruel and disrespecting the world can be sometimes. That was a big insight for me. It prompted a devastating understanding of the way the world works in the life of a farmworker.

I'm not very prolific. But I am very focused in what I write about. I don't spend time writing editorials or essays or stories, because I need—I feel in my heart of hearts that I need to make my characters into real people so that my readers can understand and not only empathize but also experience what Alejo, for example, experiences when he gets poisoned. I want people to feel his suffocation, the experience of being doused, falling from the tree, and becoming unconscious. Like with the scene with the "full of empty Quaker man," I really had to work on that scene. I was very strategic about both these scenes. Back when I was in my twenties, I did an interview where I talked about reading Third World women writers and how I wanted to write so that they would understand that I was listening to them—that I heard them screaming. That's the way I've always approached my writing: I want to write about these difficult experiences so that other people can hear the screaming. I feel the same way now, forty years later. This is the kind of commitment with which I go to my desk and write. I am committed to exposing these injustices—not just for discussion, but to make people who have never even thought or experienced such things actually experience them.

Now perhaps, as the saying goes, my ego is writing checks that my talent can't cash. But it is because I am so committed to exposing injustice that it takes me so long to write anything. I write with all of my heart and soul. Every writer pours their heart and soul into their work, but I do so also with a political commitment to expose injustices. I want to shake people up, to say "Look! Look!" I know I did that with "The Cariboo

Café." That's why I ended it in such a strange way, switching from the third-person voice to a first-person voice so that I could get the full impact of this woman who wants to take her child, who had been murdered, and just go home. I wanted all those people who are reading the "The Cariboo Café" to be indicted for their nonaction, for their nonactivism.

I have my political convictions, but I'm also a writer. I try to let my politics seep in organically. I try not to impose or manipulate, because my readers are really smart. I don't want to insult them by manipulating their minds and hearts towards my convictions. I try to allow things to happen in an organic way.

There are some issues, though, about which I am self-conscious—as you suggested, David. I understood what an incredible disruption the freeways were of the earth, of my world, of this vibrant working-class community. So I made certain kinds of decisions about how to represent freeways in *Their Dogs Came with Them*. Similarly, in *Under the Feet of Jesus*, I knew that representing the pesticide poisoning was a strategic move. I could have just said that Alejo was suffering from daño in the fields; I could have just made him be sick. But I knew that that wouldn't have been enough. I had to do something with a very visual aspect to it so that people could see it and feel it. Now you can understand why it took so long to finish!

SW: *A striking aspect of the way you represent the freeways* in Their Dogs Came with Them *is the way you attend to how people are able to move. You have several beautiful scenes in the novel about people waiting for buses or being on buses. The effect is to illustrate the role that access to cars plays. Can you speak to how transportation fits into the way that you think about the novel?*

HV: Los Angeles has always lacked good, basic transportation. Here in LA, if you don't have a car, you're screwed. Even if you do have a car, where do you go? Especially if you're isolated within a particular area? In our case, we didn't know where to go because we didn't know about a bigger world outside the confines of our neighborhood. I used to think that East Los Angeles was the whole world—a world that everybody could see. Nobody told me otherwise. It was the life I lived. It was never about looking at big cities, never about vacation, never about looking at other places and things like that.

You know, I didn't drive until I was thirty. Partly it was because I didn't want to add any more pollution to the air. I was a big transit person. I mean, I used to take all these buses all the time. When I was attending UC Irvine back in 1979, I took five buses to get there. Five buses! I didn't have a car and I didn't drive, so I would find out the route and do it. It would take me a long, long time, but I managed to figure things out. This was to get to the workshop on Tuesday afternoons. Then, on

Wednesday mornings, I would get up early and take the 7:00 a.m. library van. Students who wanted to do work at UCLA library could take the library van to UCLA. I would get off at UCLA and take another bus to downtown LA, and then I would go to work. That was my first year at UC Irvine. I remember being soaked [by the rain] like Ermila [in *Their Dogs Came with Them*]. I remember waiting for the bus, getting soaked, and trying to be very cool as I got on the bus completely drenched, and then going to work that way.

Transportation, in general, is becoming a bigger issue for me. It is a central preoccupation in a novel I'm writing right now about my uncles that is set in World War II–era Los Angeles and called *The Cemetery Boys*. This novel has really challenged me because, of course, I'm not a man, and I wasn't around during World War II. So I am having to do some research. In developing the setting of this novel, I begin with the East Side boys who are stationed in the Philippines. In the first section of this novel, they're traveling back to Manila as a result of a bet. As I was writing that section, I was going back and forth between the present-tense scene set in the Philippines and flashbacks to prior scenes that focus on the life in California of the private first class before he goes off to fight in the war. One of the things that happens before he goes off to fight is that he meets Filipinos working in the agricultural fields. I had started doing research on 1930s sharecropping, and I came to realize that there was an interesting mix of people in the sharecropping community. So I began to look at how they moved around. I began to look at how transportation affected deployment within the military from the 1930s until right before Pearl Harbor. I started to ask, "Why is this migration so embedded not only in farmwork but also in agricultural factories for the military industry?" Besides the military, there were other ways sharecroppers were transported. If they didn't have cars, they bartered for WPA sponsorship buses, they rode the trains, and they rode the rails, a lot. It's interesting to look at these forms of transportation for the military and the sharecroppers. I'm rotating back and forth between the flashback and the military, noticing how everybody is constantly on the move. They're arriving and departing and arriving and departing. I did not know this until I was writing this novel.

SW: *One of the controversies that arises around public transportation is when it is framed through the lens of climate change as providing alternative transportation for people who have cars. The idea is that if it's easy for them to not use their cars, then there are fewer cars and less pollution. The needs of people who don't have cars and who aren't contributing to pollution don't seem to matter. They get even more erased than they were before the conversation became one about reducing the number of cars.*

HV: Yeah, and you know what? Cars have not been reduced, let me tell you. Yesterday, when I got in from the airport and took out my rental, I was stuck on the freeway for an hour and a half. It was like a parking lot. But you're right, Sarah. People would use the Metro more if it was cheaper. I think it's expensive. For example, when I was at Smith College in Claremont, I would take the Metro, pay seven dollars, and it would drop me off in east LA at Cal State LA in forty-five minutes. Now that's damned good. No freeways, nothing to worry about. But if I were to have to do that fourteen-dollar round trip every day, five days a week, it would add up. How many people can afford that?

And then, where is the Metro? Where is it centralized? Now, of course, the Metro has come to East LA. I haven't been around enough to see how it affects the lives of residents. But I don't trust the people who design these things. When they finally connected East LA to the Metro, I knew that it would mean that some part of East LA was going to be gentrified. Because why else would the city pay attention to this part of the world if not to exploit it?

DV: *A question I have is how your work relates to other writers who write about Los Angeles. I'm thinking about people like Héctor Tobar and Karen Tei Yamashita, among others. Public transportation figures prominently in their novels, too. The relationship that the characters that you write about, and that Tobar and Yamashita and others write about, have very different relationships to transportation than the environmental issues that Sarah brings up: reducing the number of cars, reducing pollution, easing traffic, et cetera. It seems that "mainstream" environmental discourse is more about quality of life. It's a different thing for the characters in your novel to take public transportation or to see the coming of the Metro or the freeways as potential harms rather than benefits. I'm thinking of Tobar's novel* The Tattooed Soldier. *There's a really rich scene where one of the protagonists is traveling to South Central during the Rodney King Uprising and public transportation actually stops and he has to walk forty blocks to get to his destination. It is interesting to think about that differential relationship—these things are supposed to make the world better, but in some ways, they disconnect more than they connect.*

HV: But you know what? When I go to New York City, the subways are packed with all kinds of people. The majority of them are working people going to their jobs or students going to school. It would be a much better choice to go to a place where there's public transportation that is cheap than to go to a place where public transportation is unavailable. Public transportation offers impoverished people a sense of survival. How can you even begin to think of the future when you can't survive the day?

That's why the day is so long for poor people: because all they're trying to do is make an appointment to go to the doctor and then it becomes two to three hours. It's unbelievable! When getting around is so hard, how can they even think of the future? How can they even think about building something better or doing something to become something better?

So I'm very excited about transportation. It's been a challenge. But I'm beginning to feel that something is coming out of this preoccupation, and that's exciting to me. I haven't felt this way in a long time.

SW: *I'd love to hear your perspective on climate change. I was really struck by the fact that the People's Climate March in New York in September 2014 had four hundred thousand people in attendance. There was a real effort to put indigenous groups and migrant rights groups at the beginning of the march. There were these beautiful signs there that talked about decolonizing the climate, and I kept thinking about something you've mentioned in several other interviews about how you see your fiction as decolonizing the imagination. It made me curious about how you were thinking about climate change and colonialism.*

HV: That's a good question. When I refer to decolonizing the imagination, I begin with us—the colonized. We who have to question our assumptions and realities to break our chains of colonization and to decolonize ourselves into another form of thinking about who and what we are. I'm assuming that these groups are approaching climate change in similar ways. But what's so scary about climate change is that the earth is steadily getting hotter, and there's no return from it. What is so devastating and scary to me especially is that from the very beginning, conversations about global warming always made reference to those people that would be most hurt. Who are those people? Primarily Third World people and poor people. I knew immediately that this is something that we're all going to have to deal with because we won't be immune to the devastation and we will not be left in blissful ignorance. People will die because of global warming. So, Sarah, I am greatly concerned—even pissed off. I am so afraid of what is going to happen to the world. I always go back to this seventh-generation saying: that we acknowledge how seven generations ago someone did something to ensure that seven generations later you and I would be here and that we have to make sure that seven generations from now somebody else will be here. That sort of lineage of active motivation to do something that's healthy for the world, healthy for the earth, is essential, and yet nobody is thinking that far ahead. The powers that be are thinking about the gas situation, about the Keystone Pipeline, about running out of oil. Why don't we try thinking outside the box and consider the ramifications of using so many cars? Why don't we think about making some sacrifices to ensure that seven generations from now, somebody else will be here? And the thing is, Sarah, at the rate we're going, I don't think we're going to live to seven generations more. So that for me is very, very scary. I can see why now people are returning to indigenous groups. Indigenous groups are incredibly rich in the way they think about reality; I'm not just being romantic about it. You know there is something deeply, deeply, deeply and profoundly disgusting about the way the capitalist system uses the bodies of its workers, that it considers the bodies of the earth and the earth itself as available for full exploitation. It's disgusting and scary, and we're going to have to make it stop because otherwise we're not going to live for seven generations more.

That's why for me, as much as I love Los Angeles, I feel such solace when I go to Ithaca, New York, and am surrounded by trees. The feeling they give me is almost like protection. I'll do what I can to keep them going because they keep me going. It's a symbiotic relationship. I think we've severed ourselves from that symbiotic relationship in the turn to mass production. I think about the cruelty of the chicken factories and the cruelty associated with how the workers at the chicken factories are treated. I don't know what to say if we can't learn from this, if we can't work towards stopping it. If we can't do something about it, we're destined to fail as human beings. It's really sad. I remember seeing Cherríe [Moraga] back in New York when she was touring with *This Bridge Called My Back*, which has been reissued. She was saying it's all about selecting one or two things that you feel passionate about and acting upon them. She said that's what true political activism is. We don't often see our actions, our everyday realities, as being political. But if we act to help the earth's survival—perhaps something as small as recycling, perhaps working to be more aware of these chicken slaughterhouses and refusing to support the companies that run them—if we do something like that, it's a form of political activism. That makes us political people. I think we finally need to do more than that. But we start with that, we begin there.

SW: *That's really fantastic.*
DV: *Well, that seems like a pretty fabulous place to end. Thank you so much for your time, Helena.*
HV: Thank you, David, and Sarah, for everything. You guys are great!

NOTES

1. See the interviews with Castillo and Moraga conducted by Ybarra for this volume.
2. For a sample of ecocritical readings of Viramontes's work, see Fiskio; Grewe-Volpp; Huehls, "Ostension, Simile, Catachresis"; Huehls, "Private Property as Story"; Wald, "Visible Farmers/Invisible Workers." For decolonial environmental readings of her work, see Hsu; Ramírez-Dhoore; Wald, "Refusing to Halt."

3. See, for example, Curiel; Garay; Moya; Yarbro-Bejarano.
4. See also Vázquez; Ybarra 133–138.

WORKS CITED
Anzaldúa, Gloria, and Cherríe Moraga, editors. *This Bridge Called My Back: Writings by Radical Women of Color.* 4th ed., SUNY Press, 2015.
Castillo, Ana. *So Far from God.* Norton, 2005.
Curiel, Barbara Brinson. "'Had They Been Heading for the Barn All Along?': Viramontes's Chicana Feminist Revision of Steinbeck's Migrant Family." *Rebozos de Palabras: An Helena María Viramontes Critical Reader,* edited by Gabriella Gutiérrez y Muhs, U of Arizona P, 2013, pp. 27–47.
Fiskio, Janet. "Unsettling Ecocriticism: Rethinking Agrarianism, Place, and Citizenship." *American Literature,* vol. 84, no. 2, 2012, pp. 301–325.
Garay, R. Joyce Z. L. "Crowbars, Peaches, and Sweat: Coming to Voice through Image in *Under the Feet of Jesus.*" *Rebozos de Palabras: An Helena María Viramontes Critical Reader,* edited by Gabriella Gutiérrez y Muhs, U of Arizona P, 2013, pp. 192–216.
Grewe-Volpp, Christa. "'The Oil Was Made from Their Bones': Environmental (In)justice in Helena María Viramontes's *Under the Feet of Jesus.*" *ISLE: Interdisciplinary Studies in Literature and Environment,* vol. 12, no. 1, 2005, pp. 61–78. doi:10.1093/isle/12.1.61.
Hsu, Hsuan L. "Fatal Contiguities: Metonymy and Environmental Justice." *New Literary History,* vol. 42, no. 1, 2011, pp. 147–168.
Huehls, Mitchum. "Ostension, Simile, Catachresis: Misusing Helena Viramontes's *Under the Feet of Jesus* to Rethink the Globalization-Environmentalism Relation." *Discourse: Journal for Theoretical Studies in Media and Culture,* vol. 29, no. 2, 2007. digitalcommons.wayne.edu/discourse/vol29.
———. "Private Property as Story: Helena María Viramontes' *Their Dogs Came with Them.*" *Arizona Quarterly: A Journal of American Literature, Culture, and Theory,* vol. 68, no. 4, 2012, pp. 152–182. Project Muse, doi:10.1353/arq.2012.0021.
Moraga, Cherríe. *Heroes and Saints and Other Plays.* West End Press, 1994.
Moya, Paula M. L. *Learning from Experience: Minority Identities, Multicultural Struggles.* U of California P, 2002.
Ramírez-Dhoore, Dora. "Dissecting Environmental Racism: Redirecting the 'Toxic' in Alicia Gaspar de Alba's *Desert Blood* and Helena María Viramontes's *Under the Feet of Jesus.*" *The Natural World in Latin American Literatures: Ecocritical Essays on Twentieth Century Writings,* edited by Adrian Taylor, McFarland, 2010, pp. 175–195.
Tobar, Héctor. *The Tattooed Soldier.* Reprint ed., Picador, 2014.
Vázquez, David J. "Their Bones Kept Them Moving: Latina/o Studies, Helena María Viramontes's *Under the Feet of Jesus* and the Cross-Currents of U.S. Environmentalism." *Contemporary Literature,* vol. 58, no. 3, 2017, pp. 361–391.
Villa, Raúl Homero. *Barrio-Logos: Space and Place in Urban Chicano Literature and Culture.* U of Texas P, 2000.
Viramontes, Helena María. *The Moths and Other Stories.* Arte Público Press, 1995.
———. *Their Dogs Came with Them.* Atria Books, 2008.
———. *Under the Feet of Jesus.* Plume, 1996.
Wald, Sarah D. "'Refusing to Halt': Mobility and the Quest for Spatial Justice in Helena María Viramontes's *Their Dogs Came with Them* and Karen Tei Yamashita's *Tropic of Orange.*" *Western American Literature* vol. 48, nos. 1 and 2, 2013, pp. 70–89.
———. "Visible Farmers/Invisible Workers: Locating Immigrant Labor in Food Studies." *Food, Culture, and Society,* vol. 14, no. 4, 2011, pp. 567–586.

Yamashita, Karen Tei. *Tropic of Orange*. Coffee House Press, 1997.
Yarbro-Bejarano, Yvonne. "Phantoms and Patch Quilt People: Narrative Art and Migrant Collectivity in Helena María Viramontes's *Under the Feet of Jesus*." *Rebozos de Palabras: An Helena María Viramontes Critical Reader*, edited by Gabriella Gutiérrez y Muhs, U of Arizona P, 2013, pp. 67–96.
Ybarra, Priscilla. *Writing the Goodlife: Mexican American Literature and the Environment*. U of Arizona P, 2016.

10

"Between Water and Song"

Maria Melendez and the Contours of Contemporary Latinx Ecopoetry

RANDY ONTIVEROS

The last decade has been a boom time for Latinx poetry. In 2001, Chicago-born Puerto Rican poet Mayda del Valle won the National Poetry Slam individual title. In 2009 she performed her hair-raising poem "Grandmother" at the White House Poetry Jam, where she shared the stage with Lin-Manuel Miranda, a Puerto Rican poet from New York who that night debuted a new verse entitled "Alexander Hamilton." It became part of a Broadway musical that later garnered quite a few awards of its own. Eduardo C. Corral won the prestigious Yale Younger Poets award for his volume *Slow Lightning* in 2011. Richard Blanco recited his poem "One Today" at President Barack Obama's 2013 inauguration. In 2015 Ada Limón's *Bright Dead Things* was announced as a finalist for the National Book Award. Also, in 2015, Chicano poet Juan Felipe Herrera was named poet laureate of the United States. He was the first Latinx writer to hold the title.

These laurels, though, tell only a small part of the story. As impressive as they are, they barely scratch the surface of the range and depth of material available today, both online and in print. This chapter explores twenty-first-century Latinx poetry, focusing particular attention on nature as both a thematic concern and an aesthetic principle in the writings of Maria Melendez, a highly original and influential contemporary Chicana poet. Like poets of millennia prior, poets of today turn to the natural worlds that humans are part of for inspiration, instruction, comfort, argument, pleasure, and purpose. Yet unlike earlier generations, contemporary poets write at a time when the available scientific evidence of human-caused environmental devastation is overwhelming and when a complete ecological collapse, or what Elizabeth Kolbert calls "the sixth extinction," is imaginable.

What does it mean to turn to nature as a setting and a symbol when nature itself is in crisis? What is distinctive about representations of nature in contemporary Latinx verse? How does this canon contribute to our understanding of the cause and cure of environmental despoliation? Where does twenty-first-century Latinx nature poetry fit in relation to the long and diverse traditions of nature poetry in Europe, the Americas, and beyond? And what can it contribute to struggles for social, economic, political, and cultural representation? These are some of the key questions I address in the following pages. No single essay can capture the varied ways in which contemporary Latinx poets engage with nature. Rather than set out on a quixotic venture of an encyclopedic tour, the following pages take the opposite approach by zooming in on the work of Maria Melendez and in particular on her powerful 2006 volume *How Long She'll Last in This World*. Though not known by a wide reading public, Melendez is a Mexican American poet whose writing about nature, art, womanhood, war, and other subjects has been influential in Latinx poetry circles and beyond. What makes *How Long She'll Last in This World* worth our attention is the fact that it draws on thematic and formal traditions vital to Latinx poetry while also moving Latinx poetry in new directions by imagining those traditions within the generic conventions of ecopoetry. It would be a reach to call Melendez's volume the first collection of environmentalist poems in Latinx literature, but she may very well be the first Latinx poet to define herself as an ecopoet and to be received as such.

What is ecopoetry? The genre is difficult to define because "nature" as a subject is so vast and inescapable, but poet John Shoptaw defines ecopoetry simply and helpfully as verse that has two characteristics, one formal and one phenomenological. First, it is environmental, meaning that it is centrally "about the nonhuman natural world" or—even better, I would say—about the *relation* between the human and the nonhuman natural world. Second, it is environmentalist, meaning that "it aims to unsettle" the reader in its representation of the human damage done to local and global ecosystems (Shoptaw). In other words, ecopoetry attempts to use language to change the reader's perception of the relation between human and nonhuman nature and sometimes in doing so to create a change in action. For Shoptaw, these two dimensions of ecopoetry—the environment and the environmentalist, the subject of the poem and its impact on the reader—are united. *How Long She'll Last in This World* is a challenging read in some places and more accessible in others. However, all of the poems in the volume give expression on the page and in their effect on the reader to an incongruity that is more and more at the center of human experience: we are increasingly appreciative, scientifically and subjectively, of how much we are part of nature, and at the same time we are increasingly aware, scientifically and subjectively, of the danger our species poses to the planet. Melendez's poems emerge from this incongruity. They speak to the unevenness of the danger posed, for not all people are equally responsible for the environmental emergency that has been brought on by the Anthropocene. They record up close what it looks and feels like for members of marginalized communities to be impacted disproportionately by the conjoined forces of ecological harm and economic inequality. And not least, they observe in Latinx worlds the pleasure nature affords even amid crisis, as well as a measure of hope to be found in an art and a politics that balances tradition and adaptation—in other words, an art and politics made of "flexible bones."

Melendez's poetic career has been centered from the start on exploring the power and limits of language in expressing the relationship between human and nonhuman nature amid the neoliberal reshaping of global economies, rapid technological change, American-led militarism, sexism, and ecological devastation at the start of a new millennium. Her first published collection, a chapbook entitled *Base Pairs*, was published by the small press Swan Scythe in 2001. *How Long She'll Last in the World*, Melendez's first full-length collection, was published in 2006 by the University of Arizona Press. The book established her reputation as a Chicana feminist in the tradition of Gloria Anzaldúa, Cherríe Moraga, Lorna Dee Cervantes, Ana Castillo, Laurie Ann Guerrero, and Norma Cantú, among others. It was also Melendez's way of "staking my claim as an environmental writer," as she put it in a 2007 interview with Notre Dame's Institute for Latino Studies (Melendez, "Oral History"). *How Long She'll Last in the World* placed Melendez in a galaxy of American nature poets that includes Walt Whitman, Emily Dickinson, Robert Frost, Gary Snyder, Mary Oliver, Camille Dungy, Pat Mora, Lucille Clifton, and Wendell Berry. What makes the book distinctively Chicana is its sophisticated use of Mexican American iconography and narrative to bring the ecological destructiveness of modern capitalism down to a scale that is comprehensible, as well as her insistence on linking that destructiveness to the exploitation of Latinx lives and the lives of other marginalized communities.

In *Flexible Bones*, published by the University of Arizona in 2010 as part of its *Camino del Sol* literary series, Melendez once again crafted an ecopoetry written from a Latinx perspective. Both volumes make sophisticated use of free verse, subtle humor, code-switching between Spanish and English, scientific discourse, and indigenous imagery. Melendez's second volume, though, is more interior than her first. The poems in *How Long She'll Last in the World* make extensive use of description of the external world. Descriptive passages are part of *Flexible Bones*, but they tend to be shorter and more elliptical. *Flexible Bones* is also looser in its organization than the first volume. *How Long She'll Last in the World* is divided into four parts, each one describing (as Melendez puts it) "a habitat or an eco-zone" (Melendez, "Maria

Melendez"). *Flexible Bones* opens with a "Prologue" of five poems that establishes the bat (scientific order Chiroptera) as a central image and metaphor and then has two sections that move fluidly between registers. Studied together as a pair, Melendez's two collections show her range as a writer and the range of influences, images, and forms available to Latinx writers engaged with questions of environment and environmentalism.

The first poem I want to explore from Melendez's inaugural collection, *How Long She'll Last in the World*, is "An Argument for the Brilliance of All Things" ("Argument"). This poem, the second of the collection and part of the section focused on mountain regions, is a lyric that is structured as eleven tercets and a closing stanza of one line. The first two stanzas give the reader a description of a very particular location:

> *On a downed spruce at Murie Ranch,*
> *branches curve like scoured whale ribs,*
> *moss adheres as seaweed would.*
>
> *An old ruffed grouse struts through the windfall,*
> *drumming, drumming*
> *Its courtship ritual.* (Melendez 9)

Murie Ranch is a National Historic District in western Wyoming at the foot of the Grand Teton mountains. In the middle decades of the twentieth century, it was home to Mardy and Olaus Murie, prominent conservationists and nature writers who helped win passage of the Wilderness Act of 1964, a landmark piece of legislation that defined "wilderness" in American law and set aside over nine million acres of land for preservation. Melendez, who often writes autobiographically, worked for a time at the nonprofit Teton Science School based there.

The opening images of the felled spruce tree in stanza 1 and the "old ruffed grouse"—a medium-sized bird (*Bonasa umbellus*) native to Canada and the United States—in stanza 2 establish both a posture and a mood. The posture is one of observance, patience, and meticulousness. It is the posture of the scientist who (like the Muries and like Melendez herself) watches closely to gather data, to locate patterns, and to make hypotheses. Not coincidentally, it is also the posture of the nature poet who watches closely to grasp—or attempt to grasp—the external world at a moment in time and perhaps also to find in nonhuman nature a truth that will illuminate something about human nature. The mood established in and through the opening imagery is a mix of calmness, curiosity, and wonder. Both stanzas are woven together through a series of metaphors: branches like ribs, moss like seaweed, and mating that resembles drumming. From her vantage place at Murie Ranch, the speaker of "Argument" suggests that poetry and science are quite close to each other, despite popular opinion to the contrary. How is this so? Like science, poetry creates knowledge through a process that begins with observation and moves from there to questioning and to testing. Like poetry, science creates knowledge through description, classification, repetition, and measurement.[1] This analogy between two modes of human knowledge usually thought quite separate from each other is one that Melendez expands on elsewhere in *How Long She'll Last in the World*. It is also an aspect of the book that makes it particularly useful in the undergraduate classroom.

At first reading, the creative decision to begin a discursive poem like "Argument" with an image seems a strange one, since strictly speaking images do not make arguments. Not until the third stanza does the reader get a sense of the debate at hand. The speaker says:

Yet still we hear the claim "human consciousness
consummates," as though matter waits, barren,
for its better half. (Melendez 9)

The poem never gives an attribution for its quotation, but the claim about "human consciousness" sums up a popular belief that human intellect and human intellect alone is capable of making sense of the world. Melendez's choice of the verb "consummate" is indicative of her layered aesthetic. The word comes from the Latin word *consumārre*, which can mean "to perfect" and also (in postclassical Latin and in our English usage) "to complete a marriage through sexual intercourse." Melendez holds up for criticism the idea that nonhuman nature is somehow incomplete without human reason to give it meaning. The sexual denotation of the word *consummate* lends an additional layer to the argument because it feminizes the nonhuman and strips it of agency. Nature in this view is a woman and a powerless one at that, able only to wait for the seed of her "better half" to make her productive.

Melendez answers this anthropocentric argument not with abstract reasoning but with an inductive claim based on close observation:

Meanwhile, grouse sperm
Have every confidence
In the messy interlock

Of matter with matter. (Melendez 9)

The counterclaim is indirect, weird, and graphic. How many people have given much thought to grouse, let alone grouse sperm? And how many would point to grouse sperm as evidence of consciousness in the nonhuman?

Not many, I would guess. Yet Melendez summons the startling image of grouse sperm traveling in search of a grouse egg within the female body to suggest that humans are not alone in their perception of the world they inhabit. At every moment and in nearly every millimeter of Earth, innumerable living organisms do as their nature wills, without the permission and often without the knowledge of humanity. For the grouse sperm this means knowing with "confidence" that the collision of its "matter with matter" of another is right and true.

"Argument" points to all of nature's genius, in the sense (now obsolete) of "natural inclination" and in these sense (still around) of "natural ability or capacity."[2] The speaker calls on readers to appreciate this genius through another powerful image in the closing stanzas:

Know this, all humanists:

under the pure, lifeless
surface of the Sea
of Thought swims a great

gray whale, scarred
and barnacled, carrying
a calf, a great gray whale

about to breach. (Melendez 10)

Why address humanists in particular? The enjambment at lines 3 and 4 of the above excerpt may hold the answer. The line "surface of the Sea" brings momentarily into the reader's mind an image of the ocean, but that image is shifted suddenly in the following line as the ocean is made into a metaphor for the varied forms of consciousness that are found throughout nature. To the person focused on human knowledge divorced from the rest of nature, this "Sea / of Thought" seems "pure" and "lifeless." However, under the surface there is a vast, beautiful, and mysterious universe that Melendez symbolizes as a gray whale (*Eschrichtius robustus*) "carrying" its calf and "about to breach." Melendez was a new mother at the time she composed many of the poems in *How Long She'll Last in This World*, and she often meditates in the collection on motherhood as an important, though not universal, aspect of womanhood. In these closing lines, she paints a picture of a powerful female gray whale with its offspring as a way of challenging the view quoted in stanza 3 of nature as a "barren" female awaiting the masculine intervention of human reason. Through it, Melendez calls on humanists to be more attuned to "the brilliance of all things" and to be humbler about our own limited ways of knowing.

"Argument" is a good example of how Melendez's poetry frequently challenges and expands our imagination of what Latinx ecopoetry can look like. Nothing in "Argument" identifies it explicitly as a Chicana or Latina poem. There are none of the images, allusions, symbols, or other meaningful devices that we have come to associate with Latinx poetry—no border walls, no lotería cards, no Aztec or Mayan deities, no code-switching. There is, however, an intellectual, emotional, political, and creative orientation towards lives and lifeways that are devalued within the power structures of a colonial modernity. This orientation emerges from Melendez's identification with and education in Latinx poetry—a canon that is especially attuned to the ways in which differences in status and standing shape perception. Her subtle and sophisticated incorporation of this orientation into an environmentalist aesthetic is one of the main reasons why she is such an important voice both in Latinx poetry and in contemporary ecopoetry. In an essay that has been influential in the field of ecocriticism, the historian Lynn White Jr. argues that the origins of our present-day environmental emergency can be found in a medieval worldview that lent "a mood of indifference to the feelings of natural objects" because only humans were thought to have agency (White). "Argument" pushes against this perspective, which, according to White, was prerequisite to the European colonization of the globe because it made the exploitation of nature a moral imperative. Very subtly, Melendez's poem analogizes the denigration of nonhuman life and the denigration of human life.

The second poem I want to explore from *How Long She'll Last in This World* is "Llorona's Guide to Baptism," which appears (as the title suggests) in the "water" section of the volume. Unlike "Argument," this poem ("Guide") is a recognizably Latinx poem with its allusion to the legend of La Llorona. In fact, Melendez has spoken of "Guide" as a "rota" poem, or a poem that is required as proof and part of one's belonging to an order (Melendez, "Maria Melendez").[3] La Llorona, a Mexican and Mexican American folklore figure that is increasingly a part of broader American popular culture, is a woman who is said to roam the earth—usually the desert or the plains—crying out "Ay, mis hijos!" ("Oh, my children!"). Llorona is trapped in a state of perpetual grief over the death of her little ones. In some versions of the story, Llorona drowned her children with her own hands in a river, either because she was jealous of the time her husband spent with them or because her lover, a colonial Spaniard, rejected her as an indigenous woman in order to marry a woman of his own station. Often in these versions, when Llorona dies and arrives at the gates of heaven, God refuses to give her entrance until she has found the remains of her children. In other versions of the story, Llorona kills her children to protect them from European colonizers, and in still others the children die at the hands of their father, or a stranger, or by accident. The origins of the story are as phantasmic as Llorona herself.[4]

In the first stanza of Melendez's "Guide," Llorona gives the reader a rather odd piece of advice about the materials needed for baptism. She instructs the reader:

Even though the museum in Berkeley's run off with the skull,
hide the mammoth's twelve-pound hunk of broken tusk
for yourself—after all, you discovered it. (Melendez 64)

This opening tercet establishes a divide between the folkloric and the scientific, the unofficial and the official. On one side is the Berkeley museum that has "run off" with a "mammoth" fossil, likely a remnant of the woolly mammoth (*Mammuthus primigenius*) that roamed the North American continent thousands of years ago and was used extensively by modern humans (*Homo sapiens*) for housing, clothing, weapons, food, fuel, and art.[5] On the other side is the direct addressee of the poem, the "you" that is doubly Llorona and the reader. The museum will undoubtedly use the mammoth fossil for public purposes: education, modeling, fundraising, and the like. Llorona, and those who follow her instructions, will "hide" the bone and use it for private purposes not revealed until the end of the poem, and even then not fully. What is clear in these opening lines, though, is the need for self-reliance. The enjambment and the em dash that together set off the words "for yourself" in line 3 make clear that this "baptism" will require furtiveness, courage, and self-determination because it is unsanctioned by institutional gatekeepers. The divide in this stanza between the official and the unofficial brings to mind questions long central to feminist philosophy about what counts as knowledge and who counts as knowledgeable when it comes to nature and its truths. Melendez raises these questions to signal the importance of embodied experience as a source of knowledge.

The second stanza of "Guide" gives instruction about the water to be used for this enigmatic baptism. The speaker says:

As for the water: any creek
with fish storing enough mercury
to damage a human fetus
will do. (Melendez 64)

Her words seem to suggest an upending of the moral order. The mother figure seems to be calling for the destruction of her child rather than the child's protection through religious ritual, almost as if the poem was in fact a surreptitious guide to abortion. And yet this suggestion is followed immediately by the intimation that the real danger comes not from the mother but from the world outside her womb:

> *Any waterway modern enough*
> *to give you this recurring dream: Throw daughter in,*
> *then jump in after her. (Melendez 64)*

The "recurring dream" encapsulates the many ambiguities at the heart of the Llorona story. Is she her daughter's murderer or savior? Is death a mercy or a cruelty? Is Llorona victim or villain? How do we know?

Bringing a child into the world at a time of ecological peril can feel morally fraught because life-giving and death-dealing seem bound up with each other. For the mother in "Guide," this dilemma is especially acute. As in the world beyond the page, society has placed on Llorona an unequal obligation for caregiving and yet has stripped her of power over and in her environment and hence denied her the ability to fully protect her offspring. The result is a sense of helplessness rendered vividly by the image Llorona sees when she goes underwater to rescue her child:

> *There she is, on top of a gravel bar,*
> *no crawdads hiding under her yet,*
> *no aquatic plants*
> *anchored to her belly. Pull her up,*
> *why   won't   she   focus   ? (Melendez 64)*

The momentary pause between words in the last line and the isolated question mark that ends the stanza punctuates Llorona's uncertainty and her dismay. Her dream in many ways is an allegory for the worry that comes with parenting in these precarious times.

Like her use of the mammoth as image and symbol, Melendez's reference in this second stanza to mercury is nuanced. Mercury (atomic symbol Hg) is unique in nature because it is the only metal that is liquid at ordinary temperatures. Melendez captures this hybrid, seemingly paradoxical quality of mercury when she describes a "metallic creek" in stanza 5. In ancient times the element was known as *hydragyrum*, or "liquid silver," and while its dangers were known by some, it was used extensively in the Mediterranean, China, Egypt, and elsewhere for medicine, alchemy, and the arts (Enghag). (Cinnabar, the mineral source of most mercury, was and is used in paint for its distinctive red color.) Even more is known today about the element's toxicity, but mercury is still used widely and can be found at alarming levels in watersheds around the globe because of industrial discharge (Hong et al.; U.S. Geological Survey). The human fetus is especially vulnerable to mercury poisoning, even at infinitesimal levels, and so Llorona's advice to use toxic waters for this baptism is both a grim concession to ecological danger in modern times and an angry insistence on survival through imagination, here represented as a "recurring dream" in which a mother manages to pull her daughter from the poisoned depths.

Stanzas 3 through 5 of this six-stanza poem counsel the reader in reconciling herself to life in what German sociologist Ulrich Beck calls a "risk society" (*Risikogesellschaft*). According to Beck's influential account, risk society is a complex "reflexive modernity" in which human communities around the globe are confronted with the dangers caused by their industrializing activities and must as a result reorganize themselves in response to insecurity. (Beck, *Risk Society*) Llorona comes to us as a figure from so-called premodern times. Melendez, though, perceptively reimagines Llorona as a figure eminently suited for survival in a risky world. The baptism she makes available in this poem is a ritual not of salvation or purification but rather of adaptation. What she offers is a guide on "dwelling in crisis," to borrow the ecocritic Frederick Buell's phrase for the difficult balancing act of recognizing the gravity of a potential ecological apocalypse without succumbing to apathy or fatalism (Buell).

What exactly is Llorona's advice on how to dwell in crisis? Her guidance is elliptical, as if to underline how difficult and how personal this process will be, and yet there is a logic to it. She first counsels an acceptance of the intense feelings of sadness and anger that follow from an awareness of environmental danger. Llorona instructs the reader to "wander the valley and wail" at the daughter's physical vulnerability and to "hiss at the water she drinks every day." She then cautions mindfulness of the limits of individual action. No matter how sad or angry or afraid a person may be, there is no way to sidestep danger by eliminating the source of the threat ("you cannot smash the metallic creek"), by assuming blame ("nor bash in your own head"), or even by sounding an alarm ("you . . . cannot holler through the ivory millennia"). Yet all is not lost. The closing stanza of "Guide" suggests there is a bittersweet comfort to be found in nature and in the imagination. The speaker says of the mammoth fossil "washed up from the creek":

> It is not a megaphone, not a witching rod for poisons,
> not a gun. It is not a moral compass.
> It's just another world
> the winter floods washed up from the creek,
>   and time comes
>   when woman needs something heavy
>   to haul around.

Nonhuman nature alone will not save humanity by telling us what ought to be done. But encountering more-than-human nature and reflecting on it can be a reminder that "another world" has existed and will exist. The Anthropocene is but one small chapter in a much larger story of life on this planet, and Llorona's discovery suggests each person is connected to it across space and time. It is a somber realization but a hopeful one in its clarity. From it comes a determination to fight. The poem does not specify what will have to be done, but it suggests a posture of readiness and—to use a word central to contemporary ecological studies—resilience. The subtle threat at the end of Llorona's "Guide" suggests a departure from the rhetoric of passive femininity that has dominated discourse about nature in Western art and philosophy.

Recent years have seen a tremendous expansion of Latinx poetry that focuses thematically and formally on environmental questions, either to critique a global system that overruns the natural world for the sake of profit or to try to create in and through art a worldview in which human and nonhuman nature are seen as deeply connected to and dependent on each other. Melendez has been at the leading edge of this expansion, and she represents a powerful example of how contemporary writers are building on a tradition of what Priscilla Solis Ybarra has called "goodlife writing," or an aesthetic impulse within Chicano/a writing that "embraces the values of simplicity, sustenance, dignity, and respect" as part of a "reciprocal relation with the natural environment" that questions dominant ideals of possession and territory (Ybarra 4–5). Melendez's *How Long She'll Last in This World* is a remarkable achievement because it extends this tradition of "goodlife writing" into the twenty-first century by blending together the poetic lexicon of Latinx culture and history and the habits of scientific observation and ecological awareness.

NOTES

1. Willard Spiegelman makes a similar point in *How Poets See the World: The Art of Description in Contemporary Poetry*. He writes, "To the literary as well as the scientific eye, accurate description is the logical starting point for any act of understanding and appreciation." Spiegelman's volume is an impressive argument for the importance of description in nature poems, but the book is made weaker by unsubstantiated claims that contemporary literary criticism does not engage with the aesthetic. His analysis would be better if the bandwidth of poets and critics he engaged with were wider.

2. "genius, n. and adj.," *OED Online*, June 2018, Oxford UP, http://www.oed.com.proxy-um.researchport.umd.edu/view/Entry/77607?redirectedFrom=genius, accessed July 29, 2018.

3. The OED defines *rota* as "a round or routine (of duties, etc.)" and also "a habitual custom or practice." The word has ecclesiastical origins and connotations.

4. Llorona has been discussed extensively and brilliantly for decades in Chicana/o studies. See, among others, Limón; Rebolledo; Perez; Blake.

5. Melendez's choice of the mammoth as image is significant because the real-life story of the mammoth, like the legend story of Llorona, is veiled in mystery. Paleontologists believe that the woolly mammoth was made extinct nearly four thousand years ago as a

result of climate change, human overhunting, or both. The mammoth tusk can thus be read both as a symbol of the impact humans would have on the rest of nature during the Anthropocene and as a cautionary tale of the impact that climate change can have on all species, ours included. See Wade.

WORKS CITED

Beck, Ulrich. *Risk Society: Towards a New Modernity.* Sage Publications, 1992.

Blake, Debra J. *Chicana Sexuality and Gender: Cultural Refiguring in Literature, Oral History, and Art.* Duke UP, 2008.

Buell, Frederick. *From Apocalypse to Way of Life: Environmental Crisis in the American Century.* Routledge, 2003.

Enghag, Per. "Mercury." *Encyclopedia of the Elements,* John Wiley and Sons, 2008, pp. 791–804. *ProQuest Ebook Central,* http://ebookcentral.proquest.com/lib/umdcp/detail.action?docID=481983.

Hong, Young-Seoub, et al. "Methylmercury Exposure and Health Effects." *Journal of Preventive Medicine and Public Health,* vol. 45, no. 6, 2012, pp. 353–63. *PubMed Central,* doi:10.3961/jpmph.2012.45.6.353.

Kolbert, Elizabeth. *The Sixth Extinction: An Unnatural History.* Henry Holt, 2014.

Limón, José E. "La Llorona, the Third Legend of Greater Mexico: Cultural Symbols, Women, and the Political Unconscious." *Between Borders: Essays on Mexicana/Chicana History,* edited by Adelaida R. Del Castillo, Floricanto Press, 1990, pp. 399–432.

Melendez, Maria. *Base Pairs.* Swan Scythe Press, 2001.

———. *Flexible Bones.* U of Arizona P, 2010.

———. *How Long She'll Last in This World.* U of Arizona P, 2006.

———. "Maria Melendez: Spotlight on Hispanic Writers." Interview by Georgette M. Dorn, 11 Apr. 2013, https://www.loc.gov/poetry/hispanic-writers/maria-melendez.html.

———. "Oral History with Maria Melendez." Interview by Steven Cordova, 5 Apr. 2007, *YouTube,* https://www.youtube.com/watch?v=VJU3YmeaYKs.

Perez, Domino Renee. *There Was a Woman: La Llorona from Folklore to Popular Culture.* U of Texas P, 2008.

Rebolledo, Tey Diana. *Women Singing in the Snow: A Cultural Analysis of Chicana Literature.* U of Arizona P, 1995.

Shoptaw, John. "Why Ecopoetry." *Poetry Magazine,* Jan. 2016, https://www.poetryfoundation.org/poetrymagazine/articles/70299/why-ecopoetry.

Spiegelman, Willard. *How Poets See the World: The Art of Description in Contemporary Poetry.* Oxford UP, 2005.

U.S. Geological Survey. *Mercury in Aquatic Ecosystems.* 2 Apr. 2014, https://toxics.usgs.gov/investigations/mercury/index.php.

Wade, Nicholas. "The Woolly Mammoth's Last Stand." *New York Times,* 2 Mar. 2017, https://www.nytimes.com/2017/03/02/science/woolly-mammoth-extinct-genetics.html.

White, Lynn Jr. "The Historical Roots of Our Ecological Crisis." *The Ecocriticism Reader: Landmarks in Literary Ecology,* edited by Cheryll Glotfelty and Harold Fromm, U of Georgia P, 1996, pp. 3–14.

Ybarra, Priscilla Solis. *Writing the Goodlife: Mexican American Literature and the Environment.* U of Arizona P, 2016.

11

"Justice Is a Living Organism"

An Interview with Lucha Corpi

GABRIELA NUÑEZ

Born in México, Lucha Corpi came to Berkeley as a student wife in 1964. After a painful divorce, Corpi raised her son, Arturo, while earning her degree in comparative literature at University of California, Berkeley, and started her work teaching English as a second language. Corpi wrote poetry to cope with the stress of her busy life, and after publishing her poetry, Corpi ventured into prose writing, creating the first Chicana detective series. She is the author of two collections of poetry, *Palabras de mediodía / Noon Words* and *Variaciones sobre una tempestad / Variations on a Storm* (Spanish with English translations by Catherine Rodríguez Nieto); two bilingual children's books, *Where Fireflies Dance / Ahí, donde bailan las luciérnagas* and *The Triple Banana Split Boy / El niño goloso*; and six novels, four of which feature Chicana detective Gloria Damasco: *Eulogy for a Brown Angel, Cactus Blood, Black Widow's Wardrobe,* and *Death at Solstice. Confessions of a Book Burner: Personal Essays and Stories* was issued in 2014. She has been the recipient of numerous awards, including a National Endowment for the Arts and an Oakland Cultural Arts fellowship, PEN-Oakland Josephine Miles and Multicultural Publishers Exchange Literary Awards, and Latino and International Latino Book Awards for her crime fiction. A retired teacher, she resides in Oakland, California.

Corpi generously invited me to her home in Oakland, California, where we spent a day and evening discussing her literature in relation to the environment. We spoke over various cups of coffee and a plate of delicious chicken enchiladas that her husband, Carlos, brought for us from a local restaurant. We sat outside on the top-level, outdoor balcony that overlooks her lush backyard below and the Oakland channel from a distance. Much of our conversation about the environment caused Corpi to discuss her early years, growing up in the small town of Jáltipan in the state of Veracruz, Mexico. In the early 1950s, after high-grade minerals were discovered in Veracruz, both Mexican and U.S. companies invested in multimillion-dollar Frasch plants to extract sulfur. Companies such as the Texas International Sulphur Company from Houston, Texas, and Central Minera, S.A., from Mexico City secured contracts with the Mexican government that gave them the freedom to explore 123,550 acres on the Isthmus of Tehuantepec and to extract hundreds of thousands of tons of sulfur per year (Freeman 71). The environmental degradation that resulted from mineral and oil extraction are among Corpi's earliest memories of her beloved hometown. The fourth of five interviews with writers included in this volume, this conversation makes clear how Corpi gains sustenance from her surrounding ecology in a way that prioritizes a relationship grounded in equity rather than in a transcendental experience, and in this way she contributes to an expansion of the idea of environmentalism in this section on "Justice."

GN: *Do you identify as an environmentalist?*
LC: No, I don't identify myself as an environmentalist, but I guess I am in practice. I grew up in my hometown [Jatltipán] where it was lush and so pretty and so neat, until there was a sulfur company that moved in, because Veracruz is very rich in petroleum and minerals. I was fourteen years old when we finally realized what they were doing to the environment and killing the birds. And finally it dawned on me that we had to take care of our little planet. Do you remember the story of *The Little Prince*? He would get up every day and dress himself and then go take care of his planet, his little rock in space with one rose. But that was his planet, and he took care of that rose, and he took care of himself, and he took care of the environment. I always remember that. I think it's such a clever book. From a very young age I began to see what we were doing to the environment in Mexico, where there were no regulations for these companies. People were so careful to take care of the streams, the creeks, and the rivers. They would go and wash their clothes, but they were careful not to pollute the waters. We grew up in that kind of environment, so that you become an environmentalist, whether you like it or not. You begin to know that you cannot waste things just because they are there. It's really interesting because we always think that our resources will last forever, that the world has been going on for many millennia, and that it will go on. But, no. We have to be like the Little Prince. We have to take care of our little rock in space. Because we have abundance—like in this country—we developed that mentality of waste.

GN: What would you say are early childhood experiences that shaped your ideas in relation to the natural environment?

LC: My first eight years on this earth were spent in a place that is abundant in green. I mean, all sorts of different greens in the jungle, in the rivers, around the rivers. There is so much water that it was just all kinds of exuberant green. In my home, we would go from room to room turning on the lights so that it wouldn't be dark, so that the devil wouldn't come and get us in the dark. And my dad would go behind us turning them off and reminding us that, even though we could afford the electricity bill, there was no reason to have all the lights on. But the environment, whether it's city or countryside, is very important to me. I feed on that. I get my energy from the place where I live, and I've always had that.

GN: How do your detective novels address environmental crimes in relation to social justice?

LC: I do deal with what poisons the environment, because that is a crime. I deal with nature, of course, as it is, but I also deal with the connections between agribusiness and the poisoning of the water and the poisoning of the soil. In *Cactus Blood*, the planes spray at night or in the wee hours because that's when nobody's there. And they feel that by the time everybody comes to the fields, at five or six o'clock in the morning, that that will have dissipated, but a lot of it stays. And so, my character Carlota runs through those fields when they're really wet with all that poison, and she suffers.

When I was doing research for *Cactus Blood*, I came across a list of books that dealt with insecticides, the effect of insecticides and pesticides. One was called *The Pesticide Conspiracy*, written by a professor at UC Davis who was interested in the effects of long-term use of pesticides. He thought that in California agribusiness was going to contaminate streams and wells. He was ostracized by his colleagues. I mean, imagine, all of them were pro-agribusiness, and agribusiness was putting a lot of money into those programs, pretty much buying them up. But he was ostracized until he retired. I thought, "My goodness, what are we doing? What kind of world are we leaving for the next generations?" I talked to a doctor who worked with the farmworkers, and she said if you're going to give a child under a certain age fruit, take the skin off. Peel it, even if they're older and they can bite into it. The grapes are the worst. And no one peels the grapes.

GN: You describe the process of writing as informed by the "natural" environment when you say, "But my writing space, even when it has been only a narrow table in a corner of the living room, has always faced a window with natural greenery beyond it. Green is the way my spirit spells constancy and harmony. It's at once the familiar present and the connective tissue between my past and future" (Confessions 4). Does natural greenery continue to be your constant at your writing desk?

LC: Yes, in my office I have full view of the yard, of the trees, all the way to the [Oakland stream] channel, if I look closely. When I'm writing I look up and I see the avocado tree, the banana tree that never gives bananas [laughter], the cypress, the sequoias, the redwoods, the pines, and oaks. When I look up, that's what I see, and that's what calms me. The green makes me focus. If I see green, I feel not only calm, but I feel hopeful. It's sort of like knowing that the world will go on, even if I'm not in it anymore, that there is that possibility of constant renewal, as there is in nature, and that my children, my grandchildren, my great-grandchildren, will be able to enjoy that and have that sense of calm and focus also.

And there is a lot of green in California because a lot of species have been brought. The California soil is so good, and species thrive, not just animals and trees, but people too. I count in Oakland easily eighty languages spoken daily. People might come very proficient in subjects in their own language. But they come here, and they don't understand anything. Once they catch up and have the language, they will do well. But, in the meantime, they're treated as slow. They're treated as troubled children because they don't pay attention sometimes, because they are trying to absorb so much every day. So Oakland has a lot of problems, but they are problems that I like.

GN: *Which of your characters best represents your engagement with environmental issues in your work? What can Gloria teach us about the California landscape that other detectives might not?*

LC: Gloria is the one that pretty much has that eye for everything. She's very much a city person, and she's very arrogant. But at the same time, she notices the nature around her. That woman moves a lot. She has to go here and there, and it's almost like she sets herself up. And I follow her wherever she wants to go, and I do my research so she doesn't have to wonder. But it's her will that always goes in the books. I mean, when I was writing *Cactus Blood*, I was very much into her way of looking at things and thinking, which in some cases were not mine. But I trusted her. That whole focus on the cactus plant is Gloria's, and maybe for that reason in the novel there's also a lot of the Native American culture. Gloria's personality includes a love for the land, love for the landscape, and the landscape shapes her.

GN: *As an investigator Gloria Damasco does all the traditional legwork of a detective. At the same time, she trusts her instincts and clairvoyance de-*

spite the way her visions can be nebulous. In fact, her dark gift often launches Gloria into a vision where she grapples with other humans and nonhuman life. For example, there is a quote in Death at Solstice that describes Gloria's "dark gift" in relation to the natural world:

> What would happen when I entered the darkness of another recurring vision plaguing my dreams more and more often? Two pairs of black eyes watching me in the night; a phantom horse and the horseman on him; the redolence of gardenia and rose and candle wax in the night air; the black curls and sweet face of a boy toddler searching for his mother; an animal's growl; a place of worship by the water's edge, seeped in the suffering of people; the voice of a woman saying, "Find this place and you'll find me." Would I survive being trapped in a body of water unable to free myself before my breath bubbled totally out of me? (7)

What role does the natural world have in Gloria's investigative process? Is the natural world part of both the "traditional" and "nontraditional" detective methods of investigation?

LC: Gloria is a visionary. Gloria sees pieces that she has to put together in order to save someone or to do the right thing. She also functions very much at an intellectual level and questions everything, and that's why she's a good private detective. But what makes her a good human being is the fact that she accepts her instinct. She is not the gumshoe type detective. She has a very good mind, and she's very curious and uses all of this intellect to solve the case and to help other people. But she also knows how to approach people and is not judgmental. A judgmental detective is very common in a lot of the more traditional mysteries. But somehow she treats everyone more natural. She doesn't say someone is bad because they're doing this or that. She doesn't judge, and that's what I like most about her. And we're different. I don't judge that much either, but when I do I can be vicious [laughter], and she always stops me from being vicious.

That's a different kind of knowledge when Gloria is in the natural world because her instincts are different when she is in the outdoors, especially in *Death at Solstice*, where she had to do surveillance from up in the hills, in the middle of the night and no bathrooms, nothing. So she is surrounded by nature. Mountain lions and bobcats are coming down to the cities because their habitat is being destroyed by fires and by pollution. So if Gloria goes out there into the wild a little, into the foothills, she will encounter the animals, at least at a distance.

GN: *In your description of justice, you say that "justice is a living organism, mutating, evolving. Like a poem, it takes substance and form from incon-*

gruent elements at various levels of consciousness and the subconscious. Both poetry and justice, however, are elusive. They both require from us that we stop and listen—acknowledge." (Confessions 52). *Based on this definition, do your characters find or achieve justice? If so, what does that form of justice look like? If not, what does their quest for justice require for us readers to acknowledge?*

LC: Justice has a lot to do with a sense of self, in a group, in culture, in your environment. Sometimes you want justice, which is not the same as a system of law. Justice is separate from a system of law. You have personal justice, your own sense of yourself around others and others around you. So, you feel first. Your sense of justice will be totally turned around if you see a child being attacked because I think for the most part, it's in our nature as human beings, and animals do it too. Wild animals will kill if their young are threatened. But also, there are some animals that, if you touch their babies, they will not feed them anymore and abandon them because they've been touched by strangers. That one gets me, for example, because there are too many girls in the family, who are left by the river by their tribes. And it happens to a lot of young girls in the world. You begin to look at these things and you question yourself as to your sense of justice, your own sense of justice, and that has nothing to do with the law because in those countries where girls are abandoned, the law protects the people who abandoned them. Sometimes it's their own parents or grandparents. And it doesn't happen to boys because boys can work and bring some money and some food in. They're protected. But the girls, what good are the girls other than having babies, right? And so you have to calibrate your own sense of justice when you're exposed to so many different cultures. I still think that it is wrong and unjust to leave a girl, just because there are four of them and you want a boy, and that this is done by women, the women in the family. If they don't do it themselves, they go along with it. I question myself as to what their sense of justice is. Even if the law says it's okay to do it. Justice is shaped by the environment but also by the individual. There is a sense you have; you're born with it too.

Gloria might be making her decisions that you would not make if you were in her place, but on the other hand, she's opening a door for you to look at justice from a different angle. And that's why she's a complex character. She has many qualities that I really love because she has opened those doors for me that I had no idea about—situations that I had never been into and therefore I had never considered but was involved in. Gloria's decisions come from a deep-seeded desire to make the world work. Gloria might kill someone. But it wouldn't be because she was angry with that person. Somebody else would be in a position of danger by the aggressor, and the aggressor had to be eliminated in order for that person to be okay.

From the first novel (*Eulogy*), justice for Gloria is not resolved, which opens the door to explore historical justice in *Black Widow's Wardrobe*. Women were not writing history. It was always *his* history. You would have to guess who la Malinche was in reality, in real life. Everything points to the fact that she was very smart and savvy and able to use her body as part of a formula to survive. Most history has been very unfair to la Malinche because the history is written by men. But a woman understands much more and accepts even if she doesn't necessarily say, "Well, maybe you had other options." That's what women tell other women, "Maybe you had other options" [laughter]. I've heard that one too many times [laughter]. And maybe she did have other options. Maybe she didn't, but what she had, she made the most of, and in a way that was gentle. She didn't go around telling anybody what to do. And in some ways that kind of woman with her facility for languages, for her extensive knowledge at such a young age, and probably much smarter than Cortez, being sold into slavery, is an injustice.

GN: *In your essay "The ASPCA's Most Wanted: All Creatures Great, Small and Peewee," you write about cohabiting with the natural world, such as the "wild and colorful and deadly terrestrial, avian and aquatic fauna," (61) and how* curanderos *have the talent of observation that helps them learn from the natural world and apply that knowledge to their healing practices. This essay explores the tensions in the relationships between humans and wild animals such as snakes and invisible microbes. You describe animals as a threat to human lives but also as emotional companions for humans during moments of stress and trauma. Then, in a delightful moment of your essay, you imagine yourself as topping the ASPCA's most wanted list. How has your conflicted relationship with animals throughout your life affected your life as a poet and writer? Has this complex relationship with animals you describe informed your views on compassion and empathy?*

LC: Well, because I think that—first of all, they were part of the family except that they were animals [laughter]. And pets did not live in the house with us. They did not sleep in our beds. There was a separation for health reasons. Although our pets were well cared for, other animals were not. And there were cases of rabies in our hometown. My sister got bitten twice by dogs, and she had to have those preventive [shots] because they were stray dogs. There are some very aggressive dogs, but most dogs, if you leave them alone, they leave you alone. They might come and sniff you and see who you are or know you that way, but they are okay. But my sister had developed this fear for dogs. For the most part, I was okay with dogs and cats and whatever. Before his death my brother had these beautiful, award-winning palomas. His palomas were award winning world-wide. And when he died, after the mass, they released 150 of his white doves. The growing of animals is a whole process of nurturing. Everything has a special process.

GN: *There is an ongoing theme of shapeshifting in your fiction and nonfiction. For example, you say, "I perfected my camouflaging techniques. Like an iguana, a lizard or some insects, I was able to blend into an environment, undetected by people around me. Being petite, timid and tending to melancholy helped" (Confessions 94). Blending into your environment has clearly sharpened your skill as a keen observer and writer. You also relate shapeshifting to your ethnic and bicultural identity as a light-skinned Chicana and Mexicana. In what ways has blending into your environment helped you? And what challenges has shapeshifting caused in either your life or the life of your characters?*

LC: In *Cactus Blood*, Ramon was a shapeshifter. He was a guardian spirit and protector of people and of the environment, even though everyone thought he was the criminal. Josie's mother was also a little bit of a shapeshifter. She could read the people around her, and she would change her ways to shift to a personality that would be welcomed.

I think I identify with her because actually in a way that's what I do. I change when I am in a certain environment. I become a part of it, and so I blend and I'm not a threat to anybody. Nobody knows, unless I say I'm a writer. I never talk about being a writer unless I know someone very well. I've always been a very low-key person. Even though I can be high key, too. I have my temper and everything, but for the most part, I am low key. I think that comes from teaching people from all over the world in a way not to offend somebody. I had to learn about my students' cultures. I had to learn about where to step and not to overstep boundaries.

But there is something very interesting in all this because being a teacher puts you in a position where you know you're the one who knows. You know the ropes. You are what they need in terms of experience. You are the teacher. Your student may say, "I don't know how to do this." Okay, let's see what it is, and we are learning that here. So you're kind of like a procurer when you teach English as a second language or any of the languages because they don't know. You begin to teach them how to do things. I never did things for my students. I always explained what to do. And I was there if they needed me to make a phone call to explain something to a social worker or a school, another teacher at the school. I was always there, but I always prepared them as well as I could to help give them that sense of being okay.

GN: *I am interested in the literal and metaphorical process of metamorphosis that you use to introduce your essay "Morpheus Unbound: Butterflies,*

Madmen and Death Dreams." *In this essay you discuss your intense dreams and nightmares and your evolving relationship with Morpheus as the source of some of your anxiety during stressful times in your life. Do you see your evolution as a poet as a process that is similar to a butterfly's metamorphosis? What does that process mean to you as an artist who is always evolving based on your personal experiences?*

LC: Well, I think you know that I didn't start writing until I was here [in the United States] and twenty-four years old. But my introduction to poetry was the memorizing and reciting of patriotic poems as a child. They had a little stool that I could step on, so that they could see me because I was so tiny [laughter]. Well, obviously, I loved poetry from that time on. But poetry wasn't something that was just poetry. It was music as well, and there is a relationship between music and poetry. But the fact was that I was introduced to school and to poetry in the same way—as a free person. I was never asked to perform in that sense. It wasn't expected. And I did it because I chose my loves and passions at that age. Then I was introduced to other kinds of poetry. And once I was introduced to those, those were the ones I liked. And in a way, poetry explained to me the world that I had been seeing and gave voice to the thoughts I had.

Poetry helped me understand what was in my head about butterflies, for example. Seeing them from being the caterpillar, the little eggs on a leaf, and then becoming caterpillars. And then going into their cocoons, their time capsules [laughter]. That's what I used to call them, time capsules. And so, early education was like this insect that had nothing to do other than grow and develop. I was never pressured to like something or to go to school or do my homework or things like that because I loved school. I learned to love school on my own. I also learned to love silence because for a four- or five-year-old, you're wiggly, you're restless. And I could leave that classroom if I wanted. Nobody was going to say anything. I could roam around the school. There were no expectations from me, so I had the freedom to evolve.

At the same time, I was invisible. And that is where I got that ability to blend in. It's an escape to blend into a group because silence was my companion during those years. And so, I learned to love silence, too. Now, when I get up at five thirty in the morning and the house is quiet and warm and the coffee's bubbling in the coffee pot, it is the best time for me. That's when I used to and still write. I'll start a crossword puzzle when I'm having my coffee, and then I go downstairs. My mind is very active by the time I go downstairs; the brain cells are awake [laughter]. So anyway, because I was never asked to do, never forced to do anything, I learned to love knowledge. And there were many ways that I could actually feed my curiosity and find my own answers. In some ways, I had a very nice childhood even though everybody says that I skipped childhood. But I didn't; I still played with my friends, hide-and-seek and all that stuff. It wasn't like I was alienated from my environment; I was part of it. And I can be in a group; I don't get bored when people talk about things that I'm not necessarily interested in because I just listen, and I always find something to be interested in what people are saying. I might not contribute much to the conversation, but I love listening. And people can surprise you. You're in a group, or you're just listening to the conversation, and people can surprise you with the things they think about. I'm always surprised by what people think about.

I do observe the environment, obviously, but I'm not necessarily apart from it. I'm in different environments in the different novels. Some urban and some more agricultural, and they become part of me for the time that I'm writing the novel. I'm there altogether. But with the poetry, it's a different process. It's actually more natural. Poetry is more natural to the human condition, to the human beings. I think we all think poetically. All the elements of the poem you have in your head. It's just getting them to the arm and hand. When I write poetry, I am in there. My presence is completely in there, and so I am experiencing whatever it is in the environment, and then somehow it's translated into verses. And so, it's an interesting process, very different to the writing of stories, narratives. It's very different because with the novels I'm more of a spectator.

Poetry is influenced by your environment. Whatever is happening around you also goes into the poem because to write a poem you must be vulnerable. Writing poetry exposes you—it exposes you to the thing that hurt you. We know that if you're vulnerable, you're in a state of being open to the universe. And being open to the universe might mean there are black holes where you might fall.

WORKS CITED

Corpi, Lucha. "The ASPCA's Most Wanted: All Creatures Great, Small and Peewee." *Confessions of a Book Burner: Personal Essays and Stories*. Arte Público Press, 2014, pp. 61–90.

———. *Black Widow's Wardrobe*. Arte Público Press, 1999.

———. *Cactus Blood: A Mystery Novel*. Arte Público Press, 1995.

———. *Confessions of a Book Burner: Personal Essays and Stories*. Arte Público Press, 2014.

———. *Death at Solstice: A Gloria Damasco Mystery*. Arte Público Press, 2009.

———. *Eulogy for a Brown Angel: A Mystery Novel*. Arte Público Press, 1992.

———. "Morpheus Unbound: Butterflies, Madmen and Death Dreams." *Confessions of a Book Burner: Personal Essays and Stories*. Arte Público Press, 2014, pp. 123–152.

———. *Palabras de mediodía / Noon Words*. Arte Público Press, 2001.

———. *Triple Banana Split Boy / El nino goloso*. Bilingual ed., Piñata Books, 2009.

———. *Variaciones sobre una tempestad / Variations on a Storm*. Third Woman Press, 1990.

———. *Where Fireflies Dance / Ahi, donde bailan las luciernagas.* Children's Book Press, 2002.

Freeman, William M. "Mexico Pushing Sulphur Mining." *New York Times*, 6 Jan. 1954, p. 71.

Saint-Exupéry, Antoine de. *The Little Prince.* Reynal and Hitchcock, 1943.

Van den Bosch, Robert. *The Pesticide Conspiracy.* Doubleday, 1978.

Part III / The Decolonial

Alternative Kinships and
Epistemologies of Futurity

12

Memory, Space, and Gentrification

The Legacies of the Young Lords and Urban Decolonial Environmentalism in Ernesto Quiñonez's Bodega Dreams

DAVID J. VÁZQUEZ

"There is nothing unnatural about New York City."
—DAVID HARVEY, *Justice, Nature, and the Geography of Difference*

Central to Ernesto Quiñonez's 2000 novel, *Bodega Dreams*, is a crisis of affordable housing. Securing an affordable apartment in the escalating 1990s Manhattan real estate market is a preoccupation for the novel's protagonist, Chino, and his wife, Blanca. Although critics such as June Dwyer, Sean Moiles, and Ylce Irizarry have explored aspects of urban space and gentrification in *Bodega Dreams*, the novel offers a case study for how Latinxs[1] engage environmental ideas in what Priscilla Solis Ybarra describes as decolonial contexts. *Bodega Dreams* expands how such concerns as fair housing, gentrification, and urban renewal function as environmental issues for urban Latinxs.

A key aspect of how the novel represents struggles for fair housing and for affirming urban space relates to the way *Bodega Dreams* memorializes Puerto Rican culture and activism in Spanish Harlem. At stake for Bodega, Chino, and the other characters who populate the narrative are the ways gentrification erases and sanitizes the oppositional history of the Puerto Rican Movement. As Irizarry observes, "the recreation of identity and ethnonational belonging functions as a shield against urban renewal and the end of gentrification is the quest the characters in *Bodega Dreams* undertake" (Irizarry 112). Struggles for affordable housing and against gentrification in the novel are thus framed in relation to memorializing antiracist and community uplift projects undertaken by Puerto Rican activists in Spanish Harlem.[2]

Bodega Dreams is particularly concerned with mediating the goals of antigentrification and affordable housing in relation to the Puerto Rican Movement group the Young Lords, a former street gang that became a leftist political party and community organizing group during the late 1960s. In relation to the legacies of the Young Lords, the novel rejects the fragmented nature of barrio life, instead affirming culture and history as rights that are fundamental to inhabiting this space. Rather than simply striving for affordable housing or antigentrification, the novel embraces challenges to the social order in accordance with long-standing civil rights efforts, particularly the legacies of housing justice activism enacted by the Young Lords.[3]

Yet as Laura Pulido reminds us in the foreword to this volume, "by focusing on" Latinx communities as "either victim or ecological innovator, other possibilities are obscured—namely, Latinx peoples as perpetrators of environmental harms" (xiv). With Pulido's intervention in mind, we might understand how Quiñonez's novel presents us with nuanced portrayals of Latinxs as complex environmental and social actors. For characters such as Chino, Blanca, and Bodega, a primary goal is striving against aspects of environmental degradation such as housing insecurity and gentrification. At the same time, we cannot ignore how these same characters—and others with less progressive motives, such as Nazario and the New York Police Department—are also perpetrators of environmental harm that include privileging capitalist modes of empowerment that lead to gentrification.

My use of the term *gentrification* refers to neoliberal urban renewal policies that shift finite resources in urban neighborhoods away from the poor and toward middle-class, mostly white residents. While the history of urban renewal is well known, gentrification policies include "slum clearance," tax incentives for upscale housing and shopping, and "preserving" commodified ethnic culture, or what Arlene Dávila calls "marketable ethnicity" (10–13). For Dávila, "race-neutral" housing policies are never devoid of racial and ethnic considerations. Instead, they constitute one way racial projects (Omi and Winant) operate in urban contexts. As Latinx novelist and Brooklyn community organizer Daniel José Older puts it, "gentrification is violence. Couched in white supremacy, it is a systemic, intentional process of uprooting communities" (par. 6). Gentrification is rampant across the United States, but famous cases include Boyle Heights and Echo Park in Los Angeles, Humboldt Park in Chicago, and Loisaida and Harlem in Manhattan. Popular press accounts and other representations often whitewash and normalize gentrification, portraying it as having positive impacts on urban areas.[4] Communities of color perceive gentrification differently. I draw on critiques of gentrification in my discussion of *Bodega Dreams* to advance these communities' efforts to expose the racialization that underwrites gentrification.[5]

Gentrification may not at first glance appear to be an "environmental" matter. Yet the uneven environmental costs and benefits of gentrification become clear when we consider them through ecocritical lenses. For example, in a 2012 executive order, Obama administration deputy HUD secretary Shaun Donovan links healthy communities to environmental justice by "promot[ing] communities that are healthy, sustainable, affordable, and inclusive" through access to fair housing. Under this policy directive, the federal government considers access to fair and affordable housing an environmental justice issue because removing access to housing for impoverished communities exacerbates environmental injustice.

In addition to affordable housing, white gentrifiers experience environmental benefits from gentrification. For example, gentrifiers commonly gain access to mass transportation, shortening commute times and reducing reliance on personal automobiles. Gentrifiers also benefit from greenwashing policies in cities like New York that clean up contaminated sites and provide access to green space in the urban core—an issue that accelerated during the Bloomberg and de Blasio administrations in the early 2000s.[6] These benefits provide environmental advantages to middle-class residents who displace communities of color, aggravating environmental injustice.

It is worth considering that gentrification is also driven by such issues as sea level rise in places like Miami and New York. Similar dynamics operate in U.S. cities such as New Orleans, Boston, and Sacramento, which are also threatened by sea level rise and other environmental changes. In a recent issue of *The Atlantic*, journalist Matt Vasilogambros links sea level rise to a surge in gentrification in historically black and Haitian neighborhoods occupying higher ground in Miami. Even when the pressure for gentrification to occur is not as clearly environmental as climate change, it often results in environmental privileges for some and the deprivation of environmental benefits for others.[7]

Reading *Bodega Dreams* through an ecocritical lens offers a productive strategy for unpacking poorly understood forms of environmental justice and aspects of self-inflicted environmental harm, including housing security and gentrification. As I and others note elsewhere in this volume, ecocriticism provides a critical focus on aspects of environment and sustainability—a crucial intervention in light of the escalating climate crisis.[8] Environmental justice critics such as Scott Slovic, Joni Adamson, Julie Sze, and others productively extend this focus on environmental representations in literary and cultural texts. Proposing how we might extend environmental justice frameworks to ecocritical readings of literary texts, T. V. Reed proposes that environmental justice "adds an absolutely crucial dimension to our understanding of environmental problems and solutions" by entailing a "fundamental reworking of the field [ecocriticism]" (157). Reed argues that "in addition to looking for the most direct sources for environmental justice ecocriticism, theoretical imagination should encourage us to approach texts where the links are not immediately present" (153).

I concur with Reed that environmental justice ecocritical approaches are crucial for understanding how literary texts by people of color represent environmental costs and benefits that unequally affect marginalized communities. Social scientists such as Pulido, Robert Bullard, and Devon Peña have long drawn attention to instances of environmental injustice that are central for understanding how people of color are often the objects of environmental harm. Similarly, critics such as Adamson, Sze, Rob Nixon, Stacy Alaimo, Catriona Mortimer-Sandilands, Ursula Heise, Greg Garrard, and Slovic point to innovative representations in literary and cultural texts that make visible the social costs of environmental injustice.

I build on this body of criticism to suggest that novels like *Bodega Dreams* offer decolonial imaginaries that extend and augment environmental justice. Reading through a decolonial lens does not obviate environmental justice criticism. Environmental justice is an essential intervention that makes visible how mainstream environmentalism responds inadequately to the concerns of communities of color. At the same time, because some forms of environmental justice focus on instances of environmental injustice to the exclusion of other concerns, environmental justice ecocriticism can reify stereotypes about people of color as victims. By emphasizing victimhood, we often miss the innovative ways people of color respond to and resist environmental harm in ways that undermine "the category of environmentalism itself" (Ybarra 16) or the ways communities of color express love of the environment outside of the framework of harm or resistance (Finney). Likewise, communities of color are not always environmental progressives. As Pulido asks, "what about lowriders?" (foreword, this volume).

As I and a growing group of critics such as Ybarra, Sarah Wald, Sarah Jaquette Ray, Karen Salt, Nicole Seymour, Robert Hayashi, Jennifer James, Winona LaDuke, Nixon, and others who have dedicated their work to interrogating the effects of environmental harm and the imbrication of some forms of mainstream environmentalism in structures of racism, capitalism, and colonialism argue, the articulations of people of color and subalterns writing from the formerly colonized world have crucial environmental perspectives. As Ybarra puts it, decolonial environmentalisms contain "a treasure trove of knowledge virtually unknown to and unrecognized by environmental studies" (20). A decolonial environmental lens thus allows us to understand how such authors as Quiñonez intertwine environmental concerns with other social justice agendas.

Bodega Dreams represents decolonial environmental ideas through a number of narrative strategies, ranging from nature imagery in the city to emphasizing fair and affordable housing to contest gentrification. In what follows, I map how the novel offers an alternative ethos of preservation that memorializes the Puerto Rican Movement, especially the environmental activism of the Young Lords, and valorizes Latinx[9] cultural and historical ties to Spanish Harlem. While not the emphasis of this chapter, both the novel and the Young Lords advocated for decolonizing the island of Puerto Rico, which, with territories such as American Samoa and Guam, remains one of the last colonies in the world.[10] It is therefore crucial to note that one of the central claims the Young Lords and other Puerto Rican Movement groups made was the decolonization of the island.

The plot of *Bodega Dreams* revolves around the narrator Chino's struggles between his desire for upward mobility—and a presumed move to the suburbs—and his need to remain in Spanish Harlem. As June Dwyer points out, one vector through which *Bodega Dreams* represents the idea of upward mobility is its imaginative retelling of F. Scott Fitzgerald's *The Great Gatsby*. Like Fitzgerald's tale, *Bodega Dreams* underscores the pitfalls of the American Dream by representing a community uplift project engineered in the present of the novel (the early 1990s) by the drug lord William Irizarry (aka Willie Bodega, the novel's namesake). While Bodega is not immune to drug violence (an important subplot deals with the murder of a "dirty" journalist and a potential organized crime war with a rival dealer), he retains his activist roots by investing in the community through "grants," college loans, and real estate transactions designed to establish "an entire professional class in East Harlem" (71). Bodega uses these investments to preserve Spanish Harlem's Latinx presence in the face of urban renewal: "Housing. Housing, Chino. Thass how I'm going to do it. Thass the vision" (28). Bodega's hope is that real estate accumulation will help Spanish Harlem residents "knock those projects down" and "free our island without bloodshed" (107).

Bodega's housing scheme is not solely about accumulating wealth and establishing community uplift. Instead, he insists that capital accumulation provides low-cost housing to neighborhood residents as a way to stave off gentrification. These antigentrification goals are embedded in a place-making project that embraces Spanish Harlem as a home for Latinxs. Bodega's project is thus about more than housing; it posits a "romantic ideal" (Quiñonez 13–14) designed to make an ethical claim to Spanish Harlem based on historical and cultural ties to the neighborhood. Moreover, Bodega's linking of illegality, urban renewal, anticapitalism, and decolonization forms part of the narrative's charge. Chino's ambivalence about Bodega's drug sales to neighborhood Latinxs is mediated by his attraction to Bodega's vision. Consequently, even though the illegal and fraudulent features of Bodega's program are problematic and alienating for the very residents he attempts to empower, the anticapitalist and decolonial aspects hold appeal. The tension between the means and the ends of liberation here reveals a radical decolonial vision that takes seriously Edward Said's notion that "empire is" first and foremost "an act of geographical violence" (271).[11]

Yet Bodega's attempts to develop the neighborhood in an economically just manner that valorizes and preserves the legacies of Puerto Rican activism reveal fault lines in how people of color are also agents of environmental harm. Bodega's program never rethinks capitalist empowerment through wealth accumulation (for him or for others). Consequently, Bodega's vision is limited by the framework he employs for community uplift: real estate accumulation and profits garnered from his drug trade.

By reading the novel from these perspectives, it is possible to understand how Latinxs contest historical erasure and environmental degradation while falling prey to capitalist discourses that reinscribe environmental harm. The twin risks of devaluing neighborhood history and culture and losing the neighborhood to upwardly mobile gentrifiers is a form of environmental harm tantamount to recognizable environmental representations in other Latinx social and historical contexts (exposure to high levels of lead contamination or air pollution and farmworker exposure to toxic pesticides and fungicides, for example).[12] As we will see, this decolonial environmental reading of the novel demonstrates how housing reform and cultural affirmation evidence environmental engagement in urban Latinx texts.

Gentrification, Place, and the Legacies of the Young Lords in Spanish Harlem

In advocating for decolonial environmentalism, I aim to expand how we understand urban Latinxs' complex relationships to environments, including how imaginative texts engage in acts of place-making. By asserting ownership over and claims to Spanish Harlem as a particular urban place, Quiñonez resists abstracting barrio space (Villa), which would divest it of its cultural, place-based meanings. In making the distinction between space and place, I draw on urban geography scholarship by David Harvey, Henri Lefebvre, and Raúl Homero Villa that considers how geographical spaces invested with social meanings determine "place." As Lefebvre argues, the terms "space" and "spatial" emphasize the dynamic ways that "in spatial practices, the reproduction of social relations is predominant" (50). Lefebvre's analysis points to how ideas about geography, land, and property are socially constructed and suggests interplay between abstract notions of space as conceived by authorities like urban planners, the police, and city officials and the lived space of individuals. Importantly for Lefebvre, the lived space of imagination can potentially resist and refigure official conceived space.

Bodega Dreams engages in place-making based on how Puerto Ricans and other Latinxs in New York City ascribe group meaning to the barrio by asserting historical and social belonging. A key aspect of this place-making is the way the novel conjures the history of Latinx decolonial, antiracist activism in New York City—in particular the history of the Puerto Rican Movement. Similar to the process Villa describes as "re-creating and re-imagining dominant urban *space* as community-enabling *place*" (6) in relation to Chicanx communities in Los Angeles, Spanish Harlem emplaces Puerto Ricans in New York owing to the history of activism and resistance to hegemony that took place (literally) on that ground. As Dávila notes, at stake in the gentrification of Spanish Harlem is "whether El Barrio remains primarily Latino, becomes gentrified, or—in the eyes of many, and wistfully offsetting this binary vision—develops into a gentrified but Latino stronghold" (3).

Asserting an alternative ethos of preservation is a primary way *Bodega Dreams* figures place-making. The ethos of preservation that informs *Bodega Dreams* arises from the historical legacy of insurgent activism in Spanish Harlem since the early 1960s. Of key importance is the association in the novel between the history of activism in Spanish Harlem and the meanings of and relationships with urban space. The novel thus meditates on Puerto Rican Movement legacies as a key aspect of combatting housing inequality in the 1990s. Coequal with this representation is asserting social and political belonging to the space of the barrio.

Emerging out of 1960s civil rights struggles, Puerto Rican Movement groups like the Young Lords, El Comité, and the Puerto Rican Socialist Party formed a constellation of activists that advocated for social justice for Puerto Ricans living on the mainland and for the decolonization of the island. *Bodega Dreams* leverages this history by revisiting Puerto Rican Movement activism. Among the Puerto Rican Movement representations in *Bodega Dreams* are Willie Bodega's position as a former Young Lord, commemorating the Puerto Rican Movement at El Museo del Barrio, and Young Lords organizers such as Juan González and Pablo "Yoruba" Guzmán and other important Nuyorican figures such as author and activist Piri Thomas who appear as characters.[13]

As Darrel Enck-Wanzer observes, the Young Lords were part of a collective of militant groups that emerged during the late 1960s. The Lords arose from social conditions similar to those that facilitated the transition in the Student Non-Violent Coordinating Committee (SNCC) from nonviolent strategies to Black Power, the militancy and separatism of the Chicano Movement in the Southwest, and the confrontational leftist activism of the Black Panther Party. These social movements deployed confrontational political strategies as responses to intractable racial, social, and economic conditions. Developing in relation to this milieu, the Lords intertwined advocacy for decolonizing the island with contesting the characterization of Puerto Ricans (on both the mainland and the island) as "docile" (Enck-Wanzer 20–21).

While Andrés Torres and José E. Velásquez, Enck-Wanzer, and Sonia Song-Ha Lee have chronicled the history of Puerto Rican and Latinx social movements in New York City, an understudied dimension of these groups is their environmental activism. In fact, a number of Latinx movements of the period undertook forms of environmental advocacy. For example, Wald explains in relation to the United Farm Workers that "the UFW's campaign linking pesticides to consumer and worker health shaped public understanding of toxins more than did the activities of many environmentalists" (172). Similarly, Randy Ontiveros recalls that "Arturo Sandoval, a Chicano from New Mexico, was one of the principal organizers of [the first Earth Day in 1970]," undercutting the idea that the environmental movement is a "twenty-first century update to the colonial nineteenth-century 'white man's burden'" (86). Wald and Ontiveros make clear that Latinx studies has yet to engage the complex ways Latinx social movements offered radical environmental imaginaries.

Flowing from Wald's and Ontiveros's observations, I argue that the Young Lords engaged environmental ideas in substantive ways and that Latinx studies' lack of recognition of these themes replicates the erasure of Latinxs from environmental movements that Ontiveros bemoans.[14] Like Chicano Movement activists, the Young Lords engaged environmental ideas that anticipated the contemporary environmental justice movement by more than a decade.[15] As Enck-Wanzer explains, "the first issue the newly formed New York Young Lords mobilized around was garbage collection" (231), emphasizing the centrality of environmental activism to the movement. The Garbage Offensive of 1969 protested ineffective sanitation services provided to East Harlem. Between July 13 and July 27, 1969, the Lords began cleaning the streets of Spanish Harlem to draw attention to environmental degradation that resulted from the lack of sanitation services. When the Lords' demands for regular garbage removal were denied, they cleaned the streets themselves, requesting supplies (brooms, garbage cans, etc.) from city officials. When the City rejected their requests, the Lords kicked off the Garbage Offensive by piling accumulated garbage to close "the streets of Third Ave. from 110th, across to 112th and down to Second Ave." (Enck-Wanzer 231), effectively cutting off Upper Manhattan from the rest of the island.

In contrast to how scholars have understood them, the Lords were self-conscious about their environmental engagements. For example, point 7 of the Young Lords Ten Point Health Program of 1970 reads, "We want 'door-to-door' preventative health services emphasizing environment and sanitation control, nutrition, drug addiction, maternal and child care and senior citizen services," and point 8 claims, "We want education programs for all people to expose health problems—sanitation, rats, poor housing, malnutrition, police brutality, pollution, and other forms of oppression" (Enck-Wanzer 236). In its coupling of "environment and sanitation control" with "rats, poor housing, malnutrition," and "pollution," the Lords linked social and political well-being with environmental issues. Moreover, in identifying social ills with environmental degradation, the Lords expanded what constitutes environmentalism at a moment when mainstream environmentalism was preoccupied with other ideas—for example, wilderness preservation or ideas about "spaceship earth" and the "population bomb."[16]

This concern with environmental ideas was not limited to the Lords' health statements. In their founding document, the "Young Lords Party 13-Point Program and Platform," they asserted connections between land, urban environments, and social justice that were central to their activism. Point 5 reads:

> WE WANT COMMUNITY CONTROL OF OUR INSTITUTIONS AND LAND. We want control of our communities by people and programs to guarantee that all institutions serve the needs of our people. People's control of police, health services, churches, schools, housing, transportation and welfare are needed. We want an end to attacks on our land by urban removal, highway destruction, universities and corporations. LAND BELONGS TO ALL THE PEOPLE! (Enck-Wanzer 36)

The opening claim links the control of "INSTITUTIONS AND LAND," suggesting that space and social well-being depend on control of and stewardship over land. As Mary Pat Brady explains in relation to Chicanx communities in the Southwest, altering relationships with land "changes not simply the look of the land but social relationships as well" (5). Brady's point helps us understand the Young Lords' claims for community control over land and institutions as mutually constitutive. The control of land and space are thus central aspects of civil rights and self-determination.

Point 5 also stresses resisting "urban removal, highway destruction, universities and corporations." Here, the Lords' claim rests on the idea that issues of environmental security (access to housing, transportation, and stable institutions) are tantamount to community control over land and space. In this call, the Lords anticipate by nearly fifty years the concerns of antigentrification activists, who point to challenges communities of color face in the age of gentrification. In particular, this claim rests on the premise that gentrification is a racial project designed to uproot communities of color from their historical relationships to particular urban spaces.[17] As Pablo "Yoruba" Guzmán, the Lords' minister of information, recalls, "now these things . . . are considered 'of course,' but back then, bringing environmental factors like lead-based paint into the discussion—or even connecting poverty and health—that was all new" (Lee).

In addition to direct action campaigns and founding documents decrying environmental conditions in the inner city, the Lords mobilized symbolic imaginaries in their struggles for social and environmental justice. Consider *Amerikkka the Beautiful*, a photo collage depicting garbage-strewn streets of Upper Manhattan with an image of the Statue of Liberty superimposed on the horizon (Figure 12.1) that appeared on the back cover of *Palante*, the Young Lords' newspaper, in 1970.

In the garbage strewn about the foreground, the collage recalls the Garbage Offensive—a moment of the recent past where the Lords commanded political attention from city officials and the federal government (within the

Figure 12.1 *Amerikkka the Beautiful* (*Palante*, vol. 2, no. 13, 16 Oct. 1970; image provided from the personal collection of Darrel Wanzer-Serrano).

first two years of the Young Lords' existence, they came under scrutiny by COINTELPRO, the FBI's counterintelligence program). The image also leverages what Sarah Jaquette Ray describes in another context as a "poetics of trash" that "shocks [. . .], fascinates journalists, and activates public involvement" (147–148). It is also important to consider how poetics of trash were mobilized during this period to decry the wanton environmental destruction that the unrelenting trash in the image represents—perhaps most infamously in the crying Native American of the "Keep America Beautiful" television campaign of the same period.[18]

The Statue of Liberty superimposed in the background is central to the depiction. By juxtaposing the symbol of freedom with the garbage littering the foreground, the image suggests two failures of contemporary U.S. life. First, as a symbol associated with immigrant and migrant arrival (and it is crucial to recall that Puerto Ricans have been U.S. citizens since the passage of the Jones Act in 1916), the image suggests an inability to fulfill the promises of U.S. citizenship. Here, the United States is far from a land of promise and equality; instead, it is a dystopian landscape, barren of green space and polluted by garbage. In invoking the KKK, the image also implicates environmental injustice as another aspect of white supremacy.

Second, by linking social injustice for Puerto Ricans and other people of color with environmental injustice, the image calls to mind the failures of U.S. empire. Here, the metropole is a space in decay, littered with the detritus of contemporary civilization. The image thus suggests the insufficiencies of the United States as a space of empowerment for marginalized groups. Further, it emphasizes the direct threats facing Puerto Ricans, African Americans, and other people of color in inner cities and links these threats to white supremacy. Rather than imagining sustainable spaces within the urban core, the image depicts a bleak and dystopian life in the United States.

On one level, the attention the Lords paid to environmental issues as they relate to racism and inequality is unsurprising. As Pulido explains, "studying environmental racism is important for an additional reason: it helps us understand racism" ("Rethinking" 12). On another level, the Lords were ahead of their time by yoking environmental justice, social justice, housing equity, and claims to urban space. We should therefore consider that one aspect of Latinx environmentalism is an alternative environmental history that includes the United Farm Workers and the Lords alongside such figures as Rachel Carson, Aldo Leopold, and John Muir. Importantly, Chicano and Puerto Rican Movement commitments to environmental justice continue to influence how Latinx artists and activists represent environmental concerns.

It is without question that people of color experience environmental harm at higher rates than whites. According to reporting by Adrianna Quintero-Somaini and Mayra Quirindongo for the Natural Resources Defense Council, 91 percent of Latinxs live in large cities where exposure to air pollution is higher than in comparable Anglo communities. Wald writes that nearly three hundred thousand farmworkers are exposed to threatening levels of pesticides annually—a number that Farmworker Justice asserts radically undercounts actual poisonings. Seth Holmes explains that "approximately one-third to one-half of agricultural workers report chronic symptoms associated with pesticide exposure such as headache, skin and eye irritation, and flu-like syndromes" (101). It is also likely that environmental harms associated with unjust and unsustainable practices will increase as the federal government ramps up anti-immigrant and environmentally irresponsible policies. These circumstances point to the fact that Latinxs and other people of color bear the brunt of environmental dangers. They also serve as chilling reminders of dynamics that will intensify as climate change escalates over the next century.

As we will see, Quiñonez's environmental engagements are not limited to representations of victimhood or toxic exposure. Instead, *Bodega Dreams* makes a case for preserving the history and culture of Spanish Harlem as fundamental to primary security and environmental integrity in the city. Moreover, the novel posits a form of decolonial environmentalism as a remedy to runaway real estate values and the cultural integrity of El Barrio.

Bodega Dreams and Decolonial Preservation

Central to my analysis of *Bodega Dreams* is how the novel positions access to fair housing and antigentrification as environmental issues. Critics such as Susan Méndez, Irizarry, and Moiles comment on the novel's connections between neoliberalism and gentrification—a point exacerbated by urban redevelopment and greenwashing policies enacted by Mayors Bloomberg and de Blasio in the years following the publication of *Bodega Dreams*.

The novel's considerations of the threats gentrification poses to Puerto Ricans and other Latinxs in Spanish Harlem are well founded. Moiles notes that "during the 1990s . . . the Puerto Rican population of East Harlem declined from approximately 43,000 to 35,000" as rents nearly quadrupled (117–118)—a trend that has only accelerated as we move toward the third decade of the twenty-first century. As one community activist puts it, "I've been living here for over 50 years, and nobody was bothering us in Spanish Harlem. Now it seems like there's a grab bag going on" (Foxley). Dávila identifies the implications of gentrification in El Barrio by observing that fair housing and social inequality are crucial issues given East Harlem's vulnerability to neoliberal threats posed by "diminished social welfare and the privatization of government services" and "changes in public housing legislation" (8).

My reading of *Bodega Dreams* unfolds in relation to gentrification and housing security. I consider how Quiñonez interrogates housing instability and gentrification through two primary mechanisms. First, through the character Willie Bodega, Quiñonez mediates the idealism of 1960s activism with the realities of twenty-first-century urban policy as they relate to housing security. Second, by analyzing how *Bodega Dreams* imagines preserving urban space, we see Quiñonez mobilizing urban decolonial environmental themes that valorize the cultural values associated with the neighborhood. The novel combats gentrification by clearing space for alternative preservation schemes that build on the legacies of insurgent environmental activism practiced by the Young Lords.

A key aspect of Quiñonez's representation intertwines how Chino and Blanca mediate their desires for upward mobility with their need to remain rooted in El Barrio. Like many of their generation and diasporic status (both Chino and Blanca are first-generation mainland residents), they view education as a vector for economic and social empowerment. Chino and Blanca attend nearby Hunter College with hopes that their education will afford them opportunities to enhance their income and to purchase a home. As Nazario notes upon learning that Chino attends Hunter, "That's one more professional in East Harlem. Soon . . . we'll have an army of them. An entire professional class in East Harlem" (Quiñonez 71). The tension in this scene emerges from the fact that Chino's and Blanca's visions would entail a move *out* of El Barrio, perhaps to an outer borough or to suburbs upstate or in Long Island.

The impulse to leave Spanish Harlem is understandable, as until the 1990s (and despite the cleanup that took place during the Garbage Offensive) when the neighborhood became an object for gentrification, it was famous as a site of urban blight. Piri Thomas describes life in El Barrio as characterized by "hot and cold running cockroaches and king-sized rats" (333)—a condition that Chino echoes in his characterization of Spanish Harlem: one of the chapters in book 2 is titled "My Growing Up and All That Piri Thomas Kinda Crap." Consider a scene early in the novel where Chino and Sapo fly kites from the roof of their tenement. Chino muses on the possibilities of escaping the neighborhood: "You know, Sapo, . . . if we could ride on top of these things [the kites], we could get out of here." Invoking the rhetoric of upward mobility, Chino imagines how life might change by flying away from El Barrio. Moving out of the neighborhood is equated with better life chances. The novel thus figures the desire for social mobility as a consequence of urban blight and environmental degradation—a desire that Chino and Blanca imagine from the time they are children.

A blighted view of El Barrio is reinforced early in the novel, where Spanish Harlem is depicted as a neglected space in a state of rapid depopulation:

> You lived in projects with pissed-up elevators, junkies on the stairs, posters of the rapist of the month, and whores you never knew were whores until you saw men go in and out of their apartments like through revolving doors. You lived in a place where vacant lots grew

like wild grass does in Kansas. Kansas? What does a kid from Spanish Harlem know about Kansas? All you knew was that one day a block would have people, the next day it would be erased by a fire. (Quiñonez 5–6)

Chino's characterization of the neighborhood emphasizes decay (junkies, pissed-up elevators, etc.), underscoring the undesirability of Spanish Harlem for the upwardly mobile. A closer examination of the passage demonstrates how upward mobility is premised on a split between Spanish Harlem and spaces that are imagined as wild and pristine (i.e., Kansas). The novel characterizes this imagined wild space in terms of vacant lots' proliferation in Spanish Harlem like "wild grass." Paradoxically, Quiñonez mobilizes nature imagery to describe urban phenomena. In fact, vacant lots (or brownfields, so named for the frequency of environmental contamination) have become a focus of urban greenwashing policies in New York, particularly under Mayor Bloomberg's administration, which targeted such sites for urban redevelopment.[19] The mobilization of environmental ideas in the passage thus relates to Quiñonez's use of an environmental simile (like wild grass) and to the urban environmental policies that accrue around such sites.

Quiñonez's use of these signifiers turns common environmental tropes on their heads. As William Cronon and Lawrence Buell have shown, reifying unpeopled wilderness is a problematic trope of some first-wave ecocriticism. Rather than characterizing wilderness as empty space, Quiñonez presents the city as having a disappearing population: "All you knew was that one day a block would have people, the next day it would be erased by a fire." Calling to mind wildfires that raze prairies of wild grasses, the image suggests a naturalized process for depopulating El Barrio. The image also contests anxieties expressed in the early ecology movement about the so-called population bomb that considered people of color and those from the developing world as agents of uncontrolled population growth. Proponents of the population bomb surmised that uncontrolled population growth would promise global environmental catastrophe.

Moreover, the passage highlights disappearing populations in Spanish Harlem, echoing the logic of neoliberal urban redevelopment policies. As vacant lots expand owing to arson and neglect, valuable real estate is available for development. Because urban redevelopment in Manhattan neighborhoods as diverse as Tribeca, Loisaida (which was gentrified in the 1980s, displacing the Puerto Rican community that had resided there since the early twentieth century), Harlem, and SoHo has increased the number of luxury apartments and condominiums and decreased affordable housing and rent-controlled units, communities of color have been priced out of historical enclaves. Indeed, the specter of Loisaida gentrification creates urgency for Bodega's mission. As Nazario points out, "This neighborhood will be lost unless we make it ours. Look at Loisaida, that's gone.... All those white yuppies want to live in Manhattan, and they think Spanish Harlem is next for the taking. When they start moving in, we won't be able to compete when it comes to rents, and we'll be left out in the cold" (107).

Despite the challenges characters like Chino and Blanca face to remain in the neighborhood, it is interesting that Sapo forms a backstop against equating racial uplift with a move out of El Barrio. In fact, Quiñonez sets up Sapo as the moral conscience of the novel in the opening lines: "Sapo was different," and "I [Chino] loved Sapo. I loved Sapo because he loved himself. And I wanted to be able to do that, to rely on myself for my own happiness" (3). Sapo's difference centers on his ability to love himself and his place of origin. His love of self and neighborhood is reflected throughout the novel, perhaps most prominently in response to Chino's image of flying away on his kite: "Why would you wanna fucken leave this place? ... This neighborhood is beautiful, bro" (11).

Another tension between community uplift and urban flight arises in Bodega's vision for community empowerment. At numerous points, Bodega, Nazario, and Sapo outline formulations of community uplift: Bodega claims that "I'm talking about property. I'm talking about owning the neighborhood legally. The way the Kennedy's own Boston" (Quiñonez 37). Later, Sapo notes, "Bodega is going to own the neighborhood. Legally. And I want to be part of it" (41). Nazario underscores Bodega's program: "What Willie [Bodega] and I are trying to do is make sure that you, the future of the neighborhood, doesn't break its back. That this neighborhood isn't lost" (103).

In their campaigns of direct action, Nazario, Sapo, and Bodega echo Young Lords activism. When city officials failed to respond to their requests for services, the Lords implemented their own, cleaning up the neighborhood, setting up free clinics, and implementing lead testing.[20] As Bodega recalls:

> We knew we had to get the community on our side. So what did we Young Lords do? ...
> We cleaned the streets. Everybody, Chino, went home and got a broom, bought bags, rakes, Comet and Ajax for the graffiti walls, trash cans, and soon the community was for us. Soon they were cleaning the streets with us. No one feared us. They all loved us. (Quiñonez 32)

Despite Bodega's nostalgia about the 1960s, Quiñonez problematizes the Young Lord's history of community service. Bodega compares himself to Joseph Kennedy, who some argue earned his fortune by illegally importing alcohol during Prohibition.[21] Bodega's alignment with Joseph Kennedy brings into relief Bodega's conviction that the ends of community uplift justify the means to their achievement. Like Kennedy, however, Bodega's empowerment strategy is corrupt. He sells drugs to the neighborhood, redirecting wealth and writing off a class of residents: "Any Puerto Rican or any of my Latin brothers who are stupid enough to buy that shit don't belong in my Great Society" (31). In recalling Lyndon B. Johnson's Great Society initiatives and 1960s activism, Quiñonez offers what Raphael Dalleo and Elena Machado Sáez call "a eulogy for the political and artistic aspirations of the generation of the 1960s" (Dalleo and Machado Sáez 68), suggesting that the tactics of groups like the Lords represent a tension between illegality, anticapitalism, decoloniality, and co-optation.

Another tension arises from the desire to empower the neighborhood through capitalist accumulation. In this sense, Bodega's program relies on the surplus value of the real estate he purchases and rents or sells, leaving his work vulnerable to market forces. While working against gentrification is a laudable goal of Bodega's community uplift project, it risks losing its decolonial charge because of its imbrication within the market. The anticapitalist and antiestablishment aspects of Bodega's program are thus at risk because he employs the market to enact insurgent goals.

We should also recall that part of Bodega's motivation emerges from his desire to reclaim his one-time lover, Veronica Saldivia. Veronica leaves him in the 1960s because he places community activism above wealth. By shifting Bodega's motivation from community service to individual fulfillment, Quiñonez points to the co-optation of movements like the Young Lords, which dissolved in the early 1970s. The dissolution of the Lords owed in no small part to infiltration by COINTELPRO and other counterinsurgency organizations. But as Enck-Wanzer and Torres and Velásquez have documented, infighting and tribalism also contributed to the Lords' demise.

The shift from community uplift to individual fulfillment also mirrors the shift from collective action to neoliberal empowerment—strategies that have backfired for communities of color. It is no surprise that, like Fitzgerald's Daisy Buchanan, Veronica causes the unraveling of Bodega's enterprise by betraying him, killing her husband, and engineering Bodega's murder at the hands of Nazario.

Another of the novel's environmental engagements emerges from tensions between gentrification and preservation. A primary tension is the ambivalence Chino experiences in relation to Bodega's position as drug dealer/former Young Lord. As Dalleo and Machado Sáez point out, the relationship between "taking on the community's marginalization from capitalist circuits and . . . participating in that very capitalism, may not be mutually exclusive" (63). Hence, Bodega's channeling of community resources through the drug trade is not entirely objectionable to Chino. Elías Domínguez Barajas argues that, because Bodega is neither hero nor antihero, Chino's dilemma is to accept his program by making distinctions between its immoral aspects and its political efficacy (20). Under this logic, the exigencies of Manhattan real estate coupled with the persistence of Latinx racialization suggest a flexible morality. To put it crudely, given the community's limited access to finance capital, redevelopment policy, and city resources, Barrio residents do not have viable options for maintaining financial and cultural control of the neighborhood. Given this context, Bodega's redirection of neighborhood wealth may be justifiable—a point Nazario underscores: "This is not the sixties. The government isn't pouring any money in here anymore" (107).

While these issues may not on the surface appear to be "environmental," reading through an environmental lens helps us see the limits of community empowerment. At stake are the "rights" Puerto Ricans have to continue dwelling in a place they have cared for and about for generations.[22] Consequently, I do not valorize the drug trade as a means to empowerment. Neither am I advancing an "ends justifies the means" argument. I concur with Dalleo and Machado Sáez that the novel "supplement[s] the idealism of the Sixties with realism about people's needs and desires" (63). I point to the tension between a desire to preserve the neighborhood and the constraints of one of the most expensive housing markets in the United States. In this sense, the novel provides a critical dialog between 1960s activism and the exigencies of the twenty-first-century housing market—which, as the Young Lords pointed out more than fifty years ago, is an "environmental" issue. Resistance within this framework is constituted as much by realism as by idealism.

Bodega Dreams foregrounds these intersections in its questioning of housing equity and cultural preservation. In several scenes, characters like Bodega, Sapo, and Chino marvel at the beauty and cultural richness of El Barrio. For example, Chino admires the Metro North projects' "million-dollar views": "In the wintertime, when the East River freezes, the views are staggering. The ice acts like a mirror and the world seems to have two sunrises and at night two moons, one in the sky and one on the ice. . . . Above the East River the cloud formations are ever-changing, and when a dying hurricane is about to hit the city you can see how the waves and the clouds synchronize their gyrating motions, like Jupiter's red eye" (55). Chino's observation of climactic conditions that enhance the "million-dollar views" serves as an uncanny reminder of increasingly powerful storms like Superstorm Sandy that have buffeted Manhattan in recent years. While the storms may offer stunning vistas by augmenting natural light, they also replicate the specter of annihilation that gentrification poses. Likewise, although Quiñonez's lyricism emphasizes physical beauty, it also places the neighborhood within the context of "nature," countering the image of urban blight used to justify gentrification.

Quiñonez's environmental representations transcend nature imagery. In fact, much of the novel depicts a desire to preserve neighborhood space and culture. In this sense, the ethic of preservation echoes environmentalist discourses that advocate conservation as a remedy for environmental harm.[23] But as critics such as Ray and Ramachandra Guha remind us, discourses of preservation can mystify and naturalize what Nixon calls the "slow violence" of racial, social, and environmental hierarchies. Consequently, we should consider how Quiñonez combines environmental themes with a meditation on the efficacy of 1960s activism as a way to theorize alternatives to gentrification.

Among the many acts of cultural preservation that take place in the novel are Quiñonez's commemoration of the Young Lords, the Golden Age of Salsa, graffiti art, Nuyorican poets Pedro Pietri and Miguel Algarín, and allusions to such classic texts as Thomas's *Down These Mean Streets*. These allusions and commemorations suggest that preserving and leveraging the past, while not the only strategy for combating urban renewal, offers touchstones for contemporary resistance.

As Chino notes in relation to Bodega, "From his younger days as a Young Lord to his later days as Bodega, his life had been triggered by a romantic ideal found only in those poor bastards who really wanted to be poets but got drafted and sent to the front lines" (13–14). Bodega's past is both potential (a romantic ideal) and insufficiency when one remains mired in the past. Bodega's shortcoming is not only that he longs for the historical—symbolized in his desire to reunite with Veronica and in his nostalgia about the Young Lords—but that he remains stuck in it. The implication is that Chino admires and sees value in older resistance paradigms but understands that pragmatism sometimes supersedes poetry. Thus, when "drafted and sent to the front lines," one must employ both idealism and realism to resist gentrification.

Rather than foreclosing possibilities for effective antigentrification strategies, however, Quiñonez offers a hopeful vision of El Barrio that intertwines 1960s activism with renewal and preservation. Beginning with a dream Chino has of Bodega "dressed as a Young Lord" wearing his "beret and pin, a copy of *Pa'lante* [the Young Lord's newspaper] under his arm," the two men step onto a fire escape where they behold an expansive view of Spanish Harlem "loom[ing] below and ahead of" them. Bodega suggests that although his vision died with him, a new language is emerging in El Barrio, and with it a new consciousness. Calling to mind Latinx thinkers like Gloria Anzaldúa who suggest that hybridity offers spaces of possibility, the two men witness a woman speaking in a Spanglish Bodega describes as "a poem . . . a beautiful new language . . . that means a new race. Spanglish is the future. It's a new language being born out of the ashes of two cultures clashing with each other." Bodega urges Chino to "use [this] new language," to continue his vision. Even though "this new language is not completely correct," Bodega acknowledges that "few things are" (212).

In the suggestion of hybridity as possibility and in charging Chino with enacting Bodega's vision, the novel maintains hope in what decolonial indigenous scholar Linda Tuhiwai Smith calls "relentless optimism." Even in the face of the perceived "failures" of 1960s activism (symbolized by Bodega's nostalgia), the mounting challenges posed by gentrification, and the co-optation of Latinx social movements by neoliberal city and state actors, Chino cannot afford to give up on Bodega's vision: "I looked out to the neighborhood below. Bodega was right, it was alive. Its music and people had taken off their mourning clothes. The neighborhood had turned into a maraca, with the men and women transformed into seeds, shaking with love and desire for one another" (212). The image of Spanish Harlem residents as "seeds" carries the potential for rebirth, emphasizing the possibilities of Bodega's vision.

The implication is that with proper germination, Bodega's dream for resistance may survive. As the inheritor of 1960s activism, Chino is poised to leverage community uplift with pragmatism in the new millennium. Although this vision remains incomplete by the end of the novel, it seems likely that Chino and Sapo (who is positioned to inherit Bodega's drug operation) are poised to make change based on what they learn from the 1960s. Despite the fact that Bodega's vision fails, his figurative progeny hold the possibility for renovated forms of resistance that might produce change for Spanish Harlem in the twenty-first century.

Conclusion

Bodega Dreams evidences a decolonial environmental imaginary that leverages legacies of Puerto Rican activism to resist historical erasure and stake claims for Latinxs in Spanish Harlem. Reading the novel through ecocritical lenses unpacks how issues of housing reform and cultural affirmation offer an alternative ethos of preservation. Moreover, the novel's depiction of the tensions between illegality and anticapitalism form part of the charge that animates—and problematizes—Quiñonez's decolonial politics.

Even though Bodega's vision remains unfulfilled, Chino's hopeful act of taking in a recent immigrant and his grandson symbolizes the potential for renewal. But the nearly two decades since the novel's publication are part of the specter that haunts the narrative. Consequently, even in the face of Chino's hopeful act, tension remains between the decolonial desire to combat gentrification and the historical march of gentrification in Spanish Harlem and other parts of the city. In the end, we might consider *Bodega Dreams* in terms of the tensions and residues it imagines as part of the historical legacy of the Puerto Rican Movement.

NOTES

1. Flowing from observations we make in the introduction to this volume, I use the term *Latinx* to denote panethnic identities for people with roots in Latin America and the Hispanophone Caribbean. Although there is controversy about the use of this term, I deploy it to signal solidarities with LGBTQ Latinxs and to underscore the legacies of colonialism that operate in relation to U.S. race relations and race relations in Latin America. For more on the use of Latinx, see the introduction to this volume.

2. The history of Puerto Rican activism in New York City dates to the late nineteenth century. For more on the history of late nineteenth- and early twentieth-century

Puerto Rican activism in the city, see Vega, *Memoirs of Bernardo Vega: A Contribution to the History of the Puerto Rican Community in New York*; Colón, *A Puerto Rican in New York and Other Sketches*; Colón, *The Way It Was and Other Writings*.

3. I am indebted to Priscilla Solis Ybarra for this observation.

4. For a recent example in the popular press, see Avi Selk's recent reporting in *The Washington Post* on the Ink! Coffee shop in the Five Points area of Denver, Colorado. A controversy arose when the coffee house displayed a sandwich board reading, "Happily Gentrifying the Neighborhood since 2014" on one side, with the other side reading, "Nothing Says Gentrification like Being Able to Order a Cortado." Although Five Points was once the location for the majority of the African American population in Denver, much of the black population has relocated owing to urban redevelopment and gentrification that has driven up housing costs.

5. Thanks again to Priscilla Solis Ybarra for this formulation.

6. See, for example, recent reporting by Myles Miller for WCBS News on de Blasio's plans to develop East Harlem. See also Heather Rogers's reporting for *Tablet* magazine on how Mayor Bloomberg "greenwashed" New York City.

7. Thanks to Sarah D. Wald for this observation.

8. A few weeks before the final preparation of this manuscript, the Intergovernmental Panel on Climate Change (IPCC) issued its apocalyptic warning written by ninety-one scientists from forty nations that, given current emissions, the atmosphere is projected to warm by as much as 2.7 degrees Celsius by 2040. For more on the IPCC report, see http://www.ipcc.ch/report/sr15/.

9. Quiñonez is careful to note the presence of and solidarities among Latinx groups in Spanish Harlem, including Puerto Ricans/Nuyoricans, Cubans, Colombians, and others. Indeed, with a Puerto Rican mother and an Ecuadorian father, Chino embodies Latinidad. Among the other themes that articulate this nascent panethnic consciousness in the novel are a subplot involving the secret marriage of Roberto and Claudia (who is an undocumented Colombian immigrant), the tensions between Cubans and Puerto Ricans as portrayed by the police officers Ortiz and DeJesus, and Nazario's formulations of Latinidad: "We are one people, one island, one Latin continent!" (Quiñonez 147).

10. For more on the colonial history of Puerto Rico and the Puerto Rican movement relationship with advocacy related to the island, see Monge; Denis; Torres and Velázquez.

11. I am indebted to Sarah Jaquette Ray for this formulation.

12. See, for example, Markowitz and Rosner's *Lead Wars: The Politics of Science and the Fate of America's Children* and a Farmworker Justice report entitled "Exposed and Ignored" that details pesticide exposures among the nation's farmworkers. See also Wald's discussion of pesticide exposure among farmworkers in *Nature of California*, especially pp. 24–25.

13. By focusing on the Lords, I do not deny the environmental work of other Puerto Rican Movement groups. Rather, I limit my consideration to the Lords because the novel meditates on the residues of Young Lords activism as a paradigmatic aspect of the Puerto Rican Movement.

14. Again, thanks to Sarah Jaquette Ray for this observation.

15. Although the environmental justice movement has antecedents that extend to the antebellum period, many environmental justice scholars date the start of the contemporary movement to the Warren County Landfill Strike in 1982. See, for example, Bullard; Adamson et. al.

16. Although the term *spaceship earth* dates to the late nineteenth century, its contemporary usage was popularized in 1968 by Buckminster Fuller's *Operating Manual for*

Spaceship Earth. The idea gained currency with the release of the famous "Blue Marble" photograph of Earth taken from the moon by the Apollo 17 crew in 1972. The population bomb was an idea that gained popularity with the publication of Paul Ehrlich's book of the same name, also in 1968. The book made the case for a variety of social ills that would result from unchecked population growth (mass starvation, overcrowded cities, etc.). Population bomb rhetoric has been rightly debunked as a neo-Malthusian discourse that blames the Global South for environmental degradation. See, for example, Guha and Martínez-Alier's *Varieties of Environmentalism: Essays North and South*.

17. Consider a recent segment on National Public Radio describing the challenges gentrification poses for African American communities in Atlanta and Los Angeles ("There Isn't a Just Housing Choice").

18. See the original *Keep America Beautiful* PSA at https://www.youtube.com/watch?v=8Suu84khNGY.

19. For example, see a press release outlining Mayor Bloomberg's 2010 New York City Brownfield Incentive Grant that was designed to "provide financial incentives for the study and cleanup of brownfield properties in New York City." According to Bloomberg, the program incentivized "turning contaminated land into usable space [that] will allow us to develop new housing, create more open space, and spur new job growth" ("Mayor Bloomberg Launches City's Brownfield Incentive Grant").

20. Enck-Wanzer explains that the early phases of the Young Lords activism were oriented around community service: "This new group of New York Lords sought first to address change at the local level in their immediate community through 'serve the people' programs. . . . [T]hey were motivated by multiple traditions of thought and action . . . [and] were focused on practical public tasks (cleaning up garbage, testing for disease, providing social services, etc.)" (Enck-Wanzer 22–23).

21. Although the popular imaginary holds that Joseph Kennedy earned his fortune "rum running," this idea is now in question. As reporting by Noah Rothbaum for the *Daily Beast* shows, much of Kennedy's fortune was gained legally through import contracts he negotiated in conjunction with the U.S. government.

22. Once again, I am grateful to Priscilla Solis Ybarra for this generous observation.

23. In making this claim about preservation, I want to note the complex conversation within environmental studies and ecocriticism about differences between preservation (as associated with a tradition that goes back to John Muir's writings) and conservation (most commonly associated with Gifford Pinchot). For more on this debate, see Nash; Taylor.

WORKS CITED

Adamson, Joni, Mei Mei Evans, and Rachel Stein, editors. *The Environmental Justice Reader: Politics, Poetics and Pedagogy*. U of Arizona P, 2002.

Alaimo, Stacy. *Bodily Natures: Science, Environment, and the Material Self*. Indiana UP, 2010.

Anzaldúa, Gloria. *Borderlands/La frontera: The New Mestiza*. 3rd ed., Aunt Lute Books, 2007.

Barajas, Elías Domínguez. "The Postmodern Ethnic Condition in Ernesto Quiñónez's *Bodega Dreams*." *Latino Studies*, vol. 12, no. 1, 2014, pp. 7–26. doi:10.1057/lst.2014.2.

Brady, Mary Pat. *Extinct Lands, Temporal Geographies: Chicana Literature and the Urgency of Space*. Duke UP, 2002.

Buell, Lawrence. *Writing for an Endangered World: Literature, Culture, and Environment in the U.S. and Beyond*. Harvard UP, 2001.

Bullard, Robert D. *Dumping in Dixie: Race, Class, and Environmental Quality*. 3rd ed., Westview Press, 2008.
Colón, Jesús. *A Puerto Rican in New York, and Other Sketches*. Arno Press, 1975.
———. *The Way It Was, and Other Writings*. Arte Publico Press, 1993.
Cronon, William. "The Trouble with Wilderness: Or, Getting Back to the Wrong Nature." *Environmental History*, vol. 1, no. 1, 1996, pp. 7–28.
Dalleo, Raphael, and Elena Machado Sáez. *The Latino/a Canon and the Emergence of Post-Sixties Literature*. Palgrave Macmillan, 2007.
Dávila, Arlene. *Barrio Dreams: Puerto Ricans, Latinos, and the Neoliberal City*. U of California P, 2004.
Denis, Nelson A. *War Against All Puerto Ricans: Revolution and Terror in America's Colony*. Reprint ed., Nation Books, 2016.
Dwyer, June. "When Willie Met Gatsby: The Critical Implications of Ernesto Quiñonez's Bodega Dreams." *Lit: Literature Interpretation Theory*, vol. 14, no. 2, 2003, pp. 165–178, doi:10.1080/10436920306616.
Ehrlich, Paul R. *The Population Bomb*. Ballantine Books, 1968.
Enck-Wanzer, Darrel. *The Young Lords: A Reader*. New York UP, 2010.
Farmworker Justice.org. "Exposed and Ignored: How Pesticides Are Endangering Our Nation's Farmworkers." 2013, https://www.farmworkerjustice.org/sites/default/files/aExposed%20and%20Ignored%20by%20Farmworker%20Justice%20singles%20compressed.pdf.
Finney, Carolyn. *Black Faces, White Spaces: Reimagining the Relationship of African Americans to the Great Outdoors*. U of North Carolina P, 2014.
Foxley, David. "I'm the Last Man Standing in My Rent-Controlled Apartment Building." *Architectural Digest*, 13 Oct. 2017, https://www.architecturaldigest.com/story/im-the-last-man-standing-in-my-rent-controlled-apartment-building. Accessed 8 Nov. 2017.
Fuller, R. Buckminster. *Operating Manual for Spaceship Earth*. Southern Illinois UP, 1969.
Garrard, Greg. *Ecocriticism*. 2nd ed., Taylor and Francis, 2011.
Guha, Ramachandra. *The Unquiet Woods: Ecological Change and Peasant Resistance in the Himalaya*. Expanded ed., U of California P, 2000.
Guha, Ramachandra and Juan Martínez-Alier. *Varieties of Environmentalism: Essays North and South*. Earthscan Publications, 1997.
Harvey, David. *Justice, Nature, and the Geography of Difference*. Blackwell Publishers, 1996.
Hayashi, Robert T. "Beyond Walden Pond: Asian American Literature and the Limits of Ecocriticism." *Coming into Contact: Explorations in Ecocritical Theory and Practice*, edited by Annie Merril Ingram, 2007, pp. 58–75.
Heise, Ursula K. *Sense of Place and Sense of Planet: The Environmental Imagination of the Global*. Oxford UP, 2008.
Holmes, Seth. *Fresh Fruit, Broken Bodies: Migrant Farmworkers in the United States*. U of California P, 2013.
Irizarry, Ylce. *Chicana/o and Latina/o Fiction: The New Memory of Latinidad*. U of Illinois P, 2016.
James, Jennifer C. "Ecomelancholia: Slavery, War, and Black Ecological Imaginings." *Environmental Criticism for the Twenty-First Century*, Routledge, 2011.
LaDuke, Winona. *The Winona LaDuke Chronicles: Stories from the Front Lines in the Battle for Environmental Justice*. Reprint ed., Fernwood Publishing, 2017.
Lee, Jennifer. "The Young Lords' Legacy of Puerto Rican Activism." *City Room*, 24 Aug. 2009, https://cityroom.blogs.nytimes.com/2009/08/24/the-young-lords-legacy-of-puerto-rican-activism/.

Lee, Sonia Song-Ha. *Building a Latino Civil Rights Movement: Puerto Ricans, African Americans, and the Pursuit of Racial Justice in New York City.* Reprint ed., U of North Carolina P, 2016.

Lefebvre, Henri. *The Production of Space.* Blackwell, 1991.

Markowitz, Gerald, and David Rosner. *Lead Wars: The Politics of Science and the Fate of America's Children.* U of California P, 2013.

"Mayor Bloomberg Launches City's Brownfield Incentive Grant." *NYC Office of Environmental Remediation,* 21 June 2010, http://www.nyc.gov/html/oer/html/big/BIGlaunch.shtml. Accessed 10 Nov. 2017.

Mendez, Susan. "The Fire Between Them: Religion and Gentrification in Ernesto Quinonez's *Chango's Fire.*" *Centro: Journal of the Center for Puerto Rican Studies,* vol. 1, no. Spring, 2011, pp. 177–195.

Miller, Myles. "East Harlem Residents Claim de Blasio's Rezoning Plan Promotes Gentrification." https://newyork.cbslocal.com/2017/09/29/east-harlem-residents-claim-de-blasios-rezoning-plan-promotes-gentrification/. Accessed 8 Nov. 2017.

Moiles, Sean. "The Politics of Gentrification in Ernesto Quiñonez's Novels." *Critique: Studies in Contemporary Fiction,* vol. 52, no. 1, 2011, pp. 114–133.

Monge, José Trías. *Puerto Rico: The Trials of the Oldest Colony in the World.* Yale UP, 1999.

Mortimer-Sandilands, Catriona. *Queer Ecologies: Sex, Nature, Politics, Desire.* Indiana UP, 2010.

Nash, Roderick. *Wilderness and the American Mind.* 4th ed., Yale UP, 2001.

Nixon, Rob. *Slow Violence and the Environmentalism of the Poor.* Harvard UP, 2011.

Older, Daniel José. "Gentrification's Insidious Violence: The Truth about American Cities." *Salon,* 8 Apr. 2014, https://www.salon.com/2014/04/08/gentrifications_insidious_violence_the_truth_about_american_cities/.

Omi, Michael, and Howard Winant. *Racial Formation in the United States.* 3rd ed., Routledge/Taylor and Francis Group, 2015.

Ontiveros, Randy J. *In the Spirit of a New People: The Cultural Politics of the Chicano Movement.* New York UP, 2014.

Peña, Devon G. *Mexican Americans and the Environment: Tierra y Vida.* U of Arizona P, 2005.

Pulido, Laura. "Rethinking Environmental Racism: White Privilege and Urban Development in Southern California." *Annals of the Association of American Geographers,* vol. 90, no. 1, 2000, pp. 12–40.

Quiñonez, Ernesto. *Bodega Dreams.* Vintage Contemporaries, 2000.

Quintero-Somaini, Adrianna and Mayra Quirindongo. *Hidden Danger: Environmental Health Threats in the Latino Community.* NRDC, 2004. https://www.nrdc.org/sites/default/files/latino_en.pdf.

Ray, Sarah Jaquette. *The Ecological Other: Environmental Exclusion in American Culture.* U of Arizona P, 2013.

Reed, T. V. "Toward an Environmental Justice Ecocriticism." *The Environmental Justice Reader: Politics, Poetics, and Pedagogy,* edited by Joni Adamson, Mei Mei Evans, and Rachel Stein, U of Arizona P, 2002, pp. 145–162.

Rogers, Heather. "How Michael Bloomberg Greenwashed New York City." *Tablet Magazine,* 5 Jan. 2015, http://www.tabletmag.com/jewish-news-and-politics/187721/planyc-bloomberg. Accessed 7 Nov. 2017.

Rothbaum, Noah. "The Myth of Joe Kennedy's Bootlegging." *Daily Beast,* 5 Mar. 2016, https://www.thedailybeast.com/the-myth-of-joe-kennedys-bootlegging.

Said, Edward W. *Culture and Imperialism.* Vintage Books, 1994.

Salt, Karen. "Startling Feeling: Environmental Scholarship amid the Tangled Roots of Imperialism." *Resilience: A Journal of the Environmental Humanities*, vol. 1, no. 1, 2014. *JSTOR*, doi:10.5250/resilience.1.1.28.

Selk, Avi. "A Coffee Shop Celebrated Gentrification—and Is Now Profusely Penitent." *Washington Post*, 25 Nov. 2017, https://www.washingtonpost.com/news/post-nation/wp/2017/11/25/a-coffee-shop-celebrated-gentrification-and-is-now-profusely-apologizing/.

Seymour, Nicole. *Strange Natures: Futurity, Empathy, and the Queer Ecological Imagination*. U of Illinois P, 2013.

Slovic, Scott. "The Third Wave of Ecocriticism: North American Reflections on the Current Phase of the Discipline." *Ecozon@: European Journal of Literature, Culture and Environment*, vol. 1, no. 1, Apr. 2010. ecozona.eu, http://ecozona.eu/article/view/312.

Smith, Linda Tuhiwai. *Decolonizing Methodologies: Research and Indigenous Peoples*. Zed Books; U of Otago P, 1999.

Sze, Julie. *Noxious New York: The Racial Politics of Urban Health and Environmental Justice*. The MIT Press, 2006.

Taylor, Dorceta E. *The Rise of the American Conservation Movement: Power, Privilege, and Environmental Protection*. Duke UP, 2016.

"There Isn't a Just Housing Choice": How We've Enabled the Pains of Gentrification." *National Public Radio*, 28 Jan. 2018, https://www.npr.org/2018/01/28/581280992/there-isn-t-a-just-housing-choice-how-we-ve-enabled-the-pains-of-gentrification. Accessed 31 Jan. 2018.

Thomas, Piri. *Down These Mean Streets*. Thirtieth anniversary ed., Vintage Books, 1997.

Torres, Andrés, and José E. Velázquez. *The Puerto Rican Movement: Voices from the Diaspora*. Temple UP, 1998.

Vasilogambros, Matt. "Taking the High Ground—and Developing It." *The Atlantic*, Mar. 2016, http://www.theatlantic.com/business/archive/2016/03/taking-the-high-ground-and-developing-it/472326/.

Vega, Bernardo. *Memoirs of Bernardo Vega: A Contribution to the History of the Puerto Rican Community in New York*. Monthly Review Press, 1984.

Villa, Raúl. *Barrio-Logos: Space and Place in Urban Chicano Literature and Culture*. U of Texas P, 2000.

Wald, Sarah D. *The Nature of California: Race, Citizenship, and Farming since the Dust Bowl*. U of Washington P, 2016.

Ybarra, Priscilla Solis. *Writing the Goodlife: Mexican American Literature and the Environment*. U of Arizona P, 2016.

13

Postcards from the Edges of Haiti

The Latinx Ecocriticism of Mayra Montero's
In the Palm of Darkness

Ylce Irizarry

> I always keep track of the ones in the background,
> the ones who disappear for no reason, the forgotten ones.
> —Thierry Adrien, *In the Palm of Darkness*

Over the last decade, scholars have observed a turn to the historical in U.S. Latinx and Hispanic Caribbean fiction.[1] Ecological discourse accompanies this turn. Mayra Montero's novel *Tú, la oscuridad / In the Palm of Darkness* (1995; trans. 1997) juxtaposes ecological destruction with the degradation of the human environment in Haiti, situating it on the cusp of contemporary literary environmentalism.[2] The novel's action occurs between November 1992, when the country is in turmoil after the overthrow of President Jean-Bertrand Aristide[3] and February 1993, when the ferry carrying Victor Grigg, an American herpetologist, and Thierry Adrien, his Haitian guide, and the last known specimen of a rare frog species, the grenouille du sang, capsizes. Flashbacks revert some forty years to depict the protagonists' early lives, including Thierry's life during both Duvalier regimes.[4] The epigraph prompts readers to consider how ordinary Haitians are forgotten in recurring disaster narratives of the island.[5] For example, after the earthquake of 2010 that killed over 220,000 people, international media recycled the narrative of Haiti as primitive and violent, deeming Haiti's deforestation responsible for the earthquake as well as the cholera outbreak later attributed to UN workers.[6] On January 11, 2017, U.S. president Trump attempted to justify the rescinding of the asylum granted to Haitian refugees from this earthquake by including Haiti in his description of "shithole countries" from which the United States should not accept refugees or immigrants.[7]

Unlike politicians' and media portrayals of Haiti, Montero's novel does not portray Haiti as having a "fatal flaw" (Buss) or as a helpless pawn of U.S. neocolonialism (Farmer). Rather, she links her novel to the discourses created by the scientific journalism of the 1990s:[8] "That's how I got the idea for a novel about a North American herpetologist who goes to Haiti in search of a frog that is thought to be almost extinct. Once he is in Haiti, the herpetologist meets a Haitian guide and the novel becomes an exploration of the relationship between the two men and the adventures they experience in the crazy Haitian geography, which is full of dangers and frustrations" (Montero qtd. in Prieto 90). Even though her characterization belittles the complexity of Haiti and the richness of her own aesthetics, ecocriticism contextualizes the novel. *In the Palm of Darkness* was published nearly concurrently with the first era of ecocriticism; it anticipates—by more than two decades—postcolonial, feminist, and decolonial ecocriticisms illustrating the nexus of economic, political, and environmental problems of the entire Caribbean Basin.[9]

Given increased contemporary migration via the liquid borders of the Caribbean Sea, the Atlantic Ocean, and the Gulf of Mexico, it makes sense to explore the intersection of human and nonhuman migration.[10] If Latinx literary scholars and ecocritics are invested in transnational scholarship, we ought not marginalize Hispanic Caribbean writing about Haiti, the nation bordering the Hispanophone Dominican Republic.[11] By delineating Montero's narrative strategies to unite Haitian political and environmental history, I aim to perform what Rob Nixon describes as "the unrealized creative bridgework, between environmental literary studies and the social sciences" (31). This essay illustrates that *In the Palm of Darkness* positions Haiti within the global discourse of mass extinction and affirms Montero's place within a literature of the Americas tradition that includes U.S. Latinx literature.[12]

Relatively little scholarship on it exists in Haitian or U.S. literary studies or ecocriticism, despite the novel's 1995 publication date and settings in Haiti and the United States, suggesting that literary scholarship has repeated media and popular elisions of the complexity of Haiti's natural and political history.[13] In *Writing the Goodlife: Mexican American Literature and the Environment*, Priscilla Solis Ybarra foregrounds decolonial ecocriticism and asserts that the "decolonial prioritizes a non-Western theoretical basis and puts the body, a body politics of knowing at its center" (12). The novel's prescient, innovative efforts to foreground nonhuman bodies and non-Western epistemologies call for decolonial ecocritical reading. Because *In the Palm of Darkness* urges readers to stop looking at ecologic crises as nation-centered, this analysis performs a decolonial ecocritical reading that asserts the Caribbean's centrality to, rather than its existence on the edge of, literary environmentalism.

The attention to the portrayal of natural environments in Latin American literature is long-standing;[14] however, the formalization of literary ecocriticism is recognized through the 1992 establishment of the Association for the Study of Literature and Environment (ASLE).[15] The evolution of ecocriticism following the novel's publication requires consideration. Paravisini-Gebert ("He of the Trees", "Unchained Tales"), de la Fuente, Dávila Gonçalves,

Boling ("Apocalipsis"), and Kearns were the first to assert these concerns. Few scholars center the novel's ecological concerns, but most notable among them is Lizabeth Paravisini-Gebert, who asserts its centrality to Caribbean ecocriticism: "*In the Palm of Darkness* is an avowedly environmentalist novel—the region's first" ("He of the Trees" 192). In "The Trope of Nature in Latin American Literature," Boling uses an ecofeminist approach, citing Garrard and Murphy,[16] who describe ecofeminism as a methodology based "not only on the recognition of connections between the exploitation of nature and the oppression of women across patriarchal societies" but also "on the recognition that these two forms of domination are bound up with class exploitation, racism, colonialism, and neocolonialism" (2–3).[17]

U.S. neocolonialism has been operative throughout the Caribbean Basin, affecting Cuba, the Dominican Republic, Haiti, and Puerto Rico and other nations, since the nineteenth century.[18] Because of this consistent regional interference, U.S. neocolonialism in Haiti cannot be separated from the legacy of French colonial slavery or from the debt reparations that contributed to the rise of Haiti's dictatorships in the twentieth century. Montero's ethnonational identity and career reflect this history. Born in Cuba, Montero spent most of her adulthood in Puerto Rico. As a journalist, she interviewed Haitian exiles in the Dominican Republic, linking the political and environmental concerns of the nations of Caribbean Basin directly impacted by U.S. neocolonialism.[19] While U.S. Latinx literary scholars have devoted significant study to island-based Puerto Rican authors such as Rosario Ferré, Myra Santos Febres, Luis Rafael Sánchez, and Ana Lydia Vega, scholars have paid little attention to Montero. Moreover, much of the English-language literary ecocritical scholarship on the novel does not reference early Spanish-language scholarship. Spanish-language publications engaging the text's environmentalism by Rivera Villegas, de la Fuente, Dávila Gonçalves, Boling ("Apocalipsis"), and Kearns are problematically absent in English-language criticism. This essay partially addresses this elision and will illustrate that reading Montero into a U.S. Latinx tradition is not just useful but necessary.

Early but nonecocritical strands of criticism on the novel include poststructural analyses that emphasize binaries, oppositional structures, or their site of collapse (Dávila Gonçalves)[20]; a binaristic focus on its representation of Voodoo (Rivera); its discourse on creolité (Alcocer) and nation building (Humphrey). A strand of criticism particular to Spanish-language journals appears in essays on Latin American and Caribbean narrative generally or Puerto Rican women's narrative specifically (Paravisini-Gebert, "Unchained Tales"; de la Fuente; Gosser Esquilín).[21] Subsequent postcolonial and feminist readings of the novel that do not engage ecocriticism returned to analyses of its representations of epistemological systems as inherently oppositional.[22] Most recently, Gosser Esquilín and Heise used various strains of ecocriticism in their analyses of groups of novels but do not center *In the Palm of Darkness* in their publications.

Decolonizing Haiti's Narrative

In the Palm of Darkness is an ecofiction spun out of the stark historical realities of the Anthropocene. The chaos when Aristide is first deposed impacts Haiti's already compromised natural environment and the bodies occupying it. The scientific or ecological perspective represented in this novel argues that Haiti's natural environment—specifically its forests, mountains, and rivers—is failing. The failure is most visible in the material absence of its embodied organisms: its amphibians and its human animals are dying rapidly. The cultural perspective, expressed through the Haitian characters in the novel, argues the explanation for the decline of grenouille du sang is not this simple. Because of the disparity between local Haitian epistemologies and global foreign epistemologies, the explanation might not even be knowable.[23] Combining both perspectives, Montero suggests that Haiti's sociopolitical environment is responsible for the disruption of its natural environment and that this disruption causes unnatural migration of Haiti's bodies, human and nonhuman alike.

Sarah Jaquette Ray's *The Ecological Other* powerfully examines the corporeal body as a site of discourse. Ray's assertion that "environmentalism is fundamentally paradoxical: it functions as a critique of some dominant relations, especially capitalism, and yet it reinforces many social hierarchies along lines of race, class, and gender" is highly relevant to *In the Palm of Darkness*, especially the novel's depiction of Haitian life under dictatorship (4). Ray's study brings new attention to ableism and the disabled body: "To the extent that scholars are arguing that the body is the site of environmental injustice and the means of recovering from those injustices, they fail to trouble the correlation between the whole, healthy body and a whole, healthy environment, an assumption that I argue is ableist and ignores the investments in abled bodies that environmentalism has long held" (8). The novel's textual emphasis on human bodies can be read more effectively through theorizations such as Ray's than as a replication of the spectacular violence narrative of Haiti.[24]

Thierry's early discussion of Haiti's nonhuman animals sets up the text as deeply concerned with all forms of life on the island, rejecting a Cartesian view of humankind and nonhuman animals as mutually exclusive categories. Montero uses the omnipresence of fragmented human bodies and the absence of nonhuman bodies as an accurate historical representation of the violence of the Duvalier years and as a contemporary interpretation of the mutilation of a specific body politic: Haiti's function as an independent republic.[25] Postrevolution, two factors impeded Haiti's economic sovereignty: the repayment of debt to France and Haiti's elite class, which exploited constitutional structures to maintain power through collusion with foreign companies (Dubois 6–7). By 1914, a staggering 80 percent of the Haitian government's budget was spent on payment and interest to France for France's "losses" incurred by the Haitian Revolution (Dubois 8). Haiti was paying heavily for the crime of blacks obtaining their freedom.

While previous ecocritical analyses offer productive readings of the novel, they lack attention to the text's third voice, a discourse created through character development and ekphrasis. The third voice is developed through two kinds of textualized visuals: (1) a series of ekphrastic descriptions of images of both nonhuman animals and human animals and (2) ten unattributed blurbs on postcards detailing extinct or disappearing amphibians. These repeating visuals create the third voice, a narration that clarifies the novel's ultimate project: situating ecological disaster in the Caribbean as part of global environmental destruction that began in the Columbian era, escalated through nineteenth century European colonialism, was exacerbated by twentieth century U.S. neocolonialism, and persists today.

The U.S. occupation from 1915 to 1934 did not resolve Haiti's financial crisis; it made the nation's financial challenges dramatically worse. Agricultural corporations accompanied the medical and structural aid the United States provided, dispossessing Haitian small farmers and converting their land into monocultures (Dubois 207–214). Workers increasingly sought labor in urban areas via domestic immigration and via international immigration to the Dominican Republic, Puerto Rico, and the United States starting in the 1980s. The legacies of U.S. intervention in Haiti, both in its 1915–1934 occupation and in its 1994 occupation, made Haiti dependent on foreign aid for basic supplies of food and fuel.[26] In *Damning the Flood: Haiti, Aristide, and the Politics of Containment*, Peter Hallward explains, "In real terms, average wages fell by around 50% between 1980 and 1990, as import controls were removed, the value of US agricultural export to Haiti almost tripled during the last years of the decade" (15). The loss of wages and the surge in cost to feed one's family are parts of the highly complex and destructive sociopolitical environment of 1990s Haiti. In "Deforestation and the Yearning for Lost Landscapes in Caribbean Literatures," Paravisini-Gebert traces the literary response to the deforestation legacies of the conquest and the plantation economy evolving through nineteenth-century colonialism and twentieth-century neocolonialism.[27] Paravisini-Gebert discusses several novels published between 1944 and 1979 but mentions no Haitian publications after 1979.[28] The human rights violations of both of the Duvalier dictatorships and the state under Aristide made the production and dissemination of Haitian literature virtually impossible from the 1950s through the 1990s. François Duvalier's regime drove an estimated 80 percent of the professional and political class into exile (Bellegarde-Smith 116).

Given the political turmoil of 1990s Haiti, Montero faced a challenge. How could she center a politics of knowing without replicating the expected spectacle violence narrative? The novel's structure of alternating between

Thierry's and Victor's epistemologies and narrations of their lives accomplishes this. Thierry's narrations particularly manifest Nixon's concept of "slow violence," which he defines as "a violence that occurs gradually and out of sight, a violence of delayed destruction that is dispersed across time and space, an attritional violence that is typically not viewed as violence at all" (2). Nixon asserts, "The insidious workings of slow violence derive largely from the unequal attention given to spectacular and unspectacular time" (6). *In the Palm of Darkness* is an exemplar of this slow violence in that it resists portraying Haiti's environmental degradation as solely the result of the spectacular time(s) of the Duvalier regimes.[29]

Critics have paid insufficient attention to the temporal frames of Thierry's and Victor's narration. Each devotes considerable narrative time to familial and romantic relationships through individual flashbacks and ruminations on their present lives. By revisiting the sociopolitical effects of both Duvalier regimes on rural Haitians, Montero performs what Nixon articulates over a decade later: "Violence, above all, environmental violence, needs to be seen—and deeply considered—as a contest not only over space, or bodies, or labor, or resources, but also over time" (8). Though scholars tend to bifurcate the novel's epistemologies, I would like to foreground the novel's triangulated constructors of knowledge: the human characters' narrations, the ekphrastic paratexts, and the interspersed postcards. Together, the three forms of narrative reveal how Haiti itself has arrived at the edge of extinction.[30]

The novel uses its human protagonists to portray Haiti's stasis between internal corruption and neocolonial interference.[31] Montero criticizes the neocolonial discourse manifested not only in scientists such as U.S. American Victor Grigg but also in Haitian complicity in ecological destruction that Thierry represents. Grigg's version of ecology limits itself to collecting other nations' species while the human cohabitants of the nonhuman species are slaughtered toward extinction.[32] Thierry's role in Haiti's political and environmental corruption began forty years ago, when he helped another foreigner collect Caribbean species in Haiti—the Australian Jasper Wilbur. Thierry consistently uses Voodoo to interpret his world, but he is not unaware or unpracticed in forms of science; Wilbur teaches him how to identify, examine, and collect amphibians. As Alcocer suggests, "Thierry, does not reject—and in fact participates in—modern science" (131). Setting aside Thierry's need to earn money, Montero suggests Thierry finds the practice of science admirable.[33] Montero undermines the colonizer/colonized binary in a decolonial ecocritique by indicting Australians, Haitians, and U.S. Americans in the extinction of the grenouille du sang.

Gillman asserts that Grigg is "sent to Haiti by Vaughan Patterson to rescue the grenouille du sang, or blood frog, from extinction" (515). Victor does not want to *rescue* or *save* the species; he is collecting it at the behest of another scientist who removes species from their native habitats and fails to save any of them.³⁴ Victor also undertakes the quest with a particularly neocolonial motivation: if he manages to capture the frog, he may win a prestigious fellowship, in addition to the currency of scientific fame such an achievement would garner him. Victor chooses to ignore the recurring signs of Haiti's extinction audible in Thierry's stories as well as the visible warnings from renegade tonton macoutes, a paramilitary death squad created by the Duvalier regime.³⁵ Haiti's broken political environment is reflected in devastating unnatural corporeality that emphasizes punishment for transgressing the Duvaliers' spiritually ordained social order: the loss of able-bodiedness, to which Ray refers (8).

The often faceless, dismembered bodies hanging from trees in the forest and in the city of Port-au-Prince, the disappearances of children and pregnant women, and the animals set aflame in large piles in the novel all function as reminders of class, race, and power hierarchies. In portraying the remnants of the Duvalier regimes through the renewed violence and terrorism of competing factions of drug-trafficking tonton macoutes, *In the Palm of Darkness* illustrates how Haitian elites replicated colonial models of master/slave dialectics.³⁶ Thierry's narrations about his brother's participation in political violence suggest these actions inevitably result in unnatural fatalities: "Julien stank of the devil, he not only killed men, but women too, a lot of them about to give birth, and he had killed children" (145). After Aristide loses power, Julien "joined the forces with Cito Francisque," the drug lord who controls the Mont des Enfants Perdus at the time of the novel (146). Thierry explains that Julien "really went crazy" and "he settled all his past and future accounts" when his daughter was mutilated and killed by a rival drug lord (146).

Julien's violence is literally depleting the island of its living and its future people. Thierry cannot challenge his brother; his society, the Abakuá, warns him that they will stop Julien's slaughtering and Thierry cannot interfere. The novel's silence on the Duvaliers is, ironically, telling: "Papa Doc" is mentioned only twice; in both ekphrastic instances, his image is described as being on a fan with his picture on one side and a map of Haiti on the other. Thierry voices both of these descriptions. The evocation of the map signaling the equivalency of Duvalier with the geography of Haiti and its use as a fan suggesting his omnipresence cohere to expose the stark differences in power between rich and poor Haitians during the regimes. Instead of foregrounding an externally manufactured genocide, Montero highlights specific local political and socioeconomic causes of human degradation and decline.³⁷

The Haitian voices in the novel emphatically deny the possibility for understanding the animal extinctions fully and assert the urgency in understanding them in context. In his narration following Postcard 1 (9), Thierry says to Victor, "You want to know where the frogs go. I cannot say, sir. But let me ask you a question: Where did our fish go? Almost all of them left this sea, and in the forest, the wild pigs disappeared, and the migratory ducks, and even the iguanas for eating, they went too" (11). Thierry rejects Victor's single-species focus, viewing the declines as systemic: "One day a man like you will come here, someone who crosses the ocean to look for a couple of frogs, and when I say frogs, I mean any creature, and he will find only a great hill of bones on the shore" (11). Thierry's biocentric view places humans at the edges of his vision of extinction. He cautions Victor to "take a look at what's left of humans, take a careful look: You can see the bones pushing out under their skins as if they wanted to escape, to leave behind the weak flesh where they are so battered, to go into hiding someplace else" (11). While Victor's discourses reflect a Cartesian notion of the separation between humans and nonhuman animals, Thierry's discourse collapses that separation.

Montero's inclusion of topographic, scientific, and spiritual discourses seems invested in undermining the Western epistemologies developed through the Cartesian split. The first edition of the novel opens with a map of Haiti. In the upper left-hand corner, a tiny piece of the larger island of Cuba is visible. Haiti is literally centered across the two-page map, with a narrow strip of the Dominican Republic sitting at the right-hand edge of the page. The Atlantic Ocean frames Haiti from the north, and the Caribbean Sea frames it from the south. This image evokes what Nixon describes as the contrasts between official and unofficial landscapes. Thierry's Haiti is indeed a vernacular landscape, one that is "shaped by the affective, historically textured maps that communities have devised over generations, maps replete with names and routes, maps alive to significant ecological and surface geological features" (Nixon 17). The map opening the novel includes the Mont des Enfants Perdus, the mountain on which Thierry and Victor risk their lives to capture the grenouille du sang; this mountain does not actually appear on most contemporary maps of Haiti.

Dr. Emile Boukaka, the physician and herpetologist who also challenges Victor's suppositions, echoes Thierry's assertions that the exact cause of the disappearances is unknown. At the approximate midpoint of the novel, in the chapter entitled "Indian Hut," Montero introduces Boukaka as a priest of Voodoo; in doing so, she radically undermines stereotypical representations of Voodoo as irrational. Described by Thierry as "the Mpegó of Power, Priest of the Symbols, and Signs, the Master of the Casts, the Maker of the Mark," Boukaka's role is to initiate practitioners; he performs ritual scarification, as well as medical examination of his society before each zombie hunt the group performs (128). He embodies contradiction in this regard: his profession requires saving lives, but his ordained role as a Mpegó demands ending lives. Despite having access to both epistemologies, Boukaka can trace but not change the ongoing ecological catastrophe.

Boukaka's character constantly frames the mystery of the disappearances, in Ybarra's words, through "a body politics of knowing" (12). He affirms cultural ontology when he asserts farmers' explanation for the missing grenouille du sang: "They say that Agwé Taroyo, the god of the waters, has called the frogs down to the bottom. They say they have seen them leave: Freshwater animals diving into the sea, and the ones that don't have the time or strength to reach the meeting place are digging holes in the ground to hide or letting themselves die along the way" (95). He then challenges scientific ontology to illustrate its lack of explanation: "You people invent excuses: acid rain, herbicides, deforestation. But the frogs are disappearing from places where none of that has happened" (96). Boukaka's point vocalizes what the postcards in his office suggest: place-limited ecology elides global extinction. These postcards are his physical tracing—his signs, casts, and marks—of global disappearances linked inextricably to human activity.

Victor's goal is possession of the grenouille du sang; he does not care about other species Boukaka observes disappearing. Victor describes Boukaka to his wife as "the only Haitian who had become seriously interested in the declining populations, someone who wasn't even a herpetologist but a physician, a surgeon" (57). Montero implies Victor is the amateur scientist; if there were so few people concerned with the decline of the populations, shouldn't he start his field trip meeting with the one person who had knowledge about the declines? Montero provides a second affirmation of Victor's self-interest, not his ecological concern, when he recalls, "Months earlier I had reread one of his articles in *Froglog* on the decline of amphibians; it was a brief piece but I made a file for it and decided to write him. I never imagined at the time that I would meet him face-to-face in Port-au-Prince" (91). Perhaps he never imagined it because he never thought the trip worthwhile until the Australian Vaughan Patterson asked him to make it.

Once Boukaka enters, Montero uses Victor's interior monologue and the two men's dialogue to illuminate the cultural origins of this ecological problem. Victor explains, "I had thought Emile Boukaka was a mulatto; nobody had told me so but I had an image of him as a tall, gray-haired light-skinned man with spectacles, more self-conscious, less chubby and tropical than he actually was" (93). Victor assumes scientists must look like himself or any other white, Western European intellectual but finds Boukaka "absolutely black, intensely black, the skin on his arms gleamed as if he had been born in Africa," expressing an almost unbelievable ignorance of the racial origins of Haitian people (93). He additionally describes him in an equally ignorant conflation of Central American indigenous physiognomies, mapping the individuals he sees in a postcard onto Boukaka: "His hair and beard were somewhat reddish and he had an enormous round, flat face, a face like a Mexican (or a Bolivian?) tortilla patted into shape by naked Indian women" (93). He closes his physical description in what must be a verbalization of blackface—the gross distortions of physiognomy used in U.S. minstrel shows and cartoons beginning in the nineteenth century: "There, in the fat circle of that face, his nose, his bulging eyes, his thick half-smiling lips seemed to be dancing" (93).

I have presented this description at length because it is a primary example of the literary stratagem—characterization—through which Montero complicates Native/Other binaries. Caribbean people are made up of African, European, Caribbean Indigenous, and South Asian ancestries. This scene illustrates that Boukaka embodies the complex racial and cultural mixing present in Caribbean history and Haiti's contemporary social structure. The descendants of those ancestries, however, perpetuate a race war that began centuries ago during plantation colonialism, and Montero is suggesting the war is visible on the skin of Haiti's contemporary people. Victor is so consumed with the desire to find the grenouille du sang that he literally misses the forest for the trees: species disappearance is global because human and nonhuman migration, and thus impact on the environment, has always been global.

Victor arrogantly confesses, "I made an effort to handle with some grace the enormous quality of data provided by Boukaka," but undermines this compliment in the same thought: "I was amazed by his capacity for detail, his precision, I can even say at his erudition" (96–97). As he leaves, Boukaka repeats what Thierry has said is the Law of Water: "What I've learned, I learned in books. . . . But what I know, everything I know, I took from fire and water, from water and flame: One puts out the other" (97). Thierry has tried to teach Victor this law, and the reader may recall that Thierry does not teach this to Wilbur until Wilbur is already dying from a toad poison, foreshadowing Victor's death. Appearing at the novel's midpoint, the scene allows Montero to formally illustrate Voodoo's attempts to reconcile the natural and cultural in stark contrast to Cartesian and later Enlightenment discourses.

Tracing Disappearing Bodies

The first part of Haiti's econarrative is told through the characterizations of Victor, Thierry, and Boukaka. The second component comprises multiple instances of ekphrasis. The novel's ekphrastic discourse assumes the form of descriptions of sketches, paintings, photographs, and postcards. The most frequent ekphrasis discusses frogs, toads, and other amphibians or birds as they are drawn, painted, or photographed by characters. Because most of the species are difficult to capture and photograph, the sketch literally serves as an identification of the species when discussed by those collecting it. The first such ekphrastic moment occurs when Vaughan Patterson, the aging herpetologist from Australia, recruits Victor to find the grenouille du sang because he is too ill to make the trip. Victor recalls, "I had received a dinner invitation, a white card with an engraved drawing of a small gray frog: Professor Vaughan Patterson, the eminent Australian herpetologist, would expect me" (4). His description begins the novel's critique of species removal as fetish, not science: "Patterson boasted of keeping alive, when the species was already considered extinct, the last specimen of the *Taudactylus diur-*

nus, sole survivor of the colony that he himself had bred in his laboratory in Adelaide" (5). The description suggests the unnatural, forced migration of species is a major cause of their extinction. If Patterson was able to breed a colony in his lab, why did he fail to reintroduce it to its original ecosystem?

Boling summarizes the global contexts present in the novel, reminding us that "ostriches are being raised in Indiana, Indian women pray to Hindi goddesses in Haiti, a man from Vietnam works on a farm in the U.S., the African Diaspora has forever changed the face of the Caribbean" ("Trope of Nature" 250). This intersection of human and nonhuman migration is depicted in Grigg's ekphrastic recollection of how his expedition started. Victor explains that Patterson "began to draw on his napkin. I watched him become engrossed in sketching a frog, he didn't even look up when the waiter brought his drink. *Eleutherodactylus sanguineas*, he wrote in small letters when he was finished, framing the name between the animals' paws. He handed me the drawing" (5). Victor confesses, "I was so astonished by his request that I deliberately concentrated on the drawing. Patterson became aware of this and took back the napkin" (5). Patterson then uses the napkin to wipe his mouth, literally erasing the image, which Victor describes as "ruining the sketch" (5). Montero deftly foreshadows how the fetishistic desire of Patterson will catalyze the species' ruin. This exchange is also a metaphor for extinction in general: a scientist values a species for collection, but once he or she "captures" it, even figuratively through a sketch, the species' fate is to be is erased, to be rendered extinct.

Ekphrasis amplifies the tensions between the local and the foreign that Thierry and Victor embody; for example, foreign herpetologists draw a species as a test for the native guide to see how suitable he will be or to see if the local resident is lying about the species' location. To undermine this assumption of the Other being more knowledgeable than the Native, Montero decolonizes Victor's quest narrative by depicting the Native correcting the Other. Thus, when interviewing Thierry, Victor asks him to draw the frog: "Thierry sat looking at the sketch; he spent a long while deep in thought, and I assumed it was just a trick to gain time. . . . He handed back the drawing and told me that the upper arc was silvery, the lower one light brown, and the tip of the snout yellow or grayish-yellow" (19). Victor notes, "I nodded in silence, not taking my eyes off the sketch: now I was the one trying to gain a few moments" (19). Thierry then describes how the Australian herpetologist Jasper Wilbur[38] hired him "only after drawing a couple of toads on a little slate and asking if [I] could recognize them" (20).

One could interpret this scene as illustrative of Thierry being willing to play the neocolonizer's game; however, because it is situated within ekphrasis, the exchange indicates a larger point about human nature. Present in both Victor's and Thierry's narrations, descriptions of drawings, paintings, and photographs allude to lost loves or broken relationships. Jasper Wilbur and Thierry develop a father-son relationship; Thierry eventually calls him Papa Crapaud and works with him until his death.[39] Thierry may be anticipating that Victor will die too, because his relationship with both men began with sketching amphibians. While Thierry recalls his work with Papa Crapaud, Victor trails off to a memory of his mother, who painted an enormous midwife toad for him: "She began to paint it when she learned she was pregnant and finished it on the day I was born. From then on she suspected that my life, my entire adult life, would be bound up with those creatures" (21).

Sketching animals is connected to each man's past and each man's loss. When describing his father's ostrich farm to Thierry, Victor draws an image of an ostrich because Thierry is unfamiliar with the bird. As he draws it, Thierry recounts the time when Papa Crapaud drew a special toad he brought back from Guadeloupe, again linking his relationship with these men obsessed with amphibians to loss (68). Once Papa Crapaud realizes his wife, Ganesha, has been having sex with other men, he stops going on expeditions. Thierry explains, "I was the one who looked for all the frogs. The old man told me to while he stayed home keeping an eye on his wife, pretending he was drawing frogs" (70). Crapaud never realizes Thierry had also had sex with Ganesha, but Thierry feels the loss of the relationship the moment he betrays Crapaud (72).

Postcards from the Edge of Extinction

Two decades after the publication of this novel, most societies accept the evidence of global climate change and are taking steps to slow environmental degradation.[40] *In the Palm of Darkness* emphasizes the Caribbean islands' imbrication in uneven webs of global ecological devastation. Through the fictionalized scientific discourse of the interspersed postcard voice, Montero urges readers not to look at environmental literature through national lenses because events in one nation space have measurable impact in other nations. While scholars describe the blurbs I will refer to differently, I interpret them as the postcards Victor sees in the office of Dr. Emile Boukaka.[41] The postcards have no sources listed; this is consistent with the novel's refusal to identify a single, definitive explanation for the declines. The postcards repeatedly center the challenge of epistemology, highlighting the inextricable linkages of Caribbean islands with nations of the Global North to assert the traceability of planetary ecological devastation.

Before speaking with the surgeon, Victor observes the postcards "were from all over the world, France for the most part, but also some unexpected places, Bombay for example, Nagasaki, Buenos Aires, even Bafatá" (92). Victor's interest is decidedly Western/imperialist; he only mentions cities that have been centers of colonialism. Ironically, the postcard that "attracted [his] attention more than the others . . . seemed very old," "was hand-painted," and contains a coded mention of a Duvalier: "Kisses to Duval, is he still in

Port-au-Prince?" (93). Though the postcard is captioned "INDIAN HUT, BENI, BOLIVIA," it is signed *"De Pérou une photo de mes cher anthropophages"* (93).[42] Later, Victor assumes the following: "It was an Indian hut in Beni, Bolivia, which means the sender was confused or trying to confuse the recipient. Unless the postcard from Beni had been carried to Peru and sent from there, in which case it wasn't deception or confusion, but simply a whim or an oversight" (132). It is more likely that the inscription is a coded message. Beni is also a city in the Democratic Republic of Congo and Benin is a country within coastal West Africa, recognized to be a significant source of Africans kidnapped into slavery as well as being recognized as the place of origin of Vodou. It is not clear which Montero is referring to—Beni or Benin—but that is less important than the point Victor's assumptions about the postcard reflect. Victor is repeatedly exposed to significant information, but he does not unite Thierry's description of the surgeon and this postcard to understand that Boukaka is or was a Duvalier supporter, like Thierry's family.[43] Montero's further characterization suggests Victor is lazy, irresponsible, or completely self-interested, because he notes "most were simply greetings and regards, or data related to the disappearance of some amphibian" (93); he does not concern himself with the data on the other species.

Of the ten postcards appearing between Victor and Thierry's narrations, nine recount disappearances of species outside Haiti. The postcards, each dated and specific to a national location, are arranged in this order: United States, Australia, Switzerland, Costa Rica, United States, Puerto Rico,[44] Columbia, United States, Honduras, Hispaniola. The postcards mimic the vacillation between epistemologies of Victor and Thierry; because the novel starts with Victor's narration, each postcard "follows" a section of his. Postcard 1, for example, explains that the *Bufo boreas* of Colorado has succumbed to a disease that disrupts the toad's immune system but "the cause of the failure is unknown" (9).[45] Postcard 3 describes the deaths of millions of frogs in Switzerland: "For many biologists, the sudden decline of the *Rana temporaria* remains shrouded in mystery" (49). Subsequent postcards refer to indigenous explanations of the disappearances, such as in Hawaii, where the toad *Bufo marinus* has vanished and "the natives reported that the toads had simply 'gone away'" (79). The postcards reveal the slippage between Indigenous/biocentric explanations for extinctions and the Western/anthropocentric explanations. Postcard 8 relays how the *Rana cascadae*, once abundant in southern California, has become decimated: "The species has completely disappeared" despite its habitat "being a protected area that has undergone no significant environmental changes" (141). Montero implies the words "habitat," "protected," and "significant" vary in meaning and that Western/anthropocentric discourse fails to recognize the limits of its own taxonomy.

Postcard 10 closes the novel and pulls the narrative's chronology together for the reader. It begins with a description of the decline of the grenouille du sang: "In the mid-1970s, a significant decline was noted in the population of the *Eleutherodactylus sanguineus*, a small, bright-red land frog found only in the mountain regions of Hispaniola" (182–183). The postcard notes that it disappeared from the Dominican Republic first: "Ten years later, the frog disappeared from the Dominican Republic. At the same time, it was reported that the species was on the verge of extinction in Haiti, where only a few isolated specimens had been spotted on the Mont des Enfants Perdus, a mountain near Port-au-Prince" (182–183). Montero's choice to unite the two nations under their island name and indicate the Dominican Republic was first responsible for the extinction seems a pointed critique. The two nations are often compared, with Haiti being condemned for not having achieved the economic improvements and political stability that the Dominican Republic has presumably achieved.[46] In the map opening the first edition of the translated novel, the two places where the grenouille du sang has been spotted are literally depicted as the southern edges of Haiti: The Mont des Enfants Perdus is situated close to the Haitian-Dominican border in Haiti's southeastern corner. Casetaches Hill is located on the southwestern tip of the island, at nearly an opposite longitude.[47]

Uniting the fate of the frog with the fate of its seekers, Postcard 10 summarizes Victor and Thierry's search. The postcard indicates that the frog was not found on Mont des Enfants Perdus but "on the basis of private information that placed the frog on Casetaches Hill," Grigg "carried out an extensive search, and captured an adult male, which according to Grigg's own notes, was the last of its species on earth" (182–183). This portion of the text offers a clear decolonial ecocritique. The source of "private information" is Thierry's body of knowledge of Haiti's environment, but this is obscured in a colonial discourse reinscribing notions that codify the Westerner/scientist "discovery" narrative. Moreover, the source of information will be inaccessible to others, even the inhabitants of the same environment. The postcard unites these decolonial concerns with those raised by environmentalism, including the manner in which it "reinforces many social hierarchies along lines of race, class, and gender" previously described by Ray (4). The "extensive" nature of the search and the assertion that "Grigg" conducted the search obscure Thierry's role in collecting the last grenouille du sang. Montero is using these glaring obfuscations to remind readers of Thierry's role in the extinction of the grenouille du sang.

Haiti's End, World's End

In the chapter preceding Postcard 10, Montero dramatizes the discovery of the frog and links Haiti's narrative with the frog's capture. This time, however, it is Victor, not Thierry, who ponders how he could possibly continue his quest. He fears disappointing Vaughan Patterson: "If I didn't capture the frog, what would he say when I called him at his laboratory in Adelaide, how would I explain that Haiti wasn't simply a place, a name, a mountain with a frog that had survived?" (170). He then repeats the spectacular descriptions he used early in the novel: "How would I describe the streets, the open sewers, the human shit in the middle of the sidewalk, the corpses at dawn, the woman whose hands were missing, the woman whose face was missing?" (170–171). Finally able to move past the spectacle, Grigg articulates a consciousness, though ableist, of the human disaster: "How could I make him understand that Luc, the botanists' guide, had been buried without his feet and that Paul, Thierry's brother, was probably rotting somewhere, missing a piece of his body?" (171).

Tragically, Victor Grigg remains, in many ways, unchanged, because he does not see the need for biospheric egalitarianism[48] or what Heise calls "multispecies justice" (162). Humans remain at the center of Victor's ecology: "God almighty, how would I make him see that Haiti was disappearing, that the great hill of bones growing before our very eyes, a mountain higher than the peak of Tête Boeuf, was all that would remain?" (171). Victor may parrot Thierry's words, but these words do not mean the same thing to Victor. He chooses to capture the frog, a male specimen that seems old and sick. When he notes, "I felt as if I were holding an ancient survivor, a creature that had forgotten to die, or had taken refuge in a place so remote he hadn't heard the warning, if there was a warning, or the annihilation order, if that's what it was," Victor again repeats what a Haitian has said; in this case, he echoes Boukaka, who explained what Haitian farmers have told him (173). It would be comforting to think these words indicate that Victor had actually seen and heard all of the warnings against accelerating the frog's extinction, but Montero offers readers no such comfort.

After placing the frog in "the protected compartment" he had prepared, Victor's thirst is renewed, and he asks, "Don't you think another one must be around here someplace?" (173). In this one sentence, Montero portrays the consistent threat to all species: human greed. This is also the cause of human extinction. It is in this final chapter that Thierry tells Victor a story about a man who kills one of Thierry's society members over a trivial fight at work. He confesses to murdering the man at the command of the Abakuá and then recounts that he had lost his children, one by one, and was living quietly until Victor appeared. Victor compares Thierry to the aged grenouille du sang and says he "too was a dying species, a trapped animal, a man who was too solitary" (178). The irony is not lost—being too solitary is precisely what Thierry claims killed Papa Crapaud, the last foreigner to hire Thierry for help collecting Haiti's amphibians. The strong, consistent effect achieved through the postcards' ecocritical discourse is the utter denaturalization of the nation's exemption from modernity and its artificially constructed solitude. The postcards are evidence that Haiti is part of a larger, global pattern, not an isolated ecological disaster. The novel offers readers the chance to reframe their image of Haiti and its ecology into one that moves Haiti from the edge to the center of the Caribbean.

While the novel centers the loss of amphibians to foreign collection, it also signals a similar threat to the flora of the island. Two other scientists, a female U.S. American (Sarah) and a French man (Edouard), are seeking what may be the last specimen of a cactus unique to the island of Hispaniola, the *Pereskia quisqueyana*. Heise does not account for Victor and Sarah's role in the continued violence against Haiti. She asserts, "They have no clear grasp of Haiti's political landscape and naively imagine that scientists who are just looking for frogs or plants could not possibly interfere with the bands of *Tontons Macoutes*" (166). Neither of these scientists are naive; rather, they are symbols of American and French neocolonialism. They place their desire to possess something—in this case, species that will augment their knowledge and reputation—above Haiti's environmental health and their own physical safety as well as that of anyone who works as their guide. Sarah illustrates her awareness of the risk of her quest when she asks Victor what he is looking for, noting, "People don't risk coming to Haiti unless they're looking for something important" (119).

Like a postcard, *In the Palm of Darkness* intimates but cannot fully reveal the object or space it visualizes. Accordingly, the novel invites many forms of reading to analyze the problem it depicts: postcolonial, feminist, decolonial, ecocritical. Ultimately, decolonial ecocritical analysis offers readers the most substantive understanding of the novel's project. This essay has offered readers a recovery of Montero's work within Latinx literature generally. More specifically, by tracing the convergence of literary criticism on *In the Palm of Darkness* and ecocriticism, I have argued for a positioning of her work within the emerging field of Latinx literary environmentalism. The major literary devices Montero carefully employs—characterization, ekphrasis, and generic manipulation—all return the reader to the novel's central question: why is the grenouille du sang disappearing? It would take nearly twenty years before this question could be answered scientifically through the discovery of a fungus that has plagued amphibians globally.[49] Recalling Montero's long career as a journalist, it seems to me that the author offered us a postcard of the world as her tip—a place to start looking for the answers to the deeply troubling reality of mass extinction.

NOTES

1. Among monographs, see Dalleo and Machado Sáez; Sandín and Perez; Machado Sáez; Socolovsky.

2. The novel was published as *Tú, la oscuridad*; all quotations are from the 1997 translation.

3. Aristide ruled from 1990 until 1991; he returned to power with U.S. aid from 1994 to 1996 and from 2001 to 2004. He was removed from power and lived in exile until 2011.

4. François Duvalier ("Papa Doc") ruled 1954–1971; Jean-Claude Duvalier ("Baby Doc") ruled 1971–1986.

5. See Dubois for a discussion of the international discourse on the earthquake and the recycled narratives portraying Haiti as backward, corrupt, and incapable of self-governance.

6. See Roth.

7. For an extensive discussion of Haiti's history and its representation, see DuBois.

8. José Luis de la Fuente suggests Montero's reading of a 1992 news article compelled Montero to write the novel: "Por lo que se refiere a *Tú, la oscuridad*, un reportaje titulado 'Silence of the frogs' escrito por la periodista estadounidense Emily Yoffe [1992] sea la desaparición de anfibios en *The New York Times Magazine* provocaron en la novelista terror que precisó de la ficcionalización en forma de novela" (92). Translation mine: "A report entitled 'Silence of the Frogs,' by the American journalist Emily Yoffe [1992], about the disappearance of amphibians appearing in *The New York Times Magazine* provoked the novelist such that she needed to fictionalize the terror in the form of a novel."

9. For example, Huggan and Tiffin's collection, *Postcolonial Ecocriticism*, centers environmental and postcolonial concerns to discuss works globally, including from the Caribbean, Africa, India, and the Pacific Islands.

10. See essays theorizing liquid borders and identity by Frances Negrón-Muntaner, Rebeca Hey-Colón, and Marisel Moreno.

11. Montero often sets her narratives in Haiti and the Dominican Republic; the characters also often travel between islands during the course of the narrative. See Prieto for a discussion of the geographic settings of her work. Haitian American author Edwidge Danticat's work has been published about considerably; perhaps there is a linguistic component to this absence in English language scholarship.

12. I am referencing American and cultural studies discourse on inter-American, hemispheric, and continental frames of study articulated by Paul Jay in "The Myth of 'America' and the Politics of Location: Modernity, Border Studies, and the 'Literature of the Americas.'" Subsequent key discussions and expansions of these ideas appear in Fitz, *Rediscovering the New World*; Saldívar, *The Dialectics of Our America*; and Gruesz, *Ambassadors of Culture*. More recent discussions include Lowe, *The Intimacies of Four Continents*; and Riofrio, *Continental Shifts*. For a review of the work establishing these concepts, see Sadowski-Smith and Fox, "Theorizing the Hemisphere."

13. In *American Imperialism's Undead*, Raphael Dalleo illustrates how Haiti's more recent history, particularly its 1915–1934 occupation by the United States and cultural production responding to that occupation, has been largely elided in postcolonial, Caribbean, Latina American, and Africa diaspora studies ("Introduction").

14. For discussions of narratives that foreground nature as part of colonial and nation-building enterprises in the nineteenth and twentieth centuries, see Kane, *The Natural World in Latin American Literatures* and Elizabeth M. Pettinaroli, and Ana María Mutis, "Introduction," *Troubled Waters: Rivers in Latin American Imagination*.

15. This is the same year the article referenced in n12, "Silence of the Frogs," appears.

16. Their understanding draws heavily on the scientific discipline of ecology: "Ecology is not a study of the 'external' environment we enter—some big outside that we go to. Ecology is a study of interrelationship, with its bedrock being the recognition of the distinction between things-in-themselves and things-for-us" (Garrard and Murphy qtd. in Boling 250).

17. A 2012 issue of *Green Letters* reviews much of this criticism to set up that issue's focus on "the need for new modes of reading postcolonial and world literatures which

are attentive to both thematic matter and to the ideological content of form itself, thus avoiding the tendencies of earlier waves of ecocriticism to privilege 'mimetic' representation, realist modes, and 'eco-centric' themes" (Deckard 10). Within the *Oxford Handbook of Ecocriticism*, DeLoughrey's "Postcolonialism" and Paravisini-Gebert's "Extinctions" are useful for performing ecocritical readings of *In the Palm of Darkness*. Recent monographs and edited volumes addressing the problems of first-wave ecocriticism through postcolonial and ecocritical intersections include Mukherjee's *Postcolonial Environments*, Huggan and Tiffin's *Postcolonial Ecocriticism*, and Nixon's *Slow Violence and the Environmentalism of the Poor.*

18. The *Oxford English Dictionary* cites the first use of the term *neocolonialism* in relation to U.S. policy in the Caribbean Basin in Paul Johnson's "The Crisis in Central America."

19. Montero attributes the inspiration for her novels to her journalism travels: "I became friendly with several anthropologists, traveled many times to the border between Haiti and the Dominican Republic and visited the huts of Haitian laborers who work (and suffer) harvesting sugarcane in the Dominican Republic" (qtd. in Prieto 89).

20. "La propuesta es indicar cómo Ganesha es el elemento sincretizador de la heteroglossia caribeña y, por ende, del texto" (Dávila Gonçalves 31). Translation mine: "I propose to show that Ganesha is the syncretizing element of Caribbean heteroglossia and, therefore, of the whole text."

21. De la Fuente asserts, "La muestra de esos dos mundos de los protagonistas viene conformando por una estructura divisa que resulta muy común en la narrativa puertorriqueña de las ultimada décadas—así sucede en las novelas de Rosario Ferré, Olga Nolla y últimatamente en Mayra Santos-Febres" (105). Translation mine: "This exemplifies that the worlds of the protagonists are conforming to a divided structure quite common in Puerto Rican narrative of recent decades—such as in the novels of Rosario Ferré, Olga Nolla, and most recently, in the work of Mayra Santos Febres."

22. "Western/Judeo-Christian" and "Haitian/Vodou" (Rivera; Alcocer; Dávila Gonçalves; Boling, "Apocalipsis"; Kearns): this is a binary Montero routinely undermines by portraying several religious systems. The novel opens with Victor's recollection of a Tibetan astrologer's prediction of his death; Thierry's recollections of his life inform readers about the hierarchies of Vodou practitioners and the danger in transgressing other societies' territories or rules; through the character Ganesha, readers learn about the syncretism of Hindu spirituality and Haitian Vodou. The novel's structure and multiple narrative lines resist binary postcolonial readings foregrounding the Native/Other, feminist readings prioritizing the masculine/feminine, and ecocritical readings juxtaposing the human/the animal. *Ecocriticism of the Global South* contains essays that address differences in postcolonial ecocriticism and decolonial ecocriticism. For example, see De Shield's essay for a discussion of literary isomorphism as a limitation of postcolonial ecocriticism.

23. For example, Greg Garrard observed, "the relationship between globalization and ecocriticism has barely been broached" (*Ecocriticism* 178). Similar critiques can be found in Buell's *The Future of Environmental Criticism*, DeLoughrey and Handley's *Postcolonial Ecologies*, and Dimock and Buell's *Shades of the Planet*. As Buell, Heise, and Thornbur note in a special issue of *Literature and Environment*, the first wave of ecocriticism was challenged when "it became clear that ecocritical frameworks had most often been national or even nationalist, whereas postcolonialist approaches tended to focus on transnational and cosmopolitan webs of connection" (421).

24. While Montero's depiction of 1990s Haiti can be considered spectacle, it is a realistic portrayal of the violence perpetuated during the Duvalier regimes and in the

transitions to and after Aristide's rule. Boling takes a particularly stark view of Haiti, one that replicates an essentialist critique of Haiti that I do not believe Montero intended: "The national product of Haiti comes down to one, death itself. The world is upside down. Sons sleep with their mothers, children predecease their progenitors, trees bring forth 'strange fruit' . . . carcasses—both human and animal—line the streets and dot the hillsides. It is death itself that grows in Haiti" ("Trope of Nature" 250).

25. See Alcocer, "Bound Bodies," in *Narrative Mutations*, for further discussion of the representations of the body in the novel.

26. For an extensive discussion of U.S. neocolonialism in Haiti, see Farmer. For a discussion of the Caribbean cultural production critiquing U.S. colonialism, particularly its 1915–1934 occupation of Haiti, see Dalleo, *American Imperialism's Undead*.

27. Haiti's deforestation and natural disasters have been discussed frequently. There seems to be, however, inconsistency in this narrative. Buss, for example, asserts, "Haiti is an ecological disaster. Since colonial times, Haitians (and French colonists) have cut down 95% of forests without replacing them, producing major flooding in 2002, 2003, 2006, and 2007" (326). Dubois points to early preservation measures under Henry Christophe's rule: "There were also forward-thinking regulations meant to prevent deforestation: no one who rented a plantation, for instance was allowed to cut down more than one-third of the trees on the property, and they were also told to avoid cutting down trees on the summits of mountains" (65).

28. Paravisini-Gebert cites a number of texts, including novels by Chauvet that address U.S. neocolonial complicity in the deforestation of Haiti ("He of the Trees" 191).

29. Nixon makes a compelling point about the impact of chemicals such as Agent Orange that take decades to be fully understood: "More than thirty years after the last spray run, Agent Orange continues to wreak havoc, as through biomagnification, dioxins build up in the fatty tissues of pivotal foods such as duck and fish, and pass from the natural world into the cooking pot and from there to ensuing human generations" (14).

30. For a discussion of the role of tropical islands in the developments of natural sciences, see *Green Imperialism*.

31. Haiti was the first nation to proclaim its independence from colonial rule in 1804; it was, however, occupied by the United States from 1915 to 1934 and again in 1994. According to Buss, it was occupied by the United States fifteen times (325); the last intervention occurred during the Clinton administration. For more detailed recent histories of Haiti, see Farmer or Hallward.

32. For a discussion of imperialism, possession, and the concept of anti-conquest, see Pratt.

33. Alcocer makes a similar argument: "One could argue that his participation is economically driven, i.e., as an assistant to a foreign scientific research project he would probably earn more money than the average Haitian Laborer" (209n39).

34. My digital term search of the novel revealed that the word *save* appears a few times in Thierry's narrations, when he hopes to prevent Victor's death because he could not prevent Papa Crapaud's. The one-time Victor uses the word *save* is when his issue of *Froglog* has been left under a pile of human feces—a clear message for him to leave the mountain and stop his search. Victor notes, "The photo and the title of my article could not be seen under the stain left by the turds. I didn't try to save anything else" (44). The word *rescue* appears in the same section, but Victor uses it to describe a half-eaten skull in the bone pile they encounter.

35. Though Aristide started to disband the military in 1991, remaining factions of tonton macoutes still controlled rural areas and eventually were able to remove him from power.

36. Duvalier's self-representation as Baron Samedi is well documented; for a synopsis of his regime, see Buss.

37. Heise suggests the novel has a weakness in that "Montero's emphasis on the supernatural and the satanic does indeed block any detailed social and political analysis" (169). This statement conflates two distinct religious traditions: monotheistic Judeo-Christianity and the polytheistic Vodou, ultimately implying that Haiti's principal religious practice, Vodou, is "supernatural" and not a historic and extant religion. Similarly, Heise states Julien's actions within the tonton macoutes are spiritual and irrational: "It is difficult to make out any political or economic motivation—Julien seems in the grip of some evil force instead" (169). Haitian history and Thierry's narrations make it very clear that to survive the Duvalier dictatorships, one had to perform atrocities on demand. In the years following Aristide's removal, the use of rural forests and mountains for drug trafficking gave the former tonton macoutes a source of income. Anyone threatening this enterprise was tortured or murdered. Julien's actions are explicitly economically and politically motivated.

38. Wilbur represents a neocolonial paternity in which Victor hopes to inscribe himself: "I recalled that Wilbur, who was also an Australian, had been the teacher and friend of old man Patterson, and I took it as a good omen that after so much time the circle was closing at precisely this spot—with me, and the same guide grown old, and perhaps the same frogs" (21).

39. On their first meeting, Jasper Wilbur shows Thierry a photograph of a toad, which he is able to recognize. Thierry explains it is considered "the mother of all toads" (125), to which Wilbur responds that he feels like a father to the toads he collects. Thierry then nicknames him Papa Crapaud, and Wilbur hires him. Crapaud "discovers" a species of toad and names it after himself. Thierry describes an illustration that Crapaud receives and displays in a large frame. Thierry notes, "Years later the animal disappeared, it just left, vanished like so many others" (81).

40. In 2017, President Donald Trump removed the United States from the Paris Accord, codifying his refusal to acknowledge and ameliorate climate change.

41. José Luis de la Fuente asserts that the blurbs are excerpts from *Froglog* and *National Geographic Magazine* that note the final extinctions of amphibious species: "Son references a revistas como *Froglog* y *National Geographic Magazine* done se anotan las últimas extinciones de species amphibious" (106). Gillman also refers to them as postcards (518).

42. Translation mine: "From Peru, a photo of my dear cannibals." This may be a reference to an article, "My Dear Cannibals," written by a French Catholic missionary in the service of colonial missionary activities in Africa in the 1920s. See Foster, *Faith in Empire*, for a discussion of the article.

43. At the start of his narration, Thierry explains his family's relationship to Vodou: "My mother was a devotee of Baron-la-Croix, and my father had to be one too because of his profession" (11). This baron and Baron Samedi are alternative names for the Vodou god of the dead, Ghede. I interpret this comment to mean that Thierry's families were supporters of François Duvalier, who represented himself as Baron Samedi. For a discussion of the origins and variations in taxonomy of Vodou, see Ramsey.

44. Montero notes that several species of frog have disappeared from Puerto Rico (Prieto 90).

45. Boling argues this postcard evokes the discourse on Haiti and AIDS in the 1980s; see "Apocalipsis."

46. See Buss for an example of this type of comparison that suggests Haiti is incapable of stewarding its economic and ecologic resources.

47. I cannot locate either of these place names on any maps of Haiti.
48. *Biospheric egalitarianism* is a term derived from deep ecology. See Kane's "Redefining Modernity in Latin American Fiction" for a discussion of the term.
49. See Olson et al., "Mapping the Global Emergence of *Batrachochytrium dendrobatidis*, the Amphibian Chytrid Fungus."

WORKS CITED

Alcocer, Rudyard. *Narrative Mutations: Discourses of Heredity and Caribbean Literature*. Routledge, 2005.
Bellegarde-Smith, Patrick. *Haiti: The Breached Citadel*. Canadian Scholars, 2004.
Boling, Becky. "Apocalipsis en *Tú, la oscuridad* de Mayra Montero." *Letras Femeninas*, vol. 32, no. 1, 2006, pp. 313–327.
———. "The Trope of Nature in Latin American Literature: Some Examples." *Studies in 20th and 21st Century Literature*, vol. 30, no. 2, 2006, pp. 245–262.
Buell, Lawrence. *The Future of Environmental Criticism: Environmental Crisis and Literary Imagination*. Wiley-Blackwell, 2005.
Buell, Lawrence, Ursula Heise, and Karen Thornber. "Literature and Environment." *Annual Review of Environment and Resources*, vol. 36, 2011, pp. 417–440.
Buss, Terry F. "Foreign Aid and the Failure of State Building in Haiti from 1957 to 2015." *Latin American Policy*, vol. 6, no. 2, 2015, pp. 319–339.
Dalleo, Raphael. *American Imperialism's Undead: The Occupation of Haiti and the Rise of Caribbean Anticolonialism*. U of Virginia P, 2016.
Dalleo, Raphael, and Elena Machado Sáez. *The Latino/a Canon and the Emergence of Post-Sixties Literature*. Palgrave Macmillan, 2007.
Dávila Gonçalves, Michele C. "Voces en contrapunto: Dialogismo interno en *Tú, la oscuridad* de Mayra Montero." *Con-textos*, vol. 17, no. 35, 2005, pp. 30–41.
Deckard, Sharae. "Editorial." *Green Letters: Studies in Ecocriticism*, vol. 16, no. 1, 2012, pp. 5–14.
de la Fuente, José Luis. "Las novelas de Mayra Montero: Hacia una nueva magia." *Horizontes: Revista de la Universidad Católica de Puerto Rico*, vol. 45, no. 89, 2003, pp. 87–126.
DeLoughrey, Elizabeth M. "Postcolonialism." *The Oxford Handbook of Ecocriticism*, edited by Greg Garrard, Oxford UP, 2014, pp. 320–340.
———. *Routes and Roots: Navigating Caribbean and Pacific Island Literatures*. U of Hawaii P, 2007.
DeLoughrey, Elizabeth, Renee Gosson, and George B. Handley, editors. *Caribbean Literature and the Environment: Between Nature and Culture*. U of Virginia P, 2005.
DeLoughrey, Elizabeth, and George B. Handley, editors. *Postcolonial Ecologies: Literatures of the Environment*. Oxford UP, 2011.
De Shield, Christopher Lloyd. "Literary Isomorphism and the Malayan and Caribbean Archipelagos." *Ecocriticism of the Global South*, edited by Scott Slovic, Swarnalatha Rangarajan, and Vidya Sarveswaran, Lexington Books, 2015, pp. 77–91.
Dimock, Wai Chee, and Lawrence Buell. *Shades of the Planet: American Literature as World Literature*. Princeton UP, 2007.
Dubois, Laurent. *Haiti: The Aftershocks of History*. Metropolitan Books, 2012.
Esquilín, Mary Ann Gosser. "Caribbean Biota: Taming the Beasts and Tending the Gardens." *Journal of Caribbean Literatures*, vol. 7, no. 1, 2011, pp. 105–122.
Farmer, Paul. *The Uses of Haiti*. Common Courage Press, 2006.
Fitz, Earl. *Rediscovering the New World: Inter-American Literature in a Comparative Context*. U of Iowa P, 1991.

Foster, Elizabeth A. *Faith in Empire: Religion, Politics, and Colonial Rule in French Senegal, 1880-1940*. Stanford UP, 2013.
Garrard, Greg, ed. *Ecocriticism*. Routledge, 2004.
———. *The Oxford Handbook of Ecocriticism*. Oxford Handbooks, 2014.
Garrard, Greg, and Patrick D. Murphy, editors. "Introduction." *Ecofeminist Literary Criticism: Theory, Interpretation, Pedagogy*. U of Illinois P, 1998.
Gillman, Laura. "Inter-American Encounters in the Travel and Migration Narratives of Mayra Montero and Cristina García: Toward a Decolonial Hemispheric Feminism." *Signs: Journal of Women in Culture and Society*, vol. 39, no. 2, 2014, pp. 509-535.
Grove, Richard H. *Green Imperialism: Colonial Expansion, Tropical Island Edens and the Origins of Environmentalism, 1600-1860*. Cambridge UP, 1996.
Gruesz, Kristen Silva. *Ambassadors of Culture: The Transamerican Origins of Latino Writing*. Princeton UP, 2002.
Hallward, Peter. *Damming the Flood: Haiti, Aristide, and the Politics of Containment*. Verso, 2007.
Heise, Ursula K. *Imagining Extinction: The Cultural Meanings of Endangered Species*. U of Chicago P, 2016.
Hey-Colón, Rebeca L. "Toward a Genealogy of Water: Reading Julia de Burgos in the Twenty-First Century." *Small Axe: A Caribbean Journal of Criticism*, vol. 21, no. 3 (54), 2017, pp. 179-187.
Huggan, Graham, and Helen Tiffin, editors. *Postcolonial Ecocriticism: Literature, Animals, Environment*. Routledge, 2010.
Humphrey, Paul. "Gods, Gender, and Nation Building: An Alternative Concept of Nation in Four Novels by Mayra Montero." *Journal of Haitian Studies*, vol. 18, no. 2, 2012, pp. 119-134.
Jay, Paul. "The Myth of 'America' and the Politics of Location: Modernity, Border Studies, and the 'Literature of the Americas.'" *Arizona Quarterly*, vol. 54, no. 2, 1988, pp. 165-192.
Johnson, Paul. "The Crisis in Central America." *New Statesman*, 20 Jan. 1961, pp. 82-83.
Kane, Adrian Taylor. *The Natural World in Latin American Literatures: Ecocritical Essays on Twentieth Century Writings*. McFarland, 2010.
———. "Redefining Modernity in Latin American Fiction: Toward Ecological Consciousness in *La loca de Gandoca* and *Lo que Soñó Sebastian*." *Ecocriticism of the Global South*, edited by Scott Slovic, Swarnalatha Rangarajan, and Vidya Sarveswaran, Lexington Books, 2015, pp. 135-150.
Kearns, Sofia. "Nueva conciencia ecológica en algunos textos femeninos contemporáneos." *Latin American Literary Review*, vol. 34, no. 67, 2006, pp. 111-127.
Lowe, Lisa. *The Intimacies of Four Continents*. Duke UP, 2015.
Machado Sáez, Elena. *Market Aesthetics: The Purchase of the Past in Caribbean Diasporic Fiction*. U of Virginia P, 2015.
Montero, Mayra. *In the Palm of Darkness: A Novel*. Translated by Edith Grossman, HarperCollins, 1997.
Montero, Mayra. *Tú, la oscuridad*. Vol. 243. Tusquets Editor, 1995.
Moreno, Marisel. "Bordes líquidos, fronteras y espejismos: El dominicano y la migración intra-caribeña en *Boat People* de Mayra Santos Febres." *Revista de Estudios Hispánico*, vol. 1, 2018, pp. 17-32.
Mukherjee, Upamanyu Pablo. *Postcolonial Environments*. Palgrave Macmillan, 2010.
Negrón-Muntaner, Frances. "Bridging Islands: Gloria Anzaldúa and the Caribbean." *PMLA*, vol. 121, no. 1, 2006, pp. 272-278.

Nixon, Rob. *Slow Violence and the Environmentalism of the Poor*. Harvard UP, 2011.
Olson, Deanna H., et al. "Mapping the Global Emergence of *Batrachochytrium dendrobatidis*, the Amphibian Chytrid Fungus." *PLOS ONE*, vol. 8, no. 2, 2013, e56802.
Paravisini-Gebert, Lizabeth. "Deforestation and the Yearning for Lost Landscapes in Caribbean Literatures." *Postcolonial Ecologies: Literatures of the Environment*, edited by Elizabeth DeLoughrey and George B. Handley, Oxford UP, 2011, pp. 99–116.
———. "Extinctions: Chronicles of Vanishing Fauna in the Colonial and Postcolonial Caribbean." *The Oxford Handbook of Ecocriticism*, edited by Greg Garrard, Oxford UP, 2014, pp. 341–360.
———. "'He of the Trees': Nature, Environment, and Creole Religiosities in Caribbean Literature." *Caribbean Literature and the Environment: Between Nature and Culture*, edited by Elizabeth M. DeLoughrey, Renée K. Gosson, and George B. Handley, U of Virginia P, 2005, pp. 182–196.
———. "Unchained Tales: Women Prose Writers from the Hispanic Caribbean in the 1990s." *Bulletin of Latin American Research*, vol. 22, no. 4, 2003, pp. 445–464.
Pérez-Rosario, Vanessa. "On the Hispanophone Caribbean Question." *Small Axe: A Caribbean Journal of Criticism*, vol. 20, no. 3 (51), 2016, pp. 21–31.
Pettinaroli, Elizabeth M., and Ana María Mutis. "Introduction." *Troubled Waters: Rivers in Latin American Imagination. Hispanic Issues On Line*, vol. 12, Spring 2013, pp. 1–18.
Pratt, Mary Louise. *Imperial Eyes: Travel Writing and Transculturation*. Routledge, 1992.
Prieto, José M. "Interview." *Bomb*, vol. 70, 2000, pp. 86–90.
Ramsey, Kate. *The Spirits and the Law: Vodou and Power in Haiti*. University of Chicago Press, 2011.
Ray, Sarah Jaquette. *The Ecological Other: Environmental Exclusion in American Culture*. U of Arizona P, 2013.
Riofrio, John D. *Continental Shifts: Migration, Representation, and the Struggle for Justice in Latin (o) America*. U of Texas P, 2015.
Rivera, Ángel. "Silence, Vodou, and Haiti in Mayra Montero's *In the Palm of Darkness*." *Ciberletras: Revista de crítica literaria y de cultura*, vol. 4, 2001.
Roth, Richard. "UN Acknowledges Involvement in Haiti Cholera Outbreak for First Time." *CNN*, 18 Aug. 2016, https://www.cnn.com/2016/08/18/health/haiti-un-cholera/index.html.
Sadowski-Smith, Claudia, and Claire F. Fox. "Theorizing the Hemisphere: Inter-Americas Work at the Intersection of American, Canadian, and Latin American Studies." *Comparative American Studies*, vol. 2, no. 1, 2004, pp. 5–38.
Saldívar, José David. *The Dialectics of Our America: Genealogy, Cultural Critique, and Literary History*. Duke UP, 1991.
Sandín, Lyn Di Iorio, and Richard Perez, editors. *Contemporary US Latino/a Literary Criticism*. Palgrave Macmillan, 2007.
Slovic, Scott, Swarnalatha Rangarajan, and Vidya Sarveswaran, editors. *Ecocriticism of the Global South*. Lexington Books, 2015.
Socolovsky, Maya. *Troubling Nationhood in U.S. Latina Literature: Explorations of Place and Belonging*. Rutgers UP, 2013.
Villegas, Carmen M. Rivera. "Nuevas rutas hacia Haití en la cartografía de Mayra Montero." *Revista hispánica moderna*, vol. 54, no. 1, 2001, pp. 154–165.
Ybarra, Priscilla Solis. *Writing the Goodlife: Mexican American Literature and the Environment*. U of Arizona P, 2016.

14

"Against the Sorrowful and Infinite Solitude"

Environmental Consciousness and Streetwalker Theorizing in Helena María Viramontes's Their Dogs Came with Them

PAULA M. L. MOYA

Chicana author Helena María Viramontes occupies an interesting place in the field of Latinx literature. While her output remains small, she has garnered a devoted following, and her works are the frequent object of analysis by literary critics who treat a wide range of issues. Excellent essays have emerged from scholars (Latinx and otherwise) who turn to her stories and novels to meditate on such varied topics as the built environment, disability, gender roles and gender variance, sexuality and sexual violence, mother-daughter relationships, religion in everyday life, farmworker experience, metaphor and metonymy, myths in literature, and narrative structure.[1] As one who is drawn back again and again to Viramontes's fiction, I harbor a deep appreciation for her subject matter and her superb writerly craft. But what makes her fiction so enduring, I contend, are those elements of her work that contribute to a decolonial project. Viramontes's works of fiction explore the dynamics of subordination within which Latinx people are caught, thus revealing the socioeconomic and ideological forces that keep them from achieving full citizenship in the United States. But her works do more than this. They also imagine alternative—more egalitarian, more loving—ways of being in the world.

In what follows, I argue that Viramontes's masterful novel *Their Dogs Came with Them* both models and encourages decolonial thought, feeling, and action. I posit that in her depiction of a community subject to race- and place-based injustices of the type described by environmental literary critic Rob Nixon as "slow violence," Viramontes demonstrates the origins of what Nixon and the sociologists Ramachandra Guha and Joan Martinez-Alier identify as an "environmentalism of the poor."[2] Drawing additional inspiration from decolonial feminist philosopher Maria Lugones's insistence that strategic thinking can occur in those who occupy a "pedestrian" position, I focus on Ermila, one of Viramontes's four main characters, to show how she learns to perceive and resist the conditions within which she is trapped. Through close readings of several key paragraphs in *Their Dogs*, I show that by "hanging out," Ermila and her girlfriends together develop a "complex solidarity" that facilitates Ermila's growth as a "streetwalker theorizer" capable of the "resistant/emancipatory sense making" fundamental to a decolonial mode of being in the world (Lugones, *Pilgrimages*).[3] I end with a consideration of how Viramontes structures into her novel an epistemological uncertainty that allows her to extend the decolonial option outward to her readers.

Slow Violence and the Environmentalism of the Poor

Their Dogs Came with Them is an omnibus of a novel set in East Los Angeles during the 1960s and 1970s. It portrays the contiguous and occasionally intersecting daily lives of a diverse range of characters who populate the neighborhood around the Long Beach and Pomona freeway interchange during a time of intense social, political, and geographic upheaval. Taken as a whole, the novel explores what happens to the relatively powerless people who live in a largely Mexican American community that, because of how its residents are situated within the prevailing racial and socioeconomic order, is subject to a range of externally produced and pernicious structural forces. It shows how the people most adversely affected by the building of the LA freeway system—those who are displaced by the freeways or condemned to live in their shadows—first encounter the coming upheaval.[4] It then jumps forward in time by ten years to show how the neighborhood's physical dismemberment has negatively impacted its residents' already limited transportation and employment options. The effect of this temporal disjunction is to show how the freeways enact slow violence on the East LA Mexican American community.

In making this observation, I draw on postcolonial literary critic Rob Nixon's central concept in his book *Slow Violence and the Environmentalism of the Poor*. Building on sociologist Johan Galtung's concept of "structural violence," Nixon connects questions of global distributive justice to environmental concerns by foregrounding issues of time, movement, and change (11).[5] He designates as "slow violence" those "incremental and accretive" environmental harms that occur "gradually and out of sight" (2). Because they are not loud, spectacular, and instantaneous in the way a gunshot or an explosion is, harms that characterize slow violence are often not perceptible—or at least not perceptible as violence. Poisonings from chemical or radiological agents like DDT or transuranic waste, for example, are often "delayed" and "dispersed across time and space" (10). Their "calamitous repercussions," which might include an increased risk of cancer, autism, thyroid disease, or a higher-than-average incidence of birth defects, play out "across a range of temporal scales" and may not show up for generations (2). Characterized more by suffering (what Nixon calls the "long dyings") than by heroic martyrdoms, slow violence presents a range of challenges that can interfere with efforts to act decisively and mobilize politically (2). "A major challenge," he notes, is "how to devise arresting stories, images, and symbols adequate to the pervasive but elusive violence of delayed effects" (3). Confronting slow violence, Nixon says, requires "combative writers" who deploy their imaginative abilities to amplify "the media-marginalized causes of the environmentally dispossessed" (5). Such writers "plot and give figurative shape to formless threats whose fatal repercussions are dispersed across space and time" (10).

Giving "figurative shape to formless threats whose fatal repercussions are dispersed across space and time" is precisely what Viramontes does so successfully in *Their Dogs*. The freeways that hover over the neighborhood provide an important backdrop against which Viramontes builds a fictional world within which to explore the ravages of slow violence. Over the course of the novel, the freeways disappear neighbors, displace businesses, and cut off important neighborhood travel routes. The amputation of vehicular and pedestrian throughways introduces traffic gridlock, exacerbates pollution, and traps the neighborhood residents into a bounded area envisioned by city planners not as a desirable place to live but as a space to travel through on the way to somewhere else.[6] The freeways are a structural feature in the built environment within which Viramontes's characters live and move. But they also function—together with a nightly quarantine of the neighborhood that is ostensibly instituted to contain a rabies epidemic—as a metaphor for the structural violence that constrains the characters' lives.

Harboring a deep concern about "the fragmentations of self and society," Viramontes's critical project involves a diagnosis of the ills of her community. In *Their Dogs*, she employs her imagination and skill to explore how and why members of her fictional community "internalize that isolation and begin to kill each other."[7] But as I indicated above, Viramontes's project is larger than that. As I discuss throughout this essay, what makes her project decolonial is the way she moves beyond critique to highlight her characters' ingenuity, the way she succeeds in showing their creative responses to the toxic environments they live in as a result of being victim-inheritors of the genocidal racial logic of European colonialism. Because there are no saviors from outside the community who are either interested in or capable of saving those trapped by this externally produced racism and environmental degradation, Viramontes's fiction tracks the way the members of her community must themselves develop a decolonial imaginary to fuel their struggle for social justice.

Race, Literature, and the Decolonial Imaginary

Decoloniality, as I employ the term here, refers to a capacious and evolving mode of being devoted to dismantling European colonialism's pernicious legacies—particularly those related to the systemic objectification of "types" of human beings. Scholars, thinkers, and artists of the "decolonial turn" hail from several disciplines (religious studies, philosophy, political theory, literary studies, psychology, and ethnic studies) and a number of geographical spaces whose indigenous peoples have suffered the experience of colonization (the Caribbean, the Americas, and Africa, among others). Anibal Quijano and Walter Mignolo, for instance, have argued that coloniality is the "invisible" or the "darker" side of modernity. The logic of "modernity/coloniality," they contend, bolsters claims for European centrality, superiority, rationality, and universality and promotes the false belief that some groups of people (especially nonwhites of all races) are natural slaves or inherently (that is, culturally or biologically) inferior to the European (or European American) heterosexual, property-owning, able-bodied, and cisgender male. Although the varied projects of decolonial artists and scholars differ according to the contexts within which they work, they are united by their response to the legacies of European colonialism.[8] Their shared goal is not merely to overturn the colonial structures that resulted in the loss of political autonomy for native inhabitants of a colonized region but more fundamentally to overturn the matrix of being, power, and knowledge that is constitutive of the white supremacist logic inherent to Western modernity's project of civilization.[9]

What makes a project decolonial? Decolonial scholars, thinkers, artists, and activists agree on the imperative to take intentional and inventive action.[10] Neither accepting nor refusing the given, they turn aside and focus elsewhere to perceive anew. Because their starting point is the referential inaccuracy and genocidal logic of the European colonial racial imaginary, they observe and critique key aspects of that imaginary—including its commitment to autonomous individualism, abstract and binary thinking, and Eurocentrism.[11] Championing the necessity of relationality, quotidian witnessing, and rigorous self-assessment, decolonial thinkers move away from such dehumanizing binary logics as the mind/body split and the human/nature divide. Like other kinds of environmentalists, they turn toward onto-epistemological multiplicity and complex solidarities as in the development of an ecological imaginary.[12] Within such an imaginary, formerly colonized peoples are figured not as problems to be dealt with (i.e., "The Negro Problem," the "Mexican Problem," the "Indian Problem") but rather as potential resources whose ancestral forms of knowledge and current cultural self-ways can chart a path away from the master morality and penchant for war that undergirds unreconstructed Western modernity.[13] Categorically rejecting the subordination or exploitation of others as either a primary goal or an unintended consequence of caring for the self, they instead put their energy and imagination into the service of remaking themselves and the world(s) they inhabit. The goal of decoloniality is thus the creation of a new world—a different kind of world "in which many worlds fit," to borrow the words of the Zapatista Liberation Army.[14] This "new" world entails a total renovation of the current one—a reworking of subjectivity, community, institutional arrangements, and the logics by which humans live on the planet.[15] Not merely challenging current relations of power and the logics that structure them, decolonial thinkers seek to subvert a colonial way of being by setting aside inherited assumptions to envision new social, political, and environmental possibilities. By attending to occluded and denigrated perspectives, they open themselves up to previously disregarded as well as newly imagined possibilities—the exploration of which requires the kind of imagination and inventiveness found in the fiction of writers like Helena Maria Viramontes.

Elsewhere, I identify several narrative features of *Their Dogs* that contribute to making it a decolonial novel.[16] Before turning to a discussion of the relationship between environmental consciousness and the development of what Lugones calls "streetwalker theory," I want to mention some of those features here. In *Their Dogs*, Viramontes employs a multifocal narrative structure and a democratically distributed character-system to register her various characters' "active subjectivities." This enables her to create, in her readers, what the philosopher José Medina calls a "kaleidoscopic consciousness."[17] Facilitating a kaleidoscopic consciousness allows Viramontes to engage in the kind of unflinching decolonial self-examination necessary for what Lugones calls "faithful witnessing."[18] By bearing witness to her characters' lives, Viramontes performs an act of decolonial love that humanizes but does not sentimentalize her community. As one example, she explores the existence and origins of antiblack racism in one of her key characters to expose the institutions and societal arrangements that facilitate racist behaviors toward others even in those who are themselves victims of racist behaviors by others. Finally, as I discuss in some detail at the end of this essay, Viramontes structures into the novel's ending an epistemological uncertainty that allows her to extend the decolonial option outward to her readers by making us responsible for what comes next.[19] In the next section, I discuss several other important features of the novel that are central to its decoloniality.

Hanging Out, Complex Solidarity, and Streetwalker Theorizing

In an essay from her book *Pilgrimages/Peregrinajes* called "Streetwalker Theorizing," feminist philosopher Maria Lugones provides an account of the kind of complex solidarity that is represented through Ermila and her girlfriends Lollie, Mousie, and Rini.[20] Although Ermila is one of four major characters in the novel, when Viramontes represents her as part of her girlfriend group, she becomes subordinated to the group as a whole. As represented by Viramontes, the four girlfriends practice a form of mutual acceptance and collectivity that is both discerning and loving. Different from each other in stature, body type, and home situation, they actively create a sociality that allows them to thrive as part of an intentional and complex collective. One way they do this is by dressing alike, against the prevailing fashion, wearing "straight-legged Levi's blues jeans in order to make a statement about togetherness and nonconformity" (56). But they also do it as a matter of everyday practice, spending a great deal of their time just "hanging out" and telling each other stories:

> The only things they cherished, their only private property, were the stories they continued to create and re-create in a world which only gave them one to tell. And so they never tired of one another's company.... They met behind the gym, before homeroom, at the lunch benches, after school, at Concha's not-really-a-beauty-salon, in the back of the bus, and if they had the privilege, they phoned one another at home because a few hours without conversation were insufferable. With conviction, they designed escape routes, rehearsed their breakout and hurled their futures over the roadblocks of their marooned existence. Lest they forget that silence is destructive, they pitted each other against the sorrowful and infinite solitude, each and every hour, because that's what friends por vida are for. (62)

"Hanging out," explains Lugones, is a way that powerless people who occupy a "pedestrian" position within society can develop a sense of the social intricacies of their shared world (209). In the course of telling each other stories, such people listen to, learn from, and transmit to each other information that can help them navigate an unfriendly and unforgiving world. In this case, the girlfriends are quite literally pedestrians—not only are they too poor to own cars but also their neighborhood has been isolated from the rest of the city by the building of the LA freeways. As a result, their ability to move around the city has been compromised by the "phantom limbs" of the truncated streets that used to run through to their neighborhoods but now stop at the base of any number of interconnected freeways.

What makes hanging out such a powerful tool for people like Ermila and her girlfriends is that it creates the conditions within which they can, as "streetwalkers," come together and, through storytelling, collectively "gauge possibilities," develop a sense of how and when others intend them good or ill, and gain "social depth" (Lugones 209). Lugones defines streetwalkers as those people who are safer on the street, in the company of others like themselves, than they are in their own homes (209). Streetwalkers in the sense Lugones intends, the girlfriends are *not* safer in their own homes than they are in each other's company on the streets. As a result, they spend a great deal of time in public and semipublic spaces to which they have only temporary access. In her home, Ermila has to fight off the sexual overtures of her cousin, Nacho, while Rini faces a serious threat of sexual assault by her mother's boyfriend, Jan (more on this below). It is worth noting that the places where the girlfriends congregate (*behind* the gym, *before* homeroom, at the *lunch* benches, *after* school, at Concha's *not-really-a-beauty-salon*, in the *back* of the bus) suggest the extent to which they occupy public space in the margins and at the sufferance of more powerful persons who will tolerate them for only a circumscribed amount of time. The stories they tell, then, are much more than a way for the girlfriends to pass the time. They are a balm against the mistreatment meted out to them by an uncaring world and a mechanism by which they can help each other develop strategies for surviving and thriving.

It should come as no surprise that the girlfriends are not—are not allowed to be—naive. But though they are conscious of each other's small lies and foibles, they also understand how important it is to indulge each other's need for emotional and practical support. So, for example, as they sit together after school under a patio table umbrella at the Top Hat Hot Dog and Pastrami Factory, Ermila, Rini, and Mousie perceive but do not comment on Lollie's "repulsion to her body hair" and her ongoing efforts to remove it (*Their Dogs* 51). Similarly, Lollie, Ermila, and Rini listen patiently yet again as Mousie recounts some small detail of her dead brother YoYo's life.[21] They sympathize with Mousie's need to "cross-stitch him together to recapture his soul" and to recall "that he lived until his nineteenth year, and punched arms, went to school with purple lips, reeked of bargain cologne, [and] made her feel special because she was his sister" (*Their Dogs* 61). And when Ermila needs to make sense of the events of her early life—the loss of her parents, her surrender to Child Protective Services, her ambivalent reclaiming by her elderly grandparents, and the anger of the grandfather who made it clear that he preferred she not be part of his household—Rini, Mousie, and Lollie are there to create the supportive framework she requires to do it. For example, in the process of recounting her story, Ermila loses track of a crucial detail and wonders aloud about whether the car driven by Mrs. M. of Child Services was a Buick. In response, her girlfriends rally to "let Ermila got a Buick [sic]," because that is the kind of car she would have liked Mrs. M to have (51). And, most importantly, when any one of the four is threatened, they come together as a unit—they "F-troop it"—to strategize a solution that will leave them intact (individually and collectively) while delivering a serious blow to the one who presents the threat (178).

Consider, as an example of their complex solidarity, the time Rini is threatened with sexual assault in her own home by her mother's live-in boyfriend, Jan. When Rini first calls Ermila to ask for her help, Ermila is struggling with a dog-bitten hand, the unwanted sexual advances of her live-in cousin, the disapproval and unhappiness of her grandmother, a school system that is counting up her absences, and a difficult decision regarding whether or not to break up that evening with her boyfriend, Alfonso. She does not want to respond to Rini's plea; she wants to take care of her own needs first. But in order for the girlfriends' complex solidarity to be a real force, Ermila's individual needs must, in the face of Rini's more pressing dilemma, be subordinated to the collective—if only for the short term. Rini's sobs convince Ermila that, having spent months avoiding Jan, Rini has finally been cornered. And so, the girlfriends must collectively figure out a strategy to defend Rini in a way that will "hurt royally," "cut deep," and "provide [to Jan] a real bitchen hurt" (*Their Dogs* 196). Acknowledging that there is no one with greater power than themselves to whom they can turn for help—YoYo, says Mousie, "would kick his ass"—the four young women fall back on their own resourcefulness and ability to work smoothly in tandem to strike Jan where it hurts (196).

After establishing that Jan is the car-proud owner of a metallic bronze Chevy coupe with orange highlights, a car that he keeps "wax-sheen-polished like a warrior, the sun god," they hatch a plan that, in order to be successful, must be carried out collectively by people who know and trust one another implicitly (197). But it is also a plan that acknowledges and accounts for the individuality of each member of the ensemble. Carrying four squirt bottles of industrial-strength acetone nail polish remover from Concha's beauty salon, they pool their meager resources to buy a box of steel wool soap pads. In the hour-long walk back to Rini's house (bus fares were sacrificed to their plan), they build their collective confidence. Because it is a masterful description of complex solidarity in action, I cite the passage at length:

> From the east, west, north and south the girlfriends converged toward the magnet of their wrath's attention. There was no practice save for repetition of the task at hand and they knew the actual execution would have to take less than a few seconds. That's all they had. Each of them pulled out a squirt bottle filled with nail polish remover and each of them was assigned letters. They squirted the shapes of their designated letters with acetone, painfully stinging their open hangnails, and squirted until the last of the acetone resounded like farts relieved from their respective spouts. Onto the paint of the car's trunk, they scrubbed the liquid into the metal with the steel wool pads. Rini took the *O*'s, because there was something therapeutic about circling and circling, and Ermila took the *T*'s because she had one hanging on her wall and because Concha wore it years ago when she was a somebody. And Mousie took the *U* because the letter was in her name, and Lollie took the rest because she was

good at carrying more than her fair share. They squirted and scrubbed and jumped on the bumpers to reach the top of the hood. And in not more than thirty seconds they were finished. **PUTO**, the hood said to him. The return address on the trunk, **LOTE**.

And just as they had converged, they pulled away in opposite directions slowly, sluggishly lest they call attention to themselves. . . . They strolled away in separate directions, carrying the flakes of metallic paint, bluish palms, the color of yams on their hands, barely containing their collective sense of invincibility. (199)

The brilliance of Viramontes's representation of complex solidarity in the above passage must be lingered over to be fully appreciated. To begin with, the description of the girls approaching from the four cardinal directions is a subtle allusion to the Native American part of their ancestry—the part that, because of the history of European colonialism, has been for members of the Chicanx community a source of discrimination if not shame.[22] That the girlfriends activate an element of their indigenous heritage to support their collective action of female empowerment is reinforced by the reference to Jan's car looking "like a warrior, the sun god" (197).[23] The reference is to Huitzilopotchli, the Aztec god of sun and war. In the Aztec creation myth, Huitzilopotchli kills and dismembers his sister, the moon goddess Coyolxauhqui, thus initiating the ideology of male dominance that characterized the Aztec empire before the arrival of the Spanish. Although working together so smoothly that the entire operation took barely thirty seconds, the successful completion of the action required the girls to differentiate themselves in order to split up the task in a way that it would get done, with each girl choosing the letter or letters meaningful to them in some way. Making do with what they have, the girls tackle their problem with a sensibility that the Chicano art historian Tomas Ybarra Frausto has described as "rasquache."[24] Rasquachismo, according to Frausto, refers to a culturally particular sensibility in which people without much money assemble bits and pieces of ordinary or discarded materials in order to make out of them something of beauty. And, importantly, the materials with which the girls work are associated with women—their labor (soap pads) and their adornment (nail polish remover). Pulling together what is close at hand, the girls embody what the artist and writer Amalia Mesa-Bains (building on the idea of rasquachismo) calls "domesticana"—a way of being Chicana that is "defiant and inventive" and that accomplishes the goals of female expression and empowerment.[25]

I do not intend to overstate the impact of the young women's actions. The decolonial promise of Viramontes's novel does not, in the end, reside in this act of vandalism. The girls' behavior, while important and significant for their immediate safety, exemplifies what the philosopher Alisa Bierria calls "insurgent agency." Insurgent agency refers to a resistant agency that does not fundamentally transform the conditions of oppression but instead temporarily destabilizes, circumnavigates, or manipulates those conditions in order to reach specific ends. According to Bierria, insurgent agency is employed by subjects who "intentionally act in unstable and precarious circumstances that are difficult to escape or alter, and who craft provisional and makeshift practices of opposition that subvert, but still remain defined by, conditions of power" (Bierria 25–26). So while the young women's actions succeed in punishing someone who certainly deserves to be punished, their vandalism is not, on its own, decolonial. This is because decoloniality is not, in the end, anarchic or destructive. Rather, decoloniality is concerned with the process of rebuilding and renewing. It is a reworking of subjectivity, community, institutional arrangements, and the logics by which humans relate to the planet. While that which is destructive to human and environmental flourishing must be dismantled to garner the space and the building materials to create more livable and sustainable futures, destroying and dismantling can never by themselves conduce to a better world.

The Decolonial Option

At the end of *Their Dogs*, Viramontes ties up many but not all of the subplots that run through the novel. In a confluence of events that occur during a torrential early morning rainstorm, the storylines of the novel's four major characters converge—even though the characters themselves never do. Ermila is on her way to the bus station to warn her cousin, Nacho, that the McBride Boys have targeted him for killing. Turtle, high on drugs, is directed by the McBride Boys gang to murder him. After she does so, Turtle is murdered in turn by the Quarantine Authority, a city police force that, under the pretext of eliminating rabies, has turned the neighborhood every night into a virtual police state.[26] Tranquilina, who has been out searching for Ben with his sister, is an unwitting witness to both murders. The novel ends when Tranquilina, in a final paroxysm of anger and despair, refuses the Quarantine Authority's orders to freeze with her hands on her head. Instead, she moves forward into the storm with her fists clenched. The question readers are left with at the end of the novel is this: What happens to Tranquilina after she moves forward? Does she walk into gunfire and to her death? Or does she levitate into the "limitless space" of faith and infinite possibility in a reenactment of her father's mythical flight in the desert before she was born (325)? Although there are elements of Tranquilina's story that might tempt a reader to believe that she achieves transcendence within the diegetic space of the novel, there are other clues that suggest that she might be sacrificed at the hands of the Quarantine Authority.[27] The novel finally refuses to answer the question of what happens to Tranquilina, just as it leaves open many other questions of plot and interpretation that its readers might have: What happened to Ermila's parents? Where did Ermila's elderly neighbor go after she moved away? Did Ben's mother abandon the family? Has Turtle's brother been killed in Vietnam? Did Ermila arrive in time to witness her cousin's death? Where, for that matter, is Ben?

On one level, Viramontes's refusal to provide answers mimics the workings of our real social world—one in which we often do not know what has happened or will happen to ourselves or to others. But on another level, her refusal is more pointed. By not tying up the loose threads at the end of the novel, Viramontes sends her readers searching back through its multiple plotlines to look for answers, while also denying to them the catharsis that either a miracle or a tragedy might provide. The only thing the reader knows is that Ermila is the one major character who remains available to absorb the enormity of the slow violence that is being done to her community. Having intuited the unfairness of the situation, Ermila begins to stand up for herself and others in a way consistent with the mode of resistance Lugones calls streetwalker theorizing, one that involves "theorizing resistance from the subaltern position, and from within the concreteness of body-to-body engagement" (Lugones 207–210). Ermila's streetwalker theorizing shows up incipiently when she thinks to herself, "I gotta do something soon," while listening to the "earth-rattling explosive motors" and watching the invasive searchlights of the Quarantine Authority helicopters that "burst out of the midnight sky to shoot dogs not chained up by curfew" (12–13). It occurs again when she joins her friends in that carefully choreographed vandalism of Jan's treasured car, as discussed above. Although at the end of the novel Ermila lacks a fully fleshed-out analysis of her own and her friends' situations and has not yet elaborated a vocabulary to convey her insights, Ermila's positioning within the narrative suggests that she might yet develop into a streetwalker theorizer capable of leading her community toward social change.

The point is that Viramontes's choice to open up narrative possibilities at the end of the novel offers a decolonial option that extends outward to her readers by making us responsible, via our interpretive choices, for what might come next.[28] She replicates Frantz Fanon's gesture of openness at the end of his decolonial masterpiece, *White Skin, Black Masks*, even as she emphasizes the importance of the imagination to the project of making sense of the racialized *locura* that has been, ever since the Spanish conquest of the Americas, undergirded by a racist and capitalist world-system. Lastly, the novel's indeterminate ending serves to locate it within a larger ongoing decolonial struggle. To look for a solution within the novel itself would be to think of it as a discrete entity— an artwork unto itself—instead of as an intervention into an epic struggle that began much earlier and will continue long after we are gone. Consider, in this context, three of the novel's most important intertextual allusions. Viramontes takes her title and epigraph from *The Broken Spears: The Aztec Account of the Conquest of Mexico*. Originally published in Spanish in 1959 by Miguel León-

Portilla as an introduction to and compilation of accounts by the conquered peoples of Mexico of their experience of conquest, the book has since been expanded and translated into several European languages as well as the indigenous language Otomi. Viramontes's title, taken from one of the translated Nahuatl accounts, refers to the attack dogs that were used to terrify and kill the indigenous people during the Spanish conquest. Via this reference, the dogs in the novel serve to connect the kind of environmental degradation, economic decline, and social damage caused by the freeways and the fictional rabies quarantine to a longer history of militarized violence and conquest.[29] Similarly, Tranquilina is linked, through her possible levitation as well as through the name her father had wanted to give her, to the character of Remedios in Gabriel García Márquez's anticolonial masterpiece *One Hundred Years of Solitude*.[30] And finally, Viramontes's choice of the term *sharpshooters* to describe the Quarantine Authority gunmen who kill Turtle evokes the "sharp-shooting goose-steppers" whose racist bullets are "designed to kill slowly" in the Chicana poet Lorna Dee Cervantes's plaintive "Poem for the Young White Man Who Asked Me How I, an Intelligent, Well-Read Person, Could Believe in the War Between Races" in her award-winning book of poetry *Emplumada* (35–37). Cervantes writes not only about the pernicious psychological and social damage caused by race but also about the environmental, social, and psychic damage caused by the construction of Highway 280 through the middle of her own Mexican American neighborhood in San Jose, California.

In *Their Dogs*, Viramontes represents the lives of the ignored, the marginalized, the damnés de la terre in a way that humanizes but does not sentimentalize them. She concretizes in readily perceptible forms (freeways, rabid dogs, gendered dynamics, the Quarantine Authority) the environmental forces that subordinate a community, even as she registers the efforts of its residents to resist. She also creates a narrative structure and character-system that radically redistributes narrative space, thus making available multiple perspectives on the same event in a way that enables its readers to develop a kaleidoscopic consciousness and imagine complex solidarities. Finally, she opens up narrative possibilities so as to involve her readers in the creation of possible futures. In all these ways, she creates in *Their Dogs Came with Them* a novel that enacts a turning aside and a focusing elsewhere for the purpose of perceiving anew and building again. With a clear understanding that changing the world will involve changing who we are in relation to that world, Viramontes thus enacts what Walter Mignolo has called *thinking otherwise*.[31] Grounded, directional, intentional, and relational, as well as kaleidoscopic, flexible, expansive, literate, and loving, *Their Dogs Came with Them* shows Viramontes to be a decolonial writer par excellence. Her ability to make us understand and care about the people about whom she writes makes her a true visionary in the difficult process of remaking ourselves and the world in which we live.

NOTES

1. See, e.g., Brady ("Metaphors to Love By") and Wald ("Refusing to Halt") on the built environment; Hsu on metonymy; Moya on myth ("Another") and narrative structure ("Reading").

2. Martinez-Alier identifies "environmentalism of the poor" as a strain of environmental activism that demonstrates a "material interest in the environment as a source and a requirement for livelihood," that "struggles against impacts that threaten poor people," and that incorporates a "demand for contemporary social justice" (11). See also Guha and Martinez-Alier.

3. See especially Lugones's introduction and last chapter.

4. See Villa for a cogent discussion of how freeway construction in Mexican American neighborhoods has been reflected in their literature.

5. Galtung defines structural violence as that kind of violence that lacks a direct or personal actor that causes the harm. He notes that individuals may still "be killed or mutilated, hit or hurt" but there may not be any person who can be held directly responsible. Such violence, he explains "is built into the structure and shows up as unequal power and consequently as unequal life chances" (170–171).

6. For excellent analyses of the environmental impacts the building of the freeways had on the East LA neighborhoods as depicted in *Their Dogs*, see Hsu; Wald. Brady, Muñoz, and Pattison provide insightful spatial analyses of the novel.

7. Viramontes describes *Their Dogs* as being about a "lost community divided by freeways" and the "fragmentations of the self and society" (Kevane and Heredia 154). Noting that the marginalization and isolation produced by the construction of the freeways was "not our fault," Viramontes admits being "also intrigued by how we internalize that isolation and begin to kill each other" (Dulfano 653).

8. Some figures associated with decoloniality include Frantz Fanon, Gloria Anzaldúa, Nelson Maldonado-Torres, Sylvia Wynter, and Maria Lugones, among many others.

9. See Quijano; Mignolo, "Human Rights"; Mignolo, *Darker Side*; Mignolo, *Local Histories*; Mignolo, "Geopolitics of Knowledge."

10. Maldonado-Torres describes this as an "insurgent subjectivity" ("Decolonial Turn" 111). See also Lugones.

11. In addition to the previously referenced works by Quijano, Mignolo, and Maldonado-Torres, see Maldonado-Torres, *Against War*; Maldonado-Torres, "Decoloniality at Large"; Maldonado-Torres, "Thinking through the Decolonial Turn"; Mignolo, "Delinking"; Mignolo, "Zapatistas Theoretical Revolution"; Saldívar, *Trans-Americanity*; Walsh, "'Other' Knowledges"; Wynter, "On Disenchanting Discourse."

12. Barad offers the neologism "Onto-epistem-ology" to signal a refusal of the divide between knowing and being (829). In her theorizing about streetwalker theorizing, Lugones disrupts the binary logic of the strategy/tactic and mind/body divides in order to "embrace tactical strategies" as "crucial to an epistemology of resistance/liberation" (208). See also Ortega, *Between Worlds*; Hames-García, *Identity Complex*.

13. See Isasi-Díaz and Mendieta; Maldonado-Torres, *Against War*; Pérez.

14. See Mignolo, "Zapatistas Theoretical Revolution."

15. For a decolonial intervention outlining the thought behind the importance of reforming the institution of prison, see Hames-García, *Fugitive Thought*.

16. In my recent book, *The Social Imperative*, I was concerned to show how literature, as a system of social communication through which information, ideas, and norms are transmitted from author to reader and among different communities of readers, helps create the world we live in. As aesthetic objects that engage readers deeply on the

cognitive-affective level over a duration of time, works of literature make us think—but they also make us feel. They give us language while also prompting us to form in our minds images that evoke a whole variety of associations that we then carry out into the world. Literary texts have the potential to alter our perceptions and teach us how to interpret unfamiliar phenomena—especially phenomena to which we have limited exposure. They shape our cultural imaginaries and build for us schemas through which we interpret the social world.

17. For more on kaleidoscopic consciousness and a kaleidoscopic social imagination, see Medina, esp. pp. 200–202 and 309–310.

18. See Lugones, esp. p. 7; Martínez.

19. My analyses of these features of the novel will appear in *Theories of the Flesh: Latinx and Latin American Feminisms, Transformation, and Resistance*, edited by Andrea J. Pitts, Mariana Ortega, and José M. Medina, forthcoming from Oxford University Press.

20. For more on complex solidarity, see Hames-Garcia, *Fugitive Thought*, esp. pp. 208–219. See also his theorization of the relationship between multiplicity and social identity in *Identity Complex*, esp. pp. 1–37.

21. YoYo was killed while fighting in Vietnam. Mousie is traumatized not only by her brother's death but also because he had "returned from Vietnam in so many pieces" that her mother cremated him, which went against the practice of the Catholic church (*Their Dogs* 58).

22. "Grandmother had rejected Ermila's hair as if it were a personal affront. Raven-black and as straight as an arrow, her hair was proof of her father's mestizo blood" (*Their Dogs* 57). See also my essay "Another Way to Be" to illuminate Viramontes's conceptual universe.

23. The 1966 Chevrolet Biscayne Coupe muscle car was produced in a color called Aztec Bronze.

24. See Ybarra-Frausto, as well as the video of Ybarra-Frausto discussing "rasquachismo" on Latinopia Art posted by Tia Tenopia.

25. Mesa-Bains explains, "In rasquachismo, the irreverent and spontaneous are employed to make the most from the least. In rasquachismo one takes a stance that is both defiant and inventive. Aesthetic expression comes from discards, fragments, even recycled everyday materials. . . . The capacity to hold life together with bits of string, old coffee cans, and broken mirrors in a dazzling gesture of aesthetic bravado is at the heart of rasquachismo" (300).

26. For more on how Viramontes built on a real historical event to make a point about police surveillance of her community, see Kevane 11–41.

27. Tranquilina herself had harbored doubts about the reality of Papa Tomás's mythical flight, and the novel mentions that her name begins with a letter hated by her father because its cruciform shape "reinforced the cross they had to bear" (*Their Dogs* 44, 88).

28. For an astute analysis of the novel that focuses on the importance to interpretation of a reader's receptivity to the text's metaphors, see Franco.

29. For an insightful explication of this point, see Wald, esp. pp. 73–74.

30. Hsu notes that in an earlier version of the novel, Tranquilina was named Remedios after one of García Márquez's characters (167n52).

31. "Thinking otherwise" is a practice theorized by Mignolo across his most recent work. It refers to theorizing from locations and identities that are non-Western or not fully capitalist, the use of "in-between" or "border" epistemologies, the incorporation of coloniality as constitutive of modernity, and the imagining of noncapitalist economic structures.

WORKS CITED

Barad, Karen. "Posthumanist Performativity: Toward an Understanding of How Matter Comes to Matter." *Signs: Journal of Women in Culture and Society*, vol. 28, no. 3, 2003, pp. 801–831.

Bierria, Alisa. *Missing in Action: Agency, Race, and Recognition*. 2018. Stanford University, PhD Dissertation.

Brady, Mary P. "Metaphors to Love By: Toward a Chicana Aesthetics in *Their Dogs Came with Them*." *Rebozos De Palabras: An Helena María Viramontes Critical Reader*, edited by Gabriella Gutiérrez y Muhs, U of Arizona P, 2013, pp. 167–191.

Cervantes, Lorna D. *Emplumada*. U of Pittsburgh, 1981.

Dulfano, Isabel. "Some Thoughts Shared with Helena María Viramontes." *Women's Studies*, vol. 30, no. 5, 2001, pp. 647–662.

Fanon, Frantz. *Black Skin, White Masks*. 1952. Translated by Richard Philcox. Grove Press, 2008.

Franco, Dean. "Metaphors Happen: Miracle and Metaphor in Helena María Viramontes's *Their Dogs Came with Them*." *Novel: A Forum on Fiction*, vol. 48, no. 3, 2015, pp. 344–362.

Galtung, Johan. "Violence, Peace, and Peace Research." *Journal of Peace Research*, vol. 6, no. 3, 1969, pp. 167–191.

García Márquez, Gabriel. *One Hundred Years of Solitude*. 1970. Translated by Gregory Rabassa, HarperCollins, 2003.

Guha, Ramachandra, and Joan Martínez-Alier. *Varieties of Environmentalism: Essays North and South*. Oxford UP, 1998.

Hames-García, Michael R. *Fugitive Thought: Prison Movements, Race, and the Meaning of Justice*. U of Minnesota P, 2004.

———. *Identity Complex: Making the Case for Multiplicity*. U of Minnesota P, 2011.

Hsu, Hsuan L. "Fatal Contiguities: Metonymy and Environmental Justice." *New Literary History: A Journal of Theory and Interpretation*, vol. 42, no. 1, 2011, pp. 147–168.

Isasi-Díaz, Ada M., and Eduardo Mendieta. *Decolonizing Epistemologies: Latina/o Theology and Philosophy*. Fordham UP, 2012.

Kevane, Bridget. "Violence, Faith, and Active Miracles in East Los Angeles: *Their Dogs Came with Them* and *The Miraculous Day of Amalia Gómez*." *Profane and Sacred: Latino/a American Writers Reveal the Interplay of the Secular and the Religious*, Rowman and Littlefield, 2008, pp. 11–41.

Kevane, Bridget A., and Juanita Heredia. "Praying for Knowledge: An Interview with Helena Maria Viramontes." *Latina Self-Portraits: Interviews with Contemporary Women Writers*, U of New Mexico P, 2000, pp. 141–154.

León-Portilla, Miguel. *The Broken Spears: The Aztec Account of the Conquest of Mexico*. Beacon Press, 1992.

Lugones, Maria. *Pilgrimages/Peregrinajes: Theorizing Coalition against Multiple Oppressions*. Rowman and Littlefield, 2003.

Maldonado-Torres, Nelson. *Against War: Views from the Underside of Modernity*. Duke UP, 2008.

———. "Decoloniality at Large: Towards a Trans-Americas and Global Transmodern Paradigm." Introduction to Second Special Issue of "Thinking through the Decolonial Turn." *Transmodernity: Journal of Peripheral Cultural Production of the Luso-Hispanic World*, vol. 1, no. 3, 2012, pp. 3–10.

———. "The Decolonial Turn." *New Approaches to Latin American Studies: Culture and Power*, edited by Juan Poblete, Routledge, 2018, pp. 111–127.

———. "Thinking through the Decolonial Turn: Post-continental Interventions in Theory, Philosophy, and Critique—an Introduction." *Transmodernity: Journal of Peripheral Cultural Production of the Luso-Hispanic World*, vol. 1, no. 2, 2011, pp. 3–15.
Martínez, Ernesto J. "¿Con Quién, Dónde, y Por Qué Te Dejas?" *Aztlán: A Journal of Chicano Studies*, vol. 39, no. 1, 2014, pp. 237–246.
Martinez-Alier, Joan. *The Environmentalism of the Poor: A Study of Ecological Conflicts and Valuation*. Edward Elgar, 2002.
Medina, José. *The Epistemology of Resistance: Gender and Racial Oppression, Epistemic Injustice, and Resistant Imaginations*. Oxford UP, 2013.
Mesa-Bains, Amalia. "'Domesticana': The Sensibility of Chicana Rasquache." *Aztlán: A Journal of Chicano Studies*, vol. 24, no. 2, 1999, pp. 157–167.
Mignolo, Walter D. *The Darker Side of the Renaissance: Literacy, Territoriality, and Colonization*. U of Michigan P, 1995.
———. "Delinking: The Rhetoric of Modernity, the Logic of Coloniality, and the Grammar of De-Coloniality." *Cultural Studies*, vol. 21, no. 2, 2007, pp. 449–514.
———. "From 'Human Rights' to 'Life Rights.'" *The Meanings of Rights: The Philosophy and Social Theory of Human Rights*, edited by Costas Douzinas and Conor Gearty, Cambridge UP, 2014, pp. 161–180.
———. "The Geopolitics of Knowledge and the Colonial Difference." *South Atlantic Quarterly*, vol. 10, no. 1, 2002, pp. 57–96.
———. *Local Histories/Global Designs: Coloniality, Subaltern Knowledges, and Border Thinking*. Princeton UP, 2000.
———. "The Zapatistas Theoretical Revolution: Its Historical, Ethical, and Political Consequences." *The Collective Imagination: Limits and Beyond*, edited by Enrique Rodriguez Larreta, Institute for Cultural Pluralism, Universidad Candido Mendes, 2001, pp. 105–142.
Moya, Paula M. L. "Another Way to Be: Vestigial Schemas in Helena Maria Viramontes's 'The Moths' and Manuel Muñoz's 'Zigzagger.'" *The Social Imperative: Race, Close Reading, and Contemporary Literary Criticism*, 2016, pp. 79–107.
———. "Reading as a Realist: Expanded Literacy in Helena Maria Viramontes's *Under the Feet of Jesus*." *Learning from Experience: Minority Identities, Multicultural Struggles*, U of California P, 2002, pp. 175–214.
———. "'Remaking Human Being': Loving, Kaleidoscopic Consciousness in Helena María Viramontes' *Their Dogs Came with Them*." *Theories of the Flesh: Latinx and Latin American Feminisms, Transformation, and Resistance*, edited by Andrea J. Pitts, Marina Ortega, and José M. Medina, Oxford UP, forthcoming.
Muñoz, Alicia. "Articulating a Geography of Pain: Metaphor, Memory, and Movement in Helena María Viramontes's *Their Dogs Came with Them*." *MELUS*, vol. 38, no. 2, 2013, pp. 24–38, 157.
Nixon, Rob. *Slow Violence and the Environmentalism of the Poor*. Harvard UP, 2011.
Ortega, Mariana. *Between Worlds: Latina Feminist Phenomenology, Multiplicity, and the Self*. State U of New York P, 2015.
Pattison, Dale. "Trauma and the 710: The New Metropolis in Helena María Viramontes's *Their Dogs Came with Them*." *Arizona Quarterly: A Journal of American Literature, Culture, and Theory*, vol. 70, no. 2, 2014, pp. 115–142.
Pérez, Laura E. *Chicana Art: The Politics of Spiritual and Aesthetic Altarities*. Duke UP, 2007.
Quijano, Anibal. "Coloniality of Power, Eurocentrism, and Latin America." *Nepantla: Views from the South*, vol. 1, no. 3, 2000, pp. 533–580.

Saldívar, Jose D. *Trans-Americanity: Subaltern Modernities, Global Coloniality, and the Cultures of Greater Mexico.* Duke UP, 2012.

Tenopia, Tia. "Latinopia Art Tomás Ybarra-Frausto *Rasquachismo*." Latinopia.com, 15 Aug. 2011, http://latinopia.com/latino-art/latinopia-art-tomas-ybarra-frausto-rasquachismo/. Accessed 18 July 2018.

Villa, Raúl H. *Barrio-Logos: Space and Place in Urban Chicano Literature and Culture.* U of Texas P, 2000.

Viramontes, Helena M. *Their Dogs Came with Them.* Atria Books, 2007.

Wald, Sarah D. "'Refusing to Halt': Mobility and the Quest for Spatial Justice in Helena María Viramontes's *Their Dogs Came with Them* and Karen Tei Yamashita's *Tropic of Orange*." *Western American Literature*, vol. 48, no. 1–2, 2013, pp. 70–89.

Walsh, Catherine. "'Other' Knowledges, 'Other' Critiques: Reflections on the Politics and Practices of Philosophy and Decoloniality in the 'Other' America." *Transmodernity: Journal of Peripheral Cultural Production of the Luso-Hispanic World*, vol. 1, no. 3, 2012, pp. 11–27.

Wynter, Sylvia. "On Disenchanting Discourse: 'Minority' Literary Criticism and Beyond." *Cultural Critique*, vol. 7, Autumn 1987, pp. 207–244.

Ybarra-Frausto, Tomás. "*Rasquachismo*: A Chicano Sensibility." School by the River Press, 1989.

15

Oedipal Wrecks

Queer Animal Ecologies in Justin Torres's
We the Animals

RICHARD T. RODRÍGUEZ

In his pathfinding book, *The Feeling of Kinship: Queer Liberalism and the Racialization of Intimacy*, queer studies scholar David L. Eng argues that "queer diasporas fall out of normative Oedipal arrangements precisely by carving out other psychic pathways of displacement and affiliation, by demarcating alternative material structures and psychic formations that demand new language for family and kinship" (16). Linking Eng's claim to recent work in animal studies, this essay reads Justin Torres's critically lauded 2011 novel *We the Animals* as offering an alternative language of belonging that refuses the often interlocking heteronormative tenets of environment and kinship. Keying into the insights of Stacy Alaimo, the essay shows how Torres's keen deployment of animal symbolism indexes Alaimo's insistence on the potency of animal sexual diversity. For Alaimo, the "staggering expanse of sexual diversity in nonhuman creatures . . . is the very stuff of a vaster biodiversity" (59). She continues, "Environmentalists and queers can engage with accounts of the sexual diversity of animals, allowing them to complicate, challenge, enrich, and transform our conceptions of nature, culture, sex, gender, and other fundamental categories" (59). Such categories, I maintain, include family and kinship.

This essay, however, is not as much concerned with registering a sexual diversity of animals as it is focused on how the queer—or outsider—status of particular animals simultaneously forfeits their inclusion within heteronormative kinship networks while enabling bonds with others' unfeasible domestication. Torres's novel reveals the ways humans become animals as a result of their dubious inclusion within a proper family frame. Indeed, *We the Animals* engages a human-animal comparison in order to register the impossibility of queer subjects to conform to normative family ideals. These queer subjects are likened to animals not simply given the "sexual diversity" both might be said to represent but because their kinship reveals a resistance to incorporation within an Oedipally orchestrated framework structured by heterosexual identity and reproduction.

Assessing the act of "becoming-animal" (made possible by a trenchant reading of Daniel Mann's 1971 film *Willard*, about a man and his break from a "dreadful Oedipal atmosphere" through his identification with a rat named Ben), Gilles Deleuze and Félix Guattari extend the following analysis:

> It is all there: there is a becoming-animal not content to proceed by resemblance and for which resemblance, on the contrary, would represent an obstacle or stoppage; the proliferation of rats, the pack, brings a becoming-molecular that undermines the great molar powers of family, career, and conjugality; there is a sinister choice since there is a "favorite" in the pack with which a kind of contract of alliance, a hideous pact, is made . . . there is a circulation of impersonal affects, an alternate current that disrupts signifying projects as well as subjective feelings, and constitutes a nonhuman sexuality (233).

Deleuze and Guattari then make a critical point that I wish to build on and extend for this essay. They write, "And there is an irresistible deterritorialization that forestalls attempts at professional, conjugal, or Oedipal reterritorialization. . . . Are there Oedipal animals with which one can 'play Oedipus,' play family, my little dog, my little cat, and then other animals that by contrast draw us into an irresistible becoming?" (233). While the French theorists ask if "the same animal [might] be taken up by two opposing functions and movements" (233), I am much more interested in the possibility of non-Oedipal animals or animals exceeding the confines of sexual conformity and normative kinship. As some critics have questioned the tendency of writers and artists to casually engage with animal "symbolism," a move that avoids consideration of "biological animals in any meaningful ways," Paul Waldau alternatively argues that literature "can convey much about the human intersection with other-than-human animals" (136). Yet, in Justin Torres's novel *We the Animals*, "other-than-human animals" are not a totalizing entity against which humans can be measured but rather queer figures that stand in stark distinction from actors comprising Oedipal arrangements in both human and animal worlds. I am aware that contrasting queerness and animality may indeed raise serious questions, for it could very well read that I'm arguing that queers are like animals and vice versa. Yet learning from Sarah Jaquette Ray and Jay Sibara, who consider children (with and without disabilities) alongside animals, I understand Torres's narrative as a way to "provide insights into an environmental ethic that includes the more-than-human world" (18). That is, my goal is to destabilize normative framings of the environment that often cast both humans and animals in terms of heterosexual reproduction and kinship relations.

We the Animals not only adopts animals and animality for the sake of metaphor but, more significantly, underscores how an alienated, mixed-race, gay man like the narrator and protagonist of the novel is necessarily cast as a non-Oedipal animal who in turn aligns himself with those who locate their sense of being outside a conventional family environment and within a queer taxonomic fellowship. In "Changing Attitudes toward Animals among Chicanas and Latinas in Los Angeles," Unna Lassiter and Jennifer Wolch argue that "it is not surprising that nature-society relationships in general, and attitudes toward animals in particular, are renegotiated when people move from one region of the world to another" (268). I wish to extend Lassiter and Wolch's point to argue that, in Torres novel, nature-society relationships shift from the one (heteronormative) kind of family ecology to another form of (queer) kin when attitudes adopted regarding animals are renegotiated by those whose circumstances mediate the relations with whom they align and keep company.

Torres' novel has garnered broad critical acclaim since its publication in 2011, receiving rave reviews from publications as varied as the *New York Times* and *O Magazine*. The paperback edition contains nine opening pages of excerpts extoling the beauty and power of this 128-page novel—one of those nine is glossy and announces the book as a national bestseller. And the book has been adapted for the silver screen (the film was directed by Jeremiah Zagger, screened at Sundance 2018, and commercially released on August 17, 2018). A graduate of the Iowa Writers Workshop, Torres is Puerto Rican on his father's side and Irish/Italian on his mother's. Many critics often assume that the novel is autobiographical. Although Torres does not deny the occasional attributes he shares with his novel's protagonist, he consistently maintains in interviews that "the situations, the events, the scenes are all fiction, they're all fictionalized. It's all me trying to make myth out of real people, which I think is profoundly creative. I mean, what's not creative about the act of putting words down?" (Lee).

The point here about "myth making" is key to how I understand the novel; in particular, to make myth out of real people, Torres alters for queer purposes the myth of Oedipus that has been so instrumental in organizing proper (that is, hetero) sexual development and normative family romances. And while Torres's work opens up exciting exploratory vistas for Latina/o/x literary studies by broaching subjects such as mixed-race identity and rural, working-class queer lives, it also acutely reveals the promise of what feminist theorist Mel Chen has notably called "Animacy Theory," or the critical undertaking that considers "relations between the two epistemological regions of *queer* and *animal*" (102).[1] For Chen, the animal has long been an analogical source of understanding for human sexuality. Since the beginning of European and American sexology in the nineteenth century, during which scientific forays into sexuality were made, homosexuality has served both as a limit case for establishing the scientific zone of the sexual "normal" and, more recently, as a positive valuation for "naturalness" (in which what nature maps is fail-safe to the nonhuman animal, as opposed to the messy interventions of culture in the human animal). (103)

Torres's novel precisely sustains the "messy interventions of culture in the human animal" by refusing to play by the rules of heteronormative Oedipal organization. *We the Animals* unearths a queer link between non-Oedipal animals and humans refusing "proper" kinship networks and encompassing social relations positioned outside the conventional family dynamic.

Focusing on a family consisting of three brothers and their white mother and Puerto Rican father (both originally from Brooklyn but now residing and raising their sons in upstate New York), each member of the clan is consistently cast by the narrator as an animal of some kind or ascribed animal qualities. The narrator is the youngest brother, who remains nameless (unlike his older brothers, Manny and Joel), and through his animalized descriptions of his siblings and parents, one can trace the movement of his initial attempt at incorporation vis-à-vis a normative sexual development (or the aspiration for a successful passage of the Oedipus complex) to an eventual grasp of his queer zoological differences. While the queer body of Torres's narrator is progressively ostracized from the family to which he was born, it soon finds a kinship with those whose desires and sense of belonging require an alternative ecological grounding. Environmental studies scholar Giovanna Di Chiro argues that "thinking of the body as home/ecology, especially in consideration of those bodies, communities, and environments that have been reviled, neglected, and polluted, provides an apt metaphor and material grounding for constructing an embodied ecological politics that articulates the concepts of diversity, interdependence, social justice, and ecological integrity" (200). *We the Animals* issues a formidable challenge to eco-normativity by upending the ostensibly natural principles of the heteronormative family and centering the queer ties that offer sustenance and affiliation.

Born Again Animals

In the book's first chapter, "We Wanted More," the reader is introduced to the three brothers who long for more: more food, more muscles—those very things that would enable them to follow in the footsteps of their father. And yet, "We had bird bones, hollow and light, and we wanted more density, more weight. We were six snatching hands, six stomping feet; we were brothers, boys, three little kings locked in a feud for more" (1). With a dash of sibling rivalry, these three boys—in their formative stage of development with "bird bones, hollow and light"—are poised to assume their roles as men to in turn form a family of their own. And to be king, as we know from Sophocles and Freud, requires the elimination or absence of the father. Thus, the narrator continues: "And when our father was gone, we wanted to be fathers. We hunted animals. We drudged through the muck of the crick, chasing down bullfrogs and water snakes. We plucked the baby robins from their nest. We liked to feel the beat of tiny hearts, the struggle of tiny wings. We brought their tiny animal faces close to ours. . . . 'Who's your daddy?' we said, then we laughed and tossed them into a shoebox" (2). The three sons, in view of the relationship they share with their father, are much like those hunted animals and the baby robins plucked from their nest. Indeed, the father often casts his sons as animals to register their shortfalls in their aspirations to be like him. "'Mutts,' he said. 'You ain't white and you ain't Puerto Rican. Watch how a purebred dances, watch how we dance in the ghetto.' Every word was shouted over the music, so it was hard to tell if he was mad or just making fun" (10). What will enable their successful movement to take his place is their ability to secure their manhood through normative sexual development ("He was awakening us; he was leading us somewhere beyond burning and ripping, and you couldn't get there in a hurry" [2]). The violence shaping the relationships between men and boys (and directed at animals and women) in *We the Animals* recalls Laura Pulido's important work about the way environmental injustices serve as reflections of myriad forms of injustice so that our consideration of such discrepancies must extend beyond environmental racism in particular to grasp racism more broadly. Meanwhile, the boys' relationship with their mother reflects a pre-Oedipal affiliation in which established codes of gender and sexuality become strikingly scrambled.

Thus, the ensuing chapter, "Never-Never Time"—a clear allusion to "Never-Never Land" and Peter Pan ("the boy who wouldn't grow up") but with a decided shift from emphasizing a spatial to a temporal utopic ideal—captures a moment in which the fatigued mother working the graveyard shift at the brewery up the hill experiences her rebirth at the hands of her sons. While "never-never time" is no doubt a reference to the fact that the mother has difficulty distinguishing the time of day because of her work schedule ("She would wake randomly, mixed up, mistaking one day for another, one hour for the next, order us to brush our teeth and get into PJs and lie in bed in the middle of the day; or when we came into the kitchen in the morning, half asleep, she'd be pulling a meat loaf out of the oven, saying, 'What is wrong with you boys? I been calling and calling for dinner'" [5]), it is also about her desire to escape the trappings of both labor and sexuality as orchestrated by time. Outwardly unfazed, she intently observes her sons in the act of demolishing vegetables and tubes of lotion, presumably imitating the prop comic Gallagher in the space of their kitchen:

> We all three sat at the kitchen table in our raincoats, and Joel smashed tomatoes with a small rubber mallet. We had seen it on TV: a man with an untamed moustache and a mallet slaughtering vegetables, and people in clear plastic ponchos soaking up the mess, having the time of their lives. We aimed to smile like that. We felt the pop and smack of tomato guts exploding; the guts dripped down the walls and landed on our cheeks and foreheads and congealed in our hair. When we ran out of tomatoes, we went into the bathroom and pulled out tubes of our mother's lotions from under the sink. We took off our raincoats and positioned ourselves so that when the mallet slammed down and forced out the white cream, it would get everywhere, the creases of our shut-tight eyes and the folds of our ears. (4)

Studying "the clock for a good while" and shaking "her head quickly back and forth," the mother is likened to a non-Oedipal animal given its impossible domestication: "Her mascara was all smudged and her hair was stiff and thick, curling black around her face and matted down in the back. She looked like a raccoon caught digging in the trash: surprised, dangerous" (5).

Her trance broken and finally comprehending the action at the kitchen table, she calls her sons to her side, gently running "a finger across each of our cheeks, cutting through the grease and sludge.... 'That's what you looked like when you slid out of me,' she whispered. 'Just like that'" (6). Detailing how "slimy" they were when "coming out," she makes a request to her sons: "'Do it to me.' 'What?' we asked. 'Make me born.' 'We're out of tomatoes,' Manny said. 'Use ketchup'" (6–7). Adorning her with the cleanest raincoat, the boys proceed to give birth to their mother ("She got down on her knees and rested her chin on the table.... And the mallet swung through the air. Our mother yelped and slid to the floor and stayed there, her eyes wide open and ketchup everywhere, looking like she had been shot in the back of the head. 'It's a mom!' we screamed. 'Congratulations!' We ran to the cupboards and pulled out the biggest pots and heaviest ladles and clanged them as loud as we could, dancing around our mother's body, shouting, 'Happy Birthday! ... Happy New Year! ... It's zero o'clock! ... It's never-never time! ... It's the time of your life!'" (7). This symbolic act of giving birth to their mother depends on the interruption of time—or, in other words, disordering the chronological progression that guides a young girl to motherhood and whose subsequent delivery of three sons will in due time set them on the path to both manhood and fatherhood. In this scenario, the mother is cast out of the present temporal situation and returned to pre-Oedipal moment (a moment of continuous rebirth: Happy Birthday, Happy New Year, zero o'clock, never-never time) in which identification with her sons prefigures anatomical distinction and normative sociosexual development. Yet this unquestionably violent performance (albeit facilitated by the mother from whom they will soon part ways) points to a lesson on heterosexual masculinity and reproduction imparted to the young men. The lotion (formed into "grease and sludge") may very well belong to her, but its metaphorical currency as semen is theirs to claim in the name of procreation. And despite the attempt to stall the progression of normative development and delay the inevitable moment of her "baby birds" flying the coop, the violence of heteronormative masculinity continues to rage hard for securing the audacious right to be king.

Dissolution Time

In his 1924 paper "The Dissolution of the Oedipus Complex," Freud argues that "the Oedipus complex offered the child two possibilities of satisfaction, an active and a passive one. He could put himself in his father's place in a masculine fashion and have intercourse with his mother as his father did, in which case he would soon have felt the latter as a hindrance; or he might want to take the place of his mother and be loved by his father, in which case his mother would become superfluous" (318). While all three boys are initially regarded an indistinguishable trio who do the same "boys things" together in the kitchen and outside of it, the youngest brother gradually discloses his lack of various skills and masculine characteristics that would put him on par with his other brothers and dissolve the recognition of himself in his mother. In a revealing moment, the mother of the boys pleads with her youngest son to not grow up like his brothers:

> "Promise me," she said, "promise me you'll stay six forever." "How?" "Simple. You're not seven; you're six plus one. And next year you'll be six plus two. Like that, forever." "Why?" "When they ask how old you are, and you say 'I'm six plus one, or two, or more,' you'll be telling them that no matter how old you are, you are your Ma's baby boy. And if you stay my baby boy, then I'll always have you, and you won't shy away from me, won't get slick and tough, and I won't have to harden my heart" (17).

This strategy recalls Rachel, the narrator of Sandra Cisneros's short story "Eleven," who insists that "what they don't understand about birthdays and what they never tell you is that when you're eleven, you're also ten, and nine, and eight, and seven, and six, and five, and four, and three, and two and one" (6–7). Like the mother in *We the Animals*, Rachel understands how maturation entails a set of demands specific to boys and girls, so much so that Rachel wishes she could fast forward to the age of 102 to avoid gender-precise growing pains. Here, the scrambling of years, akin to the aforementioned example of time scrambling, manifests as a strategy to beat the clock of imposed normative development.

Hot on the heels of receiving a beating from her husband, the mother's words are acutely informed by her firsthand knowledge of the violence of manhood. Torres's narrative continues: "Then Ma leaned in and whispered more in my ear, told me more, about why she needed me six. She whispered it all to me, her need so big, no softness anywhere, only Paps and boys turning into Paps. It wasn't just the cooing words, but the damp of her voice, the tinge of pain—it was the warm closeness of her bruises—that sparked me" (17). This spark, it seems, underscores the son's identification with his mother. Indeed, her words prompt him not only to feel her pain but also to adopt it as his own. During this very intimate moment, the narrator grabs her bruised cheeks and attempts a kiss. Her reaction, however, is hardly accepting: "She ripped her face from mine and shoved me away from her, to the floor. She cussed me and Jesus, and the tears dropped, and I was seven" (17). On the one hand, her reaction could very well be the accentuation of pain felt when her son presses up against her bruised face. On the other hand, her rejection of her son's touch might be due to a dangerously close approximation to "this confused goose of a woman," (2) whose vulnerable female-animal qualities he is seemingly on the path to embodying or, to recall the words of Deleuze and Guattari, becoming.

The protagonist's vulnerability is therefore correspondingly predicated on his struggle to assume an animal-fashioned masculinity, and it foreshadows his eventual split from his brothers, whose masculinity will ensure their normative domestic inclusion. Not only is he initially incapable of swimming like his brothers—his mother tells him, "You grew up with all these lakes and rivers, and you got two brothers that swim like a couple of goldfish in a bowl—how come you don't swim?"—but he is cast as more like his mother given that she is also incapable of swimming. On an unbearably hot night, Paps drives the boys and Ma to a local lake to cool off. Each of them in the water, the narrator explains:

> Ma and I didn't know how to swim, so she grabbed onto Paps's back and I grabbed onto hers, and he took us on a little tour, spreading his arms before him and kicking his legs underneath us, our own legs trailing through the water, relaxed and still our toes curled backward.... Every once in a while Ma would point out some happening for me to look at, a duck touching down onto the water, his head pulled back on his neck, beating his wings before him, or a water bug with spindly legs that dimpled the lake's surface. (18)

Pointing to the animals on whom her son might focus his attention rather than the water and its association with masculinity and mastery, the surrounding environment, not unlike the reign of Oedipal expectation, represents the challenge that each son must meet head-on to acquire their manhood. Recalling a moment at the public pool when he nearly drowned but was saved by the high school lifeguard, the protagonist ponders his mother's inability to recall that past incident, which left him in tears—"as if it had only just now occurred to Ma how odd it was that I was here, clinging to her and Paps, and not with my brothers, who had run into the water, dunked each other's heads down, tried to drown each other, then ran back out and disappeared into the trees" (20). He further explains:

> Of course, it was impossible for me to answer her, to tell her the truth, to say I was scared. The only one who ever got to say that in our family was Ma, and most of the time she wasn't even scared, just too lazy to go down into the crawlspace herself, or else she said it to make Paps smile, to get him to tickle and tease her or pull her close, to let him know she was only really scared of being without him. But me, I would have rather let go and slipped quietly down to the lake's black bottom than to admit fear to either one of them. But I didn't have to say anything, because Paps answered for me. (21)

This initially serene family affair quickly becomes a fear-inducing moment as the father fails to heed his wife's warning to not travel toward the lake's "blacker and cooler" deep end. Insisting, "'He's going to learn . . . you're both going to learn'" (21), Paps lets go, releases them into the water, and offers them the sole option to sink or swim.

An experience to be permanently emblazoned on his memory, the protagonist notes how

> the incident itself played and played in my mind, and at night, in bed, I could not sleep for remembering. How Paps had slipped away from us, how he looked on as we flailed and struggled, *how I needed to escape Ma's clutch and grip*, how I let myself slide down and down, and when I opened my eyes what I discovered there: black-green murkiness, an underwater world, terror. I sank down for a long time, disoriented and writhing, and then suddenly I was swimming—kicking my legs and spreading my arms just like Paps had shown me long before. (23)

Before learning how to stay afloat, the protagonist fittingly wishes for his demise because of the prohibition placed on him to express fear, an expression of femininity and passivity equaling a fate worse than death. His success at learning how to swim, however, is met with celebratory shouting from Paps, who, "as if he was a mad scientist and I a marvel of his creation: 'He's alive! He's alive! He's alive!'" (23), is convinced he has made his son a man. Although in his father's eyes he has tallied a critical point in advancing on the path toward normative development (indeed, as a domesticated animal with proper fishbowl placement), as the narrative unfolds, the protagonist proves more of an Oedipal wreck.

The Making of a Queer Animal

Indeed, it becomes clear how the "we" in the book's title operates in two acts: at first, the "we" registers what initially appears to be a loosely congealed family arrangement of untamed animals; but as the novel comes to a close, the protagonist begins to fully discern his estrangement from Manny, Joel, and his parents because of his queer inclinations, and thus the "we" shifts to account for a different set of animals, namely the animals with whom it is impossible to, recalling Deleuze and Guattari, "play Oedipus" (or, in other words, to heterosexually domesticate). Arguably one of the defining moments of the protagonist's turning away from heterosexualization (and a moment many colleagues have described to me difficult to grasp, let alone teach) is when he and his brothers are invited in to the house of a local kid—a "headbanger," a "type of boy" from whom the brothers "kept separate, us three half-breeds in our world, and the white-trash boys in theirs" (90). Unbothered by his house's broken window caused by the brothers' rock throwing, this becomes an opportunity to show his newly found friends "something good to show and nobody to show it to" (91). Leading them past his father (who retires to his room) and into the basement, the headbanger reveals a VCR tape with a title that "had been inked out with black marker" (94). "The tape began, the image rolled a few times over the screen, then settled and sharpened. A white kid, a teenager, was on a bed, turning pages of a book. There was a knock on the door, and an older man entered; he called him Dad" (94). As the boys gaze upon a father-son gay porn scene, the protagonist recalls the moment a woman and her daughter walked into the men's room at the public pool "where my brothers, my father, myself, and other men and boys were showering, changing, clothed and naked" (95). Embarrassed by her mistake, the mother covers her daughter's eyes while letting out a "My goodness!" Incapable of forgetting this declaration charged by shame, the protagonist also remembers how the men's room incident united the men inside it, these "men—who never looked at nor spoke to each other outside their own kin . . . had suddenly looked around from one to the next, and after a pause, they had all erupted in laughter" (95).

These two intertwined scenes in many ways serve as primary lessons for the protagonist about sexuality and incest prohibition. Noting how he had seen "flesh, but still pictures, women" (and not the "alive" images of "this man, this teenager") as well as the members of his family in the nude "without any sense of shame," the protagonist experiences the pull away from his brothers, for their gaze does not meet his, thus signaling how his awakening desire is reflected by a same-sex and seeming unthinkable kinship dynamic. "'This is for—' Wasn't none of it nothing like this. 'And this is for—' Wasn't us. Didn't have nothing to do with us. 'Yeah, you like that, don't you.' Why won't you look at me, my brothers, why won't you take my eyes." Like Oedipus, the protagonist wishes his sight eliminated for fear that what he has seen has led to his psychic destruction. Yet this is only an initial reaction. But as the narrative continues to unfold, we witness—alongside the protagonist—a renewed ownership of vision and a marked departure from the demands of brotherhood.

Literally and figuratively parting ways with Manny and Joel on a cold night during which they scrounge together change to purchase milk for a stray cat with a recently birthed litter of kittens, the narrator notes, "They smelled my difference—my sharp, sad, pansy scent" (105). The night the narrator is "made" (as the chapter title declares and thus indexing his unmaking, as it were, of his early making by his father in the lake) is the night that the two older brothers discover that their youngest brother is an animal of a different kin and kind. Berating their younger brother for being the intellectually exceptional sibling and mock fighting him ("Manny pumped two fake swings; I flinched each time. Then he sighed in disgust"), the protagonist decides to leave his brothers behind. He declares, "I held my hands up in front of me, surrender style, and walked backward, keeping my eyes on them, until I reached the building's edge" (111). One brother shouts out, "'Where you going, girlie?'" The narrator continues, "I made it to the corner and turned, down the sloping path, away from their taunts. They called out after me, putting an angry question mark at the end of my name. Their voices boomed huge in the dark cold air—like waves pounding me from behind. They called and called and cackled, and the trees echoed with their noise. Shit, let them bark. Maybe it was true. Maybe there was no other boy like me, anywhere" (111–112). Unbeknownst to his brothers, the protagonist's animal instinct has led him to the local bus station's men's restroom. Identified as what he'd been up to behind their backs, were they to trail him, the brothers—akin to a wild pair of barking dogs—would, according to the protagonist, pick up this scent.

At the bus station, the protagonist finally has his first sexual encounter with a bus driver in the back of his bus. "A middle-aged man thick all over, down to his fingers" (114), the bus driver picks up on the protagonist's sexual clues ("The driver stood up from his seat. I held there for him, still. I wanted this") and thus begins the protagonist's making (or rather remaking). "'You want me to make you,' the driver said. 'I'll make you. I'll make you.' And I was made." This intergenerational, semipublic, homosexual encounter signals the protagonist's departure from the domesticized intimacies (or nonintimacies) modeled by his parents and the normative masculinities upheld by his brothers. Indeed, he instinctually locates a space in which men of his kind find pleasure with other queer animals who fall outside the Oedipal frame. Similar to the way penguins, according to Noël Sturgeon, do not simply offer a lesson on "the naturalness of gay marriage" (136), the men with whom the narrator might "become animal" make up a non-eco-normative sexual kinship formed by queer desire. That is, the goal isn't to fashion an intelligible identity or a gay version of family that might, in time, become accepted as "natural"; instead, the desire is to form an erotically animated alliance among the like-minded for whom a sexually charged, stranger-based sociality is of foremost importance.

Wild Things in the Wilderness

Returning home, the protagonist discovers that his family has found his journal in which he "had written a catalog of imagined perversions, a violent pornography with myself at the center, with myself obliterated" (116). This leads the narrator to go wild, lashing out at his parents and brothers. Physically and psychologically ravished, which leads to a period of institutionalization, he confesses, "I said and did animal, unforgiveable things. What else, but to take me to the zoo?" (118). Even after his release (and after a rather touching moment in which his father tenderly bathes him; his father who earlier confesses, "I was thinking how pretty you were" . . . *Goddamn, I got me a pretty one*), the narrator is still cast out of the kinship network framed by normative heterosexual development. ("The boys are sweeping off the truck," she tells the father. He nods. Hear the way she says it, *the boys*, how quickly and fully the son in the bathtub is excluded from that designation" [123]).

While the older brothers' bond becomes especially strong after their younger brother, who they once called "faggot" (90), is discovered to be one, the younger brother discovers his lot in life is to affiliate with non-Oedipal animals—we the wild animals who refuse domestic and masculinist containment (or what anthropologist Martin Manalansan identifies as a "wild" or "recalcitrant" subject who does not "measure up" [493]) as well as the normative family ecologies that foreclose queer desire and taxonomy. These wild animals are not unlike the citizens of Cherríe Moraga's "queer Aztlán," who, according to Priscilla Solis Ybarra, "enact a reciprocal relationship with nature in a way that sustains a broadly defined group" (152). "These days," the narrator tells us in the book's final chapter, titled "Zookeeping," "I sleep with peacocks, lions, on a bed of leaves. I lost my pack. I dream of standing upright, of uncurled knuckles, of a simpler life—no hot muzzles, no fangs, no claws, no obscene plumage—strolling gaily, with an upright air" (125). Refusing the demand to be king (Oedipus), he elects to be prince: "I sleep with other animals in cages and in dens, down rabbit holes, on tufts of hay. They adorn me, these animals—lay me down, paw me, own me—crown me prince of their rank jungles" (125). In their illuminating essay "Anzaldúa's Animal Abyss: *Mestizaje* and the Late Ancient Imagination," An Yountae and Peter Anthony Mena maintain that "the animal might signal a tactics of survival" (162). This is certainly the case for the narrator of Torres's *We the Animals*, but, in addition, the animal signals a tactics of belonging beyond the normative ecological imperatives of heterosexual reproduction and classification.

Queer theorist Carla Freccero has recently argued that "Animal theory is queer theory . . . it displaces humanism, denormativizes subjectivity, and turns us toward not difference but differences" (105). *We the Animals* charts the coordinates of animal theory's propositions by displacing kinship upholding a humanistic imperative through normalizing male (even homonormative male) subjectivity, a difference notoriously accommodated within the terms of the family, even when that family is supposedly queered. Indeed, the promise of Torres's novel lies in its reveling in an animal ecology that is simultaneously sexual, instinctual, and unapologetically nonconforming.

NOTE

1. I use "Latino/a/x" to register the historical significance of the gender politics and gender nonconformity of the terms *Latino*, *Latina*, and *Latinx*. For more on this point, see my essay "X Marks the Spot."

WORKS CITED

Alaimo, Stacy. "Eluding Capture: The Science, Culture, and Pleasure of 'Queer' Animals." *Queer Ecologies: Sex, Nature, Politics, Desire*, edited by Catriona Mortimer-Sandilands and Bruce Erickson, Indiana UP, 2010, pp. 51–72.

Chen, Mel Y. *Animacies: Biopolitics, Racial Mattering, and Queer Affect*. Duke UP, 2012.

Cisneros, Sandra. "Eleven." *Woman Hollering Creek and Other Stories*, Random House, 1992, pp. 6–9.

Deleuze, Gilles, and Félix Guattari. *A Thousand Plateaus: Capitalism and Schizophrenia*. Translated by Brian Massumi, U of Minnesota P, 1987.

Di Chiro, Giovanna. "Polluted Politics? Confronting Toxic Discourse, Sex Panic, and Eco-Normativity." *Queer Ecologies: Sex, Nature, Politics, Desire*, edited by Catriona Mortimer-Sandilands and Bruce Erickson, Indiana UP, 2010, pp. 199–230.

Eng, David L. *The Feeling of Kinship: Queer Liberalism and the Racialization of Intimacy*. Duke UP, 2010.

Freccero, Carla. "*Chercher la chatte*: Derrida's Queer Feminine Animality." *French Thinking about Animals*, edited by Louisa Mackenzie and Stephanie Posthumus, Michigan State UP, 2015, pp. 105–120.

Freud, Sigmund. "The Dissolution of the Oedipus Complex." *The Standard Edition of the Complete Psychological Works of Sigmund Freud*, vol. 19, translated by James Strachey, Hogarth Press, 1924, pp. 172–179.

Lassiter, Unna, and Jennifer Wolch. "Changing Attitudes toward Animals among Chicanas and Latinas in Los Angeles." *Land of Sunshine: An Environmental History of Metropolitan Los Angeles*, edited by William Deverell and Greg Hise. U of Pittsburgh P, 2005, pp. 267–287.

Lee, Stephan. "Justin Torres Q&A: Author of *We the Animals* Speaks to Shelf Life." *Entertainment Weekly*, 31 Aug. 2011, http://ew.com/article/2011/08/31/justin-torres-qa-author-of-we-the-animals-speaks-to-shelf-life/. Accessed 10 Mar. 2018.

Manalansan, Martin F. "Messy Mismeasures: Exploring the Wilderness of Queer Migrant Lives." *South Atlantic Quarterly*, vol. 117, no. 3, 2018, pp. 491–506.

Moraga, Cherríe. "Queer Aztlán: The Re-formation of Chicano Tribe." *The Last Generation: Prose and Poetry*. South End Press, 1993, pp. 145–174.

Pulido, Laura. "Rethinking Environmental Racism: White Privilege and Urban Development in Southern California." *Annals of the Association of American Geographers*, vol. 90, no. 1, 2000, pp. 12–40.

Ray, Sarah Jaquette, and Jay Sibara, editors. *Disability Studies and the Environmental Humanities: Toward an Eco-Crip Theory*. U of Nebraska P, 2017.

Rodríguez, Richard T. "X Marks the Spot." *Cultural Dynamics*, vol. 29, no. 3, 2017, pp. 202–213.

Sturgeon, Noël. *Environmentalism in Popular Culture: Gender, Race, Sexuality, and the Politics of the Natural*. U of Arizona P, 2009.

Torres, Justin. *We the Animals*. Houghton Mifflin Harcourt, 2011.

Waldau, Paul. *Animal Studies: An Introduction*. Oxford UP, 2013.

Ybarra, Priscilla Solis. *Writing the Goodlife: Mexican American Literature and the Environment*. U of Arizona P, 2016.

Yountae, An, and Peter Anthony Mena. "Anzaldúa's Animal Abyss: Mestizaje and the Late Ancient Imagination." *Divinanimality: Animal Theory, Creaturely Theology*, edited by Stephen Moore and Laurel Kearns, Fordham UP, 2014, pp. 161–181.

16

"The Body Knows and the Land Has Memory"

An Interview with Cherríe Moraga

PRISCILLA SOLIS YBARRA

Cherríe Moraga (1952–present) was raised in Southern California in the days when the civil rights, LGBT, antiwar, feminist, and environmental movements were changing the terms of public and private life. Her childhood home was just one long block from the San Gabriel Mission, established in 1771, and within view of the San Gabriel Mountains, smog allowing. Her mother was Mexican American and her father Anglo American, and this mixed identity factors into her work. The fifth of five interviews with writers included in this volume, this conversation with Moraga builds on her well-established reputation as a writer who often treads into the decolonial realms of a body politics of knowledge and the innovation of kinship relations, making her comments a fitting punctuation for this section on "The Decolonial" and for the volume as a whole.

As a playwright, poet, and essayist, her writings have shaped fundamental aspects of Chicana feminist thought, including debates on ethnic nationalism, indigeneity, sexuality, and social justice. Her writings often address environmental issues in multiple ways: toxic contamination, land sovereignty, labor and food justice, consumerism, and ecofeminism. Ecocritics have drawn analysis from two of her plays, *Heroes and Saints* (1994) and *The Hungry Woman: A Mexican Medea* (2001), as well as her early essay collections *Loving in the War Years* (1983) and *The Last Generation* (1993). These and her other newer works are essential reading toward understanding Latinx environmentalisms. In this interview we discuss the way her life's work asserts a connection to the land outside the limits of conventional environmentalism.

Moraga has recently completed a new memoir called *The Native Country of a Heart: A Memoir*. She discusses it in the interview below as growing out of journal entries about her mother's experience with Alzheimer's, which took her to looking at questions of cultural amnesia. Her newest play, *The Mathematics of Love*, was produced in San Francisco's Brava Theater in August 2017.

The interview took place at her home in Oakland on a cool January day at the beginning of 2017 after heavy rains had begun to break the six-year-long drought in Northern California. Our conversation ranged from the links between identity and environmentalism to the memory of land, to social justice and writer's craft, and finally to a perspective on death as a source of knowledge and power within Chicanx culture. We also laughed a lot, in mutual agreement that we cannot face this world without a sense of humor. A consistent refrain was the insistence that "the body knows" what we do not process rationally, and that "the land has memory" that we should be attentive to in order to survive.

Identity and the Environment

PY: Do you personally identify as an environmentalist?
CM: I wouldn't say that. I don't actively identify as such.

PY: How is it that you identify? When I'm writing about you, or when I'm introducing you to my classes, I describe you as a Chicana lesbian feminist.
CM: I think that's accurate. I mean I think it also depends on who's asking, right? I identify my work usually in two ways. One is in terms of women of color feminism. Sometimes I reference myself specifically as a Chicana feminist in my work, but it is always under the rubric of women of color feminism. The idea is always about connections—that in the specificity of my experience, as I describe it, the reader may draw meaning regarding their own specific conditions and shape a politics from it. Ever since [*This*] *Bridge* [*Called My Back*, 1981], that has remained my mandate: the possibility of politically engaging women of color, queer folk, and others. So one's writing always moves toward what compels you, especially as we age. In the last few decades, I have come to identify my work through the lens of Chicana indigenous thought and practice. I'm also very interested in intimately looking at questions of death and aging and dying. Those are the areas that continue to return me to questions of land and environment. I just don't use the word *environment* much, you know?

PY: Why don't you use the word environment *very much?*
CM: Well, because it's not an image. As a writer, I seek language that can hold memory and meaning, language that grounds knowledge. In *The Hungry*

Woman, Medea says [to her son Chac Mool], "You are my land." She can't really say, "You're the environment" [laughter].

PY: *When did you come into awareness of "environmentalism" as a concept?*
CM: I think my awareness about "environmentalism" began in high school because I had a couple of white girl friends who were involved in the movement. These were the hippie days—the late 1960s. I respected them, but they seemed foreign. But by the time I got to college, it was definitely something I cared about. I remember I had one of those peace symbols on my car to protest the Vietnam War. It was green, so it was also an environmental decal.

I went to Immaculate Heart College (IHC) in Hollywood. It was very small but very, very progressive, especially its faculty. The school had retained its Catholic women's college name, but by the time I got there, it became coed and utterly radical. Every day I went there, I was scared because it was so radical. The students were mostly these white, very privileged hippies. People were dropping acid and practicing "free love" and all kinds of things. I was just commuting from my little San Gabriel home. It felt just like what we see in our students a lot today—Chicanos, Mexican kids. They come to college, and they can't make the connection between the world of the university and their Mexican world at home. There were also all kinds of lesbians there, and I was scared to death of all of it. Everything was a threat and ironically also attractive to me. The politics of the place were very attractive.

My family was very removed from the Chicano movement. For my part, I was agitated by it. I wondered, "Is that me? Is it not me? I'm mixed blood." IHC was also where I discovered feminism. And it's also where I realized that I wanted to figure out how to get free. And to me, at that time, getting free had everything to do with the environment or, better said, "nature." When I was a kid, I was mostly removed from nature, but for about eighteen months of my life, when I was eight years old, my family (due to the death of my paternal grandmother) moved to Huntington Beach, and our upstairs apartment was just a stone's throw away from the ocean.

Old Huntington Beach was nothing like it is now. In 1960, there were whole huge swatches of beach with no development. Each day, my sister and my brother and I, we'd go out on the water after all the tourists had left. We'd go way past the waves, and we'd just be out there, floating on our inner tubes. During those moments in the ocean, it was completely clear to me, "This is how it feels to be free."

After college, I moved away from San Gabriel and into Los Angeles, and I started meeting people who had access to nature, who liked to hike and swim in natural lakes. These were white kids. I didn't know Mexicans who did that. My association was that only white people got to be free, and they got to be in "beautiful places." I remember being in college with this girl that I had a terrible crush on, and she invited me to go camping with her. My heart was pounding and everything [laughter], but I told her no because I would have to ask my mother permission. They were all free, but my mother was going to say, "Who is she? I don't know who she is. She has to come to the house." You can't translate your Mexican experience. You just don't want to have to go and say, "Yes, I'd like to go with you, but you have to meet my mom. My mom has to approve of you." I knew my mother was never going to approve of her. Because she was "free."

Another thing I remember, and that I felt more directly connected to, was something that happened in New York City during those years. They had a million-person march on disarmament.[1] That was when I was doing Kitchen Table: Women of Color Press [Smith]. Our organization along with some other feminist organizations formed a contingent in that million-person march. And it was this sense that, of course, it was about protecting the earth. I say that because it was also an identification with this not being a white people's thing. That this was a women of color group that we organized, and we were going to march, and we were going to represent. And there were many, many, many other people of color that were doing the same thing.

PY: I'm really intrigued by this idea of freedom that you talk about. The idea of "free" as being part of a middle- and upper-class and white experience in relationship to the natural environment. So what does "free" look like for us, for people of color? Is there a different word for us or a different conceptualization?

CM: The thing is that I was just speaking from my perspective as a teenager. And I think a lot of young people of color feel this way when they look at what white people have access to. I don't feel that way now. What I do see is that they stole it. You can go to Yosemite, you can go any place of natural beauty in this country, and they're always there. But now I know they're not entitled to it anymore.

Of course, the other response is one of irritation and anger. But I think that the sense about being free to me is that—and I remember writing this line—that nature has no prejudice. We're just human beings. So it is only in nature—like when I was eight years old and floating way out in the Pacific Ocean past the waves breaking. . . . You just lay on the tube and the sun is setting and your back is away from the city, and you're just looking out onto the horizon. It's ironically so humbling. And that kind of humbling, like in the face of death. . . . In those moments of that kind of awareness, your personality disappears. And when your personality disappears, you become part of the collective "we." And then, healing is possible. The environment can be saved, all of this is possible. So in those moments without prejudice, your little ego just goes away—because you are surrounded by something so much grander than you. And that's what we refer to as God.

That's why animism makes so much sense. You'd better pray to that [pointing to the sky]; the sun is God because without it you'd be dead. So these are beautiful, beautiful notions, and Mexican people, Chicanos, Latinos, we are from an animist people because we are indigenous peoples. Christianity is an overlay. But that's the human experience too, and that's why all those rich people spend so much money trying to buy it.

I remember moments in my trips to the ancient sites of Mexico—those outside the cities, next to the sea or deep in the jungles, where I finally felt like nobody was judging me. That I was Mexican enough, even in my solitude. Walking around with my little güera face. To be in those places that had such memory. And it wasn't like I felt like I belonged to those temple structures or that I could disappear there. I just felt like it was my Mexico. And that somehow, I had some relationship to this land, that land mass. And that's the best sense of belonging.

PY: *Yes, which seems to me to be our "free." Belonging. Connection. It's not about going out into nature and leaving everything behind. It's about affirming the connections.*
CM: Yes, yes.

PY: *And I think that's one of the fundamental dissonances between mainstream environmentalism that's about individualism and getting free of the grid or the culture or something. It's really about deepening those connections first.*
CM: Yeah. I remember that movie, *Into the Wild*, where that boy goes off and then he dies in the wilderness. It's very heart-wrenching, but some part of me asks, "Y quien te manda?" Who the hell do you think you are? Or like the other dude who got eaten up by the grizzly bear, filming his own death [*Grizzly Man*]. And you think, "Pendejo." The ego makes us so stupid, believing the grizzlies loved him. But, of course, I had compassion for the kid because he was rebelling against all the bullshit of a life bent on "success" and accumulation. But that's the only way they know how to do it? You're right. We need to see the "we" in it.

PY: *Yeah. The further you go out, the more vulnerable you become to the greater forces of nature, which are the very ones that can teach you that you need to live within limits.*
CM: Yes. You got to come home.

PY: *Is environmentalism ultimately about justice, or is justice ultimately about our relationship with the earth?*

CM: How do we write about environmental issues if not about injustice? Take Standing Rock, for example.[2] The Sierra Club didn't do that. The Sierra Club is not on hand, you know? This is not what they had in mind. And to act like somehow the Sierra Club members are better guardians of the earth than native people is to me one of the biggest lies. It is completely unconscionable. Their formula to protect so-called native land or pristine land absolutely has no relationship to the people that have a history of knowing how to garden the earth. You know, to *guard* the earth. And this has been my critique ever since I was a very young person. I grew up in the smog basin of San Gabriel, and I always thought, "How the hell do I get out of here?" When I first finally got the opportunity to actually "be," you know, "to backpack," to be alone in the forest . . . I knew even then that the Sierra Club was not my people. Then once you get consciousness and you can make political connections, you see that something like the Sierra Club is single-issue. As long as you have a progressive movement that's a single-issue movement, it's never going to be an effective movement. If you can't deal with the impoverished conditions of the people who are living in the environment that you want to protect, it's not going to work.

What would it take to just live an equitable life? And by equitable I mean in relationship to nature and those resources that are not "ever bountiful." You start to think about infrastructure questions. For example, with water—if they would teach us how to install water catchments with incentives and financial support to do it. Your mind goes and on and on. I think about these things all the time, and I think that's why Standing Rock becomes emblematic of so much, because it is about our relationship to water. The Winnemem Wintu of Mount Shasta are another example [further details in the "Social Justice and Craft" section of this interview].[3] It's the same kind of conflict about protecting ceremonial sites while the water privatizers want to continue to build that reservoir higher and higher just to take water down to LA. You begin to think about how everything is going to run out. You just can't have a relationship to nature that thrives on privatization. It just won't work.

So your original question was, "Is environmentalism ultimately about justice, or is justice ultimately about environmentalism?" I would tend to say the latter based on what we were just talking about, but it is a reciprocal relationship. Injustices started when we began to lose our relationship to nature and treat it just as a resource to be commodified. And with the ownership of land came the ownership of women, since the earliest notions of "property."

If we look at it historically, what we are seeing is that the injustices come about by a disregard for a balanced relationship with nature and its protectors, indigenous peoples. We have also lost track of the fact that the guardians of the earth and the people that, traditionally, were connected most to the land were women. They have worked to maintain el hogar, the protocols and ceremonial life constructed to keep harmony with the elements of the planet: earth, fire, water, and wind. Traditionally, women have resisted the idea that land is property, that you can put a flag on it and own it, like you can the moon. A pinche flag on the moon? That is the height of patriarchal ignorance, really, right?

I feel like I'm very ignorant, but some of the most valuable lessons I've learned about living with some kind of balance in the world has something to do with this sense that land has memory. And I experienced that before I consciously knew that this was so. When you understand that land has memory, if you violate the land ignoring its origins, then it just brings bad blood. And that is a foundational component of indigenous thought. Even globally, a foundational component of indigenous thought is that land is not property. And so, when you make land property, then anybody who was originally on it has no entitlement to it. And in that land grab you have genocide. And you can call genocide by the name of a lot of religions. Spanish colonialism is a good case in point.

Land and Memory

PY: *You said that at a certain point you knew that land had memory, or you had a feeling, intuited, that land had memory before you knew that that was so. Do you have some particular memories of how you learned this?*

CM: As I was growing up, throughout the whole San Gabriel Valley and Los Angeles basin, the smog was off the hook. As a kid, I used to look for the San Gabriel Mountains. They were maybe about five miles away from our home. And they are huge, beautiful. And most days we couldn't see them because of the smog. Five miles away, and we couldn't see them! And then, once in a while, the Santa Ana winds would come up. And they would clear the valley. And all of a sudden you see these mountains, and it was the most beautiful, beautiful thing, like they were really alive, holding that space in the sky for us. And it always made me feel free. But then the smog returned, and the Catholicism never left, and all of that made me feel imprisoned remained. So I always knew I had to get out.

The other thing I remember is when I was about nine years old, we took the only road trip of my childhood to see our relatives in Phoenix. My mother's sister, Hortensia, lived there with her family on this little piece of land in a really humble house where my cousin, now in his seventies, still lives. This piece of land was right at the foot of Camelback Mountain. They had a few acres, a couple horses; my tía kept her jardín. They were living a more traditional life than us, closer to our Sonoran Desert origins. And I remember driving back to LA, riding through the desert in the back of our Buick station wagon. It was so hot, we had the tailgate down and all the windows open. And I'm just sitting back there, watching the stars in the sky, the mountains, black shadows in the distance. And I get this feeling ... that I've been there before, not just been, but a sense of a whole life. It was like I just knew it, you know? And it was the weirdest thing for me because at the time, I didn't really know anything about being from that place. I knew that my grandparents were from Sonora and that we had relations in Arizona. Later, I came to learn that all of the mestizaje that is Moraga is from that area, from northern Sonora/Southern Arizona (as is so with my abuela). Later I wondered, "What was that?" Since then I have returned many, many times to the Sonora desert, and each time I remember that nine-year-old moment: the smell was right; the heat was right. It's still unshakeable for me.

In the eighties, I spent a good amount of time in the Southwest and Texas, where I encountered native women, Chicanas, having a ceremonial life. I began to witness more and more women of color just being out on the land, working it, enjoying it, cultivating an honorable relationship to it. Suddenly it was somehow "cultural" and collective to be out on the land—not like I'm just singly taking my young lesbian self out to the mountains and backpacking. During those years, the sense of land somehow holding memory began to grow for me.

It was also during this time, while living in New York, that I started to know puertorriqueñas, dominicanas, and cubanas. And it immediately hit me how they were so *not* Indian but so utterly black. Their cultura—the ritmo and tenor of it—was so very Africano and so strong. I met people deeply involved in Santeria, as well as Yoruba practitioners. Their openness to me and their drive to return to their origins spiritually showed me I had a right to an indigenous identity. Regardless of blood quantum. They taught me that my culture, like theirs, was actually a mestizo culture, and I had a right to it.

All this in many ways prepared me for my relationship with Celia (we've been together for twenty years).[4] She had a very long history of walking the red road. And I found myself with her and our queer family much, much more involved in a relationship to ceremony that had everything to do with the land and its elements. That's what ceremony is. To get well you have to have that relationship to land and come to understand time and space differently from our mundane and linear perceptions.

I have to say again that I am ignorant. I don't know a lot, but I know what I experienced. That intuitive sense that "I've been here before" reminds us, tells you again that you're not crazy. This invisible place of knowing is actually quite visible, quite material, made manifest through the natural world. That's what I now understand as an indigenous point of view. But at eight, I just knew it was so—and how does that happen?

How do we allow for people to know at that deeper level when the pace of things grows increasingly fast? You have to slow down for that to happen.

PY: *It sounds from what you're saying that learning that land has memory has been a journey of embracing your indigenous identity as a Chicana.*
CM: Yes, but it's also a work in progress [laughter]. I mean, I have always experienced my Mexican-ness as mestizo. I've never experienced it as Spanish. I'm not saying there's no Spanish elements in it; I mean, certainly there's Catholicism. But the Catholicism that I learned at those mission schools versus what I learned at home was quite distinct. My mother's altar was spiritual, not necessarily religious. Through her I understood "spirit." And that spirit has power.

The border between who is indigenous or Chicana or Mexican American is just an external imposition. If you look at who we are, our home values and daily practices, our relationship to land, even if it's just caring for a geranium in a coffee can, we may recognize that they are indigenous American ways. And I think if one thinks that's true, then one has to say that those external categories, along with the whole question of "environmentalism" as a category, are not making us any healthier in terms of our relationship to the earth. As raza, we have to feel like we're not stealing anything by claiming an indigenous identity. We have to feel like this is a gesture to get us all well. You can't talk about the environment without talking about those indigenous relationships to the land.

PY: *And it's about the practices, really. So the way that Chicano nationalism invoked an indigenous identity—I think that was akin to a colonial move because it was about what was seen as a past culture that they were then claiming to revive and refiguring into a negative or exclusionary kind of nationalism. But the Chicana feminists intervened in that move and said it's not about our connection to a perceived dead past, but it's more of our continuity with practices alive today and that we can identify as we move forward. That's the Chicana feminist version of indigeneity that can be very resonant and, of course, has a very, very close relationship to renewing one's awareness of the earth. So I totally agree with you—we have to do that; we don't have any choice.*
CM: I think your critique of Chicano nationalism as an exclusionary kind of nationalism is quite right; it was also a product of its time, trying to find justification for our right to be a sovereign pueblo, much like black nationalism. Like Black Power, its failure resided in a view of nation as another patriarchal state (to say nothing of COINTELPRO). But also, the Aztecs aren't dead. The Aztecs are alive and well, and Mexica culture still finds expression today among its descendants.

Social Justice and Craft: The Materiality of Metaphor

PY: *To what extent is our responsibility as writers and thinkers and teachers to connect with those movements going on in other parts of the world? How do we balance our connections to the wider movements with our local efforts?*

CM: I think those connections happen organically. Celia and I belong to a group called La Red Xicana Indigena. Through that group we became aware of the Winnemem Wintu and their struggles around water rights. They are fighting for access rights to the McCloud River, which is the Winnemem River, where they have lived since the beginning of their existence. They are protectors of the salmon; that's how they identify as a people. Through a series of connections, they began to work with aboriginal folks from New Zealand, who are also protectors of the salmon. Their elders are my age now, and those elders talk about how, back in the day, *their* elders described how the rivers used to be so thick when the salmon were spawning, you could walk across the river on the backs of those salmon! That's such a great image. Talk about metaphor. It's real. It's real, right? [smiling] It's material! But now, because of all of the diversions to take water to the Central Valley and to LA, the salmon can't even make it up to spawn.

The Winnemem are a very small nation of people, but they had this great moment when they learned that the eggs of their original salmon had been exported more than a century before to the rivers of New Zealand. And so they journeyed to visit the Maori there and to bring their salmon home to revive the population here. It was this beautiful thing. That's transnational environmentalism among indigenous peoples. It's not making a big splash; it just is so. There's incredible progressive consciousness that comes with seeing how all of it is related. You can't dump in one place and think you're immune from its effects, which is what the West does. We do not have to be Western thinkers. What goes around comes around. For better or worse.

PY: *When we were discussing the word* environment, *you described your process of finding "language that grounds knowledge." How do you perceive the material nature of metaphors that emerge in your work? Do you think that writers who are concerned more centrally with social justice have a different relationship to metaphor than writers who do not focus on social justice per se?*

CM: Perhaps. I would say for the writer concerned with social justice, the metaphors may be more grounded in the mundane, the ordinary, as a way to tie the language to social condition; as opposed to abstract language or metaphor that obfuscates. One poet that I feel writes about social justice incredibly strongly is Lorna Dee Cervantes. Sometimes she just really lands on it. There's her long poem called "Coffee." It goes through the whole history of coffee and exploitation of Centro Americanos, and it eventually arrives at the portrait of these little gentrifiers naively drinking their coffee in their cafés. It's just so amazing—the breadth and particularity of her critique. Her intention is absolutely to awaken the reader to injustice by drawing the lines of connection for us. You could equally say that about her relationship to the land and the environment in her writing. She writes as a native woman (Chumash). She experiences her world through that body and that conciencia.

It's like Gloria's [Anzaldúa] incredible metaphor from *Borderlands/La Frontera*: the border as "una herida abierta" (an open wound). Yes, that is it exactly to any Mexican who has ever crossed the border, legally or not. It is a wound between a people, and it still bleeds. When you land on those moments in your writing, you become like the scribes [tlacuilos] of Mesoamerica. You record histories as you prophesize through metaphor—because the body knows before the writer has fully inhabited her words.

This is what Malinxe speaks of in my play [*The Mathematics of Love*]. Lamenting the loss of indigenous Mexico, she states, "I could not presage that one day the descendants of the Cholulans, the Tlaxcalans, the Mexicas would return en masse to Aztlán. Their bellies scraped raw, dragging their bodies like criminal reptiles across the border sands of Sonora. I could not have known. But there *was* a calling in me . . . that I suppressed, I admit. Or perhaps . . . I misinterpreted. Perhaps it was just the cry of a woman wanting freedom." All of what Malinxe says is absolutely material to me. There is nothing for us that is just "sort of." It's the materiality, the viscerality that creates the metaphor and for la meXicana, the metaphor is the real wound. To me, that's the challenge of writing: to try to make it increasingly visceral so that you can't distance yourself through metaphor from what is actually taking place. I don't have any plan in regard to the materiality of metaphor. I think that all I do is to try to make it as hard as it is. That's all.

Death as Humility and Power

PY: *In your essay "Weapons of the Weak" in the collection* A Xicana Codex of Changing Consciousness, *you talk about your relationship with death and how affirming its place in your life "helps you toward a daily practice of an ethos of justice." How do you see this value appear in your literary works? How can death help us better understand the human place in nature?*

CM: [laughter] Huge questions. [pause] While I was working on my memoir [*The Native Country of a Heart*], I was going through the process of watching my mother die. Because of her Alzheimer's, it was a long process of progressive loss over time. What I thought was going to be the most horrible experience in the world ended up being one of the most valuable. I realized that the two most critical events in my life have been the near loss of my son at birth and now the loss of my mother. Death and near-death reminds you that "you're not all that." [smiling] That you're going to die even if you have a long, long life, regardless of what you think about the afterlife or spirit world. Probably the dis-ease of so much of Western civilization is that we imagine we can escape death. And so when you realize you're not all that, there's a kind of humility to be found there. Our ego is just vanities, although I struggle with this daily.

In witnessing death, you begin to see yourself as a member of this creation and that there's an inherent sense of reciprocity and a sense of interdependence and respect that can come of that. It's only when you think you're special and you deserve more that the destructiveness comes in.

It's not about humiliation; it's the opposite of that. There's a freedom in this realization that you're not special. The denial and fear of death makes possession, possessiveness, and overconsumption possible. If we would just pull back a bit, slow down and ask the "why" of each of our actions, based on the utter assurance of death, we would all be better off environmentally.

My mother was the deepest love of my life. I watched her go. I had to let her go. And she wanted to be let go. I'm not talking about suicide. She was just "done." Why suffer as fools here, man? [laughter] People are much better on the other side! [laughter] On the last day of her life, I watched my mother speak to those people, her hands waving in the air. She was alive with dying.

We are mortal. That's what I liked about your book [*Writing the Goodlife: Mexican American Literature and the Environment*]. You know, growing up, we never practiced Day of the Dead; it wasn't our tradition. But we do it now because we need to remember our mortality. At least once a year. It just seems healthy.

PY: *Yes. And your comments bring to mind the deep irony of what we do. We talk about, write about, teach about whatever we can do to bring attention to the value of our culture. But one of the most fundamental values of our Mexican American culture is humility [laughter].*

CM: I know. I love it; it's such a contradiction! [laughter]

PY: *And death, or acceptance of death, is part of that humility. Our culture is okay with letting go, and that's something really important that we can share, that people can learn from. In an essay from* Xicana Codex, *"An Irrevocable Promise," you state that a major refrain in your work is to insist on a presence where before only absences have been perceived. What are the presences and absences of Chicana environmentalisms?*

CM: What comes to me is just what I said before about being a child and knowing truly "in my bones" that I knew that Sonoran Desert once as home. Coming to consciousness changes your mind. Your mind suddenly comes into a focus that wasn't there before, and what had been invisible becomes visible to you alone. It remains absent from the larger literal world. This very present sense about what is absent from the larger world is all that I've known as a writer. I only write what's absent, in order to perhaps justify its presence in the world, believing this will make a better world, a more balanced environment. I have to honestly say, it has at times been a very painful road, this writer's life when I, myself, have often been made invisible. But I have also had enormous affirmations. To go places and have a young person come up to you and say, "You changed my life"; it still matters above all else.

I've had a blessed life. In the late 1970s when I began writing *Loving in the War Years*, it was to make visible our existence. Chicana lesbian literature did not exist. And that's what you're doing here. You're trying to fill in a blank that is a lie. It isn't really blank—that's why you work to fill it in. The blank is a lie.

NOTES

1. See Paul L. Montgomery's news article about this event.
2. See Saul Elbein's magazine article about this event.
3. See Marc Dadigan's magazine article about this event.
4. Celia Herrera Rodríguez, Moraga's partner, is a painter, performance and installation artist, and educator.

WORKS CITED

Anzaldúa, Gloria. *Borderlands/La Frontera: The New Mestiza*. Aunt Lute, 1987.
Cervantes, Lorna Dee. "Coffee." *Drive: The First Quartet, New Poems, 1980–2005*. Wings Press, 2006, pp. 9–19.
Dadigan, Marc. "The Shasta Dam Killed Off This Tribe's Salmon—or So They Thought." *Yes! Magazine*, 9 Oct. 2017. https://www.yesmagazine.org/planet/california-tribe-wants-to-bring-their-salmon-home-from-new-zealand-river-20171009.
Elbein, Saul. "The Youth Group That Launched a Movement at Standing Rock." *New York Times Magazine*, 31 Jan. 2017. https://www.nytimes.com/2017/01/31/magazine/the-youth-group-that-launched-a-movement-at-standing-rock.html.
Grizzly Man. Werner Herzog, director. Lions Gate Films, 2005.
Into the Wild. Sean Penn, director. Paramount Home Entertainment, 2007.
The Mathematics of Love. By Cherríe Moraga with Ricardo A. Bracho, directed by Cherríe Moraga, 10–27 Aug. 2017, Brava Theater Center, San Francisco, CA. Performance by Brava! For Women in the Arts.
Montgomery, Paul L. "Throngs Fill Manhattan to Protest Nuclear Weapons." *New York Times*, 13 June 1982, pp. 1, 43.
Moraga, Cherríe. *Heroes and Saints and Other Plays*. West End Press, 1994.

———. *The Hungry Woman: A Mexican Medea / The Heart of the Earth: A Popol Vuh Story*. West End Press, 2001.

———. *The Last Generation*. South End Press, 1993.

———. *Loving in the War Years / Lo que nunca pasó por sus labios*. 1983. South End Press, 2000.

———. *The Native Country of a Heart: A Memoir*. Farrar, Straust, and Giroux, 2019.

———. *Waiting in the Wings: Portrait of a Queer Motherhood*. Firebrand Press, 1997.

———. *Watsonville: Some Place Not Here / Circle in the Dirt*. West End Press, 2002.

———. *A Xicana Codex of Changing Consciousness: Writings 2000–2010*. Duke UP, 2011.

Moraga, Cherríe, and Gloria Anzaldúa, editors. *This Bridge Called My Back: Writings by Radical Women of Color*. 1981. 4th ed., SUNY Press, 2015.

Moraga, Cherríe, Alma Gómez, and Mariana Romo-Carmona, editors. *Cuentos: Stories by Latinas*. Kitchen Table: Women of Color Press, 1983.

Smith, Barbara. "A Press of Our Own Kitchen Table: Women of Color Press." *Frontiers: A Journal of Women's Studies*, vol. 10, no. 3, 1989, pp. 11–13.

Ybarra, Priscilla Solis. *Writing the Goodlife: Mexican American Literature and the Environment*. U of Arizona P, 2016.

Afterword

*What Is Absent: Fields, Futures,
and Latinx Environmentalisms*

STACY ALAIMO

In this political moment, when racism and xenophobia have become more rampant, vile, and overt and the threats to ecologies and species have accelerated, it is hard to imagine a more necessary scholarly intervention than this provocative collection, which presents incisive analyses of the historical and ongoing entanglements of environmentalism with racism and colonialism, along with gathering together rich traditions of environmental thought and practice specific to Latinx literatures, art, and cultures.[1] *Latinx Environmentalisms: Place, Justice, and the Decolonial*, considered in tandem with Priscilla Solis Ybarra's *Writing the Goodlife: Mexican American Literature and Environment*, presents a stunning expanse of decolonizing modes of ecological thought, literary creation, and practice. The arguments and analyses in these volumes put the very term *environmentalism* in question, which in and of itself suggests how generative *Latinx Environmentalisms* will be for the environmental humanities. The recovery work that this volume accomplishes changes the conversation about academic fields, political identities, and future imaginaries related to environmentalism and social justice. As Sarah D. Wald, David J. Vázquez, Priscilla Solis Ybarra, and Sarah Jaquette Ray state in their introduction, one of the ways that a recovery model is valuable is that it "demonstrates the myriad ways that communities excluded from the dominant environmental and national imaginary have long held environmental values and continue to create new ways of thinking about environmental issues."

As scholarship and interest in the environmental humanities grow, a centripetal drive to locate a center, the innermost or most pure region of the field itself, is too often discernible. This dynamic has played out not only in environmental studies but also in posthumanism, animal studies, and new materialisms, wherein what is designated as field defining or central is the work that is unmarked by gender, race, sexuality, or dis/ability. As the center is shored up, other work is relegated to the margins, rendering it supplemental rather than primary. Histories of ecocriticism, which employ the wave metaphor, wittingly or unwittingly promote such mappings, as they assert that attention to race and gender *followed* scholarship devoted purely to nature. There were already scholars, immersed in theory and cultural studies in the early 1990s, who were writing ecocritical (or eco-cultural, ecofeminist, or green science studies) projects that interrogated race, gender, and sexuality. And to some of us, it seemed like "ecocriticism" proper had been constituted both from a sincere commitment to the environment and, unfortunately, from the desire to clear a space that was free from the analyses of race, class, gender, and sexuality that were emerging in critical theory, cultural studies, gender studies, and race and ethnic studies. A place to contemplate nature without the uncomfortable clamor, a move that ironically echoes the histories of removing peoples in order to create wilderness areas. The seeming escape from the political was, as is often the case,[2] an utterly political move. Although that was several decades ago, the centripetal force to circumscribe the ostensibly unmarked center has not disappeared, and in some ways, as the environmental humanities (with its benign name) gains ground within academic institutions and grant agencies, it is intensified. I narrate this microhistory in order to underscore a rather direct point: I hope this potent volume, *Latinx Environmentalisms*, along with *Writing the Goodlife*, will be widely received, across race and ethnic studies, gender and sexuality studies, ecocriticism, the environmental humanities, and cultural studies, as well as in other areas within the rapidly expanding posthumanities, as undeniably central to the daunting intellectual and political challenge of imagining antiracist and decolonial environmentalisms.

Readers are called to take up the challenge suggested by the editors: "The question shifts from 'How do we get more diversity in environmental humanities?' to 'How can environmental humanists recognize the ways that diverse groups have always been "environmental"?'" As scholarship in indigenous studies, critical race studies, and the decolonial expands, the environmental humanities and environmentalism as a social movement need to be regenerated not only by disarticulating environmentalisms from racism and colonialism but through recovery projects that delve deeply into multiple traditions that are often ignored or marked as not "universal." As David J. Vázquez argues in "Memory, Space, and Gentrification: The Legacies of the Young Lords and Urban Decolonial Environmentalism in Ernesto Quiñonez's *Bodega Dreams*," "the articulations of people of color and subalterns writing from the formerly colonized world have crucial environmental perspectives." Ideally, the environmental humanities would be reconstituted without an unmarked center and would become, instead, an entirely intersectional intellectual space of collisions, tensions, overlaps, alliances, and new figurations. These are and will continue to be fraught terrains, with cultural appropriation on one side and marginalization, ignorance, or dismissal on the other.

After reading this volume, some readers may be dismayed by the sense that just when we need environmentalism the most, both its history and many of its contemporary manifestations are so riddled with racism, settler colonialism, elitism, capitalism, and consumerism that the very term is tainted, perhaps broken beyond repair. Christopher Perreira, for example, argues in "Speculative Futurity and the Eco-cultural Politics of *Lunar Braceros: 2125–2148*" that the novel "tells us something about the environment as imagined through capital and therein offers a cultural response to those eco-dreams and desires." Sarah Jaquette Ray, in "Environmental Justice and the Ecological Other in Ana Castillo's *So Far from God*," offers a biting and revelatory analysis of how ecocritics have overlooked the novel's strong indictment of mainstream environmentalism. She argues that the novel "does not just add an environmental justice lens; it indicts dominant environmentalism for socially oppressive values and discourses." The powerful and unflinching essays in this volume made me reconsider the very use of the term *environmentalism*. It is a testimony to the smart, keen arguments in this collection, as well as to the range of Latinx "environmentalisms" included here, that the critique of dominant environmentalisms is rendered in fresh, urgent, and newly provocative ways, since scholars have, for some time, critiqued the racism and classism within mainstream ecology movements. In my first book, *Undomesticated Ground: Recasting Nature as Feminist Space*, for example, I criticized the classism and racism in William Hornaday's *Our Vanishing Wildlife* (1913), the speeches of the Progressive Women's Conservation movement, and other texts that assert an entitlement to natural "resources" with explicit or implicit white supremacist arguments.[3] Similarly, in her chapter, Ray analyzes the designations of "ecological illegitimacy" (and presumably ecological legitimacy) that operate as "a way for those in power to maintain power, using preservation of 'nature' as an excuse for social control." Reading the interviews with writers whose work is being put forward in this volume as vital for Latinx "environmentalisms" but who do not embrace the identity category of "environmentalist" is, in and of itself, a strong indication that something is seriously wrong with environmentalism, both historically and currently. When asked by Priscilla Solis Ybarra, for example, whether she identifies as "an environmentalist," Cherríe Moraga answers, "I wouldn't say that. I don't actively identify as such." Later she explains that "their formula to protect so-called native land or pristine land absolutely has no relationship to the people that have a history of knowing how to garden the earth."

As an Angla, middle-class settler colonialist with white privilege and class privilege, complicit with colonialisms, capitalism, and extractivism,[4] Ray's interpretation of the end of Castillo's novel, which references "endangered species," is unsettling. She argues that "dominant environmentalists" package "their hidden attachment to white supremacy in animal love." While such damning insights provoke thoroughgoing interrogations of one's own identities, ethics, and politics, as well as the investigation of similar formulations across texts, discourses, communities, and political groups, I nonetheless cannot imagine not defining myself in terms of being an environmentalist and an animal lover as well as an antiracist, queer feminist. These things are easy to list, hard to live. Ethics and politics take place in the midst of the messy world, "staying with the trouble," as Donna Haraway puts it, with no ideal place to escape. Identity categories endure and transform through continual critique, disidentification, transformation, and rearticulations. Sarah D. Wald's superb essay in this volume, "The National Park Foundation's 'American Latino Expedition': Consumer Citizenship as Pathway to Multicultural National Belonging," offers sharp and rigorous analyses that guide us through perplexing political terrains. Her argument that "emergent Latinx outdoor identities may fit into narratives of U.S. exceptionalism and U.S. colonialism and simultaneously offer models to resist their confines" demonstrates the difficulty of constructing identities within layered and conflicting economic and political realities.

As an academic in ecocultural studies, environmental science studies, and feminist theory, I have long pondered the ethics and politics of epistemological positioning and would like to suggest here not only that this volume productively scrambles field maps with unmarked centers but that the "goodlife" model fully articulated by Ybarra and present through many of the interviews, the essays, and the introduction to this collection is consonant with the sort of environmentalisms emerging not only from environmental justice movements and scholarship but also those pertaining to climate change, sustainability, and the Anthropocene, all of which challenge the idea that nature is a separate place, apart from the human. Both multispecies justice and environmental justice concerns can be located across all of the naturecultures in the Anthropocene, expanding environmental practice through nearly every aspect of life and revealing the systems of oppression and injustice that configure the material world. As Julie Avril Minich argues in "Greenwashing the White Savior: Cancer Clusters, Supercrips, and *McFarland, USA*," "human-altered landscapes and social environments work to enable some while disabling others." And the peoples within those landscapes, as they are differentially positioned, encultured, and embodied, may perceive even the most apparent things in distinctly divergent ways. In Jennifer Garcia Peacock's gorgeous essay, "Sun Ma(i)d: Art, Activism, and Environment in Ester Hernández's Central Valley," for example, even the light within a "landscape" is seen differently: "Hernández and other Chicanx cultural producers have seen different forms of light in the Sierra's granite: not Muir's diffuse and heavenly glow but the fragmented glitter of the granitic crystalline forms themselves, sharp facets that might become the faux jewels on a pair of jeans or the diamond dust look of a painting on velvet." This tender attention to the aesthetic is rather breathtaking, especially since this aesthetic survives in a place profoundly altered by the corporate agriculture of Sun Maid: "When Hernández walked out of her mother's kitchen, left behind Luz's boiling water, and stepped into the garden; when she drove into and out of Dinuba; when she descended from Pacheco Pass—in each case, Sun Maid structured her life." Garcia Peacock's careful attention to the geographical elements of Hernández's life allows her to map the aesthetics and politics of place in revealing and elegant ways.

The interwoven politics of place, culture, and identity arise through many memorable moments in the remarkably informative and inspiring interviews with Ana Castillo, Helena Viramontes, Lucha Corpi, Héctor Tobar, and Cherríe Moraga. Not only will many scholars, readers, and students learn so much from these revealing discussions but by gathering these interviews together, the volume suggests a vast archive of Latinx environmental literatures. Throughout these interviews and in several of the essays, the question of what is "environmental" in Latinx lives, culture, art, and literature reappears; the radically open nature of the question enables ways of being, knowing, and acting in the world to emerge through methodologies of recovery that do not extract discrete texts from their contexts but instead transform fields and frameworks through embedded epistemologies. Ana Castillo, for example, states that she is "environmentalist in practice and consciousness." The question of what is "environmental" could be understood though an intersectional model of ecomaterialism[5] in which peoples' immersion within particular landscapes and environments; within matrices of cultural texts, histories, beliefs, and practices; and within multiple, interlocking systems of oppression results in differing "environmentalisms" that are lived and practiced without the requirement that they be already named as such. Immersed onto-epistemologies—ways of being, knowing, and acting through multiple, intersecting forces—need not be trammeled by discursively constituted frames, routes, or disciplinary divides but are instead created from within particular places constituted by multiple forces. To discern and gather what has not already been categorized in predetermined terms is, in my mind, invaluable and rather formidable intellectual and political work.

The interviews and essays in this volume engage with a vertiginous range of topics, including outdoor adventures, toxins, "supercrips," queer animals, urban gentrification, and sea level rise. The topics extend in multiple directions, resisting any coherent delineation or categorization. This vast field of subjects is certainly a strength of this volume, not only because it offers a range of topics but because it suggests that modes of Latinx "environmentalisms" need not be conceptual in an abstract sense of having already been written or codified—they instead may operate through practices and modes of interconnected knowing and being that open out onto places and events. In other words, it attests to how intra-active material-cultural agencies result in modes of being, knowing, and acting that are more rich, variegated, and complicated than what could be extracted as a kind of transcendent, circumscribed definition of "environmentalism." Moraga, explaining what she calls "an indigenous point of view," stresses the visibility of invisible places and materialities: "This invisible place of knowing is actually quite visible, quite material, made manifest through the natural world." Within my own theoretical frameworks, I understand some aspects of recovery work, especially that which is related in some way to "the environment," as a mode of new materialism that enables "captures" of material-discursive practices and onto-epistemologies. The concepts, figurations, formulations, practices, and arguments that are discerned or constructed can reconfigure fields of knowledge as well as onto-epistemologies.

I would like to conclude with one more quote from Moraga, which I believe is a testament to the value of the arts and humanities generally as well as to the environmental humanities and Latinx environmentalisms. It can challenge and inspire the work we do, through various methodologies, media, and means, to make the absent present: "I only write what's absent, in order to perhaps justify its 'presence' in the world, believing this will make a better world, a more balanced environment." Working to uncover, articulate, and circulate such absent presences may be the key to more ecologically balanced and socially just futures. And this extraordinary collection will no doubt contribute to that work.

NOTES

1. Many thanks to Sarah D. Wald, David J. Vázquez, Priscilla Solis Ybarra, and Sarah Jaquette Ray for inviting me to write an afterword for this collection.

2. See, for example, my argument about the "contest of mapping" in the section on "Nature as Political Space" in *Undomesticated Ground: Recasting Nature as Feminist Space*.

3. See *Undomesticated Ground*. See also Aileen Moreton-Robinson, *The White Possessive*, which argues that "white subjects are disciplined, though to different degrees, to invest in the nation as a white possession that imbues them with a sense of belonging and ownership" (52). And see Dorceta Taylor's work on race and environmentalism. Taylor concludes her monumental study, *The Rise of the American Conservation Movement: Power, Privilege, and Environmental Protection*, with this understated point: "The legacy of race and class discrimination and the practice of separating environmental issues from those of social inequality are challenges that the conservation movement has had a difficult time overcoming" (397).

4. Macarena Gómez-Barris explains extractivism: "Historically, the extractive view rendered Native populations invisible, which legally rendered the settlement of foreign populations onto communal properties, and facilitated the taking of those territories' resources. European colonization throughout the world cast nature as the other and, through the gaze of terra nullius, represented Indigenous peoples as non-existent. If settler colonialism and extractive capitalism reorganized space and time, then vertical seeing normalized violent removal" (6).

5. See Iovino and Opperman, *Material Ecocriticism*; Alaimo, *Bodily Natures*.

WORKS CITED

Alaimo, Stacy. *Bodily Natures: Science, Environment, and the Material Self.* Indiana UP, 2010.

———. *Undomesticated Ground: Recasting Nature as Feminist Space.* Cornell UP, 2000.

Gómez-Barris, Macarena. *The Extractive Zone: Social Ecologies and Decolonial Perspectives.* Durham: Duke UP, 2017.

Haraway, Donna J. *Staying with the Trouble: Making Kin in the Chthulucene.* Duke UP, 2016.

Hornaday, William. *Our Vanishing Wildlife*, Charles Scribner's Sons, 1913.

Iovino, Serenella, and Serpil Opperman. *Material Ecocriticism.* Indiana UP, 2014.

Moreton-Robinson, Aileen. *The White Possessive: Property, Power, and Indigenous Sovereignty.* U of Minnesota P, 2015.

Taylor, Dorceta. *The Rise of the American Conservation Movement: Power, Privilege, and Environmental Protection.* Duke UP, 2016.

Ybarra, Priscilla Solis. *Writing the Goodlife: Mexican American Literature and the Environment.* U of Arizona P, 2016.

Contributors

Stacy Alaimo is Professor of English at the University of Oregon. Her essays appear in *Queer Ecologies, Prismatic Ecologies, Material Ecocriticism, Thinking with Water*, and the *PMLA*. Her books include *Undomesticated Ground: Recasting Nature as Feminist Space* (Cornell UP, 2000), *Bodily Natures: Science, Environment, and the Material Self* (Indiana UP, 2010), and *Exposed: Environmental Politics and Pleasures in Posthuman Times* (U of Minnesota P, 2016). She coedited *Material Feminisms* (Indiana UP, 2008) and edited *Matter*, a volume for the Gender series of Macmillan Interdisciplinary Handbooks (2016). She is currently completing the book *Composing Blue Ecologies: Science, Aesthetics, and the Creatures of the Abyss* and coediting a book series at Duke UP called "Elements."

Shane Hall is Assistant Professor of Environmental Studies at Salisbury University, Maryland. He studies how the relationships between racism, militarism, and climate change are represented in U.S. literature and popular culture. He is the coeditor of an anthology, *Teaching Climate Change in the Humanities* (2017), with Stephen Siperstein and Stephanie LeMenager, and his work on teaching climate change through creative writing has been published in *Resilience: A Journal of the Environmental Humanities* (2015). His current research explores the cultural construction of "environmental" and "climate" migrants and how depictions of migrants figure centrally in militarized narratives of climate futures. At Salisbury University, Shane teaches courses such as Environmental Justice, War and Environmental Conflict, and Introduction to Environmental Humanities.

Ylce Irizarry is Associate Professor of English at the University of South Florida. Her research specialties include Chicanx, Latinx, and Hispanic Caribbean cultural production, narrative theory, and testimonio. Her book, *Chicana/o and Latina/o Fiction: The New Memory of Latinidad* (U of Illinois P, 2016), is the recipient of the MLA Prize in United States Chicana and Chicano and Latina and Latino Literary and Cultural Studies (2017) and the National Association for Chicana and Chicano Studies Book Award

(2018). The book has been reviewed in journals including *American Literary History*, *MELUS*, and *Salon SX*. Her essays and reviews have appeared in journals including but not limited to *Antípodas*, *Centro*, *Contemporary Literature*, *LIT*, and *Symbolism*. She is working on a new book about cultural productions responding to the Spanish Archive; the working title is *The Arts as Archive: Decolonizing the Encounter in Circa 1992 Fiction*.

Julie Avril Minich is Associate Professor in the Departments of English and Mexican American & Latina/o Studies at the University of Texas at Austin, where she teaches courses in U.S. Latinx literary and cultural studies, disability studies, and feminist/LGBTQ studies. Minich is author of the book *Accessible Citizenships: Disability, Nation, and the Cultural Politics of Greater Mexico* (Temple UP, 2014), winner of the 2013–2014 MLA Prize in United States Latina and Latino and Chicana and Chicano Literary and Cultural Studies. Additionally, her articles appear in journals such as *GLQ*, *Modern Fiction Studies*, *MELUS*, and the *Journal of Literary and Cultural Disability Studies*, as well as in several anthologies. She is currently working on a new book about U.S. Latinx literature, compulsory able-bodiedness, and the racialization of health, which is tentatively titled *Enforceable Care: Health, Justice, and Latina/o Expressive Culture*.

Paula M. L. Moya is Danily C. and Laura Louise Bell Professor of Humanities and Burton J. and Deedee McMurtry University Fellow in Undergraduate Education at Stanford University. She is appointed in the Department of English and, by courtesy, Iberian and Latin American Cultures. Her books include *The Social Imperative: Race, Close Reading, and Contemporary Literary Criticism* (Stanford UP, 2016) and *Learning from Experience: Minority Identities, Multicultural Struggles* (UC Press, 2002). She has also coedited three collections of original essays: *Doing Race: 21 Essays for the 21st Century* (W. W. Norton, 2010), *Identity Politics Reconsidered* (Palgrave, 2006), and *Reclaiming Identity: Realist Theory and the Predicament of Postmodernism* (UC Press, 2000).

Gabriela Nuñez is Associate Professor in the Department of Chicana and Chicano Studies at California State University, Fullerton, where she teaches courses in literature and U.S. cultural studies. Nuñez's current research examines cultural production depicting the intersections of food and labor and the relationship between Latinas/os and the environment.

Randy Ontiveros is Associate Professor of English and an affiliate member of U.S. Latina/o studies, women's studies, and Latin American studies at the University of Maryland. His first book, *In the Spirit of a New People: The Cultural Politics of the Chicano Movement* (NYU Press, 2013), explores the relationship between art, social movement, and historical memory. He is currently writing a book on Latinos/as and the American suburbs.

Jennifer Garcia Peacock is the James B. Duke Pre-Tenure Professor of Environmental Studies at Davidson College in Davidson, North Carolina. Her research specializes in twentieth-century U.S. and Latinx history, environmental history, and visual culture, and she is particularly interested in issues related to environmental justice, borderlands and the American West, rural place-making and spatial formation, and community-based learning. Her research examines the ways that Chicanx cultural producers such as artists and activists have (re)shaped the cultural landscape of California's Central Valley during the second half of the twentieth century through visual products such as murals, poster art, pilgrimage, altars, gardens, and roadside shrines.

Christopher Perreira is Assistant Professor of American Studies at the University of Kansas, where he teaches courses on Chicanx-Latinx literatures and cultures, race and ethnic studies, and the carceral state. His essays and reviews are published in the *Journal of Transnational American Studies, English Language Notes, American Quarterly*, and in the volume *Captivating Technology: Race, Carceral Technoscience, and Liberatory Imagination in Everyday Life* (Duke UP, 2019). He is completing his manuscript, *Manufacturing Prisoner-Patient Consent: Race, Memory, and Violence in the Medical Archive*, under contract with University of Minnesota Press.

Laura Pulido is Professor and Head of Ethnic Studies and Professor of Geography at the University of Oregon, where she teaches and studies race, relational ethnic studies, environmental justice, landscape, and public memory. She is the author of numerous books, including *Environmentalism and Economic Justice: Two Chicano Struggles in the Southwest, Black, Brown, Yellow and Left: Radical Activism in Los Angeles*, and *A People's Guide to Los Angeles* (with Laura Barraclough and Wendy Cheng).

Sarah Jaquette Ray is Associate Professor of Environmental Studies at Humboldt State University, where she also leads the BA in environmental studies program and is an affiliated faculty member in the environment and community master's program. Ray's research focuses on how the idea of "nature" functions as a kind of social control. Her 2013 book, *The Ecological Other: Environmental Exclusion in American Culture* (U of Arizona P), outlines the sources of conflict between environmental and social justice efforts. Her subsequent work seeks to link various projects in social justice identity politics with environmentalism: in addition to *Latinx Environmentalisms, Disability Studies and the Environmental Humanities: Toward an Eco-crip Theory* (U of Nebraska P, 2017), coedited with Jay Sibara, brings together fields that have heretofore not been in dialogue. Another coedited book with Kevin Maier, *Critical Norths: Space, Nature, Theory* (U of Alaska P, 2017), uses a critical environmental studies lens to examine Northern studies. Ray has published on immigration, disability, gender, indigeneity, and eco-media, all toward the end of theorizing conditions for environmental justice, and is working on a book, *A Field Guide to Climate Anxiety: How to Keep Your Cool on a Warming Planet* (spring 2020, U of California P).

Richard T. Rodríguez is Associate Professor of Media and Cultural Studies at the University of California, Riverside. He is the author of *Next of Kin: The Family in Chicano/a Cultural Politics* (Duke UP, 2009) and numerous articles and reviews. He is currently working on two manuscripts: "Undocumented Desires: Film Fantasies of Latino Male Sexualities" and "Latino/U.K.: Postpunk's Transatlantic Touches."

David J. Vázquez is Associate Professor and Head of English and an affiliated faculty member in the Department of Ethnic Studies and the Program in Environmental Studies at the University of Oregon. His work focuses on comparative Latinx literature, comparative ethnic American literature, environmental justice, and twentieth-century U.S. literature. His first book, *Triangulations: Narrative Strategies for Navigating Latino Identity*, published with the University of Minnesota Press in 2011, explores how Latinx authors in late twentieth-century America employ the coordinates of ideas of self in autobiographical texts to find their way to new, complex identities. His other publications have appeared or are forthcoming in the journals *Symbolism, Latino Studies, CENTRO, Ari-*

zona Quarterly, and the *Journal of Transnational American Studies*, and in the collections the *Routledge Companion to Latina/o Literature* (Routledge, 2012) and *Erasing Public Memory: Race, Aesthetics and Cultural Amnesia in the Americas* (Mercer, 2007).

Sarah D. Wald is Associate Professor of Environmental Studies and English at the University of Oregon. She is the author of *The Nature of California: Race, Citizenship and Farming since the Dust Bowl* (U of Washington P, 2016). The book focuses on the role nature plays in the construction of legal and cultural citizenship. She has also published in the journals *Díalogo*; *Food, Culture, and Society*; and *Western American Literature* as well as the anthologies *Asian American Literature and the Environment*; *Service Learning and Literary Studies in English*; *American Studies, Ecocriticism, and Citizenship: Thinking and Acting in the Local and Global Commons*; and *The Grapes of Wrath: A Reconsideration*. She is in the process of writing a new book exploring diversity initiatives among public land advocates and agencies.

Priscilla Solis Ybarra is Associate Professor in the Department of English at the University of North Texas. Her book *Writing the Goodlife: Mexican American Literature and the Environment* (U of Arizona P, 2016) was chosen for the 2017 Thomas J. Lyon Award in Western American Literary and Cultural Studies and was selected as one of the six finalists for the 2017 ASLE Ecocriticism Book Award. She has published in the anthologies *Environmental Criticism for the Twenty-First Century* (Routledge, 2011), *New Perspectives on Environmental Justice: Gender, Sexuality, and Activism* (Rutgers, 2004), *Teaching North American Environmental Writing* (MLA, 2008), and in the journal *MELUS*. She serves on the Executive Council of the Association for the Study of Literature and Environment (ASLE), and she served a three-year term on the Board of Directors for *Orion Magazine*.

Index

Page numbers followed by the letter f refer to figures.

Ableism, 53, 230, 241
Activism, 157, 174, 203, 208, 209, 283; Barrio Logan, 87–88. *See also* Puerto Rican Movement
Africa, 93
Afro-Caribbean, 235–236
Agricultural labor. *See* Farm labor
Alaimo, Stacy, 12, 13, 267. *See also Bodily Natures*; *Undomesticated Ground*
Alcocer, Rudyard, 229, 230, 245n33
Altermundos, 92
Alternative kinships, 13, 15, 18–19, 20; queer, 267–270. *See also Lunar Braceros*: alternative kinships in; *We the Animals*: alternative kinships in
American exceptionalism, 53, 55, 57, 66
American Latino Expedition (ALEX), 14–15, 52–71 *passim*; bloggers, 52, 57, 58–59, 63–68; consumption and, 54, 60, 63, 64, 70; corporate sponsorship, 54, 60, 62; Latinx identity and, 54, 58–59, 68–69; multiculturalism and, 60; national identity and, 54, 57–60, 63, 69; neoliberalism and, 60–61, 64, 70; settler-colonialism and, 64, 70
American Latino Heritage Fund, 52, 55–56, 57, 64

Amerikkka the Beautiful, 211, 212f, 213
Animacies, 269–270. *See also* Chen, Mel Y.
Animals, 20, 155–156, 157, 195–196, 242, 267; queer animals, 267–268, 276. *See also* Animal studies; *How Long She'll Last in the World*: animals in; *In the Palm of Darkness*: frogs in; *We the Animals*
Animal studies, 162n1, 267–268, 279, 296, 297–298
Anthropocene, 179, 186, 188, 230, 241, 298
Antiracism, 8, 55; as neoliberal, 60–61; as state policy, 15, 60, 71
Anzaldúa, Gloria, 220, 262n8. *See also Borderlands/La Frontera*
Aponte, Midy, 56, 70. *See also* American Latino Heritage Fund
Aramark, 14, 52, 56
Aristide, Jean-Bertrand, 227, 230, 231, 233, 242n3, 245n35
Association for the Study of Literature and Environment (ASLE), 228
Aztec creation myth, 258

Barad, Karen, 12, 262n12
Barajas, Elías Domínguez, 218
Barbarian Nurseries, The, 80, 83

Barrio Logan, 87–88, 90, 98
Beck, Ulrich, 186
Bierria, Alisa. *See* Insurgent agency
Bilingualism, 68
Biospheric egalitarianism, 241
Black Dove, 132
Blackwell, Maylei, 106
Bloomberg, Michael, 205, 214, 216, 223n19
Bodega Dreams, 19, 203, 206–209, 214–221 *passim*; capitalism in, 218; criminality in, 217–218; as decolonial, 19, 203, 206, 207, 215, 218, 221; environmental justice in, 206, 219; gentrification and, 19, 207, 214–215, 216–217, 218–220; housing in, 207, 214, 219; preservation and, 209, 214, 218–220; Puerto Rican movement in, 209, 217, 220, 221; Spanish Harlem in, 208, 215–216, 220, 221
Bodies, 37–38, 46–47, 150, 152, 230, 233, 270, 282, 291. *See also* Health
Bodily Natures, 10, 12, 206, 300n5
Boling, Becky, 229, 237, 243, 244n22, 245n24
Borderlands/La Frontera, 21, 148, 291
Brady, Mary Pat, 95, 101n14, 211
Braun, Bruce, 58
Buell, Frederick, 186
Buell, Lawrence, 8
Burns, Ken, 57, 58

California Special, 122, 123f
Cancer clusters, 14, 35, 37, 49n1, 169
Capitalism, 6, 13, 60, 69, 78, 93, 96, 98, 141. *See also* Environment: capitalism and; Neoliberalism; Racial capitalism
"Cariboo Café, The," 165, 169–170
Caro, Niki, 38–39, 42. See also *McFarland, USA*
Carson, Rachel. See *Silent Spring*
Cartesian dualism, 4, 6, 230, 234, 253
Castillo, Ana, 16, 131–144, 147, 299; "environmentalist" and, 137–139; on food, 139–140; on gender, 132–133, 138, 141; on healing, 134; on hope, 142–143; mestiza identity and, 135, 137–138; on social justice, 136, 138–141; on spirituality, 132–133, 134, 139; on toxicity, 140–141; United Farm Workers and, 135–136. See also *Black Dove*; *Give It to Me*; *So Far from God*
Central Valley, 108, 109–111, 168

Cervantes, Lorna Dee, 261, 290–291
Chang, Justin, 39, 42–43
Chavez, Cesar, 122, 133, 135, 169
Chen, Mel Y., 100n5, 269. *See also* Animacies
Chicana feminism, 136, 179, 281, 282. *See also* Moraga, Cherríe: and feminism
Chicanafuturism, 92
Chicanx environmentalisms, 20–22, 147, 155, 160, 164, 298. *See also* Latinx environmentalisms; *So Far From God*
Cisneros, Sandra, 273
Clare, Eli, 36
Climate change, 173–174, 179, 205, 214, 222n8, 238, 295, 298
COINTELPRO, 213, 218, 289
Colonialism, 4, 7, 64, 88, 90, 95, 137, 151, 206–207, 253, 300n4; aesthetic and, 53, 57; impacts on environment, 2, 3, 4, 5, 18, 20, 77, 90, 173, 183, 231; waste and, 101n13, 101n18. *See also* Decolonial; Environmentalism: as colonial; Indigeneity; *Lunar Braceros*: representations of colonialism; Settler colonialism
Columbia Sportswear, 52, 56, 62
Commodification, 54, 61, 62. *See also* Consumption
Conservationism, 25n2, 61, 62
Consumer citizenship, 14, 54, 63. *See also* American Latino Expedition: consumption and; Commodification; Consumption
Consumption, 14, 54, 63; of land, 61–62, 64; as subject formation, 69. *See also* American Latino Expedition: consumption and; Commodification; Consumer citizenship
Corpi, Lucha, 1, 17–18, 189–198; animals and, 195–196; biography, 189–191, 195–196; on gender, 194, 195; on green (color), 191–192; on justice, 193–194; poetry, 197–198; relationship to environment, 190–191; shapeshifting and, 196–197; on teaching, 196. *See also* Gloria Damasco series
Cosgrove, Denis, 8, 154
Cosmic Cruise, 119f, 120
Costner, Kevin, 35, 42, 49n2
Critical geography, 5
Critical race theory, 4, 5, 9–10
Cronon, William, 57, 216
Curandera/as, 134, 149, 151, 175

Dalleo, Raphael, 218, 219, 243n13
Danticat, Edwidge, 243n11
Dávila, Arlene, 68–69, 204, 209
Dávila Gonçalves, Michele C., 229, 244n20, 244n22
de Blasio, Bill, 205, 214, 222n6
Deckard, Sharae, 243–244n17
Decolonial, 5, 6, 7, 25n6, 206, 228, 250–251, 253, 259, 260; definition, 253–254; as epistemology, 5, 13, 19, 228, 254; stance toward climate and environment, 6, 173, 253–254, 259, 295. See also *Bodega Dreams*: as decolonial; Colonialism; Futurity: decolonial; Indigeneity; Latinx environmentalisms: as decolonial; Narrative: decolonial forms; Settler colonialism; *Their Dogs Came with Them*: as decolonial
Deep Down Dark, 77, 82
de la Fuente, José Luis, 229, 243n8, 244n21, 246n41
Deleuze, Gilles, 268, 274, 276
Descartes, René. See Cartesian dualism
Di Chiro, Giovanna, 156, 270
Dinuba, CA. See Hernández, Ester
Disability studies, 14, 36–38, 230. See also Environmentalism: cripped; Supercrip
Disney. See *McFarland, USA*
Domesticana, 258
Dominican Republic, 229, 231, 240
Donovan, Shaun, 204–205
Dubois, Laurent, 245n27
Duvalier, François "Papa Doc," 227, 230, 231, 233, 243n4, 244–245n24, 246n36

Early, Jack, 37
Eco-cosmopolitan, 150, 151
Ecocriticism, 8, 9, 183, 205, 228, 296; Chicanx literature and, 21–22, 147; decolonial, 228, 242, 244n22; first wave, 8, 216, 228, 243–244n17, 244n23; globalization and, 244n23; postcolonial, 22, 230, 234, 244n22; race and, 8, 9–10, 216, 296; recovery model, 10–11; U.S. Western bias of, 22. See also Environmental humanities
Ecofeminism, 148, 149, 229
Ecomaterialism, 299
Ecopoetry, 17, 178–179, 183. See also *How Long She'll Last in the World*
Ecological essentialism, 158, 159
Ecological legitimacy, 157–159

Ecology, 90, 155, 228, 230, 235; definition, 243n16; queer, 270, 278
El Comité. See Puerto Rican Movement
Enck-Wanzer, Darrel, 209, 210, 223n20
Endangered Species Act, 3, 155
Eng, David L., 267
Environment, 4–5, 9, 10, 22, 78, 109–110; agriculture and, 111; capitalism and, 3, 61–62, 72, 93, 141, 150, 179, 207–208; definition, 3, 25n2, 91; national parks and, 52–63. See also Colonialism: impacts on environment; Environmental justice; Environmental; Environmental racism; Environmentalism; Land; Latinx environmentalisms; Neoliberalism: environmental effects
Environmental, 178; conventional definition of, 1–2, 4, 16; expanded definition of, 17, 18, 210, 299. See also Ecocriticism; Environmental justice; Environmentalism; Environmentalist; Latinx environmentalisms
Environmental humanities, 8, 10, 13, 36, 295–296. See also Ecocriticism
Environmental imaginary/ies, 15, 88–89, 96, 99, 221. See also Latinx environmentalisms
Environmentalism, 1–3, 6, 8, 9, 10, 17, 24nn2–3, 62, 138, 141–142, 147, 159, 222n15, 285, 289, 295, 297; animals and, 155–156, 159, 298; capitalism and, 147–148, 297; as colonial, 3, 147–148, 154, 206, 286, 297–298; cripped, 37–38; preservation and, 57, 157, 223n23; race/racism and, 1–3, 8, 98, 156, 157–158, 160–161, 162, 206, 285, 297; wilderness and, 2, 3, 8, 25n5, 109–110. See also Latinx environmentalisms; *So Far from God*: critique mainstream environmentalism
Environmentalism of the poor, 251, 262n2
Environmentalist, 138, 178; resistance to term, 1, 3, 18, 190, 282, 297
Environmental justice, 2, 5, 9, 10, 13, 16, 20, 25n6, 57, 71, 87–88, 93, 104, 139, 147, 148, 153, 156, 164, 191, 205–206, 210–211, 286, 298
Environmental literature, 147, 150–151. See also Ecopoetry
Environmental racism, 2, 22, 36, 96, 138–139, 140, 150, 205–206, 213–214. See also *McFarland, USA*: naturalization of environmental racism

310 / Index

Epistemology, 4–5, 6, 19, 23, 230, 241; feminist, 184; onto-epistemology, 262n12, 299. See also Decolonial: as epistemology; In the Palm of Darkness: epistemology in
Extinction, 19, 178, 228, 230, 236, 237, 241, 242. See also In the Palm of Darkness: ecological destruction in
Extractivism: 300n4

Fanon, Frantz, 260, 262n8
Farm labor, 93, 110–111, 166–167, 168–169; in Muir, 110; risks, 39–40, 105, 140; supercrip narrative, 39. See also Under the Feet of Jesus; United Farm Workers
Farrell, Amy Erdman, 46
Federation for American Immigration Reform, 61
Fiction, 80–82
Flexible Bones, 179–180
Food, 139–140. See also Food justice
Food justice, 164, 166–167, 281
Formalism, 11–12, 254
Freccero, Carla, 279
Freeways, 78, 100n3, 107, 166. See also Los Angeles: freeways and; Their Dogs Came with Them: freeways in; Transportation
Freud, Sigmund, 273
Friedman, Milton, 16, 142, 143
Fuller, Buckminster. See Spaceship Earth
Futurity, 4, 88, 89, 95, 99; speculative fiction and, 92; decolonial, 254, 259; Latinx, 59, 66, 141. See also Chicanafuturism; Migrant futures

Galtung, Johan, 262n5
García Márquez, Gabriel, 261
Garrard, Greg, 244n23
Gender, 53, 132, 133, 193. See also How Long She'll Last in the World: gender in; Masculinity; Patriarchy; We the Animals, gender in; Women
Genre. See specific genres
Gentrification, 19, 203–204, 211, 215, 216, 221, 222n4; environmental implications, 204–205, 208; race and, 204, 214, 223n17. See also Bodega Dreams: gentrification and
Gilmore, Ruth Wilson, 40, 41
Give It to Me, 139
Gloria Damasco series, 18, 191, 192, 193, 194–195

Gómez-Barris, Macarena, 300n4
Goodlife, 55, 64, 187, 298. See also Writing the Goodlife; Ybarra, Priscilla Solis
Greenwashing, 99, 205, 214, 216, 222n6
Grizzly Man, 285
Guatemala, 77, 78, 79, 83
Guattari, Félix, 268, 274, 276
Guha, Ramachandra, 219, 250. See also Environmentalism of the poor
Guthman, Julie, 46
Guzmán, Pablo "Yoruba," 211, 223n20

Haiti, 19, 227–231, 234, 236, 240, 241–242, 245n27, 245n31; US and, 229, 231, 243n13, 244n19, 245n26, 245n28. See also In the Palm of Darkness
Hallward, Peter, 231
Halperin, Laura, 147–148, 151, 153
Haraway, Donna, 298
Harvey, David, 150
Health, 35–38, 39–40, 46–48, 54, 140, 151, 210–211, 230; racial disparities in, 46–47. See also Cancer clusters; Obesity epidemic; Pesticides; Toxicity
Heise, Ursula K., 150, 162n1, 241, 242, 246n37. See also Eco-cosmopolitan
Hernández, Ester, 15, 104, 106–109, 111–127 passim, 128n8; childhood of, 111–115; cultural landscape and, 106, 115–116, 117, 120–121; family of, 112, 116–118, 120, 124. See also California Special; Cosmic Cruise; Mis Madres; Ofrenda, La; Sun Mad
Heroes and Saints, 35, 38, 164, 281
Heteronormativity, 4, 20, 53, 267, 269, 271
History, 83, 88, 94
Holmes, Seth, 39–40, 48, 214
Hornaday, William Temple, 297
Housing, 203, 204–205
How Long She'll Last in the World, 178–87 passim; "An Argument for the Brilliance of All Things," 180–183; animals in, 180, 181–182; as ecopoetry, 178–187; decentered human in, 182–183, 186–187; gender in, 181, 182, 184, 187; "Llorona's Guide to Baptism," 183–187; maternity in, 182, 184–185; science in, 180, 181, 184, 187
Huerta, Dolores, 136
Hungry Woman, The, 281, 282–283

Imperialism. *See* colonialism
Indigeneity, 157–158, 162, 174, 258, 286–287, 289. *See also* Moraga, Cherrié: on indigeneity
Indigenous studies, 2, 7
Industrialization, 121
Insurgent agency, 258–259
In the Palm of Darkness, 19, 227–242 *passim*; as decolonial text, 19, 232, 233, 237, 240, 242; bodies in, 233; ecocriticisms in, 228–229, 231; ecological destruction in, 230–242 *passim*; ekphrasis, 231, 232, 233, 236–237; epistemology in, 230, 232, 234, 236, 239; form, 232, 235, 236, 242; frogs in, 230, 232–241; Haitian history in, 230, 232–233, 236; neocolonialism in, 232, 233, 240, 242, 246n38; temporality, 232
Into the Wild (2007 film), 285
Irizarry, Ylce, 100n7, 203

Japanese Americans Citizens League, 53
Jarvis, Jonathan B., 53
Jay, Paul, 243n12
Johnson, Gary M., 48

Kafer, Alison, 37–38
Keywords in Environmental Studies, 25n5
Klein, Naomi, 142–143
Kolbert, Elizabeth, 178
Kosek, Jake, 26, 53, 57–58, 61, 64

La Llorona, 183–187, 187n4
La Malinche, 195
Land, 109–111, 211, 286, 287; human relationship to, 20; Latinx relationships to, 63–64, 65, 288; reclamation, 7. *See also* Consumption: of land; Landscape
Landscape, 8, 40, 57, 109–110; vernacular, 106, 115, 234
Lassiter, Unna, 269
Latino movement, 132, 136
Latino Outdoors, 53
Latinx as term, 11, 22–23, 71n3, 221n1, 279n1
Latinx environmental, 7, 55, 131, 204, 209
Latinx environmentalisms, 3, 16, 62, 88, 99, 147, 160, 161, 164–165, 213, 242, 285, 292–293, 296–297, 299–300; as decolonial, 6, 18, 161, 206, 208, 228, 240, 250, 252; *See also* Environmentalism; Chicanx Environmentalisms; Moraga,

Cherrié: environment and; *So Far from God*, Chicanx environmentalisms in; Viramontes, Helena María: as environmentalist
Latinx identity, 7–8, 68, 72n6, 135, 141; consumer citizenship and, 54, 68, 70; integration into US narrative, 57. *See also* American Latino Expedition, Latinx identity and
Latinx poetry, 177, 178, 179, 183, 189; ecopoetry, 17, 178, 183, 187. *See also* Melendez, Maria
Latinxs and environmental harm, 11, 204, 206, 207–208. *See also* Settler colonialism, Latinx participation in
Lefebvre, Henri, 208
León-Portilla, Miguel, 260–261
Liberal multiculturalism, 55, 60, 69, 71
Lipsitz, George, 8, 156
Little Prince, The, 190
Lorde, Audre, 142, 154. *See also* Master's tools
Los Angeles, 19, 77, 79–80, 165, 168, 204, 208; freeways and, 78, 79, 251, 262n6
Lowe, Lisa, 100n6
Lugones, Maria, 251, 254–255, 262n8, 262n12. *See also* Streetwalker theory
Lunar Braceros, 15, 88–99 *passim*, 297; alternative kinships in, 15, 89, 94–95; critique of capitalism, 90, 95, 96–98; environmental frameworks, 89, 93, 95; futurity in, 15, 89, 94, 95, 96, 97, 99; nation and, 90–91, 93; representations of colonialism, 88–91, 95; social protest in, 92, 96–97; toxicity in, 92–93, 99; US history in, 90, 94, 95, 98, 99. *See also* Nanotext

Machado Sáez, Elena, 218, 219
Mainstream environmentalism. *See* Environmentalism
Manalansan, Martin F., 278
Marez, Curtis, 93
Martinez-Alier, Joan, 25n5, 250, 262n2. *See also* Environmentalism of the poor
Masculinity, 20, 53, 273, 274. *See also* Gender; Patriarchy
Massey, Doreen, 148, 150
Master's tools, 154, 160
Mathematics of Love, The, 282, 291

McFarland, CA, 35, 37, 39–49 *passim*; agriculture, 39–40; demographics, 44; health crisis, 35–36, 44–45, 47–48, 49n1; parents, 44–45; prison-industrial complex, 41–42. See also *McFarland, USA*

McFarland, USA, 14, 35, 38–49 *passim*; as neoliberal, 48–49; naturalization of environmental racism, 36, 37, 39–42, 46–47, 49; obesity in, 45–47; parenting in, 43–45; supercrip figure in, 36, 38, 39, 40, 44, 47; white savior narrative, 35, 40, 42–44; white supremacist patriarchy in, 41, 42, 43, 45. See also McFarland, CA

Medina, José, 254, 263n17

Melamed, Jodi, 13, 15, 55, 60, 69

Melendez, Maria, 17; 178–180. See also *Flexible Bones*; *How Long She'll Last in the World*

Memory, 95–96

Mena, Peter Anthony, 279

Mercury (element), 185

Merla-Watson, Cathryn Josefina, 92

Mesa-Bains, Amalia, 128, 263n25. See also Domesticana

Mestiza/o, 135, 137–138, 288–289

Metzl, Jonathan M., 47

Mignolo, Walter, 6, 23, 253, 261, 263n31

Migrant futures, 92

Migration, 117, 135, 167–168, 228, 231

Military-industrial complex, 151–152, 171

Mis Madres, 117, 119f, 120

Modernity, 57, 60, 101n16, 186, 253, 263n31; as toxic, 88, 90, 91, 93

Moiles, Sean, 203, 214

Montero, Mayra, 19, 227–228, 229, 231, 242, 243n11, 244n19. See also *In the Palm of Darkness*

Moraga, Cherríe, 1, 20, 24, 35, 174, 278, 281–293, 300; biography, 283–284; on death, 291–292; environment and, 283, 284–285, 286; and feminism, 282, 283, 287; freedom and, 283, 284–285; identity and, 282, 289; on indigeneity, 286–287, 289–290; on justice, 286; idea of land, 20, 286–289; term "environmentalist" and, 282–283, 289. See also *Heroes and Saints*; *Hungry Woman, The*; *Mathematics of Love, The*; *Xicana Codex of Changing Consciousness, A*

Moreton-Robinson, Aileen, 5, 72n8

Mount Whitney, 109

Moya, Paula, 11–12. See also *Social Imperative, The*

Muir, John, 24n2, 58, 109–111, 298

Murie Ranch, 180

NAACP, 53

Nanotext, 15, 88, 94, 95, 99

Narrative, 14, 46, 48, 81–82, 89, 206; collective forms, 94–95, 96; decolonial forms, 254, 260, 261; environmental racism and, 36–37, 41–42, 49

National identity, 54–55, 57, 69; consumption and, 63; Latinx revisions of, 58–59; national parks and, 53; view of nature and, 53, 57–58. See also American exceptionalism; Consumer citizenship; Nation-building

National Park Foundation, 14, 52, 55, 61. See also American Latino Expedition; American Latino Heritage Fund; National parks

National parks, 52–71 *passim*; diversity and, 52–53, 55–56, 59, 60–62; imperialism and, 61, 64–65; national identity and, 53, 58; social media, 52, 54, 56, 57, 63

National Park Service, 53, 57, 64

Nation-building, 56–58, 61, 99

Nature of California, The, 21, 222n12

Negrón-Muntaner, Frances, 22–23

Neocolonialism, 229, 231, 244n18

Neoliberalism, 49, 54–55, 60, 71, 218; consumption and, 55, 69; environmental effects, 14, 16, 47; gentrification and, 204, 216. See also Capitalism

Neoliberal multiculturalism, 55, 60, 69, 71

New materialism, 12, 151, 296

Next 100 Coalition, 53, 61–62

Nixon, Rob, 3, 77, 151, 228, 234, 245n29. See also Slow violence

Nuñez, Gabriela, 96

Obama, Barack, 53, 70–71

Obesity epidemic, 46–48

O'Brien, Jean, 101n16

Oedipus (Freudian concept), 268, 269–270, 271, 273, 276

Ofrenda, La, 119f, 120–121

Older, Daniel José, 204

Olguín, B. V., 92

Ontiveros, Randy, 1, 21, 106, 209–210

Outdoor Afro, 53

Paravisini-Gebert, Lizabeth, 229, 231
Patagonia (retailer), 63
Patriarchy, 43, 133. *See also* Gender; Masculinity; *McFarland, USA*: white supremacist patriarchy and
Pellow, David Naguib, 71, 93, 98, 100n11, 101n18
People's Climate March, 173
Pesticide Conspiracy, The, 191
Pesticides, 37, 104–105, 124, 168–169, 191, 209, 214. *See also* Toxicity
Pita, Beatrice. See *Lunar Braceros*
Place, 13, 21, 15, 80, 148, 208. *See also* Place-making
Place-making, 107, 117, 208
Platt, Kamala, 147, 149, 153
Poetry, 177–178, 197–198. *See also* Ecopoetry; *How Long She'll Last in the World*; Latinx poetry
Population bomb, 210, 216
Posthumanism, 20, 296
Postpositivist realism, 12
Poverty, 140–141
Preservationism, 57, 219–220, 223n23
Prison Alley. *See* Gilmore, Ruth Wilson
Prison-industrial complex, 39, 40–42
Puentes, Victor, 41
Puerto Rican Movement, 19, 22, 203, 206, 208–214, 221, 221–222n2, 222n10, 222n13. See also *Bodega Dreams*: Puerto Rican Movement in; Young Lords
Puerto Rican Socialist Party. *See* Puerto Rican Movement
Puerto Rico, 65–66, 138, 222n10. *See also* Puerto Rican Movement
Pulido, Laura, 11, 13–14, 36, 45, 62, 100n12, 157–159, 204, 206, 213, 271

Queer theory, 267–268, 278, 279. *See also* Alternative kinships; Heteronormativity; *We the Animals*
Queer zoology. See *We the Animals*
Quijano, Anibal, 6, 253
Quiñonez, Ernesto. See *Bodega Dreams*

Racial capitalism, 13, 15, 88, 90–91
Ramírez, Catherine, 92, 101n16
Ramírez, Tanisha Love, 23
Rasquachismo, 128n8, 258, 263n25
Ray, Sarah Jaquette, 25n6, 54, 62, 213, 230, 268

Reed, T. V., 205
REI, 14, 52, 53, 54, 56, 67–68, 72n4. *See also* Consumer citizenship
Roberts, Dorothy E., 47
Robinson, Cedric, 13. *See also* Racial capitalism
Rodriguez, Ralph E., 12
Rodríguez, Richard T., 20
Roosevelt, Theodore, 25n2, 61
Rosales, Connie, 44–45. *See also* McFarland, CA: parents

Sadowski-Smith, Claudia, 21
Said, Edward, 5, 207
Salazar, Ken, 56
Sánchez, Rosaura. See *Lunar Braceros*
Sandahl, Carrie, 40
San Diego, 87
Sandoval, Chela, 7–8
San Joaquin Valley, 35, 39, 41, 42, 45, 107; natural landscape of, 109–110. *See also* McFarland, CA; *Sun Mad*
Schalk, Sami, 36, 39
Settler colonialism, 7, 53, 61, 64, 70, 95–96; Latinx participation in, 7, 61, 137
Shepheard, Paul, 128n8
Shoptaw, John, 178
Sibara, Jay, 268–269
Sierra Club, 286
Sierra Crest Range, 109, 111
Sierra Nevada, 109, 110, 115, 128n6. *See also* Sierra Crest Range
Silent Spring, 6, 122, 150, 165
Sleep Dealer, 90
Slow violence, 9, 19, 22, 37, 150, 219, 232, 250, 251–252
Smith, Linda Tuhiwai, 220
Social Imperative, The, 11–12, 262–263n16
Social justice, 136, 142, 153, 209, 252, 286; environmentalism and, 16–17, 139, 141, 162, 213; writing and, 290–291. *See also* Environmental justice
So Far from God, 17, 131, 134, 137, 139, 147–160 *passim*, 164; as Chicanx/ecofeminist, 149, 152–153, 156; Chicanx environmentalisms in, 147, 155, 160; colonialism and, 151–152, 157, 160; critique mainstream environmentalism, 17, 148, 150, 153–156, 159–160, 162; as eco-cosmopolitan, 150–151, 153; environmental justice in, 147–148, 149, 150, 151, 153; military-industrial

So Far from God (continued)
  complex in, 150, 151–152; use of strategic essentialism, 158–159; toxicity in, 149, 150
Spaceship Earth, 17, 166, 210, 222–223n16
Spanish Harlem, 19, 203, 206, 207, 208, 209, 210, 214, 215, 221. See also *Bodega Dreams*
Speculative fiction, 89, 90–91, 92. See also *Lunar Braceros*
Spiegelman, Willard, 187n1
Spivak, Gayatri, 158
Standing Rock Movement, 2, 286
Strategic essentialism, 158
Streeby, Shelley, 92
Streetwalker theory, 19, 251, 255–256, 260. See also *Their Dogs Came with Them*: streetwalker theory in
Sturgeon, Noël, 9–10, 278
Sublime, 53, 57, 58
Sun Mad, 15–16, 104–107, 125; cultural significance, 106, 127, 127n4; formal analysis, 104, 105f, 106; pesticides and, 124–125; place-making in, 107; vernacular landscape of, 106–107, 125, 127
Supercrip, 36, 39, 40; See also *McFarland, USA*: use of supercrip figure
Sze, Julie, 9, 37, 47, 205, 206

Tattooed Soldier, The, 77, 80, 172
Taylor, Dorceta E., 2, 300n2
Temporality, 18–19, 271–272. See also Futurity; *We the Animals*: queer temporality
Their Dogs Came with Them, 19, 164, 170, 250, 254–261 *passim*; as decolonial, 250, 252, 254, 259–260, 261; form, 254, 259–260, 261; freeways in, 251–252, 255; slow violence and, 250–252, 260; solidarity in, 255–258; streetwalker theory in, 19–20, 251, 255–256, 260
This Bridge Called My Back, 282
Thomas, Piri, 215
Tobar, Héctor, 15, 76–86, 172; biography, 77–79; environment and, 77–79; history and, 83; Los Angeles and, 77, 78–80; writing and, 80–81, 82–85. See also *Barbarian Nurseries, The*; *Deep Down Dark*; *Tattooed Soldier, The*
Torres, Justin, 20, 267, 269. See also *We the Animals*
Toxicity, 40, 45, 88, 90, 93, 97, 138–139, 140–141, 149, 185, 222n12, 245n29, 251–252. See also Pesticides
Transportation, 170–173, 252; public, 172–173, 205. See also Freeways
Treaty of Guadalupe Hidalgo, 90
Trump, Donald, 70–71, 85–86n1, 98, 141, 143, 227, 246n40. See also Xenophobia: in Trump administration
Tuck, Eve, 7, 8
Turner, Frederick Jackson, 58

Under the Feet of Jesus, 17, 164–170
Undomesticated Ground, 297
United Farm Workers, 133, 135, 168, 209, 213
Urban identity, 88
Urbanization, 78, 111–112
U.S. demographics, 52, 61–62

Vázquez, David J., 10
Veracruz, 190
Vernacular landscape, 106, 115, 234
Villa, Raúl Homero, 88, 100n3, 166
Viramontes, Helena María, 6, 17, 19, 164–174, 250, 261, 262n7; on climate change, 173–174; as decolonial, 173, 250, 261; as environmentalist, 17, 164–166, 168; on justice, 168–170, 172–173; on transportation, 166, 170–173; on writing, 169–170. See also "Cariboo Café, The," *Their Dogs Came with Them*; *Under the Feet of Jesus*

Wahl, Chris, 98
Wald, Sarah D., 47, 209–210, 214. See also *Nature of California, The*
Waldau, Paul, 268
We the Animals (2018 film), 269
We the Animals, 20, 267, 268–279 *passim*; alternative kinships in, 20, 269–270, 277–278; animals in, 268–279 *passim*; gender in, 271–276; incest taboo in, 276–277; queer birth in, 271–272; queerness in, 268–270, 276, 277, 278–279; queer temporality, 271–272, 273–274; title, 276
White, Jim, 35, 43–44, 49n3; fictional representation of, 39–45. See also *McFarland, USA*
White, Lynn, Jr., 183
White savior, 35, 40, 42–43. See also *McFarland, USA*: white savior narrative
Wilderness, 53, 57, 180, 216; and subject formation, 57–58; as masculine, 53, 149
Wilderness Act, 180

Will in the World, 85
Willard (1971 film), 268
Winnemem Wintu, 286, 290
Wolch, Jennifer, 269
Women, 20, 133, 138, 141, 152, 195, 287
Wrath of Grapes, The, 14, 35, 38
Writing the Goodlife, 9, 21, 161, 228, 292, 295. *See also* Goodlife; Ybarra, Priscilla Solis

Xenophobia, 61, 99, 295; in Trump administration, 98–99; 101nn20–21, 214, 227
Xicana Codex of Changing Consciousness, A, 291–292

Yamashita, Karen Tei, 172
Yang, K. Wayne, 7, 8
Ybarra, Priscilla Solis, 9, 21, 55, 62, 95, 101n15, 187, 203, 206, 228, 234, 278, 295. *See also* Goodlife; *Writing the Goodlife*
Ybarra-Frausto, Tomás. See *Rasquachismo*
Young Lords, 203, 206, 209–213, 217, 218, 222n13, 223n20; environmentalism and, 209–213; sanitation and, 210–213, 215
Yountae, An, 279

Zagger, Jeremiah, 269
Zapatista Liberation Army, 254
Zehle, Soenke. *See* Ecological essentialism

www.ingramcontent.com/pod-product-compliance
Lightning Source LLC
Chambersburg PA
CBHW022009300426
44117CB00005B/95